KT-178-473

Successful Cooking

Successful Cooking

Over 400 recipes for every occasion

SAFEWAY/GOOD HOUSEKEEPING

Published exclusively for
Safeway
6 Millington Road, Hayes, Middlesex UB3 4AY
by Ebury Press
A division of Random House
20 Vauxhall Bridge Road
London SW1V 2SA

First published 1993

Edited by Felicity Jackson and Carol McGlynn
Designed by Peartree Design Associates
Special photography by Ken Field
Food stylist Kerenza Harries
Photographic stylist Suzy Gittins

The paper in this book is acid-free

Typeset by Textype Typesetters, Cambridge
Printed in Italy

ISBN 0 09 182107 X

The recipe for *Mushroom Strudels* on page 128 is
reproduced courtesy of Roselyne Masselin of
La Cuisine Imaginaire Cookery School.

COOKERY NOTES

All spoon measures are level unless otherwise stated.

Size 2 eggs should be used except when otherwise stated.

Granulated sugar is used unless otherwise stated.

The oven should be preheated to the required temperature unless otherwise stated.

Contents

GUIDELINES FOR HEALTHY EATING
· 6 ·

FOOD STORAGE
· 8 ·

STOCKS AND SOUPS
· 11 ·

STARTERS
· 23 ·

FISH
· 43 ·

POULTRY AND GAME
· 61 ·

MEAT
· 81 ·

VEGETARIAN DISHES
· 113 ·

RICE, GRAINS AND PASTA
· 131 ·

SALADS AND VEGETABLE ACCOMPANIMENTS
· 141 ·

DESSERTS
· 161 ·

BAKING
· 187 ·

ENTERTAINING
· 214 ·

GLOSSARY
· 217 ·

INDEX
· 221 ·

Guidelines for Healthy Eating

'You are what you eat' – it's an old saying but like many proverbs it contains a great deal of truth. There have been far too many reports in the last few years for us to ignore the fact that what we eat can have a significant effect on our health.

Medical experts agree that most people eat too much fat (particularly saturated fat), sugar and salt and not enough foods rich in starch and fibre. There is an increasing amount of evidence to suggest that diet is at least partly responsible for many of the diseases common in this country today. Diseases such as coronary heart disease, certain types of cancer, dental caries, obesity and many more can all be related to our poor eating habits. In Britain we are now in the unenviable position of being among the world leaders in deaths caused by these diseases.

But, by making a few simple changes to your diet, combined with other changes like taking more exercise and stopping smoking, you give yourself the best chance of living a fitter and healthier life. Fortunately healthy eating doesn't mean you're condemned to a life of eating cottage cheese – it's simply a question of eating less of some food and more of others. There are no 'good' and 'bad' or 'healthy' and 'unhealthy' foods.

The following simple changes will help you to improve your diet:

Eat Less Fat, Particularly Saturated Fat

- Use skimmed or semi-skimmed milk instead of full-fat.
- Spread butter, margarine or low-fat spread thinly.
- Choose lean meat. Trim away any visible fat before cooking. Eat more poultry and white fish, both of which are lower in fat. Remove the skin from chicken before eating.
- Avoid fatty meat products such as burgers and sausages.
- Use less fat in cooking. Grill, bake, boil or microwave rather than fry. When you do use oil for cooking, use an oil that is high in polyunsaturated fat or olive oil.
- Use low and reduced fat alternatives when available, such as reduced fat pâté, cheese, crisps etc. But be aware that most of these products still contain significant amounts of fat.
- Cut back on foods such as cakes, biscuits, pastry etc, all of which are high in fat.

Eat Less Sugar

- Aim to reduce the sugar you add to foods; better still don't add any at all.
- Avoid sweet fizzy drinks and squash. Choose the low calorie or sugar-free varieties.
- Eat fewer sugary snacks such as cakes, sweets and biscuits.
- Choose reduced sugar products where available, such as reduced sugar jam and sugar-free muesli.
- Don't be misled into thinking that honey is better for you than sugar or that brown sugar is better than white.

Eat Less Salt

- Add less salt to your food during cooking and at the table.
- Eat fewer salty foods such as bacon and crisps.

Eat More Starch and Fibre

- Eat more bread, especially wholemeal bread.
- Eat more potatoes, pasta, rice and breakfast cereals.
- Eat more beans and pulses.

Eat Plenty of Fruit and Vegetables

- Try fruit for snacks.
- Liven up salads with chopped mushrooms, onions, peppers, sweetcorn and carrots.
- For convenience, use frozen vegetables.

Watching Your Weight

It's not good for our health to be significantly over or under the suitable weight for our height. Being overweight means you are much more likely to suffer from problems such as heart disease, high blood pressure and diabetes; if you don't eat enough, you might not be getting all the nutrients you need.

Weight gain occurs when energy (calories) consumed exceeds the energy you expend. In this situation, the end result is that excess energy is stored in the body as fat. In order to lose weight you need to create an energy deficit; in this situation the body will draw on fat reserves to provide the energy it needs. The easiest way to do this is by reducing energy consumed (i.e. restricting calorie intake) and increasing energy expenditure (i.e. exercise).

It is never a good idea to restrict your intake to a level of less than 1000 calories a day without seeking medical advice. A lower calorie intake than this could lead to loss of lean tissues as well as fat.

Our metabolic rate is determined partly by the amount of lean tissue that we have, so losing lean tissue may make it harder to maintain energy balance in the future.

To maintain weight loss, you need to make permanent changes to your diet. Crash diets and miracle cures may promise rapid and spectacular weight loss but they are rarely successful in the long term.

Dieting is never easy, and when you have to combine watching your weight with feeding your family it can seem impossible! But counting calories doesn't have to mean endless cottage cheese salads.The key to successful dieting is knowing what foods to eat and in what quantities to eat them.

Some foods, particularly fatty foods, such as cheese, cream, butter, oil, etc are highly calorific, but this doesn't necessarily mean that you need to avoid them completely, simply that they should be consumed in much smaller quantities. Other foods, such as fruit, vegetables, lean meat, fish and chicken, are much lower in fat and calories and therefore can be consumed in more generous quantities.

Starchy foods such as bread, potatoes, pasta, cereals and rice are often wrongly accused of being fattening. In fact a slice of bread has only 80 calories. It's what you put with them that does the damage – spread a generous helping of butter and you could easily double the calorie content.

Calorie Saving Tips

- Weight for weight, fat provides more than twice as many calories as carbohydrates, so it's best to concentrate your efforts on cutting right back on the amount of fat you eat
- Choose lean meat and trim away any visible fat.
- Use more poultry, game and fish, all of which are lower in fat and calories. Remove the skin from poultry before cooking it.
- Extend or bulk savoury dishes by adding plenty of vegetables, which are low in calories.
- Use low-fat cooking methods, i.e. grilling, baking, boiling, steaming or microwave cooking rather than frying. When you do use oil for cooking use either a vegetable oil, which is high in polyunsaturated fats, or olive oil.
- Use fat reduced alternatives where available, such as reduced fat Cheddar, skimmed or semi-skimmed milk, low-fat yogurts etc.
- Use butter, margarine or low-fat spread sparingly. The term 'low-fat spread' is slightly misleading: although most contain less than half the fat and calories of butter or margarine, they do still contain fat.
- To make gravies and sauces creamy, add low-fat natural yogurt or fromage frais rather than cream. Stir in at the end of cooking to prevent curdling.
- Don't be afraid to occasionally use high-calorie foods such as cheese and bacon. You only need to use small quantities to add a lot of flavour.
- Choose high-fibre accompaniments, such as brown rice and wholemeal pasta, when possible. High-fibre foods, such as wholemeal bread, are more filling than their refined alternatives and are therefore more satisfying.

Making The Most Of Your Vitamins

There are various ways you can improve the vitamin and mineral content of your diet by buying, storing and preparing food wisely. Follow these tips to get the most from your food.

- The water soluble vitamins B and C are very easily destroyed by storage, heat and light. Try to buy fruit and vegetables little and often rather than in huge quantities. Look for firm produce, avoid limp wilting greens. Buy from a shop that you know has a quick turnover.
- Store the vegetables in a cool dark place, ideally for no more than 3 days.
- Never leave vegetables standing in water before cooking.
- Do not add bicarbonate of soda to the water when cooking vegetables.
- Ideally cook vegetables using little or no water. Boiling vegetables in large quantities of water can destroy up to 70% of the Vitamin C.
- Keep peeling to a minimum, since the highest concentrations of vitamins are found directly under the skin. Cut vegetables into large chunks so less surface area is exposed (Vitamin C is a lost when cut surfaces are in contact with air).
- Eat food soon after it is prepared; keeping food warm results in vitamin loss.
- Never leave milk outside all day on the doorstep, as up to 70% of the riboflavin (Vitamin B2) can be lost in this way.

Food Storage

Correct food storage is vitally important for ensuring that you avoid food poisoning, and for good nutrition. Today, most of us don't have a larder, but we do have freezers, refrigerators, and access to canned and dried foods – all of which extend the life of various foods.

Good food storage requires planning and effort and doesn't just happen by chance. To start with your kitchen and food storage areas need to be hygienic.

Rules For Kitchen Hygiene

- Keep your kitchen as clean as possible.
- Pets should be kept out and certainly discouraged from walking or sitting on worktops.
- Wash down and dry surfaces, sinks, floor and the refrigerator regularly.
- Wash your hands before handling food and again between handling different types of food (e.g. raw and cooked meat where you could transfer bacteria from one to the other).
- Never put cooked or ready-to-eat foods on to a surface which has just had raw food on it.
- If you don't own a dishwasher, change drying up cloths and cleaning cloths every day.
- Scrub wooden chopping boards thoroughly, if necessary scraping them occasionally with a knife blade. Plastic chopping boards are more hygienic as they can be washed in very hot water or put in a dishwasher. Ideally keep separate boards for different foods, e.g. meat, fish and vegetables.
- Even if your washing machine is in the kitchen, do not sort dirty laundry on the worktops. Wash your hands after handling dirty washing.
- If you cut yourself, cover the wound with a clean sterile dressing. Never handle food with an uncovered cut.

Handling Perishable Foods

- Do not shop for perishable foods unless you are taking them home immediately. Time spent in a shopping bag or car can cause growth of bacteria.
- Use a thermometer to check that your refrigerator is running at the correct temperature. This should be between 0°C and 5°C to prevent the development of micro-organisms. This temperature will not kill micro-organisms which are already present in food but keep them dormant, which is why it's vital to refrigerate perishables as soon as possible.
- Do not put warm or hot food in a refrigerator as it can raise the temperature of items already in there and cause bacterial growth.
- When cooking food which you intend to refrigerate, cool it as quickly as possible. Transfer it from the cooking container into a cool container and stand it on a rack to allow air to circulate all round. With large quantities, lower the container into a bowl of iced water which may need to be changed several times.
- Defrost the refrigerator regularly (unless it is self defrosting) and wash it out from time to time with a solution of bicarbonate of soda in warm water. Detergent and washing up liquid should not be used because they tend to leave a smell which can transfer to food.
- Don't open the refrigerator door more often than necessary since this allows warm air to get in.
- Don't overfill the refrigerator. Cool air needs to be able to circulate round the products.
- Keep all foods in covered containers.
- When using frozen poultry, make absolutely sure it is completely thawed before cooking it..

Refrigerator Storage

The following chart is an approximate guide to refrigerator storage times. You should adhere to the 'use by' dates on packaging. If you transfer something to another container use a chinagraph (freezer) pen to mark the date on which you opened it and by when you should use it. Your refrigerator should be set at an operating temperature between 1-5°C (34-41°F). You should regularly use a refrigerator thermometer to check this.

It is important to keep all food stored in the refrigerator covered so that cross-communication of flavours does not occur. Strongly flavoured items like mature cheese and fish can easily affect less strongly flavoured foods such as milk and chicken.

Foods should be stored in particular parts of the refrigerator for two reasons:

- Because some areas are cooler than others.
- To prevent things like raw meat juices dripping out on to other items.

Storing Frozen Food In The Refrigerator

Some refrigerator models have a frozen food compartment for storing ready-frozen food. Only those which carry the four-star symbol ∗∗∗∗ can be used for freezing fresh food. An appliance with a lower star rating is only suitable for storing ready-frozen foods as follows:

∗ up to 1 week ∗∗ up to 1 month ∗∗∗ up to 3 months

Storing Canned Food

Canned food is commercially cooked in the can so that the food and its nutrients are sealed in and the bacteria are sealed out. It keeps longer than other preserved foods, but it is important to rotate your stock of cans and to check that they show no signs of rust, denting or 'blowing' at the seam which means the contents can be damaged.

Cans now carry a 'use by' date which means you can keep an eye on your stock and ensure that older cans are used up first.

Once opened, canned food should be treated as fresh. Contents should be transferred to a clean, covered container, stored in the refrigerator and used within 2 days.

Storing Dried Food

Dried food has a long life if stored correctly in clean, dry containers that are tightly sealed to prevent damp and infestation getting in. It is important never to add newly bought dried food, such as flour, to an existing half-used pack. It should be put into a separate container which has been washed and thoroughly dried.

Strongly flavoured dried foods such as coffee and spices should be bought in only small quantities as they quickly lose their aroma when exposed to air. Ideally they should be moved to ever-smaller containers as you use them up but since this is impractical it is best to buy in quantities which will be used up fairly quickly.

Check the 'use by' date on packaging to ascertain how long dried food can be stored.

Approximate Refrigerator Storage Times

Raw meat		Cooked meat		Dairy produce	
joints	3 days	joints	3 days	milk	
poultry	2 days	casseroles/stews	2 days	(pasteurised, homogenised)	4-5 days
raw sliced meat	2 days	sliced meat	2 days	cheese, hard	7-14 days
minced meat	1 day	ham	2 days	cheese, semi-hard	7-10 days
offal	1 day	meat pies	2 days	cheese, soft	2-3 days
sausages	3 days			eggs (stored pointed end down)	2 weeks
bacon	7 days	**Vegetables**			
bacon					
(in unopened vacuum pack)	2-3 weeks	salad leaves	2-3 days		
fish	should be eaten on day of purchase	green vegetables	3-4 days		

Where To Store Food In The Refrigerator

Top and centre shelves		Bottom shelf/shelves (above salad drawer)		Salad drawer	
butter	lard	fresh meat	cooked meat	fruit	vegetables
margarine	spreads	ham	sausages		
cheese	preserves	fish	shellfish	**Door**	
salad dressings	mayonnaise	milk products	cream		
sauces	eggs			milk	fruit juice
convenience foods	cooked items				

NOTE: All meats should be packaged separately and raw meat and poultry stored below cooked meat and dairy products.

Stocks and Soups

There is nothing as satisfying as a really good home-made soup packed with flavour. Soups range from light consommés and creamed soups to thick hearty potages which are a meal in themselves. They are relatively quick and easy to make, and it's a great way to use up odds and ends of vegetables. If you make your own stock as well, you'll find it adds an extra special flavour to your soups.

Left: Stilton and Celery Soup (page 21)
Right: Chilled Tomato and Basil Soup (page 15)

Stocks

Using home-made stocks will undoubtedly produce a better flavoured soup – and stock-making needn't be a chore. Get into the habit of using leftover bones, poultry carcasses and vegetables to make full-flavoured stocks. Use whatever stock is required and freeze the remainder in sensible quantities for future occasions.

If you haven't time to make your own stock, then try one of the milder-flavoured stock cubes, but remember that stock cubes are inclined to be strong and salty, so make sure you adjust the seasoning.

TIPS FOR MAKING STOCK

1. Use the whole chicken carcass for a jellied chicken stock

2. Don't cover your stock pot completely. It needs to reduce well and if you keep the steam in it will go cloudy.

3. Skim your stock frequently: scum and fat in the stock will cause cloudiness.

4. When straining, allow the stock to drip through a sieve. Trying to squeeze the vegetables through causes cloudiness.

5. Allow stock to cool and remove the layer of fat from the surface before storing.

6. To freeze, reduce stocks well by boiling, then cool and freeze. Small quantities can be frozen in ice cube trays.

7. If you store stock in the refrigerator, boil it up every day. Meat and chicken stocks will keep refrigerated for 4 days, fish stocks for 2 days, vegetable stocks for 1-2 days.

Consommé à la Jardinière (page 14)

Beef Stock

Makes about 900 ml (1½ pt)

450 G (1 LB) SHIN OF BEEF, CUT INTO PIECES

450 G (1 LB) MARROW BONE OR KNUCKLE OF VEAL, CHOPPED

BOUQUET GARNI

1 ONION, SKINNED AND SLICED

1 CARROT, SCRUBBED AND SLICED

1 CELERY STICK, WASHED AND SLICED

½ × 5 ML TSP SALT

1. To give a good flavour and colour, brown the bones and meat in the oven before using them. Put in a saucepan with 1.8 lt (3 pt) water, the herbs, vegetables and salt. Bring to the boil, skim, partially cover and simmer for 2 hours.
2. Or pressure cook on High (15 lb) pressure for 1 hour, using 1.5 lt (2½ pt) water. If using marrow bones, increase the water to 1.8 lt (3 pt) and cook for 1¼ hours. Strain the stock and when cold remove any trace of fat.

VARIATION

Replace the shin of beef with fresh or cooked meat bones.

Chicken Stock

Makes about 900 ml (1½ pt)

1 CHICKEN CARCASS

1 ONION, SKINNED AND SLICED

1 CARROT, SCRUBBED AND SLICED

1 CELERY STICK, WASHED AND SLICED

1 BAY LEAF

SALT

1. Break up the carcass and put in a large saucepan with any skin and chicken meat. Add 1.8 lt (3 pt) water, the flavouring vegetables, bay leaf and salt. Bring to the boil, skim, partially cover and simmer for about 2 hours.
2. Or pressure cook on High (15 lb) for about 1 hour, using 1.5 lt (2½ pt) water.
3. Strain the stock and, when cold, remove all traces of fat.

Fish Stock

Makes about 300 ml (10 fl oz)

1 FISH HEAD OR FISH BONES AND TRIMMINGS

SALT

BOUQUET GARNI

1 ONION, SKINNED AND SLICED

1. Put the head and fish trimmings into a pan, cover with 450 ml (16 fl oz) water and season with salt. Bring to the boil, then skim.
2. Reduce the heat and add the bouquet garni and onion. Cover and simmer for 20 minutes. Strain and leave to cool.
3. Use on the same day, or store in the refrigerator for not more than 2 days.

Brown Onion Stock

Makes about 900 ml (1½ pt)

2 × 15 ML TBS VEGETABLE OIL

2 LARGE ONIONS, SKINNED AND ROUGHLY CHOPPED

2 GARLIC CLOVES, SKINNED AND HALVED

2 CELERY STICKS, WASHED AND CHOPPED

2 CARROTS, WASHED AND CHOPPED

FEW SAGE LEAVES, THYME STALKS AND PARSLEY STALKS

2 BAY LEAVES

1 × 5 ML TSP YEAST EXTRACT SAVOURY SPREAD (OPTIONAL)

SALT

1. Heat the oil in a large, heavy-based saucepan. Add the onions, and cook, stirring all the time, for about 10 minutes or until they turn a dark golden brown; be careful not to let them burn.
2. Add the remaining vegetables, herbs and yeast extract, if using. Cook over a high heat for 4-5 minutes or until the vegetables are lightly browned.
3. Add 1.2 lt (2 pt) water and bring to the boil. Season with salt, lower the heat and simmer gently for 30 minutes. Strain through a fine sieve into a jug or bowl.
4. The stock is now ready to use, or it can be returned to a clean saucepan and boiled rapidly to reduce the quantity and intensify the flavour. Cool and store in the refrigerator for 2-3 days or freeze for later use.

Vegetable Stock

Makes about 1.2 lt (2 pt)

2 × 15 ML TBS VEGETABLE OIL

1 ONION, SKINNED AND FINELY CHOPPED

1 CARROT, SCRUBBED AND DICED

50 G (2 OZ) TURNIP, SCRUBBED AND DICED

50 G (2 OZ) PARSNIP, SCRUBBED AND DICED

4 CELERY STICKS, WASHED AND CHOPPED

VEGETABLE TRIMMINGS, SUCH AS CELERY TOPS, CABBAGE LEAVES, MUSHROOM PEELINGS, TOMATO SKINS

BOUQUET GARNI

6 BLACK PEPPERCORNS

1. Heat the oil in a saucepan, add the onion and fry gently for about 5 minutes until soft and lightly coloured.
2. Add the vegetables with the trimmings and 1.8 lt (3 pt) water. Add the bouquet garni and peppercorns.
3. Bring to the boil, partially cover and simmer for 1½ hours, skimming occasionally.
4. Strain the stock and leave to cool. Store in the refrigerator and use within 1-2 days.

Mushroom Stock

Makes about 1.5 lt (2½ pt)

1 × 15 ML TBS VEGETABLE OIL

175 G (6 OZ) OPEN-CUP MUSHROOMS, ROUGHLY CHOPPED

1 ONION, SKINNED AND ROUGHLY CHOPPED

2 CARROTS, WASHED AND ROUGHLY CHOPPED

½ HEAD OF FENNEL, ROUGHLY CHOPPED

FEW FRESH HERB SPRIGS, SUCH AS THYME, ROSEMARY AND PARSLEY

SALT AND PEPPER

1. Heat the oil in a large saucepan. Add the mushrooms, onions, carrots and fennel and fry for 5 minutes or until softened.
2. Add the herbs and 1.8 lt (3 pt) water. Bring to the boil and simmer for 45-50 minutes.
3. Strain the stock through a fine sieve into a jug or bowl and season with salt and pepper. The stock is now ready to use, or it can be returned to a clean saucepan and boiled rapidly to reduce the quantity and intensify the flavour. Cool and store in the refrigerator for 2-3 days or freeze for later use.

Consommé

Serves 4

1.5 LT (2½ PT) BEEF STOCK (SEE PAGE 13)
115 G (4 OZ) LEAN BEEF STEAK, SUCH AS RUMP, SHREDDED
150 ML (5 FL OZ) COLD WATER
1 CARROT, PEELED AND QUARTERED
1 SMALL ONION, SKINNED AND QUARTERED
BOUQUET GARNI
1 EGG WHITE
SALT

1. Remove any fat from the stock. Soak the meat in the water for 15 minutes. Put the meat and water, vegetables, stock and bouquet garni into a deep saucepan and add the egg white. Heat gently, whisking continuously until a thick froth starts to form. Stop whisking and bring to the boil. Reduce the heat immediately, cover and simmer for 2 hours. If the liquid boils too rapidly, the froth will break and cloud the consommé.
2. Scald a clean muslin cloth or jelly bag, by pouring boiling water through it, wring it out, tie it to the four legs of an upturned stool and place a bowl underneath. Pour the soup through the cloth, keeping the froth back at first with a spoon, then let it slide out on to the cloth. Pour the soup through the cloth and through the filter of egg white a second time. The consommé should now be clear and sparkling.
3. Reheat the consommé, season with salt if necessary.

VARIATIONS

Consommé Julienne

Cut small quantities of vegetables such as carrot, turnip and celery into thin strips and boil separately; rinse before adding to soup.

Consommé à La Jardinière

Prepare a mixture of vegetables such as finely diced carrots and turnips, tiny florets of cauliflower and green peas. Cook in boiling salted water until just tender, rinse and add to the soup before serving.

Jellied Consommé

Cold consommé should be lightly jellied. It makes a good summer soup. Leave consommé to cool, then chill until set. Chop roughly and serve in individual dishes.

VARIATIONS FOR JELLIED CONSOMMÉ

1. Add 2-3 × 15 ml tbs chopped fresh herbs (chives, parsley and tarragon) to the consommé. Garnish with whipped cream, flavoured with curry powder or sprinkled with toasted flaked almonds.
2. Add 2-3 × 15 ml tbs chopped fresh mint leaves to the consommé. Garnish with whipped cream mixed with chopped mint.

COOK'S TIPS

A classic consommé is a completely clear, well flavoured broth, made from good brown stock. Both the stock and the utensils must be quite free from any trace of grease, to prevent droplets of fat forming on the surface of the soup.

To prevent the consommé becoming cloudy, rinse the garnish in water and add it to the hot liquid just before it is served.

Carrot and Coriander Soup

Serves 4

40 G (1½ OZ) BUTTER OR MARGARINE
175 G (6 OZ) TRIMMED LEEKS, WASHED AND THINLY SLICED
450 G (1 LB) CARROTS, PEELED AND THINLY SLICED
2×5 ML TSP GROUND CORIANDER
1×5 ML TSP PLAIN WHITE FLOUR
1.2 LT (2 PT) CHICKEN STOCK (SEE PAGE 13)
SALT AND PEPPER
150 G (5 OZ) NATURAL YOGURT
FRESH CORIANDER LEAVES AND CROÛTONS, TO GARNISH

1. Heat the butter in a large saucepan. Add the vegetables, cover and cook gently until they begin to soften but not colour.

Carrot and Coriander Soup

2. Stir in the coriander and flour and cook for about 1 minute before pouring the stock in. Bring to the boil, stirring all the time, season, cover and simmer for about 20 minutes or until the vegetables are tender.
3. Cool slightly then purée until smooth. Return to the rinsed-out pan and stir the yogurt in. Reheat carefully but do not boil. Adjust seasoning before serving garnished with fresh coriander leaves and croûtons.

COOK'S TIP
Use a good home-made stock for this soup, if you can, as it adds far greater depth of flavour than packet stock cubes.

Chilled Tomato and Basil Soup

Serves 4

1 × 15 ML TBS SUNFLOWER OIL
1 ONION, SKINNED AND CHOPPED
1 POTATO, PEELED AND CHOPPED
450 G (1 LB) RIPE TOMATOES, SKINNED, QUARTERED AND SEEDED, RESERVING JUICES
1 × 15 ML TBS TOMATO PURÉE
10 BASIL LEAVES
300 ML (10 FL OZ) VEGETABLE STOCK (SEE PAGE 13)
SALT AND PEPPER
225 ML (8 FL OZ) THICK GREEK-STYLE YOGURT
1 GREEN PEPPER, SEEDED AND CHOPPED
½ CUCUMBER, CHOPPED
1 × 15 ML TBS CHOPPED FRESH BASIL
FRESH BASIL, TO GARNISH

1. Heat the oil in a large saucepan, add the onion and fry gently for 5 minutes, then stir in the potato.
2. Add the tomatoes, their juices, tomato purée, basil leaves, stock and seasoning. Bring to the boil, reduce the heat, cover and simmer for 20 minutes, until the potato is tender. Cool.
3. Purée the soup with half the yogurt. Cover and chill. Place the pepper, cucumber, chopped basil, seasoning and the rest of the yogurt in a food processor. Blend until fairly smooth. Chill.
4. Pour the tomato soup into four bowls. Swirl the green sauce in the centre. Garnish with a sprig of basil to serve.

Lettuce and Mangetout Soup

Serves 4

1 × 15 ML TBS SUNFLOWER OIL
2 SHALLOTS, SKINNED AND CHOPPED
2 × 15 ML TBS CHOPPED CELERY LEAVES
900 ML (1½ PT) CHICKEN OR VEGETABLE STOCK (SEE PAGE 13)
225 G (8 OZ) SMALL MANGETOUT
½ COS LETTUCE, FINELY SHREDDED
SALT AND PEPPER
1 × 5 ML TSP SOY SAUCE
1 × 15 ML TBS CHOPPED FRESH MINT OR LEMON BALM
3 × 15 ML TBS CHOPPED FRESH PARSLEY OR CHERVIL

1. Heat the oil in large saucepan. Add the shallots and fry gently until softened – about 5 minutes. Add the celery leaves and stock and bring to the boil. Simmer, partly covered, for 5 minutes.
2. Meanwhile top and tail the mangetout if necessary; halve if large. Add these and the lettuce to the pan with the seasoning and soy sauce; return to the boil.
3. Simmer for 5 minutes, or until the lettuce is wilted, then stir in the herbs. Serve hot.

MELBA TOAST

Serves 4

4 SLICES OF READY-SLICED WHITE OR BROWN BREAD

1. Preheat the grill to high and toast the bread lightly on both sides. Cut off the crusts, then holding the toast flat, slide a sharp knife between the toasted edges to split the bread in half.
2. Cut each piece into 4 triangles, then toast under the grill, untoasted side uppermost, until golden and the edges curl. Serve warm. Alternatively make earlier in the day and warm for a short time in the oven at 160°C/325°F/Gas Mark 3 before serving.

Andalusian Summer Soup

Serves 4-6

4 × 15 ML TBS OLIVE OIL
1 LARGE ONION, SKINNED AND ROUGHLY CHOPPED
2 GARLIC CLOVES, SKINNED AND CHOPPED
2 LARGE RED PEPPERS, CORED, SEEDED AND ROUGHLY CHOPPED
450 G (1 LB) RIPE TOMATOES, CHOPPED
900 ML (1½ PT) WATER
2 × 15 ML TBS WHITE WINE VINEGAR
1 DRIED RED CHILLI, FINELY CHOPPED
SALT AND PEPPER
4 × 15 ML LOW-FAT MAYONNAISE
FINELY CHOPPED CUCUMBER, ONION, GREEN OR RED PEPPER AND CROÛTONS, TO SERVE

1. Heat the oil in a large saucepan, add the onion and garlic and fry gently for 5 minutes or until soft but not coloured. Add the red peppers and fry for a further 5 minutes, stirring constantly, then add the tomatoes and stir to break them up.
2. Add the water, wine vinegar and chilli. Season. Bring to the boil, then lower the heat, cover and simmer for 45 minutes.
3. Sieve the soup or purée it in a blender or food processor. If using a blender or processor, pass the puréed soup through a sieve afterwards to remove the tomato skins.
4. Put the mayonnaise in a large bowl and gradually whisk the soup in. Taste and adjust the seasoning, if necessary. Chill in the refrigerator for at least 4 hours before serving with chopped vegetables and croûtons.

COOK'S TIP
Serve this version of gazpacho, the classic chilled tomato soup, with bowls of finely chopped cucumber, onion and green or red pepper, plus herb croûtons (see page 16). Guests can help themselves to the accompaniments, sprinkling them over individual bowls of soup.

Creamy Carrot and Celeriac Soup

Serves 6

2 × 15 ML TBS OIL

225 G (8 OZ) ONION, SKINNED AND ROUGHLY CHOPPED

900 G (2 LB) CARROTS, PEELED AND ROUGHLY CHOPPED

900 G (2 LB) CELERIAC, PEELED AND ROUGHLY CHOPPED

1.8 LT (3 PT) CHICKEN STOCK (SEE PAGE 13)

1 × 5 ML TSP SOY SAUCE

FINELY GRATED RIND AND JUICE OF 1 ORANGE

300 ML (10 FL OZ) SINGLE CREAM

SALT AND PEPPER

HERB CROÛTONS (SEE RIGHT) AND PARSLEY, TO GARNISH

1. Heat the oil in a large saucepan and add the vegetables. Fry for 5 minutes, stirring frequently. Add the stock, bring to the boil, cover and leave to simmer gently for 20 minutes.
2. Stir in the soy sauce, orange rind and 4 × 15 ml tbs orange juice. Cover and simmer for 20 minutes.

Creamy Carrot and Celeriac Soup

3. Cool slightly, then blend in a food processor until smooth. For an extra-velvety texture, push through a sieve.
4. Stir the cream in and reheat gently. Season; serve garnished with herb croûtons and parsley.

HERB CROÛTONS

Serves 8-10

50 G (2 OZ) BUTTER

2 × 15 ML TBS CHOPPED FRESH CORIANDER OR PARSLEY

5 MEDIUM SLICES OF BREAD

1. Beat the butter until soft, then mix in the coriander or parsley. Spread one side of the bread slices with the butter mixture. Using a small cutter, stamp out croûtons, discarding crusts.
2. Place on a baking tray, butter side up, and grill until golden brown. Keep warm, uncovered.

Curried Parsnip Soup

Serves 6

40 G (1½ OZ) BUTTER OR MARGARINE
1 ONION, SKINNED AND SLICED
675 G (1½ LB) PARSNIPS, PEELED AND FINELY DICED
1×5 ML TSP CURRY POWDER
½×5 ML TSP GROUND CUMIN
1.2 LT (2 PT) CHICKEN STOCK (SEE PAGE 13)
SALT AND PEPPER
150 ML (5 FL OZ) SINGLE CREAM OR MILK
PAPRIKA, TO GARNISH

1. Melt the butter in a large saucepan, add the onion and parsnips and fry gently for about 3 minutes. Stir in the curry powder and cumin and cook the vegetables for a further 2 minutes.
2. Add the stock, season and bring to the boil, then reduce the heat, cover and simmer for about 45 minutes, until the vegetables are tender.
3. Allow to cool slightly, then sieve or purée in a blender or food processor until smooth.
4. Return the purée to the rinsed-out pan and adjust the seasoning. Add the cream and reheat but do not boil. Serve sprinkled with paprika.

Cauliflower and Almond Cream Soup

Serves 6

FEW SAFFRON THREADS
4×15 ML TBS BOILING WATER
115 G (4 OZ) FLAKED ALMONDS
50 G (2 OZ) BUTTER OR MARGARINE
1 ONION, SKINNED AND CHOPPED
1 SMALL CAULIFLOWER, BROKEN INTO FLORETS
1.3 LT (2¼ PT) CHICKEN STOCK (SEE PAGE13)
FRESHLY GRATED NUTMEG
SALT AND PEPPER
150 ML (5 FL OZ) SINGLE CREAM

1. Soak the saffron in the boiling water for 2 hours. Toast half the almonds on a sheet of foil under the grill, turning them frequently. Leave to cool.
2. Melt the butter in a large saucepan, add the onion and fry gently until soft. Add the cauliflower and the untoasted almonds and stir; cover and cook gently for 10 minutes.
3. Add the stock and stir well, then strain in the yellow saffron liquid. Add nutmeg and season to taste. Bring to the boil, lower the heat, cover and simmer for 30 minutes, or until the cauliflower is very tender.
4. Purée the soup in a blender or food processor until smooth (you may have to do this twice to break down the almonds). Return to the rinsed-out pan, add half the cream and reheat gently. Taste and adjust seasoning, then pour into a warmed tureen.
5. Swirl the remaining cream in and sprinkle with the toasted almonds and a little extra nutmeg, if liked. Serve immediately.

Cauliflower and Almond Cream Soup

MIXED BEAN AND VEGETABLE SOUP

Serves 6 as a main course

1 × 15 ML TBS OLIVE OIL

1 ONION, SKINNED AND ROUGHLY CHOPPED

450 G (1 LB) MIXED ROOT VEGETABLES, INCLUDING CARROTS, POTATOES AND PARSNIPS, PEELED AND ROUGHLY CHOPPED

450 G (1 LB) OTHER MIXED VEGETABLES, SUCH AS PEPPERS, CELERY AND FENNEL, PREPARED AS NECESSARY AND ROUGHLY CHOPPED

1 GARLIC CLOVE, SKINNED AND CRUSHED

2 × 5 ML TSP MILD CURRY POWDER

2 BAY LEAVES

ABOUT 1.2 LT (2 PT) VEGETABLE STOCK (SEE PAGE 13)

430 G CAN RED KIDNEY BEANS, DRAINED AND RINSED

430 G CAN BLACK-EYE BEANS, DRAINED AND RINSED

2 COURGETTES, TRIMMED AND SLICED

3 × 15 ML TBS CHOPPED FRESH PARSLEY OR CORIANDER

SALT AND PEPPER

1. Heat the oil in a large, heavy-based saucepan. Add all the vegetables, except the beans and courgettes, and cook over a high heat for 4-5 minutes, stirring all the time. Add the garlic, curry powder and bay leaves and continue cooking for 2-3 minutes.
2. Pour the stock in. (There should be enough to cover the vegetables; if not, add a little more.) Bring to the boil, then reduce the heat, cover and simmer for 20 minutes.
3. Add the beans and cook for a further 10 minutes. Remove the bay leaves. Purée about half the soup in a blender.
4. Return the puréed soup to the remaining soup in the saucepan and bring to the boil. Add the courgettes and herbs. Season to taste and simmer gently for 3-4 minutes or until the courgettes are just tender. Add extra stock, if necessary, to thin the soup.

COOK'S TIP

Freshly cooked beans could be used, but using cans makes the soup quick to cook. Cut the vegetables into generous chunks to give the soup a good, hearty texture.

SHROPSHIRE PEA SOUP

Serves 6

50 G (2 OZ) BUTTER OR MARGARINE

1 SMALL ONION, SKINNED AND FINELY CHOPPED

900 G (2 LB) FRESH PEAS, SHELLED

1.2 LT (2 PT) CHICKEN STOCK (SEE PAGE 13)

½ × 5 ML TSP SUGAR

2 LARGE SPRIGS OF FRESH MINT

SALT AND PEPPER

150 ML (5 FL OZ) DOUBLE CREAM OR MILK

MINT SPRIG, TO GARNISH

1. Melt the butter in a large saucepan, add the onion and cook for 5 minutes, until soft. Add the peas, stock, sugar and sprigs of mint. Bring to the boil, cover and cook for about 30 minutes.
2. Allow to cool slightly, then sieve or purée in a blender or food processor until smooth. Return to the pan and season to taste.
3. Stir the cream into the soup and reheat, stirring. Adjust the seasoning.
4. Transfer to a warmed tureen and garnish with a sprig of fresh mint.

CHESTNUT AND ROASTED GARLIC SOUP

Serves 8

2 × 250 G PACK COOKED WHOLE CHESTNUTS

4 LARGE GARLIC CLOVES, UNPEELED

3 × 425 G CANS BEEF CONSOMMÉ

PINCH OF FRESHLY GRATED NUTMEG

SALT AND PEPPER

115 ML (4 FL OZ) GREEK-STYLE YOGURT

1 × 5 ML TSP CURRY PASTE

FRESHLY MILLED BLACK PEPPER, TO GARNISH

1. Place the garlic cloves with the chestnuts on a baking tray and roast in the oven at 200°C/400°F/Gas Mark 6 for 15-20 minutes or until the garlic is soft to the touch and the chestnuts are browning. Cool, then pop the garlic cloves out of their skins.
2. Place the garlic, chestnuts and consommé in a blender or food processor and process until smooth. Pour into a saucepan, bring almost to the boil and season to taste with nutmeg, salt and pepper. Simmer very gently for 5 minutes to allow the flavours to blend. If necessary, add a little water to thin.
3. Mix the yogurt with the curry paste. Serve the soup in warmed bowls with a spoonful of yogurt, garnished with freshly milled black pepper.

Mixed Bean and Vegetable Soup (left)
Chestnut and Roasted Garlic Soup (opposite)

French Onion Soup

Serves 4

50 G (2 OZ) BUTTER OR MARGARINE

2 LARGE ONIONS, SKINNED AND SLICED

2×15 ML TBS PLAIN WHITE FLOUR

900 ML (1½ PT) BEEF STOCK (SEE PAGE 13)

SALT AND PEPPER

1 BAY LEAF

4 SLICES OF FRENCH BREAD

75 G (3 OZ) GRUYÈRE CHEESE, GRATED

1. Melt the butter in a pan and fry the onions for 5-10 minutes, until browned.
2. Stir in the flour and cook gently for 1 minute, stirring. Remove pan from the heat and gradually stir in the stock, seasoning and bay leaf. Bring to the boil slowly and continue to cook, stirring, until thickened. Cover and simmer for about 30 minutes. Remove the bay leaf. Adjust the seasoning.
3. Put a slice of bread into each individual soup bowl, pour the soup over the bread and top with cheese.

Celery and Stilton Soup

Serves 4-6

40 G (1½ OZ) BUTTER OR MARGARINE

4 CELERY STICKS, WASHED, TRIMMED AND CHOPPED

3×15 ML TBS PLAIN WHITE FLOUR

300 ML (10 FL OZ) MILK

600 ML (20 FL OZ) CHICKEN STOCK (SEE PAGE 13)

225 G (8 OZ) STILTON CHEESE, CRUMBLED

SALT AND PEPPER

1. Melt the butter in a saucepan, add the celery and cook gently for about 5 minutes, until softened but not coloured.
2. Stir in the flour and cook gently for 1 minute, stirring. Remove from the heat and gradually stir in the milk and stock. Bring to the boil, cover and simmer for about 15 minutes, until the celery is tender.
3. Gradually add the Stilton and stir until melted. Season to taste and reheat gently.

Roquefort and Watercress Soup

Roquefort and Watercress Soup

Serves 4

8 LARGE GARLIC CLOVES, UNPEELED

2×15 ML TBS OIL

225 G (8 OZ) ONIONS, SKINNED AND CHOPPED

175 G (6 OZ) OLD POTATOES, PEELED AND DICED

1.2 LT (2 PT) VEGETABLE STOCK (SEE PAGE 13)

2 BUNCHES WATERCRESS, WASHED AND STALKS REMOVED

175 G (6 OZ) ROQUEFORT CHEESE (OR STILTON), CRUMBLED

SALT AND PEPPER

SINGLE CREAM AND CRUMBLED ROQUEFORT, TO SERVE

1. Roast the garlic on a baking tray at 200°C/400°F/Gas Mark 6 for 25 minutes until charred. Cool.
2. Heat the oil in a pan, add the onion and cook for 5 minutes, until beginning to soften. Add the potatoes and stock, bring to the boil, cover and simmer for 20 minutes, until the potatoes are cooked.
3. Stir the watercress sprigs in, bring to the boil and simmer for 1 minute. Pop the garlic cloves out of their skins and add to the soup. Cool, then purée.
4. Return to the rinsed-out pan and whisk the cheese in. Reheat and season to taste. Do not boil. Serve hot or chilled with cream and extra crumbled Roquefort.

Fennel and Onion Soup

Serves 6

450 G (1 LB) FENNEL, WIPED AND FINELY SLICED, DISCARDING ANY BRUISED OUTER SECTIONS

4×15 ML TBS SUNFLOWER OIL

900 G (2 LB) ONIONS, SKINNED AND FINELY SLICED

1.8 LT (3 PT) BROWN ONION STOCK (SEE PAGE 13)

2×15 ML TBS DIJON MUSTARD

SALT AND PEPPER

50 G (2 OZ) SOFTENED BUTTER OR MARGARINE

75 G (3 OZ) CHEDDAR OR GRUYÈRE CHEESE, GRATED

6 LARGE SLICES BREAD, CRUSTS REMOVED

1. Reserve fennel tops for garnish, refrigerating them in a polythene bag. Heat the oil in a saucepan and add the fennel and onion. Cover and cook over a moderate heat until beginning to soften and brown.
2. Pour in the stock, bring to the boil then stir in half the mustard and the seasoning. Cover and simmer for 15-20 minutes, or until the vegetables are quite tender.
3. Meanwhile, beat together the butter, remaining mustard, grated cheese and seasoning. Toast the bread on both sides. Spread one side with the cheese mixture and grill until golden. Cut into neat triangles and float on the soup to serve. Garnish with fennel tops.

Chicken Soup with Dumplings

Serves 4 as a main course

1.1-1.4 KG (2½-3 LB) OVEN-READY CHICKEN, SKINNED

1 ONION, SKINNED AND CHOPPED

1 LT (1¾ PT) CHICKEN STOCK (SEE PAGE 13)

335 G (12 OZ) CARROTS, PEELED AND SLICED

SALT AND PEPPER

115 G (4 OZ) CELERY STICKS WITH LEAVES, CHOPPED

— DUMPLINGS —

75 G (3 OZ) MATZO MEAL OR OATMEAL

8×15 ML TBS BOILING WATER

1 EGG, BEATEN

SALT

1. Put the chicken, onion, stock, carrots and seasoning into a large saucepan and bring to the boil. Reduce the heat, cover and simmer for about 1 hour, until the chicken is tender. Remove the chicken and leave to stand for a few minutes. Strain the stock into a saucepan and heat to just simmering while you make the dumplings.
2. Mix together the matzo meal, boiling water, egg and salt. Shape into small marble-sized dumplings with your hands.
3. Add the dumplings and celery to the simmering soup and cook gently for about 20 minutes.
4. Meanwhile, carve the chicken off the bones. Cut the meat into small chunks, stir into the soup and heat through. Taste and adjust seasoning and serve immediately.

PRODUCE OF FRANCE

STARTERS

Starters are a very important part of a meal because they stimulate the appetite and set the scene for the rest of the meal that is to follow. Apart from soups, you can serve pâtés, mousses, seafood dishes or cold meats or vegetables as a starter – the choice is endless. Remember, though, that starter portions should be small, so they do not take the edge off the appetite, and attractively presented.

Bacon and Pistachio Terrine (page 37)

Mushroom Fritters

Serves 6

175 G (6 OZ) ONIONS, SKINNED AND FINELY CHOPPED

175 G (6 OZ) PLAIN FLOUR

½×5 ML TSP SALT

¼×5 ML TSP BAKING POWDER

½×5 ML TSP CHILLI POWDER

2×5 ML TSP SNIPPED FRESH CHIVES OR 1 × 5 ML TSP DRIED

2×5 ML TSP DRIED FENUGREEK (OPTIONAL)

2×5 ML TSP LEMON JUICE

1×5 ML TSP CUMIN SEEDS

175 ML (6 FL OZ) COLD WATER

OIL FOR DEEP-FRYING

450 G (1 LB) BUTTON OR BROWN-CAP MUSHROOMS, WIPED AND TRIMMED

LEMON SLICES AND FRESH CORIANDER, TO GARNISH

CORIANDER AND CHILLI RELISH, TO SERVE (SEE COOK'S TIPS)

1. Mix together the first nine ingredients. Gradually add enough of the cold water to make a batter the consistency of thick cream. Cover and leave to stand for 10 minutes.
2. Heat the oil in a deep-fat fryer to 180°C/350°F or in a deep saucepan until a cube of bread sizzles and turns golden brown in about 30 seconds.
3. Dip the mushrooms into the batter and deep-fry a few at a time until golden brown. Drain on absorbent kitchen paper and keep warm, uncovered, in a low oven while frying remaining mushrooms. Serve as soon as possible, garnished with the lemon slices and fresh coriander, and served with a bowl of coriander and chilli relish.

COOK'S TIPS

Serve these spicy fritters the minute they're cooked. If kept warm for any length of time, they become soft.

To make a coriander and chilli relish to serve with the fritters, blend together 1 large bunch of fresh coriander, roughly chopped, 1 salad onion, trimmed and chopped, 3-5 medium green chillies, seeded and chopped, 1 green pepper, seeded and chopped, ½ × 5 ml tsp salt, 2 × 15 ml tbs lemon juice, strained, and a few fresh mint leaves in a processor until well combined.

Goat's Cheese and Roasted Pepper Salad

Serves 6

6 LARGE PEPPERS (PREFERABLY A MIXTURE OF RED, GREEN AND YELLOW)

3-4 LARGE GARLIC CLOVES, UNPEELED

1×5 ML TSP DIJON MUSTARD

1×5 ML TSP CLEAR HONEY

SALT AND PEPPER

2×15 ML TBS WHITE WINE VINEGAR OR LEMON JUICE

6×15 ML TBS OLIVE OIL

12 THIN SLICES OF FRENCH BREAD

6 SMALL RINDLESS GOAT'S CHEESES, EACH WEIGHING ABOUT 50 G (2 OZ)

MIXED SALAD LEAVES

FEW SESAME SEEDS, TOASTED

FEW CHOPPED FRESH HERBS (OPTIONAL)

1. Grill the whole peppers and garlic cloves under a very hot grill for 10-15 minutes or until soft and blackened all over, turning occasionally. Leave until cool enough to handle.
2. Remove the skin from the garlic and squeeze the soft insides into a jug. Add the mustard, honey and plenty of salt and pepper. Beat together with a fork, mashing the garlic as you beat. Gradually beat in the vinegar or lemon juice followed by the oil. Taste and add more seasoning if necessary.
3. Carefully peel the blackened skin from the peppers, halve and seed them. Cut the flesh into strips and place in a shallow dish. Pour the dressing over the peppers and leave to marinate for at least 1 hour.
4. Just before serving, toast the bread slices on both sides. Halve the cheeses and place one half on each slice of toast. Arrange on a baking tray and bake in the oven at 180°C/350°F/Gas Mark 4 for 8-12 minutes or until the cheese is soft and warmed through, but not completely melted.
5. Meanwhile, arrange the salad leaves on six plates, and spoon the peppers and marinade over them. Arrange the bread slices and baked cheese on top and sprinkle with a few toasted sesame seeds and fresh herbs, if using. Season with black pepper and serve immediately.

VARIATION

For a less substantial dish, omit the goat's cheese and serve the salad with French bread rubbed with garlic. This would also make the dish into a suitable starter for a vegan meal.

Pizzettas

Serves 6

213 G PACKET CHILLED PUFF PASTRY

3 SALAD ONIONS, TRIMMED AND FINELY CHOPPED

25 G (1 OZ) BUTTER, MELTED

FINELY GRATED RIND AND JUICE OF 1 LEMON

SALT AND PEPPER

335 G (12 OZ) TOMATOES

225 G (8 OZ) COURGETTES

2×15 ML TBS PESTO SAUCE

FRESHLY GRATED PARMESAN CHEESE, TO SERVE

1. Roll out the pastry. Cut out six 11 cm (4½ in) rounds and place on an edged baking tray. Prick all over with a fork. Bake at 230°C/450°F/Gas Mark 8 for about 8 minutes, or until lightly risen and golden.
2. Meanwhile, stir the onions into the butter, together with the grated lemon rind and 1 × 15 ml tbs lemon juice. Season well. Cut the tomatoes and courgettes into thin slices.
3. Remove the pastry circles from the oven. (They may have puffed up quite a bit.) Spread each pastry circle with 1 × 5 ml tsp pesto sauce. Arrange slices of tomato and courgette overlapping on top of each circle and season well. Brush with the melted butter mixture.
4. Return to the oven for 10-12 minutes or until the tomatoes and courgettes have softened and the edges of the pastry are puffed and golden brown. Serve immediately, sprinkled with freshly grated Parmesan cheese.

Pizzettas

Tomato Bruschetta

Serves 4

675 G (1½ LB) VERY RIPE, JUICY TOMATOES, ROUGHLY CHOPPED

PINCH OF SUGAR

SALT AND PEPPER

2-3 LARGE GARLIC CLOVES, SKINNED

1 × 15 ML TBS OLIVE OIL

8-10 THICK SLICES OF GOOD WHITE BREAD, SUCH AS CIABATTA, CUT FROM A DAY-OLD LOAF

FEW BASIL LEAVES

FEW BLACK OLIVES (OPTIONAL)

1. Put the tomatoes in a bowl, add the sugar and season generously with salt and pepper. Crush one of the garlic cloves and add it to the tomatoes with the olive oil. Cover and leave to stand for about 30 minutes–1 hour.

2. Lightly toast the bread on both sides until golden brown. Cut the remaining garlic cloves in half and rub all over both sides of the toast. (The more you rub, the stronger the garlic flavour will be.)

3. Arrange the toast on four individual serving plates. Spoon the tomatoes on top with a little of their juice. Tear the basil leaves into small pieces and sprinkle over the bruschetta. Scatter olives, if using, on top and serve.

COOK'S TIP

Bruschetta is Tuscan garlic bread made with dense Italian bread, rich green virgin olive oil and garlic. The success of this dish depends entirely on the ingredients; soggy pre-sliced white bread and bland vegetable oil just will not do!

Warm Houmous with Feta Cheese

Serves 6

75 G (3 OZ) SESAME SEEDS

2 × 15 ML TBS POLYUNSATURATED OIL

6 × 15 ML TBS LEMON JUICE

8 × 15 ML TBS WATER

2 LARGE GARLIC CLOVES, SKINNED AND ROUGHLY CHOPPED

2 × 430 G CANS CHICK-PEAS, DRAINED

1 BUNCH SALAD ONIONS, TRIMMED AND ROUGHLY CHOPPED

150 G (5 OZ) FETA CHEESE, CRUMBLED

6 × 15 ML TBS CHOPPED FRESH CORIANDER

½ × 5 ML TSP CHILLI POWDER

3 × 15 ML TBS MILK

4 × 15 ML TBS BUTTER OR POLYUNSATURATED MARGARINE, MELTED

SALT AND PEPPER

PITTA CRISPS (SEE COOK'S TIP) AND CRUDITÉS, TO SERVE

1. Spread the sesame seeds on a baking tray and brown lightly in the oven at 180°C/350°F/Gas Mark 4 for 8-10 minutes. Cool. Place in a blender with half the oil and 1 × 15 ml tbs lemon juice. Blend to a paste. Add the remaining lemon juice, water, garlic and chick-peas and blend again until smooth. Transfer to a bowl.

2. Place the salad onions, cheese, 5 × 15 ml tbs coriander, chilli powder, milk and butter in the blender. Blend for 2-3 minutes. Stir into the chick-pea mixture and season.

3. To serve, heat the remaining oil in a fondue dish or saucepan. Add the houmous and stir over a medium heat until heated through and bubbling. Serve in the fondue dish over a burner or spoon into a warmed heatproof dish. Sprinkle with remaining coriander. Serve immediately with Pitta Crisps and crudités.

COOK'S TIP

To make Pitta Crisps, split 12 white pitta breads in half horizontally; cut each half into four. Blend together 75 g (3 oz) butter or margarine with a crushed garlic clove. Spread the cut surface of each piece of pitta bread lightly with the mixture. Place on a baking tray, buttered side up, and bake at 200°C/400°F/Gas Mark 6 for 5-7 minutes or until golden and sizzling. Serve hot.

Sesame Cheese Pastries

Serves 6

115 G (4 OZ) READY-MADE HOUMOUS

175 G (6 OZ) LOW-FAT SOFT CHEESE

1 GARLIC CLOVE, SKINNED AND CRUSHED

BLACK PEPPER

6 LARGE SHEETS FILO PASTRY

50 G (2 OZ) MELTED BUTTER

SESAME SEEDS

150 ML (5 FL OZ) OLIVE OIL

2 × 15 ML TBS WHITE WINE VINEGAR

SALT

CRISPY FRIED AUBERGINE SLICES (OR SALAD LEAVES), TO GARNISH

1. Beat together the houmous, soft cheese, garlic and pepper.

2. Cut each filo pastry sheet into four squares, each about 13 cm (5 in), making 24 in total.

3. Brush one square lightly with melted butter. Spoon a little of the houmous mixture into the centre and fold the pastry over to enclose it, like a parcel. Butter another square of pastry, place the houmous parcel in the centre and fold up to enclose as before. (This double layer helps to stop the parcels from bursting while cooking.) Brush lightly all over with butter, sprinkle with sesame seeds and place on a baking tray. Repeat until all the filling and pastry is used. Chill the pastries in the refrigerator for 20 minutes.

4. Whisk together the oil and vinegar with some toasted sesame seeds to make a dressing. Season. Cook the pastries at 190°C/375°F/Gas Mark 5 for about 25-30 minutes or until golden brown and crisp. Serve the pastries with a little dressing drizzled over, garnished with fried aubergine slices or salad leaves.

COOK'S TIP

These crispy pastries are the ideal starter or savoury to serve with drinks, as they can be made ahead and cooked from frozen. They will keep warm and crisp, uncovered, in a low oven for an extra 10-15 minutes.

Sesame Cheese Pastries

Three-Cheese Aubergine Tart

Serves 6

SHORTCRUST PASTRY, MADE WITH 225 G (8 OZ) FLOUR (SEE PAGE 212)

3 × 15 ML TBS OLIVE OIL

450 G (1 LB) AUBERGINES, DICED

450 G (1 LB) FRESH RIPE TOMATOES, DICED

3 × 15 ML TBS CHOPPED FRESH BASIL OR MARJORAM

SALT AND PEPPER

450 G (1 LB) FROZEN LEAF SPINACH, THAWED

PINCH OF MACE

175 G (6 OZ) SOFT CHEESE (SUCH AS RICOTTA, CURD, FULL-FAT SOFT OR SOFT GOAT'S CHEESE)

200 G (7 OZ) MOZZARELLA CHEESE

3 × 15 ML TBS FRESHLY GRATED PARMESAN CHEESE

SALAD LEAVES, TO SERVE

1. Roll out the pastry and use to line a 23 cm (9 in) diameter, 5 cm (2 in) deep, fluted flan tin. Bake blind until set and lightly browned. Cool.
2. Heat the oil in a pan, add the aubergine and cook gently for 10 minutes or until beginning to soften, stirring occasionally. Add the tomato and basil; season.
3. Meanwhile, place the spinach in a frying pan and cook over a high heat for about 3-5 minutes or until all excess moisture has been driven off; season well and add the mace.
4. Spread the soft cheese over the base of the tart. Top with the spinach then the aubergine and tomato mixture. Dice the Mozzarella and scatter it over the tart. Sprinkle the Parmesan over the top.
5. Stand the tin on a baking tray and bake at 190°C/375°F/Gas Mark 5 for about 50 minutes or until golden brown and heated through. Serve with salad leaves.

Blue Brie Toasts

Makes about 60

335 G (12 OZ) BLUE BRIE CHEESE, RIND REMOVED AND CUT INTO SMALL PIECES

3 × 15 ML TBS LOW-FAT MAYONNAISE

SALT AND PEPPER

10 THICK SLICES OF CRUSTLESS BREAD

SOFTENED BUTTER, FOR SPREADING

1. Beat together the cheese, mayonnaise and seasoning.
2. Spread one side of each slice of bread with butter, the other with the cheese and mayonnaise mixture, and cut into triangles.
3. Place buttered side down, on baking trays and bake at 220°C/400°F/Gas Mark 6 for 12 minutes or until crisp and brown underneath. Serve hot.

Three-Cheese Aubergine Tart

Aubergine Blinis

Serves 6

1 AUBERGINE, WEIGHING ABOUT 450 G (1 LB)

OLIVE OIL

115 G (4 OZ) PLAIN FLOUR

1 × 5 ML TSP BAKING POWDER

3 EGGS

2 GARLIC CLOVES, SKINNED AND CRUSHED

SALT AND PEPPER

ABOUT 115 G (4 OZ) BABY CARROTS, TRIMMED AND SCRAPED

115 G (4 OZ) LARGE MUSHROOMS, WIPED AND THICKLY SLICED

3 MEDIUM COURGETTES, TRIMMED AND THICKLY SLICED

GREEK-STYLE YOGURT, CRÈME FRAÎCHE OR MAYONNAISE, TO SERVE

1. Prick the aubergine all over with a fork and rub the skin with a little olive oil. Bake in the oven at 200°C/400°F/Gas Mark 6 for about 30 minutes or until soft when pressed. Cool slightly, then halve and scrape out the flesh.
2. Mash the aubergine flesh with a potato masher, then add the flour, baking powder, eggs and one garlic clove. Mix well to make a fairly stiff batter. Season generously and set aside.
3. Heat a little olive oil in a large saucepan, add the carrots and remaining garlic and fry over a high heat for 1-2 minutes. Lower the heat and continue to cook while frying the blinis.
4. To fry the blinis, heat a little olive oil in a large, heavy-based frying pan. Drop tablespoons of batter into the oil and fry for 2-3 minutes or until firm and golden brown underneath. Turn the blinis and fry for a further 2-3 minutes or until the second sides are golden brown. Remove from the pan and keep warm while frying the remaining blinis. There should be enough batter to make about 20 blinis.
5. When all the blinis are cooked, increase the heat under the carrots, add the remaining vegetables and cook for 2-3 minutes or until the mushrooms and courgettes are just tender, shaking the pan continuously.
6. Arrange the blinis on warmed serving plates and top with the vegetables and a spoonful of yogurt, crème fraîche or mayonnaise. Grind black pepper over the top and serve immediately.

COOK'S TIP

These are tiny, well flavoured pancakes, topped with sautéed vegetables and yogurt, crème fraîche or mayonnaise. If you increase the portion size, they make a good main course.

Fried Courgettes with Rosemary Aïoli

Serves 4

1 × 5 ML TSP FRESH ROSEMARY, VERY FINELY CHOPPED

2 GARLIC CLOVES, SKINNED AND CRUSHED

SALT AND PEPPER

150 ML (5 FL OZ) MAYONNAISE

900 G (2 LB) THIN COURGETTES, TRIMMED

PLAIN FLOUR FOR COATING

OIL FOR DEEP-FRYING

ROSEMARY SPRIGS, TO GARNISH

1. To make the aïoli, put the rosemary, garlic and a little salt in a bowl and mash with a fork until a paste is formed. (It won't be perfectly smooth because of the rosemary.) Add the mayonnaise. Season with pepper, cover and leave the aïoli to stand for at least 1 hour to allow the flavours to develop.
2. Just before serving, thinly slice the courgettes. Put some flour in a bowl and season it. Add the courgettes and toss until coated.
3. Heat the oil in a deep-fat fryer to 190°C/375°F or in a deep frying pan until a cube of bread sizzles in it. Put enough courgette slices into the frying basket to quarter fill it, shaking off excess flour, and lower the basket into the oil. Cook for 3-4 minutes or until golden brown. Drain on crumpled absorbent kitchen paper and keep warm while cooking the remainder.
4. Pile the fried courgettes on to warmed individual serving plates and add a spoonful of aïoli. Garnish with sprigs of rosemary and serve immediately.

Cheese and Sesame Aigrettes

Serves 8

115 G (4 OZ) PLAIN FLOUR

SALT AND PEPPER

½ × 5 ML TSP DRY ENGLISH MUSTARD POWDER

¼ × 5 ML TSP CAYENNE PEPPER

75 G (3 OZ) BUTTER OR MARGARINE

225 ML (8 FL OZ) WATER

3 EGGS, LIGHTLY BEATEN

50 G (2 OZ) MATURE CHEDDAR CHEESE, FINELY GRATED

2 × 5 ML TSP SESAME SEEDS

OIL FOR DEEP-FRYING

FRESHLY GRATED PARMESAN CHEESE, TO SERVE

1. Sift the flour with the seasoning, mustard and cayenne pepper on to a piece of absorbent kitchen paper.
2. Place the butter in a medium-sized saucepan with the water. Stir over a low heat until the butter is completely melted. Bring to a full rolling boil. Tip in the seasoned flour. Remove the pan from the heat at once and beat the mixture with a wooden spoon until it leaves the sides of the pan. Cool for 10 minutes.
3. Gradually add the beaten eggs to the flour mixture, beating well between each addition. Add the cheese and sesame seeds.
4. Heat the oil in a deep-fat fryer or deep saucepan until a piece of bread sizzles vigorously in it. Drop 3 or 4 small spoonfuls of mixture into the oil at a time and cook for 5 minutes or until puffed and golden.
5. Lift out on to absorbent kitchen paper, using a slotted spoon. Fry remaining mixture a few spoonfuls at a time. Serve at once sprinkled with Parmesan.

COOK'S TIP

These crisp savouries are quick to cook and delicious to serve with pre-lunch drinks. The mixture can be made the day before and refrigerated, so it's ready to cook when required.

Prawn Puris

Serves 8

2 × 15 ML TBS VEGETABLE OIL

1 ONION, SKINNED AND FINELY CHOPPED

2 GARLIC CLOVES, SKINNED AND CRUSHED

450 G (1 LB) COOKED PEELED PRAWNS, DRAINED AND DRIED IF FROZEN

1-2 × 5 ML TSP CHILLI POWDER, TO TASTE

8 RIPE TOMATOES, SKINNED, SEEDED AND ROUGHLY CHOPPED

150 ML (5 FL OZ) COCONUT MILK

2 × 5 ML TSP LIME OR LEMON JUICE

SALT AND PEPPER

— PURIS —

225 G (8 OZ) PLAIN WHOLEMEAL FLOUR

PINCH OF SALT

2 × 5 ML TSP VEGETABLE OIL

90-150 ML (3½-5 FL OZ) WATER

VEGETABLE OIL FOR DEEP-FRYING

CHOPPED FRESH CORIANDER, TO GARNISH

1. Heat the oil in a heavy flameproof casserole, add the onion and cook gently, stirring frequently, for 5-7 minutes until softened. Add the garlic, prawns and chilli powder, increase the heat to moderate and stir-fry for just 2-3 minutes. Remove with a slotted spoon and set aside.
2. Add the tomatoes and coconut milk to the casserole and bring to the boil, stirring. Simmer until the tomatoes are broken up and the sauce is thickened, stirring frequently, then return the prawn mixture and its juices to the pan and stir well to mix. Add the lime or lemon juice and salt and pepper to taste, then remove from the heat.
3. To make the puris, put the flour, salt and oil in a bowl and mix together. Gradually stir in enough tepid water to make a fairly stiff dough. Knead on a floured surface for at least 5 minutes, until smooth and elastic, then return to the bowl, cover with a damp cloth and leave to rest for 15 minutes.
4. Divide the dough into eight equal pieces and roll each one out to a round about 13 cm (5 in) in diameter. Cover each one as you finish rolling, to prevent drying out.
5. Heat about 5 cm (2 in) oil in a deep, heavy frying pan until hot. Add the puris one at a time and deep-fry for about 10-15 seconds on each side until puffed and golden. Remove with a slotted spoon, drain on absorbent kitchen paper and keep warm.
6. Return the prawn mixture to the heat and bring quickly to the boil, stirring. Place a puri on each of eight plates and top with the prawn mixture. Sprinkle with chopped fresh coriander and serve immediately.

Prawn Puris

Warm Salad of Mushrooms

Serves 8

SELECTION OF MIXED SALAD LEAVES, CLEANED AND TRIMMED

175 G (6 OZ) BABY SPINACH LEAVES, CLEANED AND TRIMMED WEIGHT

175 G (6 OZ) SMOKED STREAKY BACON, DERINDED AND CUT INTO STRIPS

6 × 15 ML TBS OLIVE OIL

675 G (1½ LB) OYSTER, SHIITAKE OR CUP MUSHROOMS, OR A COMBINATION, WIPED AND CUT INTO THICK SLICES

1 GARLIC CLOVE, SKINNED AND CRUSHED (OPTIONAL)

SALT AND PEPPER

1½ × 15 ML TBS TARRAGON VINEGAR

1. Arrange the salad leaves and spinach on eight plates.
2. Heat a heavy-based frying pan and fry the bacon until the fat runs. Increase the heat and fry for a couple of minutes until crisp, then remove to one side. Add the oil and mushrooms to the pan and cook over a high heat for 3-4 minutes until the mushrooms are just tender. Add the garlic, if using, and the pepper and cook for a minute longer.
3. Using a slotted spoon, remove the mushrooms from the pan and scatter over the salad leaves, with the crisp bacon. Quickly add the vinegar to the juices remaining in the pan and boil rapidly for 2 minutes. Season with salt and pepper. Pour over the salads and serve immediately.

COOK'S TIP

Instead of the tarragon vinegar, experiment using different flavoured vinegars. Try cider vinegar or red or white wine vinegars and for a particularly distinctive taste include ½ × 15 ml tbs balsamic vinegar in the total amount used.

Warm Salad of Mushrooms

Chillied Pork Dim Sum

Serves 8

1 × 15 ML TBS VEGETABLE OIL
115 G (4 OZ) LEAN PORK, MINCED
1 GARLIC CLOVE, SKINNED AND CRUSHED
½ ONION, SKINNED AND VERY FINELY CHOPPED
1 × 15 ML TBS FINELY CHOPPED BAMBOO SHOOTS
2 WHOLE DRIED RED CHILLIES, FINELY CHOPPED
2 × 5 ML TSP DARK SOY SAUCE
1 × 15 ML TBS OYSTER SAUCE
2 × 5 ML TSP TOMATO PURÉE
1 × 5 ML TSP SESAME OIL
115 G (4 OZ) SELF-RAISING FLOUR
SEVERAL GOOD PINCHES OF SALT
20 G (¾ OZ) LARD
1 × 15 ML TBS CASTER SUGAR
2 × 5 ML TSP SESAME SEEDS
ABOUT 4 × 15 ML TBS WATER

— DIPPING SAUCE —

115 ML (4 FL OZ) DRY SHERRY
115 ML (4 FL OZ) SOY SAUCE
2 GARLIC CLOVES, SKINNED AND CRUSHED
1 × 5 ML TSP CASTER SUGAR
1 × 5 ML TSP LEMON JUICE

1. Heat the oil in a frying pan, add the pork, garlic, onion, bamboo shoots and chillies and stir-fry for 5 minutes. Add the soy sauce, oyster sauce and tomato purée and cook for 5 minutes, stirring occasionally. Stir the sesame oil in and leave to cool.
2. Sift the flour and salt in a bowl and rub in the lard finely. Stir in the sugar and sesame seeds. Mix in enough water to form a soft dough. Divide into 24 portions. Form each into a ball and roll out on a lightly floured surface to a 9 cm (3½ in) round.
3. Put a teaspoonful of pork mixture into the centre of each round. Dampen the edges and gather together, sealing well. Form each into a little 'pouch' by twisting the tops together, sealing the edges well.
4. To make the sauce, mix all the ingredients together in a small serving bowl.
5. Cook the pork in a bamboo steamer (or conventional steamer) over simmering water for about 15 minutes until cooked through. Serve hot, accompanied by the dipping sauce.

Chillied Pork Dim Sum

Cauliflower Soufflés

Serves 8

225 G (8 OZ) CAULIFLOWER FLORETS
SALT AND PEPPER
GRATED PARMESAN CHEESE
40 G (1½ OZ) BUTTER OR MARGARINE
3 × 15 ML TBS PLAIN FLOUR
200 ML (7 FL OZ) MILK
1 × 15 ML TBS WHOLEGRAIN MUSTARD
115 G (4 OZ) GRUYÈRE CHEESE, GRATED
4 EGGS, SEPARATED

1. Just cover the cauliflower with salted water, cover the pan and simmer, until tender; drain. Grease eight 150 ml (5 fl oz) ramekin dishes; dust out with Parmesan.
2. Prepare a white sauce from the fat, flour, milk, mustard and seasoning. Purée the sauce and cauliflower until almost smooth. Place in a large bowl and cool slightly. Stir in the Gruyère cheese with the egg yolks.
3. Whisk the egg whites until stiff but not dry and fold into the sauce mixture. Spoon into the ramekin dishes. Bake in the oven at 180°C/350°F/Gas Mark 4 for 25 minutes, or until well browned and firm to the touch. Serve immediately.

COOK'S TIP

If the sauce base is left to cool before you complete the soufflés, bake for about 10 minutes longer.

Baked Avocado and Mushrooms

Serves 4

50 G (2 OZ) BUTTER OR MARGARINE
75 G (3 OZ) BUTTON MUSHROOMS, WIPED AND QUARTERED
1 GARLIC CLOVE, SKINNED AND CRUSHED
3 × 15 ML TBS CHOPPED FRESH PARSLEY
2 SMALL RIPE AVOCADOS
1 × 15 ML TBS LEMON JUICE
SALT AND PEPPER
4 × 15 ML TBS FRESH BROWN BREADCRUMBS
GREEN SALAD AND CRUSTY BREAD, TO SERVE

1. Melt the butter in a small saucepan and add the mushrooms and garlic. Cook over a gentle heat for 3-4 minutes or until the mushrooms soften. Stir the parsley into the pan. Divide the mushrooms between four ramekin dishes with half the butter.
2. Peel and dice the avocados; add to the ramekins with lemon juice and seasoning. Sprinkle 1 × 15 ml tbs breadcrumbs over each ramekin and top with the remaining butter.
3. Bake at 200°C/400°F/Gas Mark 6 for about 12 minutes, or until really hot. Serve immediately with a crisp green salad and plenty of crusty bread.

Cauliflower Soufflés

Aubergine and Red Pepper Roulade

Serves 6

— ROULADE —

2 RED PEPPERS, ABOUT 300 G (11 OZ) TOTAL WEIGHT

1 MEDIUM, LONG AUBERGINE, ABOUT 300 G (11 OZ) TOTAL WEIGHT

OLIVE OIL

2 × 5 ML TSP CORIANDER SEEDS

SALT AND PEPPER

— SESAME RELISH —

25 G (1 OZ) SESAME SEEDS

25 G (1 OZ) FRESH BASIL, STALKS REMOVED

25 G (1 OZ) FRESHLY GRATED PARMESAN CHEESE

1 GARLIC CLOVE

1 × 15 ML TBS SESAME OIL

50 ML (2 FL OZ) OLIVE OIL

FRESH BASIL LEAVES, TO GARNISH

1. Cut a piece of greaseproof paper into a rectangle about 35 × 30 cm (14 × 12 in).
2. Grill the peppers under a hot grill, turning occasionally until the skin is charred, about 20 minutes
3. Slice the aubergine lengthways as thinly as possible. Brush liberally with olive oil and place on a grill pan. Grill in batches for about 2-3 minutes on both sides until softened and slightly charred. Drain on absorbent kitchen paper.
4. Place the slices lengthways in a single layer on the greaseproof paper, overlapping the slices by about 1 cm (½ in) to form a rectangle about 35 × 18 cm (14 × 7 in). Sprinkle over half the crushed coriander seeds; season.
5. Remove stalks, seeds and skins from the peppers under cold water. Cut the peppers into quarters and lay over the aubergines, overlapping as before. Sprinkle with remaining coriander; season.
6. Use the greaseproof paper to help you to roll the roulade up tightly, from the short side, like a swiss roll. Wrap and chill overnight in the refrigerator.
7. Place the sesame seeds in a dry saucepan and stir over a medium heat until starting to turn golden brown. Tip into a processor with remaining relish ingredients. Process until smooth. Spoon into a jar, cover with a layer of olive oil and store in the refrigerator. Bring both relish and roulade to room temperature before serving.
8. To serve, unwrap the roulade and slice thinly with a very sharp knife. Place two or three slices on each of six small plates. Spoon a generous serving of relish on the side and garnish the roulade with fresh basil leaves.

Aubergine and Red Pepper Roulade

Asparagus in a Citrus Dressing

Serves 6

900 G (2 LB) FRESH ASPARAGUS

SALT AND PEPPER

RIND AND JUICE OF 2 LIMES

JUICE OF 1 RUBY GRAPEFRUIT

3 × 15 ML TBS POLYUNSATURATED OIL

1. Cut the woody ends off each asparagus spear then, using a potato peeler or small knife, scrape the stalk to remove any coarse spines. Cook the asparagus in simmering salted water for about 8-10 minutes or until just tender. Drain carefully.
2. Meanwhile, pare the rind from one lime, then cut it into fine needle shreds; blanch in boiling water for 1 minute only, drain and reserve. Whisk together 2 × 15 ml tbs strained lime juice, 3 × 15 ml tbs strained grapefruit juice, the oil and seasoning.
3. Place the hot asparagus in the dressing and allow to marinate for about 15 minutes. Arrange the still warm asparagus on individual serving plates, spoon a little of the dressing over the top and garnish with the shreds of lime peel.

COOK'S TIP

Choose slender asparagus spears (not the very thin ones known as 'sprue') as these have most flavour and make a more attractive display.

Fresh Herb Cheese

Serves 4-6

450 ML (16 FL OZ) LOW-FAT NATURAL YOGURT

SALT AND PEPPER

1 × 5 ML TSP SNIPPED FRESH CHIVES

1 × 5 ML TSP CHOPPED FRESH TARRAGON

FEW BASIL LEAVES, TORN INTO SMALL PIECES

1 GARLIC CLOVE, SKINNED AND CRUSHED

2 × 5 ML TSP EXTRA VIRGIN OLIVE OIL

1 BUNCH OF RADISHES, WASHED AND TRIMMED

BLACK OLIVES

PITTA BREAD, CUT INTO FINGERS AND TOASTED

FRESH HERBS, TO GARNISH

1. Line a nylon sieve with absorbent kitchen paper or clean muslin and set it over a bowl. Mix together the yogurt and ½ × 5 ml tsp salt. Pour into the sieve and leave in the refrigerator for at least 24 hours, until the yogurt is firm and the whey has drained through into the bowl.
2. Turn the yogurt into a bowl and discard the whey. Mix in the herbs, garlic and seasoning to taste. Transfer to a small serving bowl or plate and drizzle the oil over the top.
3. Serve the cheese with radishes, olives and toasted pitta bread. Garnish with herbs.

COOK'S TIP

Use runny yogurt, not the set variety, for this recipe.

VARIATION

Instead of the herbs suggested above, add whatever fresh herbs you have available, and in whatever combination you prefer.

SMOKED SALMON ROULADES

Serves 8

275 G (10 OZ) CREAM CHEESE, AT ROOM TEMPERATURE

2 × 15 ML TBS LOW-FAT MAYONNAISE

FINELY GRATED RIND AND JUICE OF 1 LIME OR LEMON

1 × 15 ML TBS POWDERED GELATINE

4 × 15 ML TBS COLD WATER

8 LARGE THIN SLICES SMOKED SALMON

4-5 × 15 ML TBS FINELY CHOPPED FRESH DILL

225 G (8 OZ) COOKED PEELED PRAWNS (THAWED, DRAINED AND THOROUGHLY DRIED IF FROZEN), FINELY CHOPPED

PEPPER

LIME OR LEMON TWISTS AND FRESH DILL SPRIGS, TO GARNISH

1. Beat the cream cheese in a bowl with the mayonnaise and lime or lemon rind.
2. Sprinkle the gelatine over the water in a small heatproof bowl. Leave for about 5 minutes until spongy, then stand the bowl in a saucepan of gently simmering water and heat until dissolved. Remove from the water and leave to cool for a few minutes.
3. Stir the dissolved gelatine into the cream cheese mixture until evenly blended, then stir in 2 × 15 ml tbs lime or lemon juice. Cover the bowl and chill in the refrigerator for about 30 minutes, or until the mixture is just firm enough to hold its shape.
4. Spread about 1½ × 15 ml tbs cream cheese mixture over each salmon slice, then sprinkle evenly with dill.
5. Sprinkle the prawns over the dill and press down gently with your fingertips. Grind pepper over the top. Carefully roll up the salmon slices from one of the short ends, then place seam side down on a plate. Cover and chill in the refrigerator for at least 2 hours, until firm.
6. To serve, cut each salmon roll diagonally into eight neat slices, then arrange the slices, slightly overlapping, on individual plates. Garnish with the lime or lemon twists and the dill sprigs and serve at room temperature.

COOK'S TIP

These pretty smoked salmon and cream cheese rolls can be prepared well ahead of time. Serve them with warm crusty granary or wholemeal rolls.

Smoked Salmon Roulades

POTTED SEAFOOD PÂTÉ

Serves 8

SUNFLOWER OIL
225 G (8 OZ) SALMON FILLET
1 BAY LEAF
225 G (8 OZ) FRESH HADDOCK FILLET
225 G (8 OZ) COOKED PEELED PRAWNS
225 G POT RICOTTA OR LOW-FAT SOFT CHEESE
4 × 15 ML TBS MAYONNAISE
GRATED RIND OF 1 LEMON AND 2 × 5 ML TSP JUICE
115 G (4 OZ) BUTTER OR MARGARINE, MELTED
SALT AND PEPPER
WHOLE COOKED PRAWNS, OAKLEAF LETTUCE AND LIME SLICES, TO GARNISH

— PEPPER MAYONNAISE —

1 SMALL GREEN PEPPER, SEEDED AND ROUGHLY CHOPPED
2-3 SALAD ONIONS, TRIMMED AND CHOPPED
3 × 15 ML TBS CHOPPED FRESH PARSLEY
1 CLOVE GARLIC, SKINNED
300 ML (10 FL OZ) MAYONNAISE
SALT AND PEPPER

1. Wash and thoroughly dry two empty 900 ml (1½ pt) food cans (large baked-bean cans or fruit cans are ideal). Lightly oil the bases and sides and line with non-stick baking parchment.
2. Place the salmon and bay leaf in a small saucepan and cover with cold water. Bring to the boil. Cover and simmer gently for about 5 minutes, or until just cooked. Remove with a slotted spoon and cool. Place the haddock in the salmon poaching liquid. Add extra water to cover if necessary. Bring to the boil, cover and simmer for about 8 minutes, depending on the thickness of the fillet. Remove with a slotted spoon and cool.
3. Flake the fish, discarding the skin. Roughly chop the prawns and reserve half. Place half the prawns and all the remaining ingredients (except the garnishes) in a blender or food processor and blend until just combined but not smooth. Fold the remaining prawns in and adjust seasoning. Spoon the mixture into the prepared cans, pressing it down lightly. Cover and refrigerate overnight.
4. Ease a round-bladed knife or skewer between the can and the lining paper. Turn the pâté out on to a wooden board, remove paper and thickly slice. Arrange on a serving dish and garnish.
5. Serve with pepper mayonnaise, made by blending all the ingredients together for 2-3 minutes, until combined. (Transfer to a serving bowl, cover and refrigerate until required.)

MUSHROOM AND CASHEW NUT PÂTÉ

Serves 8

3 × 15 ML TBS VEGETABLE OIL
50 G (2 OZ) UNSALTED CASHEW NUTS
675 G (1½ LB) MEDIUM OPEN-CUP MUSHROOMS, WIPED AND CHOPPED
2 GARLIC CLOVES, SKINNED AND CRUSHED
1 × 5 ML TSP DRIED THYME
½ × 5 ML TSP CAYENNE PEPPER
½ × 5 ML TSP GROUND ALLSPICE
200 G (7 OZ) SILKEN TOFU
2 × 15 ML TBS CHOPPED FRESH PARSLEY (OPTIONAL)
SALT AND PEPPER

1. Heat the oil in a large, heavy-based frying pan and fry the cashews for 2-3 minutes or until browned on all sides. Remove from the oil with a slotted spoon and leave to cool.
2. Add the mushrooms, garlic, thyme, cayenne and allspice to the pan and cook, stirring, for about 10 minutes, or until the mushrooms are very soft. Cool slightly.
3. Meanwhile, put the nuts in a food processor and process until finely chopped. Tip them into a bowl. Put the tofu in the food processor and process until smooth, then add the mushrooms and process until finely chopped. Remove these to the bowl. Add the parsley, if using, and season with salt and pepper and a little extra cayenne and allspice, if liked.
4. Spoon the pâté into a serving dish, cover and chill until ready to serve. Remove from the refrigerator 30 minutes before serving.

COOK'S TIP

Serve this protein-rich pâté with chunks of warm granary bread, or use it to top baked potatoes.

BACON AND PISTACHIO TERRINE

Serves 8-10

25 G (1 OZ) SHELLED PISTACHIO NUTS
115 G (4 OZ) HAZELNUTS
175 G (6 OZ) ONION, SKINNED AND ROUGHLY CHOPPED
15 G (½ OZ) BUTTER OR MARGARINE
4 EGGS
18 RASHERS RINDLESS STREAKY BACON, ABOUT 450 G (1 LB)
450 G (1 LB) MINCED PORK
175 G (6 OZ) FRESH WHITE BREADCRUMBS
1 × 5 ML TSP DRIED THYME
6 × 15 ML TBS SINGLE CREAM
SALT AND PEPPER
GREEN SALAD, TO SERVE

1. Cover the pistachio nuts with boiling water. Leave for about 1 minute, then drain, skin and reserve. Toast the hazelnuts, remove skins by rubbing the nuts in a teatowel. Cook the onion in butter to soften, then cool. Hard boil 2 eggs, then cool.
2. Stretch 6 rashers of bacon with the back of a round-bladed knife and use to line a 900 g (2 lb) loaf tin. Place another 6 rashers of bacon with the pork, onions, breadcrumbs, thyme, hazelnuts, the hard-boiled and remaining raw eggs in a blender or food processor and blend until thoroughly combined. Work in batches, if necessary. Beat in the cream and seasoning.
3. Spoon a third of the mixture into the prepared tin. Cover with half of the remaining bacon and half the pistachio nuts. Spoon on half the remaining minced mixture, top with the remaining bacon and pistachio nuts and finish with a layer of the minced mixture.
4. Cover with foil and place in a roasting tin half-filled with water, then Bake at 180°C/350°F/Gas Mark 4 for about 2 hours or until firm to the touch and the juices run clear when the terrine is pierced with a fine skewer. Remove from the oven and weight down for 2 hours, or preferably overnight, in the refrigerator.
5. Turn out and serve, thickly sliced, with a green salad. Covered, the terrine will keep in the refrigerator for 7-10 days.

MIXED VEGETABLE TERRINE

Serves 6

335 G (12 OZ) PARSNIPS, PEELED AND THINLY SLICED

335 G (12 OZ) BROCCOLI, DIVIDED INTO FLORETS WITH STALKS THINLY SLICED

335 G (12 OZ) BRUSSELS SPROUTS, TRIMMED

SALT AND PEPPER

3 EGGS

3 × 15 ML TBS SINGLE CREAM

BUTTER FOR GREASING

115 G (4 OZ) ONION, SKINNED AND FINELY CHOPPED

2 × 15 ML TBS POLYUNSATURATED OIL

1 × 5 ML TSP PLAIN FLOUR

450 G (1 LB) TOMATOES, SKINNED, SEEDED AND ROUGHLY CHOPPED, RESERVING THE JUICES

6 × 15 ML TBS WATER

1 GARLIC CLOVE, SKINNED AND CRUSHED

PINCH OF SUGAR

1 × 15 ML TBS TOMATO PURÉE

FRESH DILL, TO GARNISH (OPTIONAL)

1. Cook the parsnips, broccoli and sprouts in boiling salted water in separate pans until tender; drain well. Allow to cool, then place each vegetable separately in a blender or food processor with one of the eggs, 1 × 15 ml tbs cream and seasoning. Blend until smooth; adjust seasoning.
2. Grease and base-line a 1.4 kg (3 lb) non-stick loaf tin. Carefully spoon in first the broccoli mixture, then the parsnip purée and finish with a sprout layer; level the surface. Cover tightly with greased foil.
3. Stand in a roasting tin with enough water to come halfway up the sides of the loaf tin. Bake at 170°C/325°F/Gas Mark 3 for about 1¼ hours, or until firm to the touch. Cool, then refrigerate until firm. Turn out, cover and return to the refrigerator.
4. Meanwhile, make the sauce. Cook the onion in the oil until soft but not coloured. Stir the flour in followed by the chopped tomatoes, reserved juices and water. Bring to the boil, stirring. Mix in the garlic, sugar, tomato purée and seasoning. Simmer for about 5 minutes, then cool in a bowl until ready to serve.
5. To serve, thinly slice the terrine and serve with the tomato sauce. Garnish with fresh dill, if wished.

Mixed Vegetable Terrine

SMOKED TROUT AND APPLE MOUSSE

Serves 6-8

2 WHOLE SMOKED TROUT, ABOUT 335 G (12 OZ) TOTAL WEIGHT

275 G (10 OZ) LOW-FAT SOFT CHEESE

4 × 15 ML TBS LEMON JUICE

150 ML (5 FL OZ) NATURAL GREEK-STYLE YOGURT

2 SMALL TART EATING APPLES

75 G (3 OZ) BUTTER OR MARGARINE

1 × 5 ML TSP POWDERED GELATINE

1 × 15 ML TBS COLD WATER

PEPPER

75 G (3 OZ) STREAKY BACON, DERINDED

CHIVES, SALAD LEAVES AND LEMON SLICES, TO GARNISH

MELBA TOAST, TO SERVE (SEE PAGE 15)

1. Remove the head, skin and bones from the trout; there should be about 225 g (8 oz) flesh. Place in a blender or food processor with the soft cheese, lemon juice and yogurt.
2. Peel, core and roughly chop one apple. Put it with the butter into a small saucepan and cook, stirring, over a low heat until the apple softens; cool slightly. Add to the trout mixture and purée until smooth.
3. Sprinkle the gelatine over the water in a small heatproof bowl. Leave for about 5 minutes until spongy, then stand the bowl in a saucepan of gently simmering water and heat until dissolved. Stir into the trout mixture and season with pepper. Spoon into a deep dish, cover with clingfilm and refrigerate to set – about 3 hours. Grill the bacon until very crisp. Drain well on absorbent kitchen paper towels, then crush or cut into fine strips.
4. To serve, spoon the trout mousse on to serving plates and sprinkle with the bacon. Garnish with slices of the remaining apple, chives, salad leaves and lemon slices and accompany with Melba toast.

Smoked Trout and Apple Mousse

Avocado with Fennel and Prawns

Serves 8

3 × 15 ML TBS LIGHT SALAD OIL

1 × 15 ML TBS LEMON JUICE

SALT AND PEPPER

1 BULB OF FENNEL

2 RIPE AVOCADOS, PEELED AND STONE REMOVED

225 G (8 OZ) COOKED PEELED PRAWNS OR 16 LARGE COOKED PRAWNS

2 × 15 ML TBS FRESH CHOPPED DILL

BROWN BREAD AND BUTTER, TO ACCOMPANY

1. Whisk together the oil, lemon juice and seasoning.
2. Cut the fennel and avocados into neat strips. Arrange on a serving plate with the prawns.
3. Spoon the dressing over, sprinkle with dill and serve immediately, with brown bread and butter.

Devilled Whitebait with Deep-Fried Parsley

Serves 8

8 × 15 ML TBS PLAIN FLOUR

½ × 5 ML TSP CURRY POWDER

½ × 5 ML TSP GROUND GINGER

½ × 5 ML TSP CAYENNE

SALT

1.1 KG (2½ LB) WHITEBAIT, FRESH OR FROZEN, THOROUGHLY DRIED

OIL FOR DEEP-FRYING

25 G (1 OZ) PARSLEY SPRIGS

SEA SALT

4 LEMONS, CUT INTO WEDGES

1. Sift the flour, curry powder, ginger, cayenne and salt together into a large plastic bag. Put a quarter of the whitebait into the bag and shake well to coat in the flour mixture. Lift the fish out and shake in a sieve to remove excess flour. Repeat with the remaining whitebait.
2. Heat the oil in a deep-fat fryer to 190°C/375°F or in a deep saucepan until a cube of bread sizzles. Put a single layer of whitebait into the frying basket and lower it into the oil. Fry for 2-3 minutes, shaking the basket occasionally, until the whitebait make a rustling sound as they are shaken. Tip out on to a warmed plate lined with absorbent kitchen paper. Fry the remaining whitebait in the same way.
3. Allow the oil temperature to reduce to about 186°C/365°F. Deep-fry the parsley for a few seconds until it stops sizzling. Drain on absorbent kitchen paper, then sprinkle with sea salt.
4. Divide the whitebait between eight warmed serving plates. Scatter the parsley sprigs over the top and garnish with lemon wedges.

Saffron Prawns with Melon

Serves 4-6

1 SMALL RIPE MELON

225 G (8 OZ) COOKED PEELED PRAWNS, RINSED

FEW SAFFRON THREADS

2 × 15 ML TBS BOILING WATER

5 × 15 ML TBS LEMON MAYONNAISE

SALT AND PEPPER

OAKLEAF LETTUCE, COARSELY SHREDDED

BROWN BREAD ROLLS AND BUTTER, TO ACCOMPANY

1. Scoop the melon into small balls or cut into neat dice; reserve any juices. Pat the prawns dry with absorbent kitchen paper.
2. Infuse the saffron in the water. Leave to stand for about 10 minutes, then strain the water into the lemon mayonnaise.
3. Mix the melon and juices with the prawns, mayonnaise and seasoning. Cover and refrigerate for about 2 hours.
4. Arrange the oakleaf lettuce in individual dishes and top with the prawn mixture. Serve with bread rolls and butter.

COOK'S TIP

Just a hint of saffron is enough to add fragrance to the prawns.

Mediterranean Seafood Cocktail

Serves 4

GRATED RIND AND JUICE OF 1 GRAPEFRUIT

3 × 15 ML TBS POLYUNSATURATED OIL

2 × 15 ML TBS DRY SHERRY

1 × 15 ML TBS SOY SAUCE

1 GARLIC CLOVE, SKINNED AND CRUSHED

1 × 15 ML TBS CLEAR HONEY

SALT AND PEPPER

225 G (8 OZ) READY-PREPARED SEAFOOD COCKTAIL

1 SMALL GREEN PEPPER, SEEDED AND FINELY SLICED

1 SMALL YELLOW PEPPER, SEEDED AND FINELY SLICED

75 G (3 OZ) RED-SKINNED ONION, SKINNED AND FINELY SLICED

LAMB'S LETTUCE

MELBA TOAST, TO ACCOMPANY (SEE PAGE 15)

1. In a medium-sized bowl whisk together the rind of the grapefruit with 115 ml (4 fl oz) juice, the oil, sherry, soy sauce, garlic, honey and seasoning. Stir the seafood cocktail into this marinade.
2. Mix the peppers and onion into the marinade. Cover tightly and leave to marinate in the refrigerator overnight.
3. Arrange the lamb's lettuce in four individual serving dishes and top with the fish mixture. Serve with Melba toast.

COOK'S TIP

Packets of ready-prepared seafood cocktail contain a mixture of squid, mussels and prawns, which is ready to eat and can be used hot or cold in a wide variety of quick, easy-to-prepare dishes. Add to salads and starters, heat in a sauce to serve with pasta or use in pilaffs and risottos. The possibilities are endless.

Mediterranean Seafood Cocktail

Corbières
BLANC DE BLANCS
PRODUCE OF FRANCE
SELECTED BY SAFEWAY
75cl ℮

FISH

Fish is both nutritious and versatile, providing a valuable source of protein, plus minerals and vitamins. All fish are classified into three groups: white fish, oily fish and shellfish. There are two types of white fish: round, such as cod or haddock; and flat, such as plaice. Fish is sold whole, and as cutlets, steaks and fillets, and can be used in a variety of ways to produce recipes to suit all the family.

Left: Fillets of Trout with Prawns and Dill (page 54)
Right: Casserole of White Fish and Vegetables (page 51)

DILL-GLAZED SALMON

Serves 8

1.4 KG (3 LB) SALMON OR SEA TROUT, RINSED UNDER COLD RUNNING WATER

DRY WHITE WINE

ONION AND CARROT SLICES, BLACK PEPPERCORNS AND BAY LEAF FOR FLAVOURING

1 SMALL BUNCH OF FRESH DILL

½×5 ML TSP POWDERED GELATINE

GREEN SALAD LEAVES AND LEMON AND LIME SLICES, TO GARNISH

LEMON MAYONNAISE, TO ACCOMPANY

1. Remove the head and tail if wished and place the salmon in a fish kettle or large roasting tin. Pour in just enough cold water and a little wine to cover the fish. Add the flavouring ingredients and dill stalks. Divide the feathery dill tops into small sprigs, cover and refrigerate.
2. Cover the salmon with lid or foil and bring the liquid slowly to the boil. Simmer for 5 minutes, then turn off the heat and leave the salmon (still covered) in the liquid until cold.
3. Carefully remove the salmon from the poaching liquid. Strain and reserve 150 ml (5 fl oz) liquid. Carefully skin the salmon, gently scraping away any dark brown flesh.
4. Place the salmon on a flat serving platter. If the head and tail are still on, cut a 'V' shape into the tail to neaten it. Cover the salmon with clingfilm and refrigerate – for at least 30 minutes.
5. Place the reserved poaching liquid in a small bowl. Sprinkle over the powdered gelatine and leave to soak for 3-4 minutes. Place the bowl in a saucepan of simmering water and heat gently until the gelatine has completely dissolved. Cool the liquid until just beginning to thicken.
6. Brush a little of the poaching liquid over the salmon. Press the reserved dill sprigs onto the exposed salmon flesh. Brush all over with more liquid. Return to the refrigerator to set.
7. To serve the salmon, garnish with green salad leaves and lemon and lime slices. Accompany with lemon mayonnaise.

Dill-Glazed Salmon

HOT SALMON AND MUSHROOM CRISP

Serves 8

3×15 ML TBS OLIVE OIL

225 G (8 OZ) MIXED BUTTON AND WILD MUSHROOMS, WIPED AND CHOPPED

175 G (6 OZ) BULB OF FENNEL, TRIMMED AND CHOPPED

1×15 ML TBS CHOPPED FRESH TARRAGON

SALT AND PEPPER

213 G PACKET CHILLED PUFF PASTRY

1.6 KG (3½ LB) SALMON, PREPARED AND COOKED AS IN STEPS 1-4 OF DILL-GLAZED SALMON (SEE OPPOSITE), RESERVING 600 ML (20 FL OZ) POACHING LIQUID

50 G (2 OZ) BUTTER, MELTED

ABOUT 150 G (5 OZ) FILO PASTRY

150 ML (5 FL OZ) WHITE WINE

150 ML (5 FL OZ) DOUBLE CREAM

1. Heat the oil in a frying pan, add the mushrooms and fennel. Cook over a moderate heat until all excess moisture has evaporated, about 4-5 minutes. Place in a bowl. Stir in 1×5 ml tsp tarragon and seasoning. Cool, cover and chill until required.
2. Roll out the puff pastry to a rectangle about 18×40 cm (7×16 in). Place on a wet baking tray and prick well. Bake at 200°C/400°F/Gas Mark 6 for about 15 minutes. Cool and return to the baking tray.
3. Bone the salmon as for Celebration Salmon (see page 46). Place one side of the salmon on the puff pastry. Spoon over the mushroom mixture and top with the remaining side of salmon. Trim any excess pastry, about 2.5 cm (1 in) away from the edge of the fish.
4. Brush the exposed pastry edges with melted butter and then cover the fish with over-lapping layers of filo pastry, brushing with butter between the layers. Tuck the edges underneath to form a parcel. Top with crumpled pieces of filo pastry; brush with butter.
5. Bake at 200°C/400°F/Gas Mark 6 for 35-40 minutes, covering loosely with foil.
6. Bubble the reserved poaching liquid with the wine until 300 ml (10 fl oz) remains. Add the cream and simmer for 5 minutes to thicken. Add the remaining tarragon. Simmer for 1-2 minutes and season.
7. Serve the salmon warm, accompanied by the sauce.

Celebration Salmon

Serves 10-12

1 × 5 ML TSP SAFFRON THREADS

1 × 15 ML TBS BOILING WATER

1 BUNCH OF WATERCRESS, RINSED

300 ML (10 FL OZ) LEMON MAYONNAISE

3 × 15 ML TBS SINGLE CREAM

SALT AND PEPPER

115 G (4 OZ) LONG-GRAIN AND WILD RICE MIXED

½ CUCUMBER, PEELED AND DICED

115 G (4 OZ) SMOKED SALMON TRIMMINGS, FINELY CHOPPED

115 G (4 OZ) COOKED PEELED PRAWNS

LEMON JUICE

1.8-2 KG (4-4 ½ LB) SALMON OR SEA TROUT, PREPARED AND COOKED AS IN STEPS 1-4 OF DILL-GLAZED SALMON (SEE PAGE 45)

115 G (4 OZ) LARGE SLICES OF SMOKED SALMON

VERY THIN SLICES OF LEMON AND CUCUMBER, AND WATERCRESS SPRIGS, TO GARNISH (OPTIONAL)

1. Cover the saffron with the boiling water and leave to stand for 15 minutes. Strain and keep the liquid. Place half the watercress in a food processor with the lemon mayonnaise and strained liquid and blend until the watercress is finely chopped. Place in a bowl and stir the cream in. Season.
2. Prepare the stuffing. Cook the rice in boiling salted water until tender; drain well. Sprinkle the cucumber with salt and leave for 20 minutes; rinse under cold water and drain well. Finely chop the remaining watercress and mix with the rice, cucumber, smoked salmon trimmings and prawns, and about 4 × 15 ml tbs of the saffron mayonnaise to bind. Season and add lemon juice to taste.
3. Using a small, sharp knife, carefully cut down the whole central line of the flatter side of the salmon. Ease the top fillets away from the bone. Place these fillets together again, skin side down, on a serving dish. Spoon the stuffing over the fillet.
4. Lift and ease the bone off the remaining side of salmon. Run your fingers along the fillet to ensure all bones are removed. Turn the fillet over. Cover the salmon with the smoked salmon slices. Place the fillet on top of the stuffing.
5. Garnish with cucumber and lemon slices and watercress sprigs, if you wish. Cover and refrigerate. Serve accompanied by the watercress and saffron mayonnaise.

COOK'S TIP

This makes the ideal buffet dish as the boned fish is so easy to serve. There is plenty of stuffing so that there is a generous layer between the fish fillets. If there is any left over it can be served separately

Celebration Salmon

Outrageous Salmon Fishcakes

Serves 8

335 G (12 OZ) COOKED FRESH SALMON, FLAKED

225 G (8 OZ) SMOKED SALMON, ROUGHLY CHOPPED

335 G (12 OZ) FRESHLY COOKED MASHED POTATO

1 × 15 ML TBS LEMON JUICE

PEPPER

75 G (3 OZ) BUTTER, MELTED

3 × 15 ML TBS CHOPPED FRESH DILL OR 1 × 15 ML TBS DRIED DILL WEED

2 EGGS, BEATEN

ABOUT 225 G (8 OZ) DRIED WHITE BREADCRUMBS

VEGETABLE OIL FOR FRYING

1. Mix the two salmons with the mashed potato, lemon juice, pepper to taste, butter and dill. Add just enough beaten egg to bind the mixture together. It should be firm, not sloppy. Cool, then refrigerate for 1 hour until very firm.
2. Shape the mixture into 16 cakes about 2.5 cm (1 in) thick. Brush with some of the remaining beaten egg and coat with breadcrumbs. Chill for 30 minutes to firm. Coat the cakes with egg and crumbs once more. Chill again until firm.
3. Shallow fry the cakes in batches for 3-4 minutes on each side, or until golden brown. Drain on absorbent kitchen paper and keep warm in the oven.

Salmon Noisettes with Black Bean Dressing

Serves 6

6 SALMON STEAKS, ABOUT 175 G (6 OZ) EACH
1 BUNCH OF SALAD ONIONS, TRIMMED AND CHOPPED
2.5 CM (1 IN) PIECE OF FRESH ROOT GINGER, PEELED AND GRATED
LIGHT SESAME OIL
4 × 15 ML TBS BLACK BEAN SAUCE
4 × 15 ML TBS DRY SHERRY
4 × 15 ML TBS ORANGE JUICE
BLACK PEPPER
1 LIME, THICKLY SLICED
198 G PACKET CHINESE MEDIUM EGG NOODLES
STIR-FRIED BROCCOLI, TO ACCOMPANY

1. Carefully remove centre bones from the salmon steaks. Cut in half; remove skin. Curl each salmon piece round to form a small noisette. Tie with string.
2. Mix the salad onions and ginger with 75 ml (3 fl oz) sesame oil, the black bean sauce, sherry, orange juice and pepper.
3. Heat 2 × 15 ml tbs sesame oil in a non-stick frying pan. Brown the noisettes lightly on each side with the lime slices, a few noisettes at a time. Place in an edged dish; spoon the black bean mixture over, cool, cover and chill for at least 1 hour, turning once.
4. Meanwhile, cook the noodles in boiling, salted water for 4-5 minutes or according to the instructions, until just tender. Drain well; rinse in cold water to stop noodles cooking further. Place in a large bowl; mix with 3 × 15 ml tbs sesame oil. Cover and chill until required.
5. Lift the noisettes out of the marinade; remove string. Toss the noodles with the marinade. Cut six pieces of non-stick baking parchment, about 38 cm (15 in) square. Spoon the noodle mixture into the middle of each and top with two noisettes and some lime slices. Bring up the corners of the paper to form a loose bundle. Tie around the top with string.
6. Bake the parcels in the oven at 200°C/400°F/Gas Mark 6 for 20 minutes. Serve on heated plates; untie the string. Accompany with stir-fried broccoli.

COOK'S TIPS

If you don't want to prepare the salmon noisettes, use the steaks just as they are, but skin them before cooking.

The black bean sauce tends to be quite salty, so you only need to add pepper to the marinade.

Salmon Noisettes with Black Bean Dressing

Wine-Simmered Fish

Serves 6

675-900 G (1½-2 LB) SKINNED COD FILLET
3 × 15 ML TBS COGNAC
2 × 15 ML TBS OLIVE OIL
225 G (8 OZ) ONIONS, SHALLOTS OR LEEKS, SKINNED AND CHOPPED
1 GARLIC CLOVE, SKINNED AND CHOPPED
600 ML (20 FL OZ) FRUITY, DRY WHITE WINE
FRESH PARSLEY
FRESH THYME
FRESH BAY LEAVES
75 G (3 OZ) BUTTER, SOFTENED
1 × 15 ML TBS PLAIN WHITE FLOUR
18 BUTTON ONIONS, SKINNED
225 G (8 OZ) BUTTON MUSHROOMS, WIPED
1 LEMON
SALT AND PEPPER
CHOPPED FRESH PARSLEY AND 6 HEART-SHAPED CROÛTES, DIPPED IN CHOPPED PARSLEY, TO GARNISH

1. Place the fish in a non-metallic dish. Add the Cognac and oil. Cover; marinate overnight in a cool place.
2. Place the onion and garlic in a saucepan with the wine and herbs. Bring to the boil and simmer for about 30 minutes. Cool.
3. In a small bowl, blend 50 g (2 oz) of the butter with the flour to form a paste.
4. Place the fish and marinade in a saucepan. Strain the wine over the fish until it just covers it. Simmer for 10 minutes or until tender.
5. Simmer the button onions for 12 minutes. Drain. Fry the mushrooms for about 5 minutes in 25 g (1 oz) butter; add a squeeze of lemon juice.
6. Remove the fish with a slotted spoon, cover and keep warm. Boil the cooking liquid for 2-3 minutes until slightly reduced. Keep boiling and whisk in the butter paste a little at a time until the sauce is lightly thickened. Stir in the onions and mushrooms. Season, spoon the sauce over the fish and garnish with parsley and croûtes.

Sliced Fish Pot

Serves 8-10

3 MEDIUM-SIZED RED MULLET, CLEANED, ABOUT 675 G (1½ LB) TOTAL WEIGHT
675 G (1½ LB) COD, FILLETED WEIGHT
335 G (12 OZ) PIECE SALMON TAIL
1 BAY LEAF
300 ML (10 FL OZ) COLD WATER
2 × 15 ML TBS POLYUNSATURATED OIL
450 G (1 LB) CARROTS, PEELED AND CUT INTO THIN STRIPS
225 G (8 OZ) FENNEL, TRIMMED AND CUT INTO THIN STRIPS
225 G (8 OZ) ONIONS, SKINNED AND THINLY SLICED
1 GARLIC CLOVE, SKINNED AND CRUSHED
2 × 5 ML TSP TURMERIC
300 ML (10 FL OZ) DRY WHITE WINE
150 ML (5 FL OZ) SINGLE CREAM
SALT AND PEPPER
1 BUNCH OF SALAD ONIONS, TRIMMED AND CUT DIAGONALLY INTO THIN STRIPS

1. Thickly slice the mullet, placing heads and tails in a medium-sized saucepan. Trim the cod of any skin and slice into bite-sized chunks. Add any trimmings to the pan. Skin and thickly slice the salmon, discarding bones. Add the skin to the other trimmings with the bay leaf and the cold water. Bring to the boil, cover and simmer for 20 minutes. Strain and reserve the liquid.
2. Heat the oil in a large flameproof casserole and sauté the vegetables with the garlic and turmeric for 3-4 minutes, or until golden. Add half the wine. Boil the mixture until most of the liquid has evaporated and the vegetables are glazed. Add the remaining wine and boil again until reduced by half.
3. Stir in the reserved fish stock, half the cream, the cod and seasoning. Cover and bake in the oven at 160°C/325°F/Gas Mark 3 for 15 minutes. Add the mullet and salmon, cover and return to the oven for a further 15 minutes or until the fish is cooked through.
4. Gently stir the remaining cream into the casserole and sprinkle with the salad onions to serve.

Salmon with Tomato Vinaigrette

Serves 6

OLIVE OIL
1 × 15 ML TBS DIJON MUSTARD
50 ML (2 FL OZ) WHITE WINE VINEGAR
75 G (3 OZ) SHALLOTS, SKINNED AND FINELY CHOPPED
2 GARLIC CLOVES, SKINNED AND CRUSHED
1 × 15 ML TBS CASTER SUGAR
565 G (1¼ LB) TOMATOES, PREFERABLY PLUM, SKINNED, SEEDED AND DICED
4 × 15 ML TBS CHOPPED FRESH CHIVES
2 × 15 ML TBS CHOPPED FRESH TARRAGON
SALT AND PEPPER
6 × 200 G (7 OZ) SALMON FILLETS OR STEAKS, SKINNED
SALAD LEAVES, FRESH HERBS AND LIME WEDGES, TO GARNISH

1. First, make a vinaigrette with 200 ml (7 fl oz) oil, mustard, vinegar, chopped shallots, crushed garlic and sugar. Add the diced tomatoes to the vinaigrette with the chives and tarragon. Season.
2. Brush the salmon with oil and season. Grill until tender and well browned, about 10-15minutes (salmon steaks take a little longer, and need more oil).
3. Place the fish on serving plates and half-cover with the vinaigrette. Garnish with salad leaves, fresh herbs and lime wedges.

VARIATION

Instead of using chives and tarragon in the vinaigrette, add whatever suitable fresh herbs you have available, in whatever combination you like. Chopped fresh basil or mint would work well in this dish.

Salmon with Tomato Vinaigrette

Salmon Pie with Parmesan Crust

Serves 8

225 G (8 OZ) BUTTER

50 G (2 OZ) ONION, SKINNED AND FINELY CHOPPED

400 G (14 OZ) WHITE PLAIN FLOUR

450 ML (16 FL OZ) FISH STOCK

150 ML (5 FL OZ) DRY WHITE WINE

900 G (2 LB) SALMON FILLET, SKINNED AND CUT INTO BITE-SIZED PIECES

225 G (8 OZ) FROZEN QUEEN SCALLOPS, THAWED

115 G (4 OZ) GRUYÈRE CHEESE, GRATED

SALT AND PEPPER

75 G (3 OZ) FRESHLY GRATED PARMESAN CHEESE

1 EGG, BEATEN

3-4 × 15 ML TBS COLD WATER

BEATEN EGG, TO GLAZE

1. Melt 50 g (2 oz) of the butter in a medium saucepan. Sauté the onion, stirring, for 5-6 minutes or until softened but not coloured.
2. Off the heat, stir in 50 g (2 oz) of the flour, the stock and wine. Bring to the boil, stirring, then simmer for 3-4 minutes until thickened. Take off the heat, cool slightly.
3. Add the salmon, scallops and Gruyère cheese. Season; turn into a 1.8 lt (3 pt) shallow, ovenproof dish and cool.
4. Rub the remaining butter into the remaining flour. Stir the Parmesan in. Add the beaten egg and the cold water. Bind the pastry together with your hands, adding extra water, if necessary. Turn out on to a floured surface and knead lightly until smooth. Cover and chill for about 15 minutes.
5. Roll out the pastry; cover the filling, pressing edges down well. Trim excess pastry and re-roll. Cut out leaves from the trimmings. Brush pie with beaten egg; cover with leaves. Brush with egg again. Chill for 15-20 minutes.
6. Bake in the oven at 190°C/375°F/Gas Mark 5 for 45-50 minutes or until crisp, covering loosely with foil if necessary. Serve immediately.

COOK'S TIP

This pie can be cooked from the freezer so it's perfect to make ahead. Don't expect a completely smooth sauce, it's a tasty mix topped with a crisp cheese crust.

Salmon Pie with Parmesan Crust

Casserole of White Fish and Vegetables

Serves 4

225 G (8 OZ) SMALL PASTA SHELLS

SALT AND PEPPER

175 G (6 OZ) BABY CORN, CUT IN HALF

1 GREEN PEPPER, SEEDED AND CUT INTO SMALL PIECES

450 G (1 LB) WHITE FISH FILLET, CUT INTO 2.5 CM (1 IN) CUBES, DISCARDING ANY SKIN AND BONE

1 × 15 ML TBS SEASONED FLOUR

SUNFLOWER OIL

450 G (1 LB) TOMATOES, SKINNED AND CUT INTO EIGHTHS

115 G (4 OZ) BUTTON MUSHROOMS, WIPED AND HALVED

150 ML (5 FL OZ) WHITE WINE

1 × 15 ML TBS TOMATO PURÉE

1 CLOVE GARLIC, SKINNED AND CRUSHED

150 ML (5 FL OZ) WATER

CHOPPED FRESH PARSLEY (OPTIONAL)

1. Cook the pasta in boiling salted water until tender. Drain well, rinsing under warm water to remove excess starch. Blanch the corn and pepper together in boiling salted water for 2-3 minutes, then drain.
2. Toss the fish cubes in the seasoned flour, then lightly brown in a little oil in a large, shallow flameproof casserole or sauté pan. Turn the fish with care, as it breaks up very easily. Remove the fish to one side.
3. Gently stir all the remaining ingredients together into the pan with the water. Bring to the boil, cover and replace the fish, then simmer gently for 5-10 minutes or until the fish is cooked. Season with salt and pepper and mix in the parsley.

Salmon and Prawn Rice in Filo Pastry

Serves 8

75 G (3 OZ) LONG-GRAIN WHITE AND WILD RICE, MIXED

SALT AND PEPPER

1 BUNCH OF SALAD ONIONS, TRIMMED AND CHOPPED

75 G (3 OZ) BUTTER

115 G (4 OZ) COOKED PEELED PRAWNS

GRATED RIND OF 1 LEMON

1 BUNCH OF WATERCRESS, RINSED AND ROUGHLY CHOPPED

2 × 15 ML TBS CHOPPED FRESH DILL OR 1 × 5 ML TSP DRIED DILL WEED

230 G PACKET FILO PASTRY (10 SHEETS,EACH SHEET APPROX 30 × 23 CM/12 × 9 IN)

2 × 450 G (1 LB) SALMON FILLETS, SKINNED

2 × 15 ML TBS LEMON MAYONNAISE

LEMON MAYONNAISE, TO ACCOMPANY

SLICED CUCUMBER, TO GARNISH

1. Cook the rice in boiling, salted water until tender; drain well. Sauté the salad onions in 25 g (1 oz) of the butter for 2-3 minutes or until just beginning to soften. Stir into the rice with the prawns, lemon rind, watercress, dill and seasoning.
2. Melt the remaining butter. Layer up six sheets of filo pastry, brushing with butter between each sheet and overlapping the sheets so they are large enough to wrap one of the salmon fillets. Place one salmon fillet in the centre of the pastry. Spoon over the rice mixture and top with mayonnaise. Place the other salmon fillet on top.
3. Fold up the sides of the pastry, then top with three of the remaining pastry sheets to enclose the salmon completely. Brush with melted butter to seal well. Cut the remaining sheet of pastry into diamond shapes and scatter over the top. Brush with more melted butter and season with black pepper.
4. Bake in the oven at 200°C/400°F/Gas Mark 6 for 20 minutes. Cover loosely with foil and cook at 180°C/350°F/Gas Mark 4 for a further 20 minutes or until crisp and cooked through. Serve warm, accompanied by lemon mayonnaise and garnished with cucumber.

Salmon with Tarragon

Serves 4

900 G (2 LB) SALMON, SKINNED AND FILLETED

KNOB OF SOFTENED BUTTER

2 × 5 ML TSP CHOPPED FRESH TARRAGON

1 × 5 ML TSP GREEN PEPPERCORNS, SOAKED IN COLD WATER OVERNIGHT

SALT

POLYUNSATURATED OIL

25 G (1 OZ) SPINACH LEAVES, RINSED AND DRIED, REMOVING ANY THICK STALKS

4 × 15 ML TBS DOUBLE CREAM

NEW POTATOES, TO SERVE

1. Place one salmon fillet, skinned side down, on a board. Dot with a little butter and sprinkle with tarragon. Lightly crush the peppercorns and sprinkle over the top. Season with a little salt.
2. Lay the other piece of salmon on top, pressing it down lightly. Cut the fish across into four equal pieces. Lightly oil four squares of cooking foil and place a portion of salmon in the centre of each square.
3. Roll up the spinach leaves and shred them finely. Sprinkle them over the salmon and pour the cream over the top. Season with a little salt. Wrap the salmon loosely in the foil, sealing the edges.
4. Place the parcels on a baking tray and bake in the oven at 190°C/375°F/Gas Mark 5 for 12-15 minutes, until the fish is just cooked. Transfer the fish to warmed serving plates and pour over the cooking juices. Serve with tiny new potatoes.

POACHED PLAICE AND SPINACH FLAN

Serves 4

1½ × QUANTITY RICH SHORTCRUST PASTRY (SEE PAGE 212)

2 MEDIUM PLAICE, SKINNED AND FILLETED, ABOUT 450 G (1 LB) FILLETED WEIGHT, EACH FILLET HALVED LENGTHWAYS TO MAKE 8 FILLETS

300 ML (10 FL OZ) MILK

FEW BLACK PEPPERCORNS

1 BAY LEAF

115 G (4 OZ) FRESH SPINACH OR 50 G (2 OZ) FROZEN CHOPPED SPINACH

25 G (1 OZ) BUTTER

20 G (¾ OZ) PLAIN WHITE FLOUR

SALT AND PEPPER

50 G (2 OZ) BRIE, RINDED AND ROUGHLY CHOPPED

2 × SIZE 4 EGGS

1 × 15 ML TBS FRESHLY GRATED PARMESAN CHEESE

1. Roll out the pastry on a lightly floured surface and line a 34 × 11 cm (13½ × 4½ in) loose-based, fluted tranche tin. Chill for 10-15 minutes. Place tin on a flat baking tray and bake blind for about 20 minutes or until just cooked through (see page 212).
2. Roll up the fillets, skinned side out. Place in a saucepan into which they will just fit and pour the milk over. Add the peppercorns and bay leaf. Cover and bring slowly to the boil, simmer for about 2 minutes or until the fillets are just cooked. Remove with a slotted spoon, dry on absorbent kitchen paper. Strain and reserve the liquid.
3. If using fresh spinach, wash, trim and, without drying it, place in a medium-sized saucepan. Cover and cook over a gentle heat for 3-4 minutes or until wilted. Drain well. Squeeze out any excess liquid and finely chop.
4. Melt the butter in a medium-sized saucepan. Stir the flour in and cook, stirring, for 1-2 minutes before adding 200 ml (7 fl oz) of the reserved poaching liquid. Season and bring to the boil. Simmer for 2-3 minutes until thickened and smooth. Off the heat, beat in the Brie, eggs and spinach. Add frozen spinach at this stage, if using, stirring until it is evenly blended.
5. Place the poached fish down the centre of the prepared flan tin. Spoon over the sauce and sprinkle with the Parmesan.
6. Bake in the oven at 180°C/350°F/Gas Mark 4 for 25-30 minutes or until just set. Brown under a hot grill for 1-2 minutes. Serve warm.

GOLDEN-TOPPED FISH PIE

Serves 4

900 G (2 LB) OLD POTATOES, PEELED AND CUT INTO LARGE CHUNKS

SALT AND PEPPER

335 G (12 OZ) FENNEL, THINLY SLICED, DISCARDING ANY COARSE CORE OR STEMS (USE THEM IN THE FISH COOKING LIQUOR)

LEMON JUICE

675 G (1½ LB) FRESH HADDOCK FILLET

150 ML (5 FL OZ) DRY WHITE WINE

350 ML (12 FL OZ) WATER

115-175 G (4-6 OZ) COOKED PEELED PRAWNS

75 G (3 OZ) BUTTER OR MARGARINE

40 G (1½ OZ) FLOUR

5 × 15 ML TBS SINGLE CREAM

1 × 15 ML TBS FRESH CHOPPED DILL OR ½ × 5 ML TSP DRIED DILL WEED

ABOUT 115 ML (4 FL OZ) HOT MILK

2 × 15 ML TBS FRESH WHITE BREADCRUMBS

FRESH DILL SPRIGS, TO GARNISH (OPTIONAL)

1. Cook the potatoes in boiling, salted water until just tender; drain well.
2. Blanch the fennel in boiling, salted water with a dash of lemon juice for 5 minutes or until just tender. Drain well.
3. Place the haddock in a large frying pan or saucepan and pour the wine over together with the water; season and add the fennel core and stems. Bring slowly to the boil; cover and simmer until just tender – about 10 minutes.
4. Lift the haddock out of the pan and flake the flesh, discarding any skin and bone. Place the haddock in a 2.4 lt (4 pt) shallow ovenproof dish with the fennel and prawns.
5. Melt 50 g (2 oz) of the butter in a saucepan. Add the flour and cook for 1 minute before stirring in the strained cooking liquor. Bring to the boil, stirring all the time, and cook for a 1 minute or two. Off the heat mix in the cream and dill; adjust seasoning and pour over the fish. Allow to cool.
6. Mash the potatoes. Beat in the hot milk, the remaining butter and plenty of seasoning. Cover the fish mixture with spoonfuls of potato. Sprinkle with breadcrumbs. Brush with a little melted butter.
7. Bake in the oven at 190°C/375°F/Gas Mark 5 for about 40-45 minutes or until lightly browned and bubbling hot. Garnish with sprigs of dill.

ROLLED PLAICE WITH SMOKED SALMON

Serves 6

6 LARGE PLAICE FILLETS, ABOUT 115 G (4 OZ) EACH, SKINNED AND CUT IN HALF LENGTHWAYS

115 G (4 OZ) SMOKED SALMON, CUT INTO SIMILAR-LENGTH STRIPS

JUICE OF 1 LEMON

BLACK PEPPER

115 ML (4 FL OZ) DRY WHITE WINE

1. Lay the plaice on a board, skinned side up, and place a strip of salmon on top, patching with more salmon if this becomes necessary. Squeeze a little lemon juice over each portion and grind over plenty of black pepper. Roll up each fillet carefully.
2. Pour the wine into a flameproof casserole and add the rolls of fish in an even layer, seam side down. (The wine should just cover the base of the casserole.) Cover with a lid or foil.
3. Bring to the boil and leave to simmer gently for about 10 minutes.
4. Using a slotted spoon, carefully lift the fish rolls on to a warmed serving platter.

Golden-Topped Fish Pie

Fillets of Trout with Prawns and Dill

Serves 8

75 G (3 OZ) LONG-GRAIN WHITE RICE

SALT AND PEPPER

115 G (4 OZ) OYSTER OR BUTTON MUSHROOMS, WIPED, TRIMMED AND ROUGHLY CHOPPED

50 G (2 OZ) BUTTER OR MARGARINE

4 × 15 ML TBS CHOPPED FRESH DILL OR ¼ × 5 ML TSP DRIED DILL WEED

225 G (8 OZ) PEELED PRAWNS, CHOPPED

1 EGG

1 × 15 ML TBS LEMON JUICE

8 × 200 G (7 OZ) PINK-FLESHED TROUT, FILLETED IF POSSIBLE

200 ML (7 FL OZ) DRY VERMOUTH

200 ML (7 FL OZ) WATER

150 ML (5 FL OZ) DOUBLE CREAM

SPRIGS OF FRESH DILL, TO GARNISH

1. Cook the rice in boiling salted water until just tender; drain and cool. Sauté the mushrooms in the butter until tender; stir into the rice. Add the dill with the chopped prawns, egg and lemon juice. Season.
2. If the fish are not already filleted, cut off their heads and slit open all the way along the belly. Place on a board, flesh-side down, and press firmly along the backbone to flatten the fish and release the bone. Turn over and ease out the bones. Divide each fish into two fillets and remove the skin. Rinse and drain the fish and pat dry with absorbent kitchen paper. Divide the stuffing between the fillets, roll up and secure with wooden cocktail sticks. Place in one or two shallow ovenproof dishes into which they will just fit. Pour over the vermouth and water. Season. Cover tightly and bake in the oven at 190°C/375°F/Gas Mark 5 for about 25 minutes until the fish is tender.
3. Using a slotted spoon, lift the fish out and place in a serving dish; remove the cocktail sticks, cover and keep warm. Strain the cooking juices into a saucepan. Whisk in the cream. Bring to the boil and simmer, stirring all the time until the sauce thickens slightly. Adjust seasoning and spoon a little sauce over the fish. Garnish with fresh dill and serve the remaining sauce separately.

Crispy Layered Fish Pie

Serves 6

335 G (12 OZ) FRESH SPINACH, WASHED AND COARSE STALKS DISCARDED

75 G (3 OZ) LONG-GRAIN RICE

SALT AND PEPPER

225 G (8 OZ) FRESH HADDOCK FILLET

225 G (8 OZ) SMOKED HADDOCK FILLET

225 ML (8 FL OZ) MILK

115 G (4 OZ) BUTTER

2 × 15 ML TBS PLAIN WHITE FLOUR

1 HARD-BOILED EGG, ROUGHLY CHOPPED

230 G PACKET FILO PASTRY (10 SHEETS, EACH SHEET APPROX 30 × 23 CM/12 × 9 IN)

ASPARAGUS, TO ACCOMPANY

1. Place the spinach leaves in a saucepan with only the water that adheres to them. Cover tightly and cook over moderate heat for 5-6 minutes or until the spinach is cooked. Drain, squeezing out excess liquid, roughly chop and leave to cool. Cook the rice in boiling salted water until tender. Drain well and cool.
2. In a covered pan, poach fish in milk until just cooked. Strain and reserve the cooking liquor. Flake fish into large pieces, discarding any skin and bones.
3. Melt 40 g (1½ oz) butter in a saucepan, add the flour and cook for 1-2 minutes. Stir the reserved liquor in, bring to the boil and boil for 1-2 minutes or until thickened. Carefully stir the fish and chopped egg in. Season, then leave to cool.
4. Melt remaining butter. Grease a baking tray then place one pastry sheet on it. Brush lightly with butter and continue layering like this until half the pastry has been used. Spoon the rice on to the pastry, leaving a 2.5 cm (1 in) border all round. Cover the rice with spinach, then with fish mixture.
5. Place a sheet of the remaining pastry on top of the filling and brush with butter, then complete the layering as above. Seal the edges well and brush the top with the remaining butter.
6. Bake at 200°C/400°F/Gas Mark 6, covering lightly with foil if necessary, for about 30 minutes until the pie is crisp and golden. Serve with asparagus.

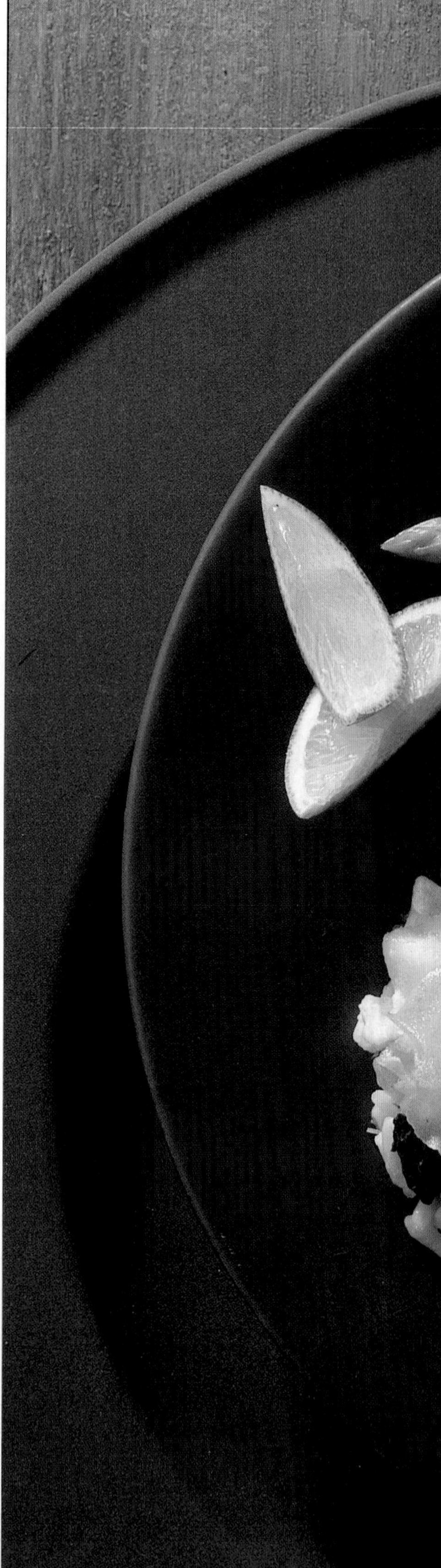

Crispy Layered Fish Pie

Prawn and Tarragon Omelette

Serves 2

4 EGGS

SALT AND PEPPER

2×15 ML TBS WATER

KNOB OF BUTTER OR MARGARINE

115 G (4 OZ) COOKED PEELED PRAWNS

1-2×15 ML TBS CHOPPED FRESH TARRAGON OR ½×5 ML TSP DRIED

1. In a bowl, whisk together the eggs, seasoning and water.
2. Heat the butter in a medium frying pan or omelette pan, preferably non-stick. When it is hot and sizzling, tip in the eggs. Cook over a moderate to high heat, drawing a fork through the mixture to allow the raw egg to run through.
3. When the omelette is lightly set, sprinkle the prawns and tarragon over. Cook for a few seconds longer then fold into three and flip out on to a serving plate. Serve immediately, cut in half.

Spicy Spinach Roulade

Serves 4-6

900 G (2 LB) FRESH SPINACH, THOROUGHLY WASHED AND LARGE STALKS DISCARDED

SALT AND PEPPER

1×5 ML TSP MUSTARD SEEDS

1×5 ML TSP CORIANDER SEEDS

½×5 ML TSP CUMIN SEEDS

225 G (8 OZ) LOW-FAT SOFT CHEESE

4 EGGS, SEPARATED

15 G (½ OZ) BUTTER

175 G (6 OZ) BUTTON MUSHROOMS, WIPED AND FINELY CHOPPED

1×5 ML TSP GROUND TURMERIC

225 G (8 OZ) COOKED PEELED PRAWNS, THOROUGHLY DEFROSTED IF FROZEN, FINELY CHOPPED

WHOLE COOKED PRAWNS AND FRESH PARSLEY SPRIGS, TO GARNISH

1. Line a greased 33×23 cm (13×9 in) swiss roll tin with non-stick baking parchment. Set aside.
2. Put the spinach leaves in a large saucepan with only the water that clings to them. Add salt to taste and cook over a gentle heat for 5 minutes, shaking the pan constantly, until the spinach wilts and shrinks. Drain well.
3. Purée the spinach in a blender or food processor. Crush the spices with a mortar and pestle, then add to the spinach with half of the cheese. Work until evenly mixed. Add the egg yolks and salt and pepper to taste and work again until smooth. Transfer to a large bowl.
4. Whisk the egg whites in a clean bowl until standing in stiff peaks. Fold into the spinach mixture, then immediately spread in the prepared tin with a palette knife. Bake in the oven at 200°C/400°F/Gas Mark 6 for 15 minutes or until firm to the touch.
5. Meanwhile, melt the butter in a saucepan, add the mushrooms and turmeric and toss over a high heat until the juices have evaporated. Add the prawns and heat through. Turn the mixture into a bowl, add the remaining cheese and salt and pepper to taste. Beat to a soft, spreading consistency. Cover and keep warm.
6. Turn the cooked roulade out on to a large sheet of non-stick baking parchment and carefully peel off the lining paper. Immediately spread with the prawn mixture. Roll up gently with the help of the parchment.
7. To serve, lift the roulade carefully on to a warm serving plate and place seam side down. Garnish with prawns and parsley.

Seafood Roulade

Serves 8

115 G (4 OZ) BUTTER

335 G (12 OZ) COOKED PRAWNS IN SHELLS

200 ML (7 FL OZ) DRY WHITE WINE

200 ML (7 FL OZ) WATER

ONION SLICES AND A BAY LEAF, FOR FLAVOURING

225 G (8 OZ) FRESH HADDOCK FILLET

200 ML (7 FL OZ) MILK

SALT AND PEPPER

PLAIN FLOUR

4 EGGS, SEPARATED

2×15 ML TBS SINGLE CREAM

FRESH HERBS, TO GARNISH

1. First prepare the paper case. Cut two sheets of foil (to use as a double layer) or one sheet of strong non-stick baking parchment into a rectangle measuring 40×30 cm (16×12 in). Fold up 2.5 cm (1 in) around the edges, then snip in at the corners and secure with paper clips or staples. Brush the case generously with melted butter.
2. To prepare the fish stock, remove the heads and shells from the prawns, reserving the flesh, and place in a small saucepan with the wine, water and the flavouring ingredients. Bring to the boil and simmer for 10 minutes. Strain into a jug and reserve.
3. Place the haddock in a saucepan with the milk and seasoning. Bring to the boil, cover and simmer for 8 minutes or until the fish is tender. Strain and reserve the liquor – there should be about 200 ml (7 fl oz). Flake the fish, discarding skin and bone.
4. Melt 50 g (2 oz) butter in a saucepan. Stir in 50 g (2 oz) flour followed by the reserved milk. Bring to the boil and cook for 1 minute, stirring, to make a very thick sauce. Take off the heat, allow to cool slightly, then mix in the flaked haddock and the egg yolks. Adjust the seasoning.
5. Whisk the egg whites until stiff but not dry. Stir one large spoonful into the fish sauce, then lightly fold in the remaining egg whites and pour into the paper case. Push the mixture out carefully to fill the case to the edges. Bake at 200°C/400°F/Gas Mark 6 for about 12 minutes or until lightly browned and just firm to the touch.
6. Melt 25 g (1 oz) butter in a saucepan and stir in 3×15 ml tbs flour, followed by the stock. Bring to the boil, stirring all the time, and cook for 1 minute. Take off the heat and mix in the prawns and cream. Adjust the seasoning and keep warm.
7. Have ready a large sheet of damp greaseproof paper. Snip the edges of the paper case, then flip the cooked roulade on to the sheet of paper.
8. Carefully ease off the paper case. Make a shallow cut along one short edge – this helps to start the roulade rolling up. Spread thinly with the sauce and fish mixture and roll up from the short edge. Lift carefully on to serving platter and garnish with fresh herbs. Serve immediately, accompanied by the remaining sauce.

Spicy Spinach Roulade

Glazed Seafood Platter

Serves 6-8

225 G (8 OZ) HADDOCK FILLET, SKINNED AND CUT INTO BITE-SIZED PIECES

450 G (1 LB) HALIBUT FILLET, SKINNED AND CUT INTO BITE-SIZE PIECES

75 G (3 OZ) FENNEL, FEATHERY TOPS REMOVED FINELY CHOPPED AND RESERVED, AND THE REST CUT INTO WAFER-THIN SLICES

300 ML (10 FL OZ) DRY WHITE WINE

150 ML (5 FL OZ) FISH STOCK

1 BAY LEAF

115 G (4 OZ) COOKED SHELLED MUSSELS

115 G (4 OZ) COOKED PEELED PRAWNS

40 G (1½ OZ) BUTTER

40 G (1½ OZ) PLAIN FLOUR

1 EGG YOLK

150 ML (5 FL OZ) DOUBLE CREAM

SALT AND PEPPER

50 G (2 OZ) EMMENTHAL CHEESE, GRATED

LEMON PEPPER SALAD (SEE PAGE 143), TO ACCOMPANY

1. Place the fish and fennel in a large shallow pan and pour the wine and stock over the top. Add the bay leaf. Bring to the boil, cover and simmer for 7-8 minutes or until the fish is just cooked.
2. With a slotted spoon, remove the fish and fennel from the cooking liquor and arrange in a single layer in a gratin dish.
3. Add the mussels to the liquid, return to the boil and immediately remove with a slotted spoon. Scatter the mussels over the fish with the prawns. Cover the platter with foil and keep warm in the oven at 160°C/325°F/Gas Mark 3.
4. Melt the butter in a saucepan. Stir the flour in and cook, stirring, for 1-2 minutes. Strain the poaching liquor in, bring to the boil, stirring all the time, then simmer for 2-3 minutes until thickened. Beat in the egg yolk, cream and seasoning.
5. Spoon the sauce evenly over the seafood and sprinkle with the cheese. Place under a hot grill until golden brown. Garnish with the reserved fennel tops. Serve immediately with the lemon pepper salad.

Barbecued Mullet Cooked in Vine Leaves

Serves 8

227 G PACKET VINE LEAVES IN BRINE

9×15 ML TBS OLIVE OIL

2×15 ML TBS WHITE WINE VINEGAR OR LEMON OR LIME JUICE

SALT AND PEPPER

8 RED MULLET, EACH WEIGHING ABOUT 275 G (10 OZ), CLEANED AND SCALED

LIME OR LEMON WEDGES AND A FEW GRAPES, TO GARNISH

1. Drain the brine from the vine leaves, put them in a large bowl and pour boiling water over them. Rinse well.
2. Whisk the oil, vinegar or lemon or lime juice together and season to taste with salt and pepper.
3. Put the fish into a shallow dish and pour over the oil and vinegar. Leave in a cool place for at least 30 minutes to marinate.

Glazed Seafood Platter

4. Remove the fish from the marinade and wrap each one in one or two of the vine leaves. Secure the leaves with string.
5. Place the fish in a greased barbecue rack and cook over a barbecue for about 12-14 minutes or until the fish is cooked, turning occasionally and brushing with the marinade. Remove string and serve on a platter lined with vine leaves, decorated with lemon or lime wedges and a few grapes.

Barbecued Fish in Satay Sauce

Serves 6

6 MEDIUM MACKEREL, ABOUT 225 G (8 OZ) EACH, GUTTED
190 G JAR SATAY SAUCE
GRATED RIND AND JUICE OF 1 LEMON
2 × 15 ML TBS LOW-FAT NATURAL YOGURT
LEMON AND LIME HALVES, TO SERVE
FRESH CORIANDER, TO GARNISH

1. Make three or four deep slashes into the mackerel flesh on both sides of the fish. Mix together the satay sauce, lemon rind and juice and the yogurt. Pour the mixture over the fish. Cover and refrigerate for at least 10 minutes.
2. Wrap each fish, together with a little of the marinade, in foil and secure with a wooden skewer or wooden cocktail stick.
3. Cook the fish on the barbecue for about 12-15 minutes, turning frequently. Alternatively, place the fish on a rack over a roasting tin and bake at 220°C/425°F/Gas Mark 7 for about 15-20 minutes. Serve immediately, with the halves of lemon and lime and garnished with the fresh coriander.

COOK'S TIP

Mackerel is used in this recipe as its strong flavour marries well with the spicy marinade. Also, the oily flesh is ideal for grilling as it stays moist. To protect the fish and all the flavours, wrap it in foil. If time allows, marinate the fish overnight.

Thai Prawn Curry

Serves 8

2 LARGE ONIONS, SKINNED AND CHOPPED
4 GARLIC CLOVES, SKINNED AND ROUGHLY CHOPPED
8 CM (3 IN) PIECE OF FRESH ROOT GINGER, PEELED AND CHOPPED
1 STALK OF LEMON GRASS, TRIMMED AND ROUGHLY CHOPPED
1-2 SMALL CHILLIES, SEEDED
1 × 15 ML TBS GROUND CORIANDER
1 × 5 ML TSP GROUND CUMIN
¼ × 5 ML TSP GROUND NUTMEG
1 × 15 ML TBS NAM PLA FISH SAUCE
4 × 15 ML TBS CHOPPED FRESH CORIANDER
FINELY GRATED RIND AND JUICE OF 2 LIMES
2 × 15 ML TBS OIL
1.8 KG (4 LB) MEDIUM OR LARGE, RAW PRAWNS IN THE SHELL
600 ML (20 FL OZ) THICK COCONUT MILK (SEE COOK'S TIP)
300 ML (10 FL OZ) FISH OR VEGETABLE STOCK
SALT AND PEPPER
VERY FINELY SHREDDED SALAD ONIONS AND CHOPPED FRESH CORIANDER, TO GARNISH

1. Put one onion, the garlic, ginger and lemon grass into a blender and process until finely chopped. Add the chillies, ground coriander, cumin, nutmeg, fish sauce, fresh coriander, lime rind and half of the oil and continue processing to make a paste.
2. Prepare the prawns, by removing most of the shell, leaving the tail piece attached. Using a small, sharp knife, cut each prawn along the outer curve, stopping at the tail shell, to expose the dark vein (take care not to split the prawn completely in half). Open each prawn and remove the dark vein. Rinse the prawns and drain thoroughly.
3. Heat the remaining oil in a large, shallow flameproof casserole dish. Add the remaining onion and cook for 5 minutes until golden brown, stirring all the time.
4. Add the spicy paste and cook over a high heat for about 5 minutes until browned, stirring all the time. Add the coconut milk and stock. Bring to the boil and simmer for 2 minutes.
5. Add the prawns and cook for a further 2-3 minutes or until the prawns are just pink. Turn off the heat and stir in the lime juice and salt and pepper to taste. Transfer to a serving dish and sprinkle with the salad onions and coriander.

COOK'S TIP

To make 600 ml (20 fl oz) coconut milk, put ½ × 200 g packet creamed coconut in a heatproof measuring jug and pour in boiling water to come up to the 600 ml (20 fl oz) mark. Stir until dissolved. For thick milk, use the whole packet.

Lemon and Mustard Mackerel

Serves 4

4 FRESH MACKEREL, ABOUT 335 G (12 OZ) EACH, CLEANED
1 × 15 ML TBS MUSTARD SEEDS
50 G (2 OZ) BUTTER, SOFTENED
GRATED RIND AND JUICE OF 1 LEMON
1 × 15 ML TBS DIJON MUSTARD
1 × 5 ML TSP GROUND PAPRIKA
SALT AND PEPPER
2 × 15 ML TBS OLIVE OIL
450 G (1 LB) CUCUMBER, FINELY DICED
4 × 15 ML TBS CHOPPED FRESH PARSLEY
FRESH PARSLEY SPRIGS AND LEMON WEDGES DIPPED IN PAPRIKA, TO GARNISH (OPTIONAL)

1. Make several deep slashes along the length of both sides of each fish; arrange them in a non-metallic dish.
2. Crush the mustard seeds with a rolling pin, and beat into the butter. Add the lemon rind, 1 × 15 ml tbs juice, the mustard, half the paprika and seasoning, mixing well.
3. Spread this butter into the slashes in the fish. Spread any remainder over the fish. Pour any remaining lemon juice over the fish, cover and leave to marinate in the refrigerator for at least 1 hour.
4. Place the fish on a wire rack in a grill pan and grill for 10 minutes on each side or until cooked through.
5. Meanwhile, heat the oil in a frying pan and add the cucumber. Sauté for 2-3 minutes, then stir in the remaining paprika and parsley. Cook for a further 1 minute. Serve with the mackerel, garnished with parsley and lemon wedges dipped in paprika.

POULTRY AND GAME

Poultry was once a rare luxury food, served only on special occasions. Developments in breeding and rearing have radically changed this, and most poultry is now plentiful and no longer expensive. Chicken has become increasingly popular as the growing awareness of healthy eating has encouraged people to eat more low-fat white meat. Also included in this chapter are pigeon, pheasant and venison.

Left: Chicken and Spiced Apricot Casserole (page 62)
Right: Peppered Poussins with Lime and Sage Crumbs (page 71)

Yogurt-Braised Chicken

Serves 4

¼×5 ML TSP CHILLI POWDER

¼×5 ML TSP TURMERIC

SALT AND PEPPER

2.5 CM (1 IN) PIECE OF FRESH ROOT GINGER, PEELED AND GRATED

1 GARLIC CLOVE, SKINNED AND CRUSHED

6 CHICKEN BREASTS ON THE BONE, SKIN REMOVED

25 G (1 OZ) BLANCHED ALMONDS

25 G (1 OZ) UNSALTED CASHEW NUTS

ABOUT 50 ML (2 FL OZ) WATER

1×5 ML TSP SAFFRON THREADS

ABOUT 75 G (3 OZ) GHEE

175 G (6 OZ) ONION, SKINNED AND ROUGHLY CHOPPED

10 WHOLE GREEN CARDAMOMS, SPLIT

2 CLOVES

1 CINNAMON STICK

2 BAY LEAVES

¼×5 ML TSP EACH GARAM MASALA, GROUND CARDAMOM AND GROUND MACE

225 G (8 OZ) LOW-FAT NATURAL YOGURT

2×15 ML TBS MILK

4 EGGS, BEATEN

115 G (4 OZ) TOMATO, SEEDED AND CHOPPED

1 GREEN CHILLI, SEEDED AND FINELY CHOPPED

2×15 ML TBS CHOPPED FRESH CORIANDER

SLIVERED ALMONDS, TO GARNISH

NAAN-STYLE BREAD (SEE PAGE 210), TO SERVE

1. Mix together the chilli powder, turmeric, salt, grated ginger and crushed garlic. Rub well into the chicken. Cover and leave to marinate for 15 minutes.
2. Place the almonds and cashew nuts in a blender or food processor. Add the water and saffron. Process it all together to form a smooth, creamy paste.
3. Heat 50 g (2 oz) ghee in a large flameproof casserole and add 115 g (4 oz) onion. Sauté, stirring, for 10-12 minutes until golden brown and soft. Remove with a slotted spoon and add to the nut mixture. Process again until smooth.
4. In the same casserole, sauté the chicken until well browned on all sides. Remove with a slotted spoon and drain on absorbent kitchen paper.
5. Stir the cardamoms, cloves, cinnamon stick, bay leaves, garam masala, ground cardamom and ground mace into the casserole. Cook for 1-2 minutes. Off the heat, add the nut mixture and yogurt. Return the chicken to the casserole and cover tightly with foil and a lid. Simmer very gently for 15-20 minutes or until the chicken is tender and cooked.
6. Add the milk and seasoning to the beaten eggs. Stir the tomatoes in, with the remaining chopped onion, chilli and the fresh coriander. Heat a little ghee in an omelette pan and make four flat omelettes with the egg mixture.
7. Remove the chicken pieces to a warm, flat serving dish. Garnish with slivered almonds and serve with the omelettes and Naan-Style Bread.

Chicken and Spiced Apricot Casserole

Serves 10

1.4 KG (3 LB) CHICKEN FILLETS, CUT INTO CHUNKS

2×15 ML TBS CHOPPED FRESH THYME OR 1×5 ML TSP DRIED

PINCH OF GROUND CLOVES

2 LARGE GARLIC CLOVES, SKINNED AND CRUSHED

18 NO-SOAK DRIED APRICOTS

2×15 ML TBS CLEAR HONEY

3×15 ML TBS WHITE WINE VINEGAR

450 ML (16 FL OZ) DRY CIDER

3 WHOLE CLOVES

3×15 ML TBS VEGETABLE OIL

450 G (1 LB) ONION, SKINNED AND CHOPPED

75 G (3 OZ) BACK BACON, RINDED AND MADE INTO SMALL ROLLS

GRATED RIND AND JUICE OF 1 LARGE ORANGE

200 ML (7 FL OZ) MARSALA

175 G (6 OZ) FRESH SPINACH

ABOUT 4×5 ML TSP CORNFLOUR

SALT AND PEPPER

1. Marinate the chicken overnight with the thyme, ground cloves and garlic. Heat the apricots, honey, vinegar, cider and whole cloves together. Remove from heat and cover. Leave overnight, then discard the cloves.
2. In a flameproof casserole, sauté the chicken and marinade in the oil until browned; remove from pan. Add onion, bacon and orange rind; sauté for 2-3 minutes.
3. Return chicken and stir in 4×15 ml tbs orange juice, the marsala, apricots and their liquid. Cover and simmer for 20-25 minutes or until the chicken is tender and cooked. Meanwhile, cook the spinach, finely chop, then stir into the casserole.
4. Thicken the juices with the cornflour. Add seasoning.

Chicken and Apple Casserole

Serves 4

2×15 ML TBS OLIVE OIL

4 CHICKEN QUARTERS, ABOUT 900 G (2 LB) TOTAL WEIGHT

900 G (2 LB) MIXED ROOT VEGETABLES, PEELED AND SLICED, LEAVING SMALL ONES WHOLE

335 G (12 OZ) ONION, SKINNED AND ROUGHLY CHOPPED

115 G (4 OZ) GREEN LENTILS, BOILED RAPIDLY FOR 10 MINUTES, THEN DRAINED

2 SMALL EATING APPLES, WASHED OR PEELED, CORED AND SLICED

200 ML (7 FL OZ) APPLE JUICE

300 ML (10 FL OZ) CHICKEN STOCK (SEE PAGE 13)

SALT AND PEPPER

1. Heat the oil in a large flameproof casserole and brown the chicken quarters well. Remove from the pan with a slotted spoon and drain on absorbent kitchen paper.
2. Add all the vegetables to the pan and sauté for 4-5 minutes or until beginning to colour. Add the lentils, apples, apple juice and stock and bring to the boil. Season well and replace the chicken quarters.
3. Cover and cook at 190°C/375°F/Gas Mark 5 for about 50 minutes or until the chicken and lentils are tender and cooked through. Adjust the seasoning before serving.

COOK'S TIP

You can add any of your favourite seasonal root vegetables to this casserole – just keep the total weight the same. If you prefer a casserole with thicker juices, simply purée some of the vegetables and stir back in.

Chicken and Apple Casserole

Marinated Chicken with Prunes

Serves 4

6 CHICKEN QUARTERS (BREAST OR LEG), ABOUT 900 G (2 LB) TOTAL WEIGHT

4 GARLIC CLOVES, SKINNED AND SLICED

2 × 5 ML TSP DRIED MIXED HERBS

2 × 15 ML TBS RED WINE VINEGAR

115 ML (4 FL OZ) VEGETABLE OIL

225 G (8 OZ) PITTED READY-TO-EAT PRUNES

2 × 15 ML TBS CAPERS, DRAINED

SALT AND FRESHLY GROUND PEPPER

300 ML (10 FL OZ) DRY WHITE WINE

25 G (1 OZ) DEMERARA SUGAR

1 × 5 ML TSP CORNFLOUR

1 × 15 ML TBS WATER

150 ML (5 FL OZ) CHICKEN STOCK (SEE PAGE 13)

JUICE OF 1 LEMON

PARSLEY, TO GARNISH

1. Place the chicken in a large non-metallic bowl with the garlic. Add the herbs, vinegar, oil, prunes and capers with plenty of seasoning; mix. Cover and marinate in the refrigerator overnight.
2. Remove the chicken and reserve the marinade. With a little oil from the marinade, brown the chicken in a large flameproof casserole that holds the chicken in a single layer. Pour the remaining marinade with the marinade ingredients and the wine over the chicken; sprinkle with the sugar. Bring to the boil.
3. Cover and bake at 180°C/350°F/Gas Mark 4 for 30 minutes, then uncover and baste. Return to the oven, uncovered, for a further 20 minutes, or until the chicken quarters are cooked through.
4. Using a slotted spoon, lift the chicken into a serving dish; cover and keep warm. Skim the juices. Mix the cornflour to a smooth paste with the water. Add to the pan juices with the stock and bring to the boil, stirring all the time. Cook for 1-2 minutes. Adjust the seasoning, add about 1 × 5 ml tsp lemon juice to taste, spoon over the chicken and serve, garnished with parsley.

Marinated Chicken with Prunes

Golden Parmesan Chicken

Serves 6

335 G (12 OZ) AUBERGINE, THINLY SLICED

VEGETABLE OIL

50 G (2 OZ) FRESHLY GRATED PARMESAN CHEESE

2 × 5 ML TSP DRIED MARJORAM

6 CHICKEN QUARTERS (BREAST AND WING), ABOUT 675 G (1½ LB) TOTAL WEIGHT

1 EGG, BEATEN

225 G (8 OZ) ONION, SKINNED AND ROUGHLY CHOPPED

2 GARLIC CLOVES, SKINNED AND CRUSHED

400 G CAN CHOPPED TOMATOES

1 × 15 ML TBS TOMATO PURÉE

PINCH OF SUGAR

SALT AND PEPPER

175 G (6 OZ) MOZZARELLA CHEESE, THINLY SLICED

CRISP SALAD, TO ACCOMPANY

1. Brush each slice of aubergine with a little oil. Cook under a moderate grill for 2-3 minutes or until golden on each side. Drain on absorbent kitchen paper.
2. Meanwhile, mix the Parmesan cheese with half the marjoram. Dip the chicken in beaten egg and then in the cheese mixture. Place on a flat baking tray. Cover and chill in the refrigerator for 10-15 minutes.
3. Heat 1 × 15 ml tbs oil in a non-stick sauté pan and gently cook the onion and garlic until softened and golden. Stir in the tomatoes, tomato purée, remaining marjoram, sugar and seasoning. Bring to the boil and simmer for 1 minute. Pour into a 2 lt (3½ pt) shallow ovenproof dish.
4. Place the chicken, aubergine slices and Mozzarella cheese in overlapping rows over the sauce.
5. Bake in the oven at 190°C/375°F/Gas Mark 5 for 40-45 minutes or until the chicken is cooked through and the cheese is golden brown. Serve immediately with a crisp salad.

Golden Parmesan Chicken

Pot-Roasted Poussins with Oatmeal Stuffing

Serves 8

225 G (8 OZ) MEDIUM OATMEAL

75 G (3 OZ) BUTTER OR MARGARINE

225 G (8 OZ) ONION, SKINNED AND ROUGHLY CHOPPED

50 G (2 OZ) CASHEW NUTS, CHOPPED

225 G (8 OZ) EATING APPLE, CORED AND ROUGHLY CHOPPED

2 × 15 ML TBS CHOPPED FRESH TARRAGON OR 1 × 5 ML TSP DRIED

GRATED RIND OF 2 ORANGES AND JUICE OF 3-4 ORANGES

4 POUSSINS, ABOUT 565 G (1¼ LB) EACH

175 G (6 OZ) MIXED CHOPPED ONION, CARROT, TURNIP AND CELERY

115 ML (4 FL OZ) WHITE WINE VINEGAR

115 ML (5 FL OZ) CHICKEN STOCK (SEE PAGE 13)

SALT AND PEPPER

4 × 15 ML TBS DOUBLE CREAM

SPRIGS OF FRESH TARRAGON AND APPLE SLICES, TO GARNISH

1. Lightly toast the oatmeal under a hot grill. Melt 50 g (2 oz) butter in a medium-sized saucepan and sauté the onion with the nuts until golden. Add the apple. Cook for 1-2 minutes before adding half the tarragon, the orange rind, 4 × 15 ml tbs orange juice and the oatmeal. Cool.
2. With the thumb and forefinger, loosen the skin away from the breast flesh of the poussins to make a pocket. Divide the stuffing mixture between the poussins, spooning as much as possible into the pocket of each bird.
3. Melt 25 g (1 oz) butter in a heavy flameproof casserole. Brown the poussins two at a time until golden on all sides, adding more butter if necessary. Drain on absorbent kitchen paper. Stir the mixed vegetables into the casserole and sauté, stirring until golden brown. Place the poussins on top of the vegetables. Mix together the vinegar, stock and 4 × 15 ml tbs orange juice and pour over the poussins. Season.
4. Bring to the boil, cover and simmer the poussins for 35-40 minutes or until just tender and cooked. Test with a skewer. The juices should run clear, not pink.
5. Remove the poussins and cut in half. Place on a warmed serving dish, cover loosely with foil and keep warm in a low oven. Strain the contents of the casserole into a small saucepan. Discard the vegetables. Stir in the cream and remaining tarragon. Boil rapidly until slightly thickened and smooth. Adjust seasoning. Spoon a little sauce over the poussins and garnish with sprigs of fresh tarragon and apple slices to serve. Serve the remaining sauce separately.

COOK'S TIP

The same stuffing can be used with boned chicken thighs or breasts for easier eating.

Mild Chicken Curry

Serves 4

2 × 15 ML TBS VEGETABLE OIL

8 BONELESS CHICKEN THIGHS, OR ABOUT 450 G (1 LB) BONELESS CHICKEN PIECES, CUT INTO LARGE BITE-SIZED PIECES

225 G (8 OZ) ONION, SKINNED AND SLICED

1 GARLIC CLOVE, SKINNED AND CRUSHED

2 × 15 ML TBS MILD CURRY PASTE

400 G CAN CHOPPED TOMATOES

200 ML (7 FL OZ) CHICKEN STOCK (SEE PAGE 13)

2 × 5 ML TSP TOMATO PURÉE

25 G (1 OZ) SULTANAS (OPTIONAL)

SALT AND PEPPER

BOILED RICE, SLICED TOMATOES, BANANAS, CUCUMBER AND MANGO CHUTNEY, TO ACCOMPANY

1. Heat the oil in a medium-sized flameproof casserole. Fry the chicken until golden, then remove from casserole.
2. Lower the heat, add the onion and garlic and cook until soft but not coloured. Stir the curry paste in and cook for 1-2 minutes.
3. Replace the chicken, mix in tomatoes, stock, tomato purée, sultanas and seasoning. Bring to the boil, stirring occasionally. Cover and simmer gently for 20-30 minutes, or until chicken is tender and cooked.
4. Serve with boiled rice and simple, colourful accompaniments such as sliced tomatoes, bananas, cucumber and mango chutney.

Spicy Coconut Chicken

Serves 6

6 CHICKEN BREAST FILLETS WITH SKIN, ABOUT 675 G (1½ LB)

3 × 15 ML TBS VEGETABLE OIL

225 G (8 OZ) ONION, SKINNED AND FINELY CHOPPED

1 GARLIC CLOVE, SKINNED AND CRUSHED

1 CM (½ IN) PIECE OF FRESH ROOT GINGER, PEELED AND FINELY CHOPPED

½ × 5 ML TSP GROUND TURMERIC

1 × 5 ML TSP EACH GROUND CUMIN, GROUND CORIANDER AND MILD CURRY POWDER

PINCH OF HOT CHILLI POWDER (OPTIONAL)

227 G CAN CHOPPED TOMATOES

75 G (3 OZ) CREAMED COCONUT, COARSELY GRATED

2 × 15 ML TBS POPPY SEEDS

300 ML (10 FL OZ) CHICKEN STOCK (SEE PAGE 13)

SALT AND PEPPER

2 × 15 ML TBS GREEK-STYLE NATURAL YOGURT

CHOPPED FRESH CORIANDER, TO GARNISH

1. Tuck the ends of the chicken breasts under to shape into neat rounds; tie with string.
2. Heat the oil in a pan and sauté the chicken fillets until golden. Remove with a slotted spoon and drain on absorbent kitchen paper.
3. Add the onion, garlic and ginger and cook, stirring, for 1-2 minutes. Add spices. Cook for a further minute, then add the tomatoes, coconut and poppy seeds. Cook for a further minute. Add the stock. Bring to the boil, and simmer for 2-3 minutes.
4. Replace the chicken, cover and simmer for about 20 minutes or until the chicken is cooked through. Remove string (see Cook's Tip).
5. Skim off any excess oil and add seasoning. Off the heat, stir the yogurt in. Serve garnished with fresh coriander.

COOK'S TIP

To keep a perfect shape, leave the string on the chicken when serving, but do remember to remove before eating.

Spicy Coconut Chicken

Cheesy Chicken and Bacon Rolls

CHEESY CHICKEN AND BACON ROLLS

Serves 4

12 BONELESS, SKINLESS CHICKEN THIGHS, ABOUT 675 G (1½ LB) TOTAL WEIGHT

2 × 15 ML TBS WHOLEGRAIN MUSTARD

115 G (4 OZ) GRUYÈRE OR CHEDDAR CHEESE, CUT INTO 12 STICKS

12 SLICES SMOKED STREAKY BACON, ABOUT 250 G (9 OZ)

1. Unroll each chicken thigh and spread the inside with mustard. Place the cheese sticks on top of the mustard. Roll up the chicken.
2. Gently stretch the bacon with the back of a knife and wrap one piece tightly around each thigh. Secure with wooden satay sticks.
3. Place in a non-stick roasting tin and bake at 190°C/375°F/Gas Mark 5 for 30-35 minutes or until cooked through and golden brown. Serve immediately.

COOK'S TIP

These rolls are delicious served with a cheese or garlic-flavoured dip.

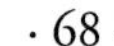

CHICKEN-STUFFED EGGS

Serves 8

10 WHOLE EGGS, PLUS 1 EGG YOLK

40 G (1½ OZ) BUTTER OR MARGARINE

50 G (2 OZ) ONION, SKINNED AND FINELY CHOPPED

175 G (6 OZ) BUTTON MUSHROOMS, WIPED, TRIMMED AND FINELY CHOPPED

1 × 15 ML TBS PLAIN WHITE FLOUR PLUS EXTRA FOR COATING

115 ML (4 FL OZ) MILK

SALT AND PEPPER

2 × 5 ML TSP DIJON MUSTARD

2 × 15 ML CHOPPED FRESH PARSLEY

115 G (4 OZ) COOKED CHICKEN, FINELY CHOPPED

115 G (4 OZ) DRIED WHITE BREADCRUMBS

VEGETABLE OIL

TOMATO SAUCE OR CHUTNEY, TO ACCOMPANY

1. Hard-boil eight eggs, then cool under cold water. Shell the eggs and halve them lengthways. Remove the yolks and push them through a sieve; keep the yolks and halved whites covered.
2. Meanwhile, melt the butter in a saucepan and cook the onion and mushrooms in the butter until all the excess moisture has evaporated.
3. Stir in the flour, milk and seasoning. Bring to the boil and cook for 1-2 minutes then stir in the raw egg yolk, mustard and parsley. Cool; beat in the finely chopped chicken and sieved, hard-boiled egg yolks. Cover and chill for several hours.
4. Stuff the mixture into the egg whites, piling it up well, and then neatly sandwich two egg halves together. Chill again to allow the filling to firm up – this can take 30-45 minutes.
5. Coat the eggs in seasoned flour, beaten egg and breadcrumbs; repeat the egging and crumbing twice to give a good coating. Chill thoroughly.
6. Heat a thin layer of oil in a roasting tin. Add the stuffed eggs and bake in the oven at 220°C/425°F/Gas Mark 7 for about 25 minutes, basting once or twice. The eggs should be well browned.
7. Serve hot with tomato sauce or cold with chutney.

ROASTED PECAN CHICKEN

Serves 4

50 G (2 OZ) CREAMY GOAT'S CHEESE

1½ × 5 ML TSP LEMON JUICE

75 G (3 OZ) PECAN NUTS

1 SMALL GARLIC CLOVE, SKINNED AND ROUGHLY CHOPPED

2 × 15 ML TBS OLIVE OIL

SALT AND PEPPER

1.6 KG (3½ LB) OVEN-READY CHICKEN

LEMON AND ONION SLICES

150 ML (5 FL OZ) DRY WHITE WINE

300 ML (10 FL OZ) CHICKEN STOCK (SEE PAGE 13)

2-3 × 5 ML TSP CORNFLOUR

ABOUT 2 × 15 ML TBS WATER

1. Place the cheese, lemon juice, nuts, garlic and oil in a blender or food processor; season with black pepper only. Blend until the mixture forms a paste.
2. Loosen the skin around the chicken breast and spread the mixture underneath the skin to form an even layer. Try not to pierce or break the skin. Secure the skin with a cocktail stick and tie the chicken legs together.
3. Place chicken in a roasting tin with the lemon and onion slices, wine and 150 ml (5 fl oz) stock. Cook in the oven at 200°C/400°F/Gas Mark 6 for about 1½ hours, basting occasionally. If necessary, cover with foil towards the end of cooking time. Test the thickest part of the thigh with a fine skewer – when cooked, the juices run clear.
4. Remove cocktail stick and string. Place the chicken on a serving platter and keep warm. Discard lemon and onion slices. Skim the fat from the juices and stir the remaining 150 ml (5 fl oz) stock in. Bring to the boil, scraping any sediment off the base of the pan. Mix the cornflour to a smooth paste with the water. Off the heat, stir it into the pan juices. Return to the heat; bring to the boil, stirring all the time. Bubble for 2–3 minutes. Adjust seasoning and serve with the chicken.

Roasted Pecan Chicken

Chicken with Vermouth and Olives

Serves 4

8 CHICKEN THIGHS, SKINNED, TOTAL WEIGHT ABOUT 900 G (2 LB)

40 G (1½ OZ) SEASONED FLOUR

50 G (2 OZ) BUTTER OR MARGARINE

300 ML (10 FL OZ) CHICKEN STOCK (SEE PAGE 13)

150 ML (5 FL OZ) DRY FRENCH VERMOUTH OR DRY WHITE WINE

1 SMALL GARLIC CLOVE, SKINNED AND CRUSHED

150 ML (5 FL OZ) SOURED CREAM

50 G (2 OZ) BLACK OLIVES, STONED AND SLICED

SALT AND PEPPER

PASTRY CRESCENTS (SEE COOK'S TIP) AND PARSLEY SPRIGS, TO GARNISH

1. Toss the chicken thighs in seasoned flour and reserve any remaining flour. Melt the butter in a flameproof casserole and brown the chicken well all over. Carefully remove the chicken with a large slotted spoon and set aside; keep warm.
2. Stir in the reserved seasoned flour and cook gently for 1 minute, stirring. Remove pan from the heat and gradually stir in the stock, vermouth and crushed garlic. Bring to the boil slowly and continue to cook, stirring constantly, until the sauce has thickened.
3. Return the chicken to the pan, cover and simmer gently for about 1 hour.
4. Transfer the chicken to a serving dish and keep warm. Stir the cream into the pan juices. Heat gently for 3–4 minutes, without boiling.
5. Just before serving, add the olives, adjust the seasoning and spoon the sauce over the chicken. Garnish with pastry crescents and parsley.

COOK'S TIP

To make pastry crescents, use 50 g (2 oz) Shortcrust Pastry made with 50 g (2 oz) flour (see page 212). Cut into crescents, place on a dampened baking sheet and bake in the oven at 220°C/425°F/Gas Mark 7 for about 12 minutes until golden brown and well risen.

Lemon and Ginger Poussins with Onions

Peppered Poussins with Lime and Sage Crumbs

Serves 6

3 LIMES

1 × 15 ML TBS COARSELY GROUND BLACK PEPPERCORNS

SALT

5 × 15 ML TBS OLIVE OIL

3 POUSSINS ABOUT 565 G (1¼ LB) EACH, HALVED, DISCARDING THE BACKBONE

1 BUNCH OF SALAD ONIONS, TRIMMED AND ROUGHLY CHOPPED

1 WHOLE BULB GARLIC, HALVED HORIZONTALLY TO EXPOSE CLOVES

2 × 15 ML TBS CHOPPED FRESH SAGE

50-75 G (2-3 OZ) BUTTER

175 G (6 OZ) FRESH WHOLEMEAL BREADCRUMBS

FRESH SAGE LEAVES AND LIME WEDGES, TO GARNISH

1. Thinly slice one lime. Grate the rind and squeeze juice from remaining two; keep separate. Mix together the lime slices, juice, peppercorns, salt and olive oil in a large, shallow, flameproof dish. Add poussins and baste with the oil mixture. If time allows, place the poussins with the oil and lime mixture in a non-metallic dish, cover and marinate in the refrigerator overnight.
2. Cook the poussins under a hot grill or on a barbecue, basting with the oil and lime mixture as they cook. Allow about 15 minutes on each side. Test with a skewer; the juices should run clear.
3. Meanwhile, place salad onions, garlic, sage and lime rind in a large sauté pan with the butter. Sauté over a high heat for 2-3 minutes, then stir in the crumbs. Continue to cook, stirring, for 3-4 minutes until golden and crisp.
4. Serve the grilled poussins on a bed of sautéed crumbs, garnished with fresh sage leaves and lime wedges.

Lemon and Ginger Poussins with Onions

Serves 6

GRATED RIND AND JUICE OF 6 LEMONS

5 CM (2 IN) PIECE OF FRESH ROOT GINGER, PEELED AND CHOPPED

8 × 15 ML TBS CLEAR HONEY

150 ML (5 FL OZ) VEGETABLE OIL

1 STALK LEMON GRASS (OPTIONAL)

SALT AND PEPPER

3 POUSSINS, ABOUT 450 G (1 LB) EACH, HALVED LENGTHWAYS

900 G (2 LB) ONIONS, SKINNED AND SLICED

75 G (3 OZ) SOFT LIGHTLY BROWN SUGAR

SLICES OF LEMON, TO SERVE

1. Whisk together the lemon rind and juice, ginger, honey and oil. Split and add the lemon grass, if using, and season. Place poussins in a non-metallic dish and pour over the marinade. Cover and refrigerate for at least 12 hours.
2. Place the poussins with half the marinade in a roasting tin, discarding the lemon grass. Bake in the oven at 200°C/400°F/Gas Mark 6 for 45 minutes or until tender and cooked, basting occasionally.
3. Meanwhile, heat the remaining marinade in a sauté pan; add onions and sugar. Bring to the boil, then simmer for about 35 minutes, stirring occasionally, until the onions soften and caramelise.
4. Lift the poussins into a serving dish, cover and keep warm. Bubble down the cooking juices to reduce.
5. Serve poussins on a bed of onions with the juices spooned over, and top each one with a lemon slice.

Turkey and Watercress Roulades

Serves 4-6

65 G (2½ OZ) BUTTER OR MARGARINE
75 G (3 OZ) BRAZIL NUTS, ROUGHLY CHOPPED
1½ × 5 ML TSP GROUND CUMIN
1 GARLIC CLOVES, SKINNED AND CRUSHED
1 BUNCH OF WATERCRESS, WASHED, TRIMMED AND FINELY CHOPPED
225 G (8 OZ) FULL-FAT SOFT CHEESE
FINELY GRATED RIND AND JUICE OF 1 LEMON
SALT AND FRESHLY GROUND PEPPER
675 G (1½ LB) TURKEY BREAST STEAKS (ESCALOPES)
2 × 15 ML TBS PLAIN WHITE FLOUR
1 × 15 ML TBS VEGETABLE OIL
300 ML (10 FL OZ) CHICKEN STOCK (SEE PAGE 13)
115 ML (4 FL OZ) DRY VERMOUTH
2 × 15 ML TBS SINGLE CREAM
WATERCRESS SPRIGS OR CHOPPED WATERCRESS, TO GARNISH

1. Heat 40 g (1½ oz) butter in a frying pan. Add the nuts, cumin and garlic and stir-fry until beginning to brown. Mix the watercress in and stir-fry until all excess moisture has been driven off. Transfer to a bowl. Cool.
2. Beat the watercress mixture together with the cheese and lemon rind. Season, cover and chill.
3. Meanwhile, place the turkey breast steaks between sheets of clingfilm and pound out until very thin. Cut them up into 10-12 even-sized pieces.
4. Divide the stuffing mixture among the turkey steaks. Roll up and secure with wooden cocktail sticks. Sprinkle the rolls with seasoned flour.
5. Heat the oil with 25 g (1 oz) butter in a shallow flameproof casserole. Brown the turkey rolls about half at a time. Remove from the casserole. Stir any remaining flour into the pan juices. Pour in the stock and vermouth and bring to the boil. Season and add 1 × 15 ml tbs lemon juice. Return the turkey rolls.
6. Cover and bake in the oven at 180°C/350°F/Gas Mark 4 for about 35 minutes or until the meat is tender and cooked. Lift the rolls out of the casserole and remove cocktail sticks. Cover and keep warm.
7. Strain the cooking juices and bubble down to reduce slightly. Take off the heat, stir in the cream and adjust the seasoning. Pour over the rolls and garnish with watercress, to serve.

Roast Turkey with Chestnut Stuffing

Serves 8

6 KG (13 LB) OVEN-READY TURKEY, WITH GIBLETS
75 G (3 OZ) BUTTER, SOFTENED
SALT AND PEPPER
WATERCRESS, TO GARNISH

— STUFFING —

115 G (4 OZ) BUTTER
2 LARGE ONIONS, SKINNED AND FINELY CHOPPED
900 G (2 LB) PORK SAUSAGEMEAT
450 G (1 LB) FRESH OR CANNED UNSWEETENED CHESTNUT PURÉE
225 G (8 OZ) FRESH WHITE BREADCRUMBS
3 × 15 ML TBS MIXED DRIED HERBS
4 × 15 ML TBS CHOPPED FRESH PARSLEY
FINELY GRATED RIND OF 1 LEMON
1 EGG, BEATEN

— GRAVY —

1 ONION, SKINNED AND ROUGHLY CHOPPED
1 CARROT, ROUGHLY CHOPPED
1 BAY LEAF
FRESH PARSLEY SPRIG
1 GARLIC CLOVE, UNSKINNED
1.2 LT (2 PT) WATER
SALT AND PEPPER
ABOUT 3 × 15 ML TBS PLAIN FLOUR
200 ML (7 FL OZ) SINGLE CREAM

1. Remove giblets from the turkey and reserve for gravy. Wipe the turkey, inside and out, with absorbent kitchen paper. Using a small sharp knife, carefully remove the wishbone from the neck cavity to make carving easier.
2. To make the stuffing, melt the butter in a frying pan. Pour off half into a small bowl and set aside. Add the onions to the frying pan and cook gently for about 10-15 minutes, until soft but not brown. Cool.
3. Put all the remaining ingredients for the stuffing into a large mixing bowl. Add the softened onions and the reserved butter, then season well. Knead together until thoroughly blended.
4. Stuff the neck end of the turkey with the stuffing, then truss the bird neatly. Place in a large roasting tin, spread with the 75 g (3 oz) softened butter, then season well. Cover the turkey with foil. Any remaining stuffing can be placed in a roasting tin and cooked for the final hour with the turkey.
5. Roast the turkey in the centre of the oven at 180°C/350°F/Gas Mark 4 for 4-5 hours, removing the foil for the last hour to

brown the skin. Baste frequently during cooking. Test to see if the turkey is done by piercing thighs at their thickest part; if the juices run clear, it is cooked (if the juices are pink, continue cooking a little longer).

6. While the turkey is cooking, prepare the stock for the gravy. Put the giblets into a saucepan with the onion, carrot, herbs and garlic. Add the water and season well. Bring slowly to the boil, then skim off any scum from the surface. Reduce the heat, partially cover the saucepan and simmer gently for about 2 hours. Strain the stock into a measuring jug, and make up to 600 ml (20 fl oz) with water, if necessary.

7. When the turkey is cooked, lift it on to a large serving dish. Loosely cover with foil and leave to stand for 30 minutes before serving.

8. To make the gravy, tilt the roasting tin and carefully skim off all the fat from the surface of the juices in the tin and discard. Stir the flour into the juices left in the tin, then whisk the turkey stock in. Bring the gravy to the boil, whisking all the time until it thickens. By this time the residue from the roasting tin will have dissolved into the gravy, so the gravy can be strained into a saucepan, for easier handling. Simmer the gravy gently for 15 minutes, season, then stir the cream in. Allow to heat through, but not to boil. Pour into a hot gravy boat.

9. To serve the turkey, remove the trussing string, then garnish with watercress.

VARIATION

Serve the turkey with poached pear halves filled with cranberry sauce and garnished with grated lime rind or herbs. Cornbread (see page 209) also goes well with this dish.

Roast Turkey with Chestnut Stuffing

Roast Duckling with Honey and Grapefruit

Serves 4

1.8 KG (4 LB) OVEN-READY DUCKLING

3 GRAPEFRUIT

50 G (2 OZ) BUTTER

1 × 5 ML TSP DIJON MUSTARD

SALT AND PEPPER

4 × 15 ML TBS CLEAR HONEY

1 × 15 ML TBS CHOPPED FRESH ROSEMARY OR 1 × 5 ML TSP DRIED

2 × 15 ML TBS BRANDY

½-1 × 5 ML TSP CORNFLOUR

1. Prick the duck skin all over with a fork. Slice one grapefruit and place two slices in the neck cavity, reserving the remainder for garnish. Place the duck breast-side down on a rack in a roasting tin.

2. Melt the butter in a pan. Pare the rind of one grapefruit and cut into fine strips. Add to the pan with 8 × 15 ml tbs juice and the mustard, seasoning, honey, rosemary and brandy. Bring to the boil, stirring, and pour the mixture over the duck.

3. Roast the duck in the oven for 15 minutes at 220°C/425°F/Gas Mark 7. Turn the duckling breast-side uppermost and baste with the mixture. Continue to roast, basting occasionally, at 180°C/350°F/Gas Mark 5 for about 1½ hours or until the duckling is tender and cooked, covering with foil if necessary.

4. Remove the roasting tin from the oven. Place the duckling on a warmed serving dish and return to the turned-off oven to keep warm. Skim the excess fat from the roasting juices and discard. Add the juice from the remaining grapefruit. Mix the cornflour to a smooth paste with a little cold water. Add to the juices in the roasting tin and bring to the boil. Simmer, stirring, for 2-3 minutes until slightly thickened. Strain the juices before serving.

5. Carve or joint the duckling, spoon a little of the sauce over it and serve the remainder of the sauce separately. Garnish with reserved grapefruit slices.

Braised Duckling with Apple

Serves 4

4 DUCKLING PORTIONS, PREFERABLY BREAST FILLETS, EACH WEIGHING 400 G (14 OZ)

4 × 15 ML TBS VEGETABLE OIL

450 G (1 LB) COOKING APPLES, PEELED, QUARTERED, CORED AND SLICED

450 G (1 LB) ONIONS, SKINNED AND SLICED

400 ML (14 FL OZ) CHICKEN STOCK (SEE PAGE 13)

150 ML (5 FL OZ) APPLE JUICE

4 × 15 ML TBS CRANBERRY SAUCE

SALT AND PEPPER

4 × 5 ML TSP ARROWROOT

FRIED APPLE SLICES AND WATERCRESS SPRIGS, TO GARNISH

1. Trim the duckling of any excess fat and halve each joint. Place on a grill rack and grill under a moderate heat for about 15 minutes or until well browned and a lot of fat has been drawn off. Pat the duckling pieces with absorbent kitchen paper to remove all fat traces.

2. Meanwhile, heat the oil in a large flameproof casserole; add the apple and onion and fry for 2-3 minutes. Stir in the stock, apple juice, cranberry sauce and seasoning. Bring to the boil, then add the duckling. Cover and bake in the oven at 180°C/350°F/Gas Mark 4 for about 50 minutes or until the duckling is tender and cooked. Using a slotted spoon, lift out the duckling and strain the cooking juices into a heatproof jug. Reserve the apple and onion slices and place in a covered dish with the duckling. Refrigerate the juices and duckling overnight.

3. The next day, remove all fat from the juices and discard. Reheat the juices in a flameproof casserole. Replace the duckling, apples and onions. Cover tightly and reheat in the oven at 200°C/400°F/Gas Mark 6 for about 30 minutes.

4. Using a slotted spoon, place the duckling on a grill rack. Grill under a high heat to brown the skin. Keep warm, loosely covered, in a low oven. Meanwhile mix the arrowroot to a smooth paste with a little water. Add to the pan juices and bring to the boil, stirring; bubble for 1 minute. Adjust seasoning and spoon a little over the duckling for serving. Pour the remainder into a sauceboat to serve separately. Garnish the duckling with fried apple slices and watercress sprigs.

COOK'S TIP

It's best to prepare this dish the day ahead so that the fat can be skimmed off the juices the next day. Just crisp up the duckling skin before serving.

Duckling with Orange Sauce

Serves 4

1.8-2.6 KG (4-6 LB) OVEN-READY DUCKLING

SALT AND PEPPER

150 ML (5 FL OZ) WHITE WINE

4 ORANGES (USE BITTER ORANGES WHEN AVAILABLE)

1 LEMON

1 × 15 ML TBS SUGAR

1 × 15 ML TBS WHITE WINE VINEGAR

2 × 15 ML TBS BRANDY OR ORANGE-FLAVOURED LIQUEUR

1 × 15 ML TBS CORNFLOUR

2 × 15 ML TBS WATER

1 BUNCH OF WATERCRESS, TO GARNISH

1. Rub the duckling skin with salt and prick the skin all over.

2. Put the duckling in the roasting tin with the wine and roast in the oven at 180°C/350°F/Gas Mark 5 for 30-35 minutes per 450 g (1 lb), basting occasionally.

3. Meanwhile, grate the rind of one orange and squeeze the juice of three oranges and the lemon. Separate the remaining orange into segments and reserve for the garnish.

4. Melt the sugar in a pan with the vinegar and heat until it is a dark brown caramel.

5. Add the brandy and the orange and lemon juice and simmer gently for 5 minutes.

6. When the duckling is cooked, remove it from the roasting tin, joint it and place the pieces on a serving dish. Keep warm.

7. Drain the excess fat from the tin and add the orange sauce and grated rind to the sediment.

8. Blend the cornflour with the water, stir into the pan juices, bring to the boil and cook for 2-3 minutes, stirring. Season and pour the sauce over the joints. Garnish with watercress.

Crispy Duck Breast with Mangetout

Serves 6

6 DUCKLING BREAST FILLETS

SALT

1½ × 15 ML TBS CLEAR HONEY

3 × 15 ML TBS VEGETABLE OIL

1 BUNCH OF SALAD ONIONS, TRIMMED AND CUT INTO 2.5 CM (1 IN) LENGTHS

1 LARGE GREEN PEPPER, SEEDED AND CUT INTO THIN STRIPS

225 G (8 OZ) MANGETOUT, TOPPED AND TAILED

2 GARLIC CLOVES, SKINNED AND CRUSHED

¼-½ × 5 ML TSP FIVE-SPICE POWDER

3 × 15 ML TBS CASTER SUGAR

3 × 15 ML TBS DARK SOY SAUCE

3 × 15 ML TBS MALT VINEGAR

16 WATER CHESTNUTS, DRAINED AND SLICED

40 G (1½ OZ) TOASTED CASHEW NUTS, CHOPPED, TO GARNISH

FRIED RICE, TO ACCOMPANY

1. Prick the duck breast skin all over with a skewer or fork and rub well with salt to help crisp the skin. Place duck, skin side uppermost, on a rack or trivet in a roasting tin.
2. Bake in the oven at 180°C/350°F/Gas Mark 4 for 15 minutes. Brush the skin with the honey and cook for a further 15 minutes or until cooked through. Remove from the oven and leave to cool. When cold, cut into thin strips.
3. In a wok or large frying pan, heat the oil. Add the salad onions, green pepper, mangetout, garlic and five-spice powder and stir-fry for 2 minutes. Add the sugar, soy sauce, vinegar and duck strips and toss them in the sauce to heat through and glaze. Add the water chestnuts and toss through lightly.
4. Serve at once, sprinkled with toasted cashew nuts and accompanied by fried rice.

Duckling and Bacon with Cranberry

Serves 8

115 G (4 OZ) STREAKY BACON, RINDED AND ROUGHLY CHOPPED

8 DUCKLING BREAST FILLETS, SKINNED AND SLICED INTO CHUNKY FINGER-LENGTHS

VEGETABLE OIL

115 G (4 OZ) SMALL BUTTON MUSHROOMS, WIPED AND HALVED, IF LARGE

450 ML (16 FL OZ) CHICKEN STOCK (SEE PAGE 13)

3 × 15 ML TBS CRANBERRY SAUCE

½ × 5 ML TSP TOMATO PURÉE

SALT AND PEPPER

2 × 5 ML TSP CORNFLOUR

CREAMED POTATO AND BROCCOLI FLORETS, TO ACCOMPANY

1. Cook the bacon in a shallow flameproof casserole until the fat begins to run. Quickly brown the duckling pieces on both sides, adding a little oil to the pan if necessary.
2. Stir in the mushrooms, the stock, cranberry sauce, tomato purée and seasoning. Bring to the boil, cover and cook in the oven at 180°C/350°F/Gas Mark 4 for about 30 minutes, or until the duckling is tender and cooked.
3. Blend the cornflour to a smooth paste with a little cold water; stir into the casserole. Bring to the boil, adjust seasoning and serve with creamed potato and broccoli florets.

Crispy Duck Breast with Mangetout

Honeyed Pigeon with Kumquats

Serves 8

8 SMALL WOOD PIGEONS, ABOUT 240 G (8½ OZ) EACH

16 RASHERS OF RINDLESS STREAKY BACON, ABOUT 275 G (10 OZ) TOTAL WEIGHT

½ × 15 ML TBS VEGETABLE OIL

40 G (1½ OZ) BUTTER OR MARGARINE

275 G (10 OZ) BUTTON ONIONS, SKINNED AND HALVED IF LARGE

1 CINNAMON STICK

1 BAY LEAF

750 ML (1¼ PT) CHICKEN STOCK (SEE PAGE 13)

300 ML (10 FL OZ) DRY CIDER

SALT AND PEPPER

3 × 15 ML TBS CLEAR HONEY

335 G (12 OZ) KUMQUATS, HALVED

3 × 15 ML TBS CORNFLOUR

1. Using strong scissors, halve the pigeons, discarding the backbones. Rinse, drain and dry on absorbent kitchen paper. Stretch the bacon with the back of a knife, then wrap around the pigeon halves. Secure with wooden cocktail sticks.
2. Heat the oil and butter in a large flameproof casserole. Put in about four pigeon halves at time and cook until browned. Remove with a slotted spoon and allow to drain on absorbent kitchen paper.
3. Lower the heat, add the onions and sauté, stirring, until golden brown. Add the cinnamon, bay leaf, stock, cider and seasoning. Return the pigeons to the casserole, bring to the boil, cover and cook in the oven at 160°C/325°F/Gas Mark 3 for 1½ hours.
4. Stir the honey and kumquats in. Cook for a further 30 minutes or until the pigeons are cooked and very tender.
5. Using a slotted spoon, lift the pigeons out of the casserole. Remove the cocktail sticks, cover the birds and keep warm. Remove the bay leaf and cinnamon stick. Blend the cornflour to a smooth paste with a little cold water. Add to the casserole and bring to the boil, stirring all the time, until the juices are lightly thickened. Adjust the seasoning before spooning the juices over the pigeons to serve.

Roast Pheasant

Roast Pheasant

Serves 4

BRACE OF YOUNG PHEASANTS, OVEN-READY

½ ONION, SKINNED AND HALVED

BUTTER FOR BASTING

SALT AND PEPPER

FEW RASHERS OF STREAKY BACON

WATERCRESS, TO GARNISH

BRUSSEL SPROUTS AND GAME CHIPS (SEE PAGE 154), TO SERVE

1. Wash the pheasants inside and out and pat dry. Put half the onion and a knob of butter inside each body cavity. Season well inside then truss.
2. Cover the breast with the bacon and roast in the oven at 230°C/450°F/Gas Mark 8 for 10 minutes, then reduce the heat to 200°C/400°F/Gas Mark 6 and cook for a further 30-50 minutes until tender and cooked, basting frequently.
3. Garnish with watercress and serve with brussel sprouts and Game Chips.

Pheasant with Chestnuts

Serves 4

2 × 15 ML TBS VEGETABLE OIL

50 G (2 OZ) BUTTER OR MARGARINE

BRACE OF PHEASANTS, OVEN-READY

225 G (8 OZ) FRESH CHESTNUTS, PEELED

2 ONIONS, SKINNED AND SLICED

3 × 15 ML TBS PLAIN WHITE FLOUR

450 ML (16 FL OZ) BEEF STOCK (SEE PAGE 13)

115 ML (4 FL OZ) RED WINE

SALT AND PEPPER

GRATED RIND AND JUICE OF ½ AN ORANGE

2 × 5 ML TSP REDCURRANT JELLY

BOUQUET GARNI

CHOPPED FRESH PARSLEY, TO GARNISH

1. Heat the oil and butter in a frying pan, add the pheasants and fry for about 5-6 minutes until golden brown. Remove with a slotted spoon and put into a casserole dish.
2. Fry the chestnuts and onions in the oil and butter for about 5 minutes, until golden brown, and add to the pheasants.
3. Stir the flour into the remaining fat and cook gently for 1 minute, stirring. Remove the pan from the heat and gradually stir in the stock and wine. Bring to the boil slowly and cook, stirring, until it thickens. Season and pour over the pheasants.
4. Add the orange rind and juice, redcurrant jelly and bouquet garni. Cover and cook in the oven at 180°C/350°F/Gas Mark 4 for 1 hour, until the pheasants are tender and cooked.
5. Remove the bouquet garni before serving and adjust the seasoning, if necessary. Sprinkle with chopped parsley.

Guinea Fowl with Grapes and Madeira

Serves 6-8

3 SMALL GUINEA FOWL, ABOUT 1.1-1.4 KG (2½-3 LB) EACH

1½ × 15 ML TBS VEGETABLE OIL

75 G (3 OZ) BUTTER OR MARGARINE

3 SHALLOTS, SKINNED AND FINELY CHOPPED

GRATED RIND AND JUICE OF 3 ORANGES

200 ML (7 FL OZ) DRY WHITE WINE

200 ML (7 FL OZ) MADEIRA

900 ML (1½ PT) CHICKEN STOCK (SEE PAGE 13)

175 G (6 OZ) WALNUT HALVES, TOASTED

SALT AND PEPPER

450 G (1 LB) SEEDLESS WHITE GRAPES

4 × 15 ML TBS CORNFLOUR

4 × 15 ML TBS CHOPPED FRESH PARSLEY

1. Using sharp scissors, halve, then quarter the guinea fowl, discarding the backbones. Heat the oil and butter in a flameproof casserole. Brown the guinea fowl and drain on absorbent kitchen paper.
2. Lower the heat and add the shallots to the pan. Sauté, stirring, until soft. Add the orange rind and juice, the wine, Madeira, stock, walnuts and seasoning.
3. Return the guinea fowl to the casserole, bring to the boil, cover and cook in the oven at 160°C/325°F/Gas Mark 3 for 1 hour. Stir the grapes in, cover and cook for a further 30 minutes or until the guinea fowl are cooked and tender.
4. Blend the cornflour to a smooth paste with a little water. Add to the casserole and bring to the boil, stirring, until the juices are lightly thickened. Stir the parsley in.

Venison and Chestnut Casserole

Serves 8

3 × 15 ML TBS VEGETABLE OIL

50 G (2 OZ) BUTTER

675 G (1½ LB) LEAN VENISON STEAKS OR HAUNCH OF VENISON, CUT INTO 4 CM (1½ IN) CHUNKS

675 G (1½ LB) LEAN STEWING BEEF, CUT INTO 4 CM (1½ IN) CHUNKS

335 G (12 OZ) CARROTS, PEELED AND SLICED

450 G (1 LB) ONIONS, SKINNED AND CHOPPED

335 G (12 OZ) CELERY, TRIMMED AND SLICED

2 LARGE GARLIC CLOVES, SKINNED AND CRUSHED

3 × 15 ML TBS PLAIN WHITE FLOUR

1.2 LT (2 PT) BEEF STOCK

300 ML (10 FL OZ) DRY SHERRY

PARED RIND AND JUICE OF 1 LEMON

2 BAY LEAVES

SALT AND PEPPER

175 G (6 OZ) NO-SOAK DRIED APRICOTS

250 G PACK COOKED WHOLE CHESTNUTS

2 × 15 ML TBS BRANDY

CHOPPED FRESH PARSLEY, TO GARNISH

1. Heat the oil and butter in a large flameproof casserole. Brown the meat in batches, adding more oil if necessary. Lift the meat out of the pan using a slotted spoon.
2. Add the carrots, onions and celery to the pan with the garlic, and lightly brown. Mix the flour in and cook for 1 minute before stirring in the stock, sherry, lemon rind and strained juice, and bay leaves. Bring to the boil, replace the meat and season. Cover tightly and bake in the oven at 160°C/325°F/Gas Mark 3 for 1½ hours.
3. Stir the apricots in, re-cover and bake for a further 1 hour, or until the meat is quite tender.
4. Stir in the cooked chestnuts and brandy and simmer for 5 minutes. Adjust seasoning and garnish with chopped parsley.

Venison Escalopes with Red Wine

Serves 6

6 ESCALOPES OF VENISON CUT FROM THE HAUNCH (LEG), ABOUT 175 G (6 OZ) EACH

1 SMALL ONION, SKINNED AND FINELY CHOPPED

1 BAY LEAF

2 FRESH PARSLEY SPRIGS

8 JUNIPER BERRIES

300 ML (10 FL OZ) DRY RED WINE

15 G (½ OZ) BUTTER

1 × 15 ML TBS VEGETABLE OIL

2 × 15 ML TBS REDCURRANT JELLY

SALT AND PEPPER

CARROTS, SPROUTS AND GAME CHIPS (SEE PAGE 154), TO SERVE

1. Put the venison in a large, shallow nonmetallic dish and sprinkle with the onion, bay leaf, parsley and juniper berries. Pour the wine over the top, cover and leave to marinate in the refrigerator for 3-4 hours or overnight, turning the escalopes occasionally.
2. Remove the escalopes, reserving the marinade. Heat the butter and oil in a large frying pan and fry the escalopes for 3-4 minutes on each side. Transfer to a warmed serving dish and keep warm while making the sauce.
3. Strain the reserved marinade into the frying pan and stir to loosen any sediment. Increase the heat and boil rapidly for 3-4 minutes, until reduced. Stir the redcurrant jelly in and season the mixture to taste. Cook, stirring, for 1-2 minutes. Pour the sauce over the escalopes and serve immediately with carrots, sprouts and Game Chips.

Venison Escalopes with Red Wine

Venison Collops with Oranges

Serves 8

1-2 × 15 ML TBS VEGETABLE OIL

8 × 115-175 G (4-6 OZ) VENISON STEAKS

600 ML (20 FL OZ) BEEF STOCK (SEE PAGE 13)

2-3 × 15 ML TBS ORANGE MARMALADE

3 JUNIPER BERRIES, CRUSHED

3 ORANGES

SALT AND PEPPER

FRESH HERBS, TO GARNISH

CELERIAC 'STRAW' (SEE PAGE 157), TO SERVE

1. Heat the oil in a heavy frying pan, until smoking. Add the venison steaks and fry for 1-2 minutes on each side until they are well browned. Transfer to a shallow ovenproof dish, cover with foil and set aside.
2. Add half the stock to the frying pan, scraping the bottom to dislodge any sediment. Add the remaining stock, marmalade and juniper berries and bring to the boil. Meanwhile, grate the rind from one of the oranges and add to the pan. Boil until reduced by half, then season with salt and pepper.
3. Cut the rind and pith from the oranges. Cut down in between each membrane to remove the segments. Cover the segments and set aside.

Venison Collops with Oranges

4. Bake the steaks in the oven at 200°C/400°F/Gas Mark 6 for 10 minutes only. Uncover and pour any meat juices into the sauce. While the meat is cooking, reheat the sauce with the orange segments over low heat.
5. Serve the steaks on individual heated plates surrounded with orange segments and a little of the sauce. Garnish with fresh herbs and serve with Celeriac 'Straw'.

COOK'S TIP

High protein, low-fat venison is ideal cooked quickly in this way, but fillet steak is an alternative if venison is unavailable.

Meat

Meat is not just the basis of a good satisfying meal, it supplies vital nutrients. In this country, beef, lamb and pork are the most popular meats, while veal is eaten to a lesser extent. Modern methods of transport and storage have done away with seasons for meat and you can buy good-quality beef, lamb and pork all year round. It is essential when cooking meat that the oven is preheated to the required temperature.

Garlic and Rosemary Rack of Lamb (page 94)

Rib of Beef with Anchovies and Walnuts

Serves 4

ABOUT 1.1 KG (2½ LB) BEEF FORERIB
50 G (2 OZ) WALNUT PIECES, CHOPPED
50 G (2 OZ) UNSALTED CASHEW NUTS, CHOPPED
50 G CAN ANCHOVIES, DRAINED
2×15 ML TBS WALNUT OIL
2×15 ML TBS OLIVE OIL
75 G (3 OZ) PARSNIP, PEELED AND GRATED
75 G (3 OZ) CARROT, PEELED AND GRATED
50 G (2 OZ) BUTTER, MELTED
SALT AND PEPPER
1×15 ML TBS PLAIN WHITE FLOUR
300 ML (10 FL OZ) RED GRAPE JUICE
300 ML (10 FL OZ) BEEF STOCK (SEE PAGE 13)
5×15 ML TBS BRANDY
BAKED POTATOES AND SOURED CREAM, TO ACCOMPANY

1. Place the meat cut-side down on a clean work surface. Using a thin-bladed sharp knife, make a horizontal cut into the meat to form a pocket, working from the side opposite the bone and reaching right through the meat almost to the bone.
2. Place the nuts, anchovies and walnut oil in a bowl and pound together with the end of a rolling pin. Use this to fill the pocket and tie up neatly at three or four intervals with fine string.
3. Heat the olive oil in a roasting tin and quickly sear the meat on both sides until quite brown. Roast at 200°C/400°F/Gas Mark 6 for 15 minutes per 450g (1 lb) plus 15 minutes for rare beef, or for 20 minutes per 450 g (1 lb) plus 20 minutes for medium-rare, turning over halfway through.
4. About 20 minutes before the end of cooking time, mix the vegetables with the melted butter and spread loosely on top of the meat. Season well and return to the oven to finish cooking. Test with a skewer or thermometer.
5. Turn off the oven and transfer the meat to a warm serving dish. Leave to rest in the oven for at least 15 minutes before carving.
6. To make the sauce, skim off any fat from the pan juices and sprinkle the flour in. Place over a medium heat and cook for 1 minute. Whisk the grape juice, stock and brandy into the sauce. Boil rapidly until reduced by half. Adjust the seasoning and strain into a warm gravy boat.
7. Remove the string carefully from the beef before carving. Serve with small baked potatoes and soured cream.

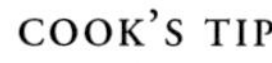

COOK'S TIP

The anchovies dissolve, leaving a savoury walnut stuffing. The 'thatch' of parsnip and carrots provides a vegetable accompaniment for this dish.

Rib of Beef with Anchovies and Walnuts

Peppered Beef

Serves 8

900 G (2 LB) FILLET OF BEEF
2×5 ML TSP MIXED PEPPERCORNS
3×15 ML TBS VEGETABLE OIL
4×5 ML TSP WHOLEGRAIN MUSTARD
1×5 ML TSP GROUND GINGER
½×5 ML TSP SALT
1×15 ML TBS SOFT LIGHT BROWN SUGAR
1 GARLIC CLOVE, SKINNED AND CRUSHED
2×5 ML TSP ENGLISH MUSTARD POWDER
FRESH CORIANDER, TO GARNISH
BROCCOLI, CELERY AND TOMATOES, TO ACCOMPANY
VINAIGRETTE, TO SERVE (OPTIONAL)

1. Trim any excess fat off the meat; tie with fine string at 2.5 cm (1 in) intervals. Place in a roasting tin.
2. Coarsely grind the peppercorns using a pestle and mortar, or in a strong bowl with the end of a rolling pin. Beat together with the next seven ingredients to form a paste. Spread the paste over the beef to cover it.
3. Roast the beef in the oven for 20 minutes at 230°C/450°F/Gas Mark 8 to seal, basting occasionally. Reduce the temperature to 200°C/400°F/Gas Mark 6 for about a further 20 minutes for medium-rare or 25 minutes for quite well done.
4. Allow to stand for 10 minutes before removing string and carving into thick slices. Garnish with coriander and serve hot with sautéed broccoli, celery and tomatoes, or cold with blanched broccoli, cherry tomatoes and a vinaigrette dressing.

COOK'S TIP

The crushed, coloured peppercorns give a festive-looking coating. You can blend your own mix of white, black, pink and green peppercorns, or buy a ready-made mix.

Peppered Beef

SPICY BEEF

Serves 6

300 ML (10 FL OZ) NEWCASTLE BROWN ALE

75 ML (3 FL OZ) OLIVE OIL

1 × 15 ML TBS DRIED MIXED HERBS

2 GARLIC CLOVES, SKINNED AND SLICED

1.1KG (2½ LB) BONED AND ROLLED RIB OF BEEF OR SILVERSIDE FOR ROASTING

1 × 15 ML TBS WHOLE CORIANDER SEEDS

1 × 15 ML TBS EACH BLACK, DRIED GREEN AND WHITE PEPPERCORNS

SALT AND PEPPER

NOODLES, CARROTS AND CARAMELISED ONIONS (SEE PAGE 110), TO ACCOMPANY

1. Mix together the ale, olive oil, herbs and garlic. Add the meat, turning well to coat; cover and leave to marinate overnight in the refrigerator, turning occasionally.
2. Crush the coriander seeds and peppercorns with a pestle and mortar or in a strong bowl with the end of a rolling pin.
3. Remove the meat from the marinade; pat dry. Press the coriander seeds and peppercorns all over the meat. Place the meat in a roasting tin and pour the marinade round. Roast for 10 minutes at 230°C/450°F/Gas Mark 8 to seal, then turn the oven down to 200°C/400°F/Gas Mark 6 and roast for 15 minutes per 450 g (1 lb) for rare or 20 minutes per 450 g (1 lb) for medium-rare.
4. Turn off the oven and transfer the meat to a serving dish; leave to rest in the oven for at least 15 minutes.
5. Skim the pan juices. Place over a medium heat and bring to the boil, adding water if the sauce is too strong. Season and strain into a warm gravy boat.
6. Remove string from the beef and slice thickly. Serve with the sauce and noodles, carrots and caramelised onions.

Spicy Beef

ITALIAN BRAISED BEEF

Serves 6

1.1 KG (2½ LB) BRAISING STEAK, CUT INTO 4 CM (1½ IN) CUBES

335 G (12 OZ) ONIONS, SKINNED AND ROUGHLY CHOPPED

2 LARGE GARLIC CLOVES, SKINNED AND THINLY SLICED

75 CL BOTTLE CHIANTI

7 × 15 ML TBS OLIVE OIL

2 × 15 ML TBS TOMATO PURÉE

1 × 15 ML TBS WINE VINEGAR

SALT AND PEPPER

BUNCH FRESH THYME OR 2 × 5 ML TSP DRIED

50 G (2 OZ) FLOUR

300 ML (10 FL OZ) BEEF STOCK (SEE PAGE 13)

175 G (6 OZ) BROWN CAP OR BUTTON MUSHROOMS, WIPED AND HALVED OR QUARTERED

400 G CAN ARTICHOKE HEARTS, DRAINED AND CUT IN HALF

ABOUT 18 STONED BLACK OLIVES

1. Place the beef, onions and garlic in a glass bowl with the wine, 3 × 15 ml tbs olive oil, the tomato purée, vinegar and seasoning. Add a bunch of fresh thyme tied in a bundle or sprinkle with the dried herb. Stir thoroughly to mix, cover and marinate in the refrigerator for at least 24 hours.
2. Strain off the marinade and reserve. Heat about 4 × 15 ml tbs olive oil in a large flameproof casserole. Brown the meat, about one quarter at a time, adding a little more oil if necessary. Remove all the meat from the casserole using a slotted spoon.
3. Stir the flour into the remaining oil and cook for about 1 minute. Pour in the marinade and stock and bring to the boil. Replace the meat.
4. Cover the casserole tightly, then cook in the oven at 170°C/325°F/Gas Mark 3 for about 2 hours, or until the meat is tender.
5. Ten minutes before end of cooking, stir the mushrooms and artichoke hearts into the casserole with the olives. Adjust seasoning and serve.

COOK'S TIP

This rich beef casserole cooks by itself, simply needing 5 minutes' attention at the end, when the artichoke hearts, mushrooms and black olives are added and warmed through.

Festive Fillet of Beef

Serves 6

115 G (4 OZ) RAISINS OR SULTANAS

200 ML (7 FL OZ) MADEIRA

75 G (3 OZ) SLICED PARMA HAM

2×15 ML TBS ROUGHLY CHOPPED FRESH PARSLEY

1.1 KG (2½ LB) FILLET OF BEEF

335 G (12 OZ) AUBERGINE, THINLY SLICED LENGTHWAYS

ABOUT 115 ML (4 FL OZ) OLIVE OIL

1×5 ML TSP EACH GROUND GINGER AND ALLSPICE

675 G (1½ LB) SHALLOTS OR SMALL ONIONS, ROOT ENDS TRIMMED, AND HALVED OR QUARTERED IF LARGE

1×15 ML TBS LIGHT MUSCOVADO SUGAR

150 ML (5 FL OZ) BEEF STOCK (SEE PAGE 13)

SALT AND PEPPER

1. Soak the raisins or sultanas in the Madeira overnight. Drain well, reserving the Madeira.
2. Cut the Parma ham into 12 long strips about 2.5 cm (1 in) wide. Dip 12 raisins in half the chopped parsley, then roll each one tightly in a strip of ham.
3. Using the point of a sharp knife, make 12 small, deep incisions in the beef. Push in the Parma ham rolls. Tie the beef at 2.5 cm (1 in) intervals with fine string to produce a neat shape.
4. Brush the aubergine slices lightly with a little of the oil. Grill for 2-3 minutes each side until golden brown. Cool.
5. Heat 3×15 ml tbs olive oil in a flameproof casserole or roasting tin. Brown the fillet all over, then remove and set aside. Add another 1×15 ml tbs oil to the pan with the spices and shallots. Sauté for 3-4 minutes or until golden, stirring occasionally.
6. Cover the fillet with the aubergine slices and return to the pan. Mix together the reserved Madeira, sugar, stock and remaining raisins and pour over the fillet. Bring to the boil and season.
7. Cook, uncovered, in the oven at 230°C/450°F/Gas Mark 8 for 35-40 minutes for medium-rare. Allow a further 10-12 minutes for well done. Stir the remaining parsley into the pan juices. Remove string and slice the beef as thinly as possible. Serve with the warmed pan juices.

Roast Spiced Beef

Serves 8

1 FILLET OF BEEF, ABOUT 900 G (2 LB)), TRIMMED OF ANY EXCESS FAT OR SINEW

2×5 ML TSP BLACK PEPPERCORNS

75 ML (3 FL OZ) VEGETABLE OIL

1 GARLIC CLOVE, SKINNED AND CRUSHED

½×5 ML TSP SALT

2×5 ML TSP DRY MUSTARD

1×5 ML TSP GROUND GINGER

2×15 ML TBS WHOLEGRAIN MUSTARD

1×15 ML TBS LIGHT SOFT BROWN SUGAR

OAK LEAF AND RADICCHIO LETTUCE AND FRESH FIGS, TO GARNISH

CARAMELISED ONIONS (SEE PAGE 110) AND VINIAGRETTE WITH CHOPPED HERBS, TO ACCOMPANY

1. Tie beef with string at 2.5 cm (1 in) intervals and place in a non-metallic dish.
2. Coarsely grind the peppercorns using a pestle and mortar, or in a strong bowl with the end of a rolling pin. Beat together with the next seven ingredients. Spread all over the beef, cover and refrigerate overnight.
3. Transfer the beef and marinade to a small roasting tin. Roast the beef for 20 minutes at 240°C/475°F/Gas Mark 9, basting occasionally. Reduce the oven temperature to 220°C/425°F/Gas Mark 7 for a further 20 minutes for medium-rare beef or 25 minutes for well done. Remove the meat from the oven and drain off any pan juices (keep and use as the basis of a sauce or gravy to accompany another dish). Allow to cool completely.
4. With a very sharp knife, remove the string and cut the beef into wafer-thin slices. Serve on a platter of oak leaf and radicchio lettuce and quartered figs, accompanied by the caramelised onions and the vinaigrette with chopped herbs.

Roast Spiced Beef

Rich Beef and Wine Casserole

Serves 12

900 G (2 LB) VENISON, CUT INTO LARGE CHUNKS
1.4 KG (3 LB) STEWING BEEF, CUT INTO LARGE CHUNKS
450 G (1 LB) ONIONS, SKINNED AND ROUGHLY CHOPPED
3 GARLIC CLOVES, SKINNED AND SLICED
75 CL BOTTLE RED WINE
4×15 ML TBS TOMATO PURÉE
2×15 ML TBS RED WINE VINEGAR
2 BAY LEAVES
5×15 ML TBS CHOPPED FRESH THYME
3 LARGE ROSEMARY SPRIGS
ABOUT 9×15 ML TBS OLIVE OIL
GRATED RIND AND JUICE OF 1 ORANGE
SALT AND PEPPER
3 STICKS CELERY, WASHED, TRIMMED AND CHOPPED
450 G (1 LB) BABY TURNIPS, PEELED AND HALVED OR QUARTERED
50 G (2 OZ) PLAIN FLOUR
600 ML (20 FL OZ) BEEF STOCK (SEE PAGE 13)
2×400G CANS ARTICHOKE HEARTS, DRAINED AND HALVED
115 G (4 OZ) BLACK OLIVES (OPTIONAL)
150 ML (5 FL OZ) PORT
SAUTÉED LEEKS WITH CREAM (SEE PAGE 150) AND SWEDE AND ORANGE PURÉE (SEE PAGE 157), TO ACCOMPANY

1. Place the meat, onions and garlic in a large non-metallic bowl with the wine, tomato purée, vinegar, bay leaves, thyme, rosemary, 3×15 ml tbs olive oil, orange rind and juice and seasoning. Stir and cover, then refrigerate overnight.
2. Next day, strain the meat and reserve the marinade, discarding the rosemary and bay leaves. Heat 6×15 ml tbs oil in a large flameproof casserole. Brown the meat and onions in batches; add a little more oil if necessary. Remove with a slotted spoon.
3. Add a little more oil to the casserole if necessary and lightly cook the celery and turnips until just brown. Stir in the flour; cook for 1 minute. Pour in the stock and marinade.
4. Replace the meat and onions, season and bring to the boil. Cover tightly and cook in the oven at 170°C/ 325°F/Gas Mark 3 for about 2 hours or until tender.
5. Add the artichokes to the casserole with the olives, if using, and the port. Cover and simmer on the hob for 15 minutes, stirring occasionally. Adjust seasoning and serve with Sautéed Leeks with Cream and Swede and Orange Purée.

Rich Beef and Wine Casserole

Hot Carpaccio with Salsa Verde

Serves 6

— HOT CARPACCIO —
450 G (1 LB) FILLET OF BEEF
6×15 ML TBS OLIVE OIL
2×15 ML TBS DARK SOY SAUCE
BLACK PEPPER
— SALSA VERDE —
3 ANCHOVY FILLETS IN OIL, DRAINED
2 GARLIC CLOVES, SKINNED AND CRUSHED
½×5 ML TSP BALSAMIC OR SHERRY VINEGAR
1×15 ML TBS CAPERS, ROUGHLY CHOPPED
4×15 ML TBS CHOPPED FRESH PARSLEY
150 ML (5 FL OZ) OLIVE OIL
PEPPER

1. With a sharp knife, cut the beef into twelve 0.6 cm (¼ in) slices. Pound out each slice between damp greaseproof paper until it has doubled in size and is almost transparent. Be careful not to tear the meat. Lay the slices of beef in a non-metallic dish.
2. Whisk together the olive oil and soy sauce with lots of black pepper. Pour this over the meat. Cover and leave to marinate for at least 2 hours, preferably overnight, in the refrigerator, turning once.
3. Meanwhile, make the Salsa Verde. Pound the anchovies in a pestle and mortar or in a strong bowl with the end of a rolling pin. Stir in the garlic and the balsamic vinegar. Beat in the capers and parsley, gradually adding the olive oil. Season with pepper. (You should not need to add any salt as the anchovies are salty.)
4. Preheat the oven to 240°C/475°F/Gas Mark 9. The oven must be very hot for this recipe. Lay the meat in a single layer on two large baking trays and cook for 2 minutes only, until it has changed colour to brown. Transfer to warm plates and serve immediately, dressed with a little Salsa Verde.

COOK'S TIP
Serve with fresh pasta with carrots and courgettes and a salad of green beans, sun-dried tomatoes and feta cheese.

Hot Carpaccio with Salsa Verde

Quick Beef and Onion Casserole

Serves 8

1×15 ML TBS VEGETABLE OIL

450 G (1 LB) LEAN RUMP STEAK, THINLY SLICED

225 G (8 OZ) BABY ONIONS

45 G (1½ OZ) PACKET BEEF CASSEROLE MIX

300 ML (10 FL OZ) WATER

115 G (4 OZ) CARROTS, PEELED AND THINLY SLICED

1-2×15 ML TBS CREAMED HORSERADISH

1 BAY LEAF

SALT AND PEPPER

1. Heat the oil in a small flameproof casserole, add the meat and onions, and cook until lightly browned.
2. Combine the casserole mix with the water and add to the meat with carrots, horseradish and bay leaf.
3. Bring to the boil, stirring; cover and bake in the oven at 180°C/350°F/Gas Mark 4 for 30-35 minutes, until cooked through and the meat is tender. Remove the bay leaf and add seasoning.

Beef Casserole with Kumquats

Serves 4

900 G (2 LB) CHUCK STEAK

40 G (1½ OZ) PLAIN WHITE FLOUR, SEASONED WITH SALT AND PEPPER

PEEL AND JUICE OF 1 TANGERINE

3×15 ML TBS VEGETABLE OIL

1 GARLIC CLOVE, SKINNED AND CRUSHED

300 ML (10 FL OZ) BEEF STOCK (SEE PAGE 13)

150 ML (5 FL OZ) RED WINE

1 BAY LEAF

225 G (8 OZ) CELERY, WASHED, TRIMMED AND THICKLY SLICED, RESERVING ANY LEAVES

335 G (12 OZ) LEEKS, WASHED AND SLICED

115 G (4 OZ) KUMQUATS, HALVED

CREAMED POTATOES AND BROCCOLI, TO ACCOMPANY

1. Trim the meat of any excess fat and cut into 5 cm (2 in) pieces. Toss in the seasoned flour. Cut the tangerine peel into needle shreds and reserve.
2. Heat the oil in a medium-sized flameproof casserole. Fry the meat, a few pieces at a time, to brown and seal. Remove with a slotted spoon.
3. Return the meat with any remaining flour. Add the garlic, stock, wine, 3×15 ml tbs tangerine juice, bay leaf and seasoning. Bring to the boil, then transfer to the oven. Cook, covered, at 160°C/325°F/Gas Mark 3 for about 1 hour.
4. Stir celery into the casserole with the sliced leeks and kumquats. Return to the oven and cook, covered, for a further 1½ hours or until the meat is tender. Remove the bay leaf. Adjust seasoning and serve garnished with shreds of tangerine peel and celery leaves. Serve with creamed potatoes and broccoli.

Beef and Pimiento Casserole

Serves 10

1.8 KG (4 LB) SHIN OF BEEF

3×15 ML TBS GROUND GINGER

2 LARGE GARLIC CLOVES, SKINNED AND CRUSHED

40 G (1½ OZ) BUTTER OR MARGARINE

450 G (1 LB) MUSHROOMS, WIPED AND FINELY CHOPPED

3 LEMONS

1.8 LT (3 PT) BEEF STOCK (SEE PAGE 13)

4×15 ML TBS VEGETABLE OIL

335 G (12 OZ) ONIONS, SKINNED AND CHOPPED

450 ML (16 FL OZ) MEDIUM-DRY SHERRY

10×15 ML TBS CHOPPED FRESH PARSLEY

450 G (1 LB) DRIED PASTA SHAPES

400 G CAN PIMIENTOS, DRAINED AND CHOPPED

SALT AND PEPPER

1. Cut the beef into chunks. Place in a large non-metallic bowl with the ginger and garlic and leave, covered, in the refrigerator overnight.
2. Melt the butter in a saucepan and sauté the mushrooms. Add the grated rind of one lemon, 6×15 ml tbs lemon juice and the stock. Simmer, covered, for 15 minutes. Press the liquid through a sieve.
3. Heat the oil in a large flameproof casserole, add the beef and brown on all sides. Remove from the casserole. Sauté the onion for 2-3 minutes. Return the beef to the casserole with the sherry, mushroom liquid and half the parsley. Cover and cook in the oven at 150°C/300°F/Gas Mark 2 for 2 hours.
4. Add the pasta and pimientos, re-cover and cook for 1 more hour, or until all the ingredients are tender. Add remaining parsley and seasoning before serving.

Spiced Meat Skewers

Serves 6

900 G (2 LB) MINCED BEEF OR LAMB

2 ONIONS, SKINNED AND GRATED

2×15 ML TBS GROUND CUMIN

1×15 ML TBS GROUND CORIANDER

6×15 ML TBS FINELY CHOPPED FRESH PARSLEY

SALT AND PEPPER

OLIVE OIL

PAPRIKA PEPPER

3 SALAD ONIONS, TRIMMED AND CHOPPED

300 ML (10 FL OZ) LOW-FAT NATURAL YOGURT

1×15 ML TBS CHOPPED FRESH MINT

LEMON WEDGES, TO ACCOMPANY

1. Mince the meat several times or chop very finely in a food processor. Knead it with the onions, cumin, coriander, 4×15 ml tbs parsley and seasoning to make a smooth paste.
2. Take 1-2×15 ml tbs of the mixture and press a flat sausage shape on to the ends of wooden skewers. Brush the meat lightly with oil and sprinkle with a little paprika.
3. Grill about half at a time under a high heat for about 5 minutes, turn, sprinkle with more paprika and grill the second side until well browned all over and cooked through. (Keep the exposed wooden sticks away from the flame.) Keep all the kebabs warm, loosely covered, until required; sprinkle with parsley.
4. Mix the salad onions, reserving a few dark green shreds for garnish, with the yogurt and mint. Garnish, then serve with the kebabs along with lemon wedges.

Beef Casserole with Kumquats

Crispy Beef and Coconut Sauté

Serves 8

50 ML (2 FL OZ) OLIVE OIL

75 G (3 OZ) ONION, SKINNED AND FINELY CHOPPED

2 GARLIC CLOVES, SKINNED AND CRUSHED

450 G (1 LB) RUMP STEAK, THINLY SLICED

115 G (4 OZ) DESICCATED COCONUT

1×15 ML TBS LEMON JUICE

1×5 ML TSP GROUND CUMIN

2×5 ML TSP GROUND CORIANDER

1×15 ML TBS DARK MUSCOVADO SUGAR

SALT AND PEPPER

LIME SLICES AND FRESH PARSLEY SPRIGS, TO GARNISH

1. Heat the oil in a large frying pan and sauté the onion and garlic until softened. Add the meat and cook, stirring, until lightly browned, about 3-4 minutes.

2. Add the remaining ingredients, then cover and simmer for about 30 minutes or until the meat is tender, stirring occasionally. There should be very little liquid left in the pan. If necessary, increase the heat to bubble away some of the juices.

3. Uncover the pan and continue to cook, stirring occasionally, until the mixture is very dry. Serve hot or cold, garnished with slices of lime and sprigs of flat-leaf parsley.

Stir-Fried Fillet Steak with Mango

Serves 4

335 G (12 OZ) FILLET STEAK

5 CM (2 IN) PIECE OF FRESH ROOT GINGER, PEELED AND FINELY CHOPPED

2-3 FRESH GREEN CHILLIES, SEEDED AND FINELY CHOPPED

2×15 ML TBS DARK SOY SAUCE

4×15 ML TBS VEGETABLE OIL

1 GARLIC CLOVE, SKINNED AND CRUSHED

SALT AND PEPPER

2 FIRM, RIPE MANGOES

2×15 ML TBS BEEF STOCK (SEE PAGE 13)

1. Shred the steak into wafer-thin slices, cutting with the grain of the meat. Place the beef, ginger and chillies in a bowl and stir in the soy sauce, half the oil, and the garlic and seasoning. Cover and refrigerate overnight.

2. Cut thick slices of mango flesh off either side of the stone, then thinly slice them. Trim off the skin, cover and refrigerate.

3. Heat the remaining oil in a large frying pan. Add the beef and cook, stirring, over a high heat for 1-2 minutes. Stir the stock into the pan and cook for a further 3-4 minutes. Add the mango and stir in carefully. Adjust the seasoning and serve.

Crispy Beef and Coconut Sauté

Stir-Fried Beef with Mixed Vegetables

Serves 4

4×15 ML TBS SOY SAUCE

6×15 ML TBS VEGETABLE OIL

1 LARGE GARLIC CLOVE, SKINNED AND CRUSHED

15 G (½ OZ) FRESH ROOT GINGER, PEELED AND FINELY CHOPPED

3-4 GREEN CHILLIES, SEEDED AND FINELY CHOPPED

565 G (1¼ LB) RUMP STEAK, CUT INTO THIN STRIPS, DISCARDING ANY FAT

SALT AND FRESHLY GROUND PEPPER

1 BUNCH OF SALAD ONIONS

175 G (6 OZ) BROCCOLI

115 G (4 OZ) BABY SWEETCORN, TRIMMED AND SLICED LENGTHWAYS INTO STRIPS

175 G (6 OZ) MANGETOUT, TOPPED AND TAILED

115 G (4 OZ) SMALL CUP MUSHROOMS, WIPED AND THINLY SLICED

75-115 ML (3-4 FL OZ) CHICKEN OR VEGETABLE STOCK (SEE PAGE 13)

FINE NOODLES, TO ACCOMPANY

1. In a bowl, whisk the soy sauce with 2×15 ml tbs oil and the garlic. Stir the ginger and half the chillies in. Tightly cover the remainder of the chillies and refrigerate.

2. Stir the beef into the bowl with plenty of black pepper but only a little salt. Cover and refrigerate overnight.

3. Divide each salad onion into two or three pieces, discarding roots and dark green leaves. Divide broccoli into small florets, trim stalks and slice lengthways into thin pieces. Blanch the corn and broccoli separately in boiling salted water for about 1 minute each. Drain well. Cover and refrigerate the vegetables separately.

4. When ready to serve, take two large frying pans and heat 2×15 ml tbs oil in each. Add the beef and marinade to one and the vegetables to the other. Stir-fry both over a high heat for 2-3 minutes only. Combine the contents of both pans, add the stock and bubble up together. Adjust seasoning, adding extra chillies to taste. Serve immediately with fine noodles.

Stir-Fried Beef with Mixed Vegetables

Spicy Lamb and Aubergines

Serves 12

OLIVE OIL

900 ML (1½ PT) MILK

SALT AND PEPPER

¼×5 ML TSP GRATED NUTMEG

175 G (6 OZ) SEMOLINA

115 G (4 OZ) FRESHLY GRATED PARMESAN CHEESE

1 EGG, LIGHTLY BEATEN

900 G (2 LB) AUBERGINES, TRIMMED AND CUT INTO ½-1 CM (¼-½ IN) SLICES

4 RED PEPPERS, HALVED AND SEEDED

1.4 KG (3 LB) MINCED LAMB

335 G (12 OZ) ONIONS, SKINNED AND CHOPPED

4 GARLIC CLOVES, SKINNED AND CHOPPED

½×5 ML TSP GROUND ALLSPICE

2×15 ML TBS MILD CHILLI SEASONING

450 ML (16 FL OZ) DRY WHITE OR RED WINE

3×15 ML TBS CHOPPED FRESH CORIANDER OR PARSLEY

2×400 G CANS CHOPPED TOMATOES

3×15 ML TBS TOMATO PURÉE

1. First make the gnocchi. Brush a swiss roll tin with oil. Bring the milk to the boil with 1½×5 ml tsp salt and the nutmeg. Turn down the heat and steadily pour the semolina in, stirring all the time. Simmer, stirring, for 2-3 minutes until the mixture is really thick. Beat the cheese and egg into the mixture. Spread evenly in the tin and level. Cool and chill for 1 hour until firm. Turn out and stamp out as many rounds as possible with a 5 cm (2 in) round cutter. Cover the gnocchi and set aside.
2. Meanwhile, brush the cut sides of the aubergine lightly with olive oil and arrange on a grill pan. Grill for 3-4 minutes on each side until golden brown. Arrange in overlapping circles in two 2.7 lt (4½ pt) ovenproof serving dishes.
3. Place the red peppers, skin side up, under a hot grill until well blackened and charred. Peel off the skin under cold water. Chop roughly and reserve.
4. Heat a frying pan and brown the meat in batches, adding a little oil if necessary. Transfer the meat to a large saucepan.
5. Brown the onion and garlic in the residual oil. Add allspice and chilli and cook for 1 minute. Stir the mixture into the lamb with remaining ingredients and season well. Simmer, uncovered, for 1 hour or until well reduced and thick. Stir in the red peppers. Spoon the spicy lamb mixture over the aubergines. Arrange the gnocchi overlapping around the edges of the serving dishes.
6. Loosely cover with foil and bake in the oven at 200°C/400°F/Gas Mark 6 for about 1¼ hours until golden brown and bubbling. Remove the foil 30 minutes before the end of the cooking time.

COOK'S TIP

Topped with golden, cheesy gnocchi, this dish has a smoky Middle Eastern flavour with its mix of aubergines and spices. Fresh Parmesan is the best cheese to use, or grated Gruyère.

Spicy Lamb and Aubergines

Roast Lamb Fillet with Garlic

Serves 6

3×275 G (10 OZ) FILLETS OF LAMB, ANY LARGE PIECES OF FAT REMOVED AND SET ASIDE

3×15 ML TBS OLIVE OIL

8-10 GARLIC CLOVES, SKINNED

LEAVES STRIPPED FROM 2 LARGE SPRIGS OF ROSEMARY

FRESH ROSEMARY, BAKED TOMATO AND FENNEL (SEE PAGE 148) AND POTATOES WITH ROAST GARLIC (SEE PAGE 150) TO SERVE

— SAUCE —

40 G (1½ OZ) BUTTER

335 G (12 OZ) LEEKS, TRIMMED, WASHED AND CHOPPED

1×15 ML TBS PLAIN WHITE FLOUR

300 ML (10 FL OZ) CHICKEN STOCK (SEE PAGE 13)

5×15 ML TBS WHITE WINE

2×15 ML TBS WHITE WINE VINEGAR

2×15 ML TBS CLEAR HONEY

2×15 ML TBS CHOPPED FRESH PARSLEY

SALT AND PEPPER

1. Place the lamb, olive oil, whole garlic cloves and rosemary in a non-metallic dish, into which they just fit. Cover and leave to marinate overnight in the refrigerator.

Roast Lamb Fillet with Garlic

2. Place the fat from the lamb in a frying pan and heat gently to extract the oil. Discard any remaining fatty pieces. When the fat in the pan is very hot, remove the lamb and garlic from the marinade and toss quickly in the pan to brown on all sides.

3. Place the lamb fillets and garlic cloves in a roasting tin with the fat from the pan. Spoon the remaining marinade over the top.

4. Roast in the oven at 200°C/400°F/Gas Mark 6 for about 15 minutes for rare meat and about 20 minutes for medium.

5. Meanwhile prepare the sauce. Melt the butter in a saucepan and sauté the leeks, stirring frequently, for about 5 minutes or until soft but not brown. Add the flour, cook for a further minute, then stir in the stock, wine, vinegar and honey and bring to the boil. Simmer for 3 minutes.

6. When the meat is cooked, add any pan juices to the sauce, then stir in the parsley and season.

7. Place the meat on a warmed serving dish on a bed of fresh rosemary surrounded by garlic cloves. Slice the meat thickly and serve with the reheated sauce and the tomato and fennel and the potatoes.

Garlic and Rosemary Rack of Lamb

Serves 6

6 LARGE GARLIC CLOVES, SKINNED

2 BEST ENDS OF LAMB, TRIMMED, WITH CHINE BONE REMOVED, ABOUT 1.1-1.4 KG (2½-3 LB) TOTAL WEIGHT

8 LONG SPRIGS OF FRESH ROSEMARY

SALT AND BLACK PEPPER

OLIVE OIL FOR BRUSHING

1×15 ML TBS REDCURRANT, MINT OR APPLE JELLY

1×15 ML TBS PLAIN WHITE FLOUR

300 ML (10 FL OZ) BEEF STOCK (SEE PAGE 13)

1×15 ML TBS CRÈME DE CASSIS, FRAMBOISE OR MÛRES

FRESH ROSEMARY SPRIGS, TO GARNISH

1. Place five cloves of garlic in a small pan of cold water. Bring to the boil and boil for 2 minutes. Drain and set aside.
2. Place one best end of lamb fat side down on a clean work surface. Lay two sprigs of rosemary along the length of the 'eye' of the meat. Slice the remaining clove of garlic and lay this on top of the rosemary. Season with black pepper. Lay the other best end on top and link the bones to form a 'guard of honour'. Using fine string, tie the lamb at regular intervals. Place in a roasting tin on top of the remaining rosemary.
3. Push the blanched garlic along the top of the lamb flesh underneath the bones. Drizzle with olive oil. Rub the outside of the lamb with a little more oil and score lightly with a sharp knife.
4. Roast in the oven at 200°C/400°F/Gas Mark 6 for about 20 minutes per 450 g (1 lb) plus 20 minutes for pink lamb (allow extra time for well-done meat). Test with a skewer or thermometer. About 30 minutes from the end of cooking time, glaze the outside of the lamb with the jelly.
5. Turn off the oven and transfer the meat to a warm serving dish. Leave to rest in the oven for at least 15 minutes before carving.
6. Heat the juices in the roasting tin, retaining the rosemary. Skim off any fat, then stir the flour in. Cook for 1 minute, stirring, then whisk in the stock and the crème de cassis. Bring to the boil and bubble rapidly for 2 minutes or until syrupy. Season to taste, then strain into a warm gravy boat.
7. Remove the string carefully from the meat. Garnish the rack of lamb with sprigs of rosemary. Serve the meat, cut into double cutlets, with the garlic cloves and gravy.

COOK'S TIPS

Serve the lamb with a selection of vegetables, such as leeks, green beans and Gratin Dauphinoise (see page 152), baked in individual ramekins for 40 minutes.

Pan-Fried Lamb

Serves 4

12 ESCALOPES OF LAMB, ABOUT 565 G (1¼ LB) TOTAL WEIGHT

50 G (2 OZ) BUTTER

115 G (4 OZ) ONION, SKINNED AND FINELY CHOPPED

2.5 CM (1 IN) PIECE OF FRESH ROOT GINGER, PEELED AND CHOPPED

2 GARLIC CLOVES, SKINNED AND CHOPPED

50 ML (2 FL OZ) WATER

PINCH OF GROUND CLOVES

2×15 ML TBS CHOPPED FRESH MINT

PINCH OF CHILLI POWDER

SALT AND PEPPER

THINLY SLICED ONIONS, LEMON WEDGES AND FRESH MINT SPRIGS, TO GARNISH

1. Place the lamb escalopes between two sheets of clingfilm or pieces of greaseproof paper. Pound them lightly with a rolling pin.
2. Heat 25 g (1 oz) butter in a small saucepan and sauté the onion for about 10 minutes, or until very soft and golden. Set aside and leave to cool.
3. Place the ginger and garlic in a blender or food processor with the water. Blend them together to a smooth paste.
4. Mix together the ginger and garlic paste with the ground cloves, chopped mint, chilli powder and cooled, sautéed onions. Season to taste. Place the lamb in a large, shallow container and spread the onion mixture over the top. Cover and leave to marinate in the mixture for 1 hour.
5. Heat 25 g (1 oz) butter in a large sauté pan and brown the lamb escalopes well on both sides before transferring them to a shallow, ovenproof casserole. Cover the dish with foil and a lid, and finish cooking the escalopes in the oven at 180°C/350°F/ Gas Mark 4 for 20 minutes. Serve garnished with sliced onion, lemon wedges and sprigs of mint.

Loins of Lamb with Oatmeal

Serves 8

2×1.1 KG (2½ LB) LOINS OF LAMB

150 G (5 OZ) LOW-FAT SOFT CHEESE

2×15 ML TBS CHOPPED FRESH THYME OR 1×5 ML TSP DRIED

2 GARLIC CLOVES, SKINNED AND CRUSHED

SALT AND PEPPER

PLAIN WHITE FLOUR

1 EGG, BEATEN

115 G (4 OZ) MEDIUM OATMEAL

VEGETABLE OIL

600 ML (20 FL OZ) BEEF STOCK (SEE PAGE 13)

SHERRY

FRESH THYME, TO GARNISH (OPTIONAL)

1. Using a sharp knife, cut all bones away from the lamb and trim off excess fat.
2. Beat together the cheese, herbs, garlic and seasoning. Spread half over the fleshy side of each boned loin. Roll up the lamb to enclose the stuffing completely. Tie with fine string. Roll the joints in a little flour then brush with beaten egg and coat with the oatmeal. Press firmly to ensure that the oatmeal clings to the joint.
3. Heat a thin coating of oil in a medium-sized roasting tin. Add the joints. Roast in the oven at 200°C/400°F/Gas Mark 6 for 45-50 minutes. Baste once during cooking. Thickly slice the joints, discarding the string; cover and keep warm in a low oven.
4. Pour off any excess fat from the roasting tin, leaving about 2×15 ml tbs. Stir in 4×5 ml tsp flour and cook, stirring, until lightly browned. Add the stock and bring to the boil, stirring. Cook for 1-2 minutes, then add a dash of sherry. Adjust the seasoning and serve with the lamb. Garnish with fresh thyme.

Loins of Lamb with Oatmeal

FRUITY LAMB

Serves 6

12 PRUNES, PITTED

300 ML (10 FL OZ) MALT VINEGAR

1 CLOVE

175 G (6 OZ) SUGAR

2.5 CM (1 IN) PIECE FRESH GINGER, PEELED AND GRATED

3×15 ML TBS VEGETABLE OIL

1.4 KG (3 LB) BONED LEG OF LAMB, CUT INTO CUBES

175 G (6 OZ) ONION, SKINNED AND ROUGHLY CHOPPED

1 GARLIC CLOVE, SKINNED

2×5 ML TSP GROUND ALLSPICE

PINCH OF GROUND CHILLI

1 CINNAMON STICK

50 G (2 OZ) PLAIN FLOUR

2×15 ML TBS CLEAR HONEY

2×15 ML TBS TOMATO PURÉE

SALT AND PEPPER

1 LT (1¾ PT) BEEF STOCK (SEE PAGE 13)

PARED RIND AND JUICE OF 2 ORANGES

PARED RIND AND JUICE OF 1 LEMON

4 FIRM PEARS

ROAST PARSNIPS AND BUTTERED CABBAGE, TO ACCOMPANY

1. Place the prunes in a large bowl. Place the vinegar, clove, sugar and ginger in a small saucepan and heat until the sugar dissolves. Cool and strain on to the prunes. Cover and leave to soak overnight.

2. Heat the oil in a flameproof casserole and brown the lamb, a few pieces at a time, adding more oil if necessary. Drain well on absorbent kitchen paper.

3. Add the onion to the casserole and cook, stirring, over a low heat until softened. Stir in the garlic and spices. Cook, stirring, for 1 minute before adding the flour, honey, tomato purée and seasoning. Stir in the stock, lamb and rind and strained juice of the oranges and lemon. Bring to the boil.

4. Cover the casserole tightly and cook in the oven at 160°C/325°F/Gas Mark 3 for 1 hour. Remove from the oven, discard the cinnamon stick, cool and refrigerate.

5. When ready to use, skim off any excess fat. Bring slowly to the boil; cover and simmer for a further 20 minutes or until the lamb is very tender.

Fruity Lamb

6. Meanwhile, halve, core and slice the pears into the soaking prunes. When the lamb is ready, drain the fruit and stir it in to the casserole. Adjust seasoning and serve with the vegetables.

LAMB CHOPS WITH TOMATO AND BASIL

Serves 4

4 LAMB CHUMP CHOPS, ABOUT 175G (6 OZ) EACH, TRIMMED OF EXCESS FAT

SALT AND PEPPER

ABOUT 1215 ML TBS PLAIN WHITE FLOUR

2215 ML TBS VEGETABLE OIL

25 G (1 OZ) BUTTER

175 G (6 OZ) ONION, SKINNED AND CHOPPED

50 G (2 OZ) CELERY, TRIMMED AND CHOPPED

1 GARLIC CLOVE, SKINNED AND FINELY CHOPPED

245 G CAN CONDENSED TOMATO SOUP

125 ML TSP DRIED BASIL

ROAST OR SAUTÉ POTATOES AND SHREDDED CABBAGE, TO ACCOMPANY

1. Coat the chops lightly in seasoned flour.

2. Heat the oil in a shallow flameproof casserole. Add the butter and when foaming fry the chops until golden on both sides; remove from the pan.

3. Lower the heat and add the onion, celery and garlic. Cook until soft but not coloured.

4. Replace the chops, stir in the tomato soup (undiluted), the basil and seasoning. Bring to the boil, cover and simmer very gently, or bake in the oven at 170°C/325°F/Gas Mark 3 for 45 minutes – 1 hour or until the chops are tender; test with a skewer to see if they are cooked.

5. Skim any fat from the surface, adjust seasoning and serve with roast or sauté potatoes and shredded cabbage.

COOK'S TIP

The long, slow cooking helps to tenderise the meat and the soup mixture develops into a rich sauce.

Lamb Noisettes with Flageolet Beans

Serves 6

200 G (7 OZ) DRIED FLAGEOLET BEANS

2×15 ML TBS CHOPPED FRESH PARSLEY

1 GARLIC CLOVE, SKINNED

SALT AND PEPPER

12 LEAN LAMB NOISETTES, ABOUT 75-115 G (3-4 OZ) EACH

FRESH ROSEMARY SPRIGS

CARROTS AND NEW POTATOES, TO ACCOMPANY

1. Rinse the beans, then place in a bowl with plenty of cold water and leave to soak in a cool place overnight. The next day, rinse the beans again and place in a saucepan with plenty of fresh water. Bring to the boil, boil rapidly for 10 minutes, then cover and boil for about 1 hour, or until just tender. Drain, reserving the cooking liquor.
2. Place three-quarters of the flageolet beans in a blender or food processor with the parsley, garlic and 450 ml (16 fl oz) reserved cooking liquor. Process until almost smooth then season to taste. Pour into a small saucepan.
3. Place the noisettes on a bed of rosemary sprigs on a wire rack and grill for 4-5 minutes on each side – the flesh should still be a little pink. Meanwhile, gently reheat the sauce, stirring frequently. Dip the whole beans in boiling water for 2-3 minutes to reheat, then drain.
4. Spoon a little of the sauce on to warmed serving plates and sit two noisettes on each plate. Garnish with the whole beans and a sprig of rosemary. Serve with carrots and boiled new potatoes.

Lamb Noisettes with Flageolot Beans

Lamb Escalopes with Oatmeal

Serves 4

2 LAMB LEG STEAKS (BONE IN), ABOUT 565 G (1¼ LB) TOTAL WEIGHT, ABOUT 2-2.5CM (¾-1 IN) THICK

DIJON MUSTARD

ABOUT 150 G (5 OZ) MEDIUM OATMEAL

1×15 ML TBS DRIED RUBBED SAGE

SALT AND PEPPER

1×SIZE 3 EGG, BEATEN

142 ML POT SOURED CREAM

GROUND PAPRIKA

VEGETABLE OIL

25 G (1 OZ) BUTTER

GREEN LEAF, ORANGE AND ONION SALAD, TO ACCOMPANY

1. Trim any excess fat off the lamb and cut out the bone. Place the meat between sheets of damp greaseproof paper and pound out until quite thin – about 0.6 cm (¼ in) thick. Cut each steak into four or six pieces.
2. Spread a little mustard over one side of each piece of lamb. Mix together the oatmeal, sage and seasoning.
3. Brush the meat with beaten egg and then coat with the oatmeal mixture; cover and chill for about 30 minutes.
4. Mix together the soured cream and 1×15 ml tbs mustard; sprinkle a little paprika over the top; cover and chill.
5. Heat a little oil in a large frying pan. Mix in the butter and, when foaming, add about half the meat.
6. Fry over a moderate heat until lightly browned and tender – about 3 minutes each side. Drain on absorbent kitchen paper. Keep warm, loosely covered, while frying the remaining lamb.
7. Serve the lamb escalopes with the soured cream sauce accompanied by a green leaf, orange and onion salad.

Lamb and Lentil Hotpot

Serves 6

1.4 KG (3 LB) MIDDLE NECK OF LAMB, DIVIDED INTO CUTLETS

VEGETABLE OIL

450 G (1 LB) ONIONS, SKINNED AND SLICED

450 G (1 LB) CARROTS, PEELED AND THICKLY SLICED

115 G (4 OZ) RED LENTILS, BOILED RAPIDLY FOR 10 MINUTES, THEN DRAINED

6×15 ML TBS CHOPPED FRESH PARSLEY

SALT AND PEPPER

600 ML (20 FL OZ) BEEF STOCK (SEE PAGE 13)

200 ML (7 FL OZ) DRY CIDER

FRESH PARSLEY, TO GARNISH

STEAMED AND SHREDDED CABBAGE, TO ACCOMPANY

1. Trim the cutlets of any excess fat and gristle. Heat a little oil in a large flameproof casserole. Add half the meat and brown well, then remove from the pan with a slotted spoon. Repeat with the remainder of the meat.
2. Add the onions and carrots and cook until lightly brown. Layer the meat, onions, carrots and lentils in the casserole with the parsley, seasoning each layer well as you add it to the casserole.
3. Pour the stock and cider over then bring to the boil. Cover tightly and cook in the oven at 150°C/300°F/Gas Mark 2 for about 1½ hours, or until the meat is quite tender.
4. Adjust seasoning, garnish with parsley and serve the hotpot accompanied by steamed cabbage.

COOK'S TIP

The lentils slowly absorb much of the liquid to give this dish its rich tasty juices.

Lamb with Olive Juices

Serves 8

50 G CAN ANCHOVY FILLETS IN OIL

1 GARLIC CLOVE, SKINNED AND CRUSHED

1 × 15 ML TBS CHOPPED FRESH ROSEMARY

2 KG (4½ LB) LEG OF LAMB

4 × 15 ML TBS OLIVE OIL

150 ML (5 FL OZ) BEEF STOCK (SEE PAGE 13)

3 × 15 ML TBS WHITE WINE VINEGAR

300 ML (10 FL OZ) DRY WHITE WINE

SALT AND PEPPER

FRESH ROSEMARY AND THYME, TO GARNISH

1. Crush the anchovies with their oil and the garlic and rosemary in a pestle and mortar. Put a rack in a roasting tin, large enough to hold the lamb. Place the lamb on the rack and spread with the anchovy paste. Pour the oil over.

2. Roast the lamb in the oven at 180°C/350°F/Gas Mark 4 for 20 minutes per 450 g (1 lb), basting occasionally with the olive oil. Transfer the lamb to a warmed serving platter and keep warm for about 15 minutes before carving.

3. To make the gravy, skim off the fat from the roasting tin. Pour the stock, wine vinegar and the wine into the tin and stir to dislodge the sediment. Bring to the boil and simmer for a couple of minutes, then season to taste with salt and pepper. Pour the gravy into a gravy boat. Serve the meat garnished with herbs.

Spiced Lamb with Potatoes

Serves 4

450 G (1 LB) LEAN BONELESS LAMB, CUT INTO SMALL SLICES

SALT AND PEPPER

2 × 15 ML TBS PLAIN FLOUR

2 × 15 ML TBS VEGETABLE OIL

115 G (4 OZ) ONION, SKINNED AND ROUGHLY CHOPPED

1 RED PEPPER, CORED, SEEDED AND ROUGHLY CHOPPED

1 × 5 ML TSP GROUND GINGER

1 × 15 ML TBS GROUND CORIANDER

450 ML (16 FL OZ) BEEF STOCK (SEE PAGE 13)

1 × 15 ML TBS SOY SAUCE

1 × 15 ML TBS WORCESTER SAUCE

335 G (12 OZ) SMALL NEW POTATOES, SCRUBBED AND HALVED

50 G (2 OZ) BLACK OLIVES (OPTIONAL)

CORIANDER LEAVES, TO GARNISH (OPTIONAL)

1. Toss the meat in seasoned flour. Heat the oil in a large flameproof casserole and brown the meat, a few pieces at a time. Remove with a slotted spoon and drain on absorbent kitchen paper.

2. Add the onion and pepper and sauté for 2 minutes. Stir in the spices and any remaining flour and cook for 1 minute. Mix in the stock, soy sauce and Worcester sauce, and return the meat to the pan with the potatoes.

3. Bring to the boil, cover and bake in the oven at 180°C/350°F/Gas Mark 4 for 40 minutes, or until the meat and potatoes are tender.

4. Stir in the olives, if using, adjust seasoning and serve garnished with coriander leaves, if wished.

Cinnamon Lamb

Serves 4

1 × 15 ML TBS VEGETABLE OIL

225 G (8 OZ) ONIONS, SKINNED AND FINELY CHOPPED

2 GARLIC CLOVES, SKINNED AND CRUSHED

2.5 CM (1 IN) PIECE OF FRESH ROOT GINGER, PEELED AND CHOPPED

675 G (1½ LB) LEAN FILLET OR LEG OF LAMB, SLICED INTO BITE-SIZED PIECES

227 G CAN CHOPPED TOMATOES

2 × 15 ML TBS DARK SOY SAUCE

2 × 5 ML TSP DARK MUSCOVADO SUGAR

¼ × 5 ML TSP GRATED NUTMEG

1 × 5 ML TSP GROUND CINNAMON

PEPPER

150 ML (15 FL OZ) WATER

— LACE PANCAKES —

150 G (5 OZ) PLAIN WHITE FLOUR

1 EGG, LIGHTLY BEATEN

300 ML (10 FL OZ) MILK AND WATER, MIXED

SALT AND PEPPER

VEGETABLE OIL

SALAD ONION SHREDS, TO GARNISH

GREEN BEANS AND QUARTERED TOMATOES, TO ACCOMPANY

1. Heat the oil in a large sauté pan, add the onions, garlic and ginger and cook for 2-3 minutes or until softened. Add the meat to the pan and cook over a high heat for 4-5 minutes or until the meat is well browned.

2. Stir in the remaining ingredients with the water. Bring to the boil, cover and simmer gently for about 20 minutes or until the meat is tender.

3. Meanwhile, make the pancakes. In a food processor, blend the first three ingredients to form a smooth, thin batter; season.

4. Lightly oil a non-stick frying pan, dip your fingers into the batter and allow it to run into the pan as you shake your hand.

5. Cook each pancake for 2-3 minutes on one side until golden, then turn it over and cook for a further 2-3 minutes. Repeat until all the batter is used.

6 Spoon the lamb over the pancakes and fold them over. Garnish with salad onion shreds and serve with green beans and tomatoes.

Cinnamon Lamb

Lamb with Peppers and Aubergines

Serves 4

50 G (2 OZ) SOFTENED BUTTER

1 × 15 ML TBS WHOLEGRAIN MUSTARD

1 × 5 ML TSP DRIED OREGANO OR MARJORAM OR 1 × 15 ML TBS FRESH

1.1 KG (2½ LB) HALF LEG KNUCKLE OF LAMB

115 ML (4 FL OZ) OLIVE OIL

450 G (1 LB) RED PEPPERS, HALVED,CORED, SEEDED AND CUT INTO LARGE CHUNKS

450 G (1 LB) AUBERGINES, TRIMMED AND CUT INTO LARGE CHUNKS

2 × 15 ML TBS CHOPPED FRESH OREGANO OR PARSLEY, TO SERVE (OPTIONAL)

SAUTÉED POTATOES WITH THYME OR ROSEMARY, TO ACCOMPANY

1. Beat the butter with the mustard and herbs. Trim the lamb of excess fat, and cut regular slits 2 cm (¾ in) deep.
2. Spread the butter all over the meat, pushing it into the slits. Sit the lamb on a wire rack that will fit over a roasting tin.
3. Pour the olive oil into the roasting tin and stir the vegetables in. Place the wire rack and lamb on top and roast in the oven at 200°C/400°F/Gas Mark 6 for 20 minutes per 450 g (1 lb) plus 20 minutes for medium lamb. Stir the vegetables twice during cooking. Test the lamb with a skewer or thermometer.
4. Transfer the meat to a serving dish and leave to rest in the turned-off oven for 15 minutes. If necessary, brown the vegetables over a high heat, stirring all the time. Stir the oregano or parsley into the vegetables. Spoon them around the lamb and serve immediately accompanied by sautéed potatoes with thyme or rosemary.

COOK'S TIP

If you love garlic, place whole cloves of unpeeled garlic among the vegetables.

Lamb with Peppers and Aubergines

Honeyed Lamb Noisettes

Serves 6

2 LARGE LEMONS

12 LEAN LAMB NOISETTES, ABOUT 75-115 G (3-4 OZ) EACH

2 × 15 ML TBS CHOPPED FRESH THYME OR 1 × 5 ML TSP DRIED

ABOUT 2 × 15 ML TBS FRESH CHOPPED ROSEMARY OR 2 × 5 ML TSP DRIED

1 BAY LEAF

2 GARLIC CLOVES, SKINNED AND CRUSHED

1 CM (½IN) PIECE OF FRESH ROOT GINGER, PEELED AND GRATED (OPTIONAL)

8 × 15 ML TBS CLEAR HONEY

4 × 15 ML TBS VEGETABLE OIL

SALT AND PEPPER

BAY LEAVES AND FRESH THYME AND ROSEMARY SPRIGS, TO GARNISH

1. Pare the rind off one lemon. Cut into fine strips. Cover and set aside.
2. Place the lamb in a shallow, non-metallic dish. Sprinkle over the herbs and add the bay leaf. Whisk together the grated rind of the remaining lemon, 6 × 15 ml tbs lemon juice, the garlic, ginger (if wished), honey, oil and seasoning. Pour the mixture over the lamb. Cover and leave to marinate in the refrigerator overnight.
3. Drain the marinade from the lamb and strain into a small saucepan. Place the meat on a grid over the grill pan. Cook under a hot grill for about 7 minutes on each side until cooked. Transfer to an ovenproof serving dish with a slotted spoon. Cover with foil and keep warm in a low oven. Carefully pour the grill pan juices into the strained marinade. Stir in the strips of lemon rind. Bring to the boil and simmer, stirring occasionally, for about 2-3 minutes, or until syrupy. Adjust seasoning. Spoon over the noisettes. Garnish with bay leaves and sprigs of fresh thyme and rosemary to serve.

Lamb with Coriander Marinade

Serves 8

2×15 ML TBS CORIANDER SEEDS

1-2 GARLIC CLOVES, SKINNED AND CRUSHED

1 HOT CHILLI, SEEDED AND CHOPPED

3×15 ML TBS CHOPPED FRESH CORIANDER

2.5 CM (1 IN) PIECE OF FRESH ROOT GINGER, PEELED AND CHOPPED

2×5 ML TSP GROUND CUMIN

1×15 ML TBS GROUND CORIANDER

2×5 ML TSP GROUND TURMERIC

600 ML (20 FL OZ) GREEK-STYLE YOGURT

SALT AND PEPPER

2×15 ML TBS LEMON JUICE

1.1 KG (2½ LB) LAMB FILLET, TRIMMED OF FAT AND CUT INTO CUBES

FRESH CORIANDER, TO GARNISH

1. Crush the coriander seeds in a pestle and mortar, or in a strong bowl with the end of a rolling pin, then add the garlic, chilli, fresh coriander and ginger and work to a paste. Add the cumin, ground coriander and turmeric and mix thoroughly together.
2. Stir the paste into the yogurt and season generously. Stir the lemon juice into the mixture. Pour the yogurt marinade into a large glass bowl, then add the lamb. Mix until all the lamb is coated with the marinade. Cover and leave in a cool place to marinate for at least 1 hour or overnight.
3. Thread the meat on to skewers. Barbecue until the meat is brown on the outside and just pink and tender on the inside, about 20 minutes. Serve on a platter, garnished with fresh coriander.

Lamb with Spinach

Serves 6

3×15 ML TBS OIL

900 G (2 LB) LEAN BONED LEG OF LAMB, TRIMMED OF FAT AND CUT INTO 4 CM (1½ IN) CUBES

115 G (4 OZ) ONION, SKINNED AND ROUGHLY CHOPPED

5 CM (2 IN) PIECE OF FRESH ROOT GINGER, PEELED AND GRATED

2 GARLIC CLOVES, SKINNED AND CRUSHED

¼×5 ML TSP CHILLI POWDER

1×5 ML TSP TURMERIC

SALT AND PEPPER

225 G (8 OZ) TURNIP, PEELED AND ROUGHLY CHOPPED

450 G (1 LB) FRESH SPINACH, WASHED AND SHREDDED

300 ML (10 FL OZ) WATER

115 G (4 OZ) TOMATO, SKINNED, SEEDED AND CHOPPED

PINCH EACH GROUND CLOVES, GROUND CARDAMOM AND GROUND MACE

1×5 ML TSP DRIED DILL WEED

RICE, TO SERVE

1. Heat the oil in a large flameproof casserole and brown the lamb. Remove with a slotted spoon and drain on absorbent kitchen paper. Sauté the onion until golden – about 5 minutes. Stir in the ginger and garlic. Cook, stirring, for 1 minute before adding the chilli powder, turmeric and seasoning. Cook for a further 1 minute before returning all the lamb to the pan with the turnip and shredded spinach.
2. Stir the water in. Bring to the boil, cover with foil and then a lid and simmer for about 1½ hours or until almost tender.
3. Add the tomato, then sprinkle the mixture with the ground cloves, cardamom, mace and dill. Re-cover the casserole and simmer for 15-20 minutes until the lamb is tender. Serve with rice.

Minted Lamb Meatballs

Serves 4

225 G (8 OZ) ONIONS, SKINNED AND CUT IN HALF

50 G (2 OZ) BUTTER OR MARGARINE

1×15 ML TBS GROUND CORIANDER

1×15 ML TBS GROUND CUMIN

335 G (12 OZ) MINCED LAMB

115 G (4 OZ) FRESH BROWN BREADCRUMBS

4×5 ML TSP MINT SAUCE

150 ML (5 FL OZ) LOW-FAT NATURAL YOGURT

1 EGG, BEATEN

SALT AND PEPPER

2×15 ML TBS VEGETABLE OIL

2×5 ML TSP PLAIN FLOUR

400 G CAN CHOPPED TOMATOES

150 ML (5 FL OZ) BEEF STOCK (SEE PAGE 13)

1. Finely chop half the onions. Melt the fat in a pan. Add the chopped onions and spices and cook gently until beginning to soften, stirring occasionally. Cool.
2. Mix together the minced lamb, crumbs, onion and spices, 1 × 15 ml tbs mint sauce, 2 × 15 ml tbs yogurt, the egg and seasoning. Beat well until evenly blended then roll into about 24 balls and place on baking trays. The mixture is quite soft to handle.
3. Heat the oil in a frying pan and brown the meatballs in two batches. Drain on absorbent kitchen paper. Place in a single layer in a shallow ovenproof dish.
4. Slice remaining onion and fry it in the residual oil for 1-2 minutes. Stir in the flour, tomatoes, stock, 1 × 5 ml tsp mint sauce and seasoning. Bring to the boil, stirring, then pour it over the meatballs.
5. Cover the dish tightly and bake at 190°C/375°F/Gas Mark 5 for about 40 minutes. Drizzle the remaining yogurt over the top to serve.

Pork Tenderloin with Watercress Sauce

Serves 4-6

2 PORK TENDERLOINS, ABOUT 565 G (1¼ LB) TOTAL WEIGHT, TRIMMED OF FAT

2 GARLIC CLOVES, SKINNED AND CRUSHED

2×15 ML TBS VEGETABLE OIL

25 G (1 OZ) BUTTER OR MARGARINE

25 G (1 OZ) ONION, SKINNED AND FINELY CHOPPED

1 BAY LEAF

½ BUNCH OF WATERCRESS, WASHED, TRIMMED AND FINELY CHOPPED

25 G (1 OZ) PLAIN FLOUR

50 ML (2 FL OZ) DRY WHITE WINE

300 ML (10 FL OZ) MILK

300 ML (10 FL OZ) SINGLE CREAM

1×5 ML TSP DIJON MUSTARD

115 G (4 OZ) GRUYÈRE CHEESE, GRATED

SALT AND PEPPER

335 G (12 OZ) MOZZARELLA CHEESE, SLICED INTO 12 PIECES

12 SLICES PROSCIUTTO CRUDO (ITALIAN DRY CURED HAM), ABOUT 150 G (5 OZ)

2×15 ML TBS DRIED WHITE BREADCRUMBS

2×5 ML TSP FRESHLY GRATED PARMESAN CHEESE

WATERCRESS SPRIGS, TO GARNISH

MIXED GREEN SALAD, FRESH PASTA AND SAUTÉED MUSHROOMS, TO ACCOMPANY

1. Cut each of the tenderloins into six pieces about 5 cm (2 in) long. Stand each one on end and pound down with a rolling pin to form small steaks. Rub with crushed garlic. Cover tightly and set aside for 1 hour in a cool place or overnight in the refrigerator.
2. Heat the oil in a large sauté pan. Brown the steaks well on all sides. Remove with a slotted spoon and pat dry on absorbent kitchen paper. Cool.
3. Melt the butter and sauté the onion with the bay leaf for 2-3 minutes until golden. Stir in the chopped watercress and flour. Cook, stirring, for 2-3 minutes, then add the wine and milk. Bring to the boil, stirring. Simmer for 2-3 minutes. Off the heat, add the cream, mustard and 75g (3 oz) grated Gruyère cheese. Remove bay leaf. Season.
4. Place a piece of Mozzarella on top of each pork steak. Season and wrap in a slice of prosciutto. Place the pork parcels in a single layer in a shallow ovenproof dish. Spoon the sauce over and sprinkle with the remaining grated Gruyère cheese, breadcrumbs and Parmesan. Bake at 180°C/350°F/Gas Mark 4 for 40-45 minutes until tender. Brown under a hot grill if necessary. Serve garnished with watercress and a mixed green salad, fresh pasta and sautéed mushrooms.

Pork Tenderloin with Watercress Sauce

Fruit-Crusted Loin of Pork

Serves 6

175 G (6 OZ) MIXED DRIED FRUIT SUCH AS PRUNES, APRICOTS, PEACHES, PEARS, FINELY CHOPPED

2×15 ML TBS MEDIUM OR FINE OATMEAL

FINELY GRATED RIND OF 1 ORANGE

½×5 ML TSP GROUND CORIANDER

½×5 ML TSP GROUND ALLSPICE

SALT AND PEPPER

500 ML (18 FL OZ) PRUNE JUICE

ABOUT 1.1 KG (2½ LB) PORK LOIN ROAST, ON THE BONE

300 ML (10 FL OZ) WATER

CREAMED POTATO AND BRAISED FENNEL OR CABBAGE, TO ACCOMPANY

1. Mix dried fruit with the oatmeal, orange rind, coriander, allspice, seasoning and about 4×15 ml tbs prune juice to bind.
2 Trim off the skin and as much excess fat from the loin as possible. Place the pork bone-side down in a roasting tin and press the fruit mixture evenly over the skinned surface of the meat. Pour the remaining prune juice around the meat and roast in the oven at 180°C/350°F/Gas Mark 4 for about 40 minutes per 450 g (1 lb) or until the meat is thoroughly cooked. Baste the meat with the prune juice after 20 minutes and occasionally throughout cooking. Test with a skewer or thermometer.
3 If the fruit crust looks as if it is burning, cover the crust only with a piece of foil, but continue to baste occasionally.
4 Turn off the oven and transfer the roast to a warm serving dish. Keep warm in the oven for at least 15 minutes before carving.
5 Boil up the juices with the water. Adjust seasoning and skim off fat; strain. Serve the meat cut into thick slices with the juices spooned over. Creamed potato and braised fennel or shredded cabbage would be good accompaniments.

COOK'S TIP

Basting with the prune juice gives the meat succulence and flavour and makes a delicious sauce.

Fruit-Crusted Loin of Pork

DIJON-GLAZED PORK MEDALLIONS

Serves 8

1.4 KG (3 LB) PORK TENDERLOIN

SALT AND PEPPER

1×15 ML TBS VEGETABLE OIL

1 ONION, SKINNED AND FINELY CHOPPED

1 GARLIC CLOVE, SKINNED AND CRUSHED

65 G (2½ OZ) BUTTER

3×15 ML TBS MADEIRA OR MARSALA

450 ML (16 FL OZ) CHICKEN STOCK (SEE PAGE 13)

1×15 ML TBS DIJON MUSTARD

175 G (6 OZ) CRÈME FRAÎCHE

1½×15 ML TBS PLAIN FLOUR

FRESH SAGE LEAVES, SHREDDED, AND CARROT AND PARSNIP MATCHSTICKS, BLANCHED, TO GARNISH

1. Slice each tenderloin into 1 cm (½ in) thick slices. Put the slices between two sheets of greaseproof paper and, using a meat mallet or rolling pin, pound out the slices firmly until they are thin. Sprinkle with salt and pepper.
2. Heat the oil in a large frying pan and gently fry the onion and garlic for about 5 minutes, then remove from pan. Add 50 g (2 oz) butter to the pan and fry the medallions, a few at a time, for 2-3 minutes until just cooked on each side. Remove and keep warm.
3. Add the Madeira to the pan and stir in the onion mixture, stock, mustard and crème fraîche. Bring to the boil and boil rapidly for about 4 minutes until partially reduced. Mix together the remaining butter and flour to form a paste. Gradually add to the sauce, stirring all the time. Boil for 2 minutes, stirring, until thickened.
4. Return the pork to the pan and heat through for 2 minutes, spooning the sauce over during heating. Serve garnished with sage and carrot and parsnip matchsticks.

COOK'S TIP

Pork tenderloin is a lean and tender choice for a special meal. Here it is cut into medallions and beaten out to form thin rounds (which cook quickly). Veal escalopes could be used instead of pork, if wished.

Dijon-Glazed Pork Medallions

LEMON-SPICED PORK

Serves 8

900 G (2 LB) PORK TENDERLOIN OR ESCALOPES

GRATED RIND AND JUICE OF 2 LEMONS

12 GREEN CARDAMOMS, SEEDS REMOVED AND CRUSHED

1×15 ML TBS GROUND CUMIN

1×15 ML TBS GROUND CORIANDER

SALT AND PEPPER

1 GARLIC CLOVE, SKINNED AND CRUSHED

6×15 ML TBS VEGETABLE OIL

225 G (8 OZ) ONIONS, SKINNED AND SLICED

25 G (1 OZ) PLAIN FLOUR

750 ML (1¼ PT) CHICKEN STOCK (SEE PAGE 13)

1 LARGE BUNCH OF WATERCRESS, TRIMMED AND FINELY CHOPPED

3×15 ML TBS SINGLE CREAM

1. Cut the tenderloin into 1 cm (½ in) thick slices or divide each escalope into two or three pieces. Put the pieces between two sheets of greaseproof paper and, using a meat mallet or rolling pin, lightly pound them out. Place in a shallow glass or china dish. Add the lemon rind and strained juice.
2. Sprinkle the cardamom seeds over the meat with the cumin, coriander and seasoning. Add the garlic, stirring well to mix. Cover tightly and refrigerate for about 24 hours, turning occasionally.
3. Heat the oil in a large, shallow flameproof casserole. Lift the meat out of the marinade and brown in the oil in several batches. Leave on one side. Add the sliced onion to the pan and lightly brown. Stir the flour in and cook for 1 or 2 minutes until it begins to brown. Pour the stock in and any remaining marinade and bring to the boil. Add the finely chopped watercress and replace the meat.
4. Cover and bake at 180°C/350°F/Gas Mark 4 for about 30 minutes or until the meat is just tender. Remove from the oven, stir in the cream and adjust seasoning.

COOK'S TIPS

For this aromatic rather than spicy dish the best accompaniment is simply boiled or baked brown rice.

The strength of cardamoms varies greatly – the fresher the better.

Chinese Spiced Pork

Serves 4

2.5 CM (1 IN) PIECE OF FRESH ROOT GINGER, PEELED AND FINELY CHOPPED

2 GARLIC CLOVES, SKINNED AND CRUSHED

200 ML (7 FL OZ) WATER

115 ML (4 FL OZ) LIGHT SOY SAUCE

1×5 ML TSP CHINESE FIVE-SPICE POWDER (NOT SEASONING)

2×15 ML TBS SOFT BROWN SUGAR

ABOUT 900 G (2 LB) BONED AND SMOKED (CURED) PORK LOIN ROAST

5×15 ML TBS DRY SHERRY OR CIDER

EGG NOODLES AND STIR-FRIED VEGETABLES, TO ACCOMPANY

1. Place the ginger in a small saucepan with the garlic, water, soy sauce, five-spice powder and sugar. Bring to the boil.
2. Place the pork in a small roasting tin. Pour the spiced soy mixture over it. Turn the meat to coat, then cover with a loose 'tent' of foil. Roast in the oven at 190°C/375°F/Gas Mark 5 for about 35 minutes per 450 g (1 lb) or until the meat is thoroughly cooked. Test with a skewer or thermometer. Remove the foil for about the last 30 minutes and baste occasionally.
3. Turn off the oven and transfer the meat to a warm serving dish. Leave to rest in the oven for at least 15 minutes. Place the roasting dish over a high heat and bubble until the juices have reduced slightly. Stir the sherry in and boil rapidly for 1 minute. Taste, and if a little salty, dilute with water. Strain into a gravy boat.
4. Serve the meat thickly carved, with the sauce poured over. Accompany with egg noodles and stir-fried vegetables.

Chinese Spiced Pork

Gammon with Crunchy Nut Glaze

Serves 8

4×15 ML TBS CLEAR HONEY

1×15 ML TBS DIJON MUSTARD

1.6-1.8 KG (3½-4 LB) PRECOOKED CORNER GAMMON JOINT

ABOUT 10 CLOVES

2×15 ML TBS SESAME SEEDS

1×15 ML TBS WHITE MUSTARD SEEDS

25 G (1 OZ) FLAKED ALMONDS

WHOLE POACHED PEARS, PEELED WITH STEM ON, TO ACCOMPANY (OPTIONAL)

1. Mix together the clear honey and the Dijon mustard.

2. With a sharp knife, carefully strip the rind from the cooked gammon joint and score the fat. Place in a roasting tin. Press the cloves into the scored fat and brush over half the honey and mustard glaze.

3. Add the remaining ingredients to the glaze and press on to the fat. Cook in the oven at 200°C/400°F/Gas Mark 6 for about 15 minutes. If necessary, protect any fleshy surfaces with foil. Serve the gammon, warm or cold, with the pears, if you wish.

Quick Pork Cassoulet

Serves 4

450 G (1 LB) FRESH PORK STREAKY RASHERS, ABOUT 2 CM (¾ IN) THICK

VEGETABLE OIL

335 G (12 OZ) ONIONS, SKINNED AND SLICED

1 GREEN PEPPER, SEEDED AND ROUGHLY CHOPPED

6 STICKS OF CELERY, WASHED, TRIMMED AND THICKLY SLICED

½×5 ML TSP CHILLI POWDER

1×5 ML TSP DRIED MIXED HERBS

400 G CAN CHOPPED TOMATOES

450 ML (16 FL OZ) CHICKEN STOCK (SEE PAGE 13)

SALT AND PEPPER

430 G CAN RED KIDNEY BEANS

FRIED WHITE BREADCRUMBS, TO TOP (OPTIONAL)

CHOPPED FRESH PARSLEY, TO GARNISH

1. Cut the rind and fat off the pork and then cut the flesh into bite-sized pieces. Lightly brown in the minimum of oil in a flameproof casserole, then remove.

2. Add the prepared vegetables to the casserole, with a little more oil if necessary; stir-fry for 2-3 minutes.

3. Add the chilli powder and cook for 1 minute before mixing in the dried mixed herbs, tomatoes and juices, stock and seasoning. Replace the meat and bring to the boil. Cover tightly and simmer for about 45 minutes, or until the meat is tender.

4 Uncover, stir in the drained beans and bubble down the juices to thicken slightly. Adjust seasoning before serving, topped with fried white breadcrumbs, if wished, and garnished with chopped fresh parsley.

Gammon with Crunchy Nut Glaze

Sausage and Bean Casserole

Serves 4-6

2×15 ML TBS VEGETABLE OIL

450 G (1 LB) PORK AND HERB SAUSAGES

225 G (8 OZ) ONIONS, SKINNED AND SLICED

225 G (8 OZ) CARROTS, PEELED AND SLICED

400 G CAN TOMATOES

430 G CAN CHICK-PEAS, DRAINED AND RINSED

430 G CAN RED KIDNEY BEANS, DRAINED AND RINSED

1×15 ML TBS CORNFLOUR

350 ML (12 FL OZ) CHICKEN STOCK (SEE PAGE 13)

1×5 ML TSP TABASCO SAUCE

2×15 ML TBS TOMATO PURÉE

SALT AND PEPPER

CRUSTY BREAD, TO SERVE

1. Heat the oil in a medium flameproof casserole. Add the sausages and brown evenly – about 5 minutes. Remove from the casserole and cut each one into two or three pieces.

2. Lower the heat, and add the onions and carrots. Cook, stirring, until they begin to soften.

3. Return the sausages to the casserole, with the tomatoes, chick-peas and kidney beans. Blend the cornflour with a little of the stock, add this to the casserole with the remainder of the stock, the Tabasco sauce, the tomato purée and seasoning. Stir.

4. Bring to the boil, cover and cook at 160°C/325°F/Gas Mark 3 for about 1 hour or longer if possible to increase the depth of flavour. Serve with lots of crusty bread to soak up the juices.

Herb Sausages with Caramelised Onions

Serves 4

25 G (1 OZ) BUTTER

2×15 ML TBS OLIVE OIL

335 G (12 OZ) BUTTON ONIONS, SKINNED AND HALVED, OR 4 MEDIUM ONIONS, SKINNED AND ROUGHLY CHOPPED

2×15 ML TBS CASTER SUGAR

450 G (1 LB) PORK SAUSAGEMEAT

1-2×15 ML TBS CHOPPED FRESH HERBS, SUCH AS MARJORAM, THYME, OREGANO

1×15 ML TBS DIJON MUSTARD

SALT AND PEPPER

GREEN SALAD, TO ACCOMPANY (OPTIONAL)

1. Heat the butter and olive oil in a frying pan. Add the onions and sugar to the pan and stir well, then reduce the heat slightly. Cover and cook for about 20 minutes or until the onions are just tender. Do not lift the lid too often or the onions will stick. Keep warm.

2. Meanwhile, use a fork to mix together the pork sausagemeat, herbs, mustard and seasoning. Shape into 12 sausages or small, flat rounds. Grill them for about 10 minutes, or until they are cooked through, turning as necessary.

3. Serve the sausages with the caramelised onions, and a green salad if wished.

Herb Sausages with Caramelised Onions

Garlic Sausages

Serves 6

115 G (4 OZ) SMOKED STREAKY BACON RINDLESS, FINELY CHOPPED

1 SMALL RED CHILLI, SEEDED AND FINELY CHOPPED

450 G (1 LB) LEAN MINCED PORK

225 G (8 OZ) PORK SAUSAGEMEAT

2 GARLIC CLOVES, SKINNED AND CRUSHED

25 G (1 OZ) FRESH WHITE BREADCRUMBS

SALT AND PEPPER

1 EGG AND 1 EGG YOLK

4×15 ML TBS OLIVE OIL

1. Mix the bacon and chilli together with the minced pork, sausagemeat, garlic, breadcrumbs and seasoning. Beat in the egg and egg yolk until thoroughly combined.

2. Shape the mixture into about 18 sausages. (There's no need to be too fussy with the shaping – the sausages should look home-made.) Cover and chill for at least 15 minutes, preferably overnight.

3. Heat the olive oil in a large roasting tin on the hob. Add the sausages in batches and brown on all sides. Return all the sausages to the roasting tin. Transfer to the oven and cook at 200°C/400°F/Gas Mark 6 for about 20-25 minutes or until cooked through. Drain on absorbent kitchen paper.

Sausage and Apple Plait

Serves 8

175 G (6 OZ) ONION, SKINNED AND ROUGHLY CHOPPED

150 G (5 OZ) RINDLESS BACK BACON, ROUGHLY CHOPPED

1×15 ML TBS OIL

1 SMALL COOKING APPLE, PEELED AND CHOPPED

½×5 ML TSP DRIED THYME

450 G (1 LB) PORK AND HERB SAUSAGES OR SAUSAGEMEAT

25 G (1 OZ) PORRIDGE OATS

SALT AND PEPPER

340 G PACKET CHILLED PUFF PASTRY

50 G (2 OZ) CHEDDAR CHEESE, THINLY SLICED

2×15 ML TBS MANGO CHUTNEY

BEATEN EGG

1. Fry the onion and bacon in the oil until the onion begins to soften. Add the apple with the thyme and cook until the apple softens; cool.
2. Skin the sausages and stir together with the cold bacon mixture and the porridge oats; season.
3. Roll out the puff pastry to a rectangle 25 × 36 cm (10 × 14 in) and place on a baking tray. Spread sausage mixture down the centre, leaving 5 cm (2 in) free at each end; top with slices of cheese and the chutney.
4. Cut the exposed pastry into 2 cm (¾ in) thick diagonal slices. Fold the end flaps and strips of pastry over the filling to form a plait effect. Then glaze with beaten egg.
5. Bake at 220°C/425°F/Gas Mark 7 for 20 minutes. Reduce the heat to 180°C/350°F/ Gas Mark 4 for a further 20-25 minutes or until golden and firm to the touch.
6. Cool, then store, wrapped, in the refrigerator until ready to serve. Cut into slices to serve.

Veal and Bacon Kebabs

Serves 6

225 G (8 OZ) STREAKY BACON, RIND REMOVED

450 G (1 LB) VEAL FILLET, CUT INTO BITE-SIZED PIECES

225 G (8 OZ) ONIONS, SKINNED AND CUT INTO 1 CM (½ IN) SQUARES

1 GREEN PEPPER, SEEDED AND CUT INTO 1 CM (½ IN) SQUARES

115 G (4 OZ) NO-SOAK DRIED APRICOTS

FINELY GRATED RIND AND JUICE OF 1 LARGE ORANGE

150 ML (5 FL OZ) PORT OR RED WINE

150 ML (5 FL OZ) WATER

½ × 5 ML TSP DRIED THYME

SALT AND PEPPER

1 × 5 ML TSP SUGAR (OPTIONAL)

1-2 × 5 ML TSP ARROWROOT

1. Stretch each bacon rasher with the back of a knife then divide in half. Roll up tightly. Thread the veal, bacon rolls, onion, pepper and apricots on to long metal or wooden skewers. Place the skewers in shallow non-metallic dishes.
2. Mix the orange rind and juice with the port, water, thyme and seasoning. If using wine, stir in the sugar. Pour over the kebabs; cover with clingfilm and refrigerate for about 24 hours. Turn the kebabs and baste occasionally.
3. Lift the kebabs out of the marinade and place on a grill pan. Grill for 15-20 minutes, in two batches if necessary, frequently turning and basting with a little marinade. Keep warm, loosely covered in a low oven. Mix half the arrowroot with a little water to form a smooth paste. Add to the remaining marinade and bring to the boil, stirring. Simmer for 1-2 minutes or until lightly thickened. (Add remaining arrowroot only if necessary.) Adjust the seasoning and serve with the kebabs.

COOK'S TIP

For all kebabs it's important to pack the skewers loosely so that the meat will cook through. Baste them frequently while grilling.

Veal with Bacon and Juniper

Serves 8

VEGETABLE OIL

1.8 KG (4 LB) DICED VEAL, TRIMMED OF FAT

225 G (8 OZ) SMOKED STREAKY BACON, RINDED AND CUT INTO THIN STRIPS

225 G (8 OZ) BUTTON ONIONS, SKINNED AND HALVED

1 GARLIC CLOVE, SKINNED AND CRUSHED

225 G (8 OZ) CARROTS, TRIMMED AND THICKLY SLICED

8 JUNIPER BERRIES, CRUSHED

4 × 15 ML TBS PLAIN WHITE FLOUR

750 ML (1¼ PT) CHICKEN STOCK (SEE PAGE 13)

300 ML (10 FL OZ) PORT

2 × 5 ML TSP TOMATO PURÉE

115 G (4 OZ) NO-SOAK, PITTED PRUNES

4 × 15 ML TBS CHOPPED FRESH PARSLEY

SALT AND PEPPER

1. Heat 4 × 15 ml tbs oil in a large, flameproof casserole. Brown the veal, a few pieces at a time, adding more oil if necessary. Remove with a slotted spoon and drain on absorbent kitchen paper.
2. Sauté the bacon until well browned. Remove with a slotted spoon and drain on absorbent kitchen paper.
3. In the same casserole, sauté the button onions, garlic, carrots and juniper berries until the vegetables turn golden. Return the veal and bacon to the casserole. Add the flour. Cook, stirring, for 1-2 minutes, then add chicken stock, port and tomato purée.
4. Bring to the boil, cover and cook in the oven at 180°C/350°F/Gas Mark 4 for 1 hour. Stir in the prunes. Re-cover and continue to cook for a further 30 minutes, or until the veal is very tender. Stir the parsley in and add seasoning before serving.

Veal Escalopes with Mineola and Herb Butter

Serves 8

4 VEAL ESCALOPES, ABOUT 115 G (4 OZ) EACH

3 × 15 ML TBS PLAIN WHITE FLOUR, SEASONED WITH SALT AND PEPPER

25 G (1 OZ) BUTTER

75 ML (3 FL OZ) DRY WHITE WINE

75 ML (3 FL OZ) CHICKEN STOCK (SEE PAGE 13)

GRATED RIND AND JUICE OF 2 MINEOLAS

1 × 15 ML TBS CHOPPED FRESH MIXED HERBS, SUCH AS ROSEMARY, PARSLEY, LEMON THYME

JUICE OF ½ LEMON (OPTIONAL)

SLICES OF FRUIT AND HERB SPRIGS, TO GARNISH

1. Place the veal escalopes between two sheets of greaseproof paper and, using a meat mallet or rolling pin, carefully pound them out. Dip into the seasoned flour, shaking off any excess.
2. Heat the butter in a large sauté pan. Cook the veal, two pieces at a time, on a high heat for 1-2 minutes, until browned on both sides. Lower the heat and cook until tender – about 4 minutes on each side. Remove from the pan and keep warm.
3. Add the wine and stock; cook over a high heat, scraping (deglazing) the pan to incorporate all juices. Reduce the heat and add the rind and about 5 × 15 ml tbs mineola juice and the herbs. Simmer gently until slightly reduced. Adjust seasoning, adding lemon juice if wished. Return the veal to the pan. Heat gently until warmed, them serve garnished with fruit and herbs.

VEGETARIAN DISHES

Vegetarian food means far more than dry nut roasts and tasteless baked vegetables. The collection of highly imaginative recipes in this chapter will provide inspiration for both committed vegetarians and for those seeking an occasional alternative to meat. The exciting and original recipes range from stir-fries and satays to Mediterranean salads, vegetable flans and rich, country casseroles.

Left: Root Vegetable Stew (page 120) Centre: Quorn Satay (page 114)
Right: Sweet Pepper and Basil Flan (page 125)

Vegetable, Fruit and Nut Stir-Fry

Serves 8

— SAUCE —

1-2 FRESH GREEN CHILLIES, HALVED, SEEDED AND CHOPPED

1×15 ML TBS DARK SOFT BROWN SUGAR

JUICE OF 1 LIME OR LEMON

2×5 ML TSP CORNFLOUR

2×15 ML TBS CRUNCHY PEANUT BUTTER

4×15 ML TBS SOY SAUCE

150 ML (5 FL OZ) COLD WATER

— STIR-FRY—

3×15 ML TBS VEGETABLE OIL

1 BUNCH OF SALAD ONIONS, TRIMMED AND CUT DIAGONALLY INTO 2.5 CM (1 IN) LENGTHS

5 CM (2 IN) PIECE OF FRESH ROOT GINGER, PEELED AND CUT INTO MATCHSTICKS

2 GARLIC CLOVES, SKINNED AND CUT INTO SLIVERS

6 CARROTS, PEELED AND CUT INTO MATCHSTICKS

3 RED PEPPERS, SEEDED AND SLICED LENGTHWAYS

225 G (8 OZ) FINE GREEN BEANS, WASHED AND CUT IN HALF DIAGONALLY, IF WISHED

225 G (8 OZ) MANGETOUT, TOPPED AND TAILED AND CUT IN HALF DIAGONALLY

1 SMALL PINEAPPLE, PEELED, CORED AND CUT INTO CHUNKS

115 G (4 OZ) BEANSPROUTS

75 G (3 OZ) DRY ROASTED PEANUTS, COARSELY CHOPPED

SALT AND PEPPER

1. To make the sauce, pound the chillies in a mortar and pestle (or using the end of a rolling pin in a strong bowl) with the sugar and lime or lemon juice. Dissolve the cornflour in a jug with a few teaspoonfuls of cold water. Add the chilli mixture, the peanut butter and soy sauce and stir well to mix, then stir in the cold water.

2. Heat a wok until hot. Add 2×15 ml tbs oil and heat until hot but not smoking. Add the salad onions, ginger and garlic and stir-fry for about 5 minutes to flavour the oil. Remove from the pan with a slotted spoon and set aside to drain on absorbent kitchen paper.

3. Add the remaining oil to the wok, heat, add the carrots and stir-fry for 3 minutes, then add the peppers and stir-fry for 2-3 minutes. Next add the beans and mangetout and stir-fry for 2-3 minutes until evenly mixed but still very crisp. Remove all the vegetables from the wok and set aside with the salad onion mixture.

4. Stir the sauce ingredients in the jug, then pour into the wok. Stir over high heat until thickened and dark, then return all the vegetables to the wok. Add the pineapple, beansprouts and two-thirds of the peanuts and stir-fry for a few minutes until heated through and evenly mixed with the vegetables. Add salt and pepper to taste, then place in a warmed large serving bowl. Sprinkle with the remaining peanuts and serve hot.

Quorn Satay

Serves 4

450 G (1 LB) QUORN, IN LARGE, EVEN-SIZED CHUNKS

VEGETABLE OIL, FOR BRUSHING

— MARINADE —

2 GARLIC CLOVES, SKINNED AND CRUSHED

2.5 CM (1 IN) PIECE OF FRESH ROOT GINGER, PEELED AND GRATED

3×15 ML TBS SOY SAUCE

2×5 ML TSP SOFT BROWN SUGAR

3×15 ML TBS WATER

— SAUCE —

50 G (2 OZ) CREAMED COCONUT, ROUGHLY CHOPPED

150 ML (5 FL OZ) BOILING WATER

5×15 ML TBS CRUNCHY PEANUT BUTTER

2×15 ML TBS SOY SAUCE

1×5 ML TSP SOFT BROWN SUGAR

1 GARLIC CLOVE, SKINNED AND CRUSHED

1×5 ML TSP CHILLI POWDER, OR TO TASTE

1×5 ML TSP CHOPPED FRESH LEMON GRASS OR FINELY GRATED LEMON RIND

NOODLES AND A MIXED SALAD, TO SERVE

FRESH CORIANDER OR PARSLEY AND LIME WEDGES, TO GARNISH

1. Mix all the ingredients for the marinade in a large shallow dish. Add the quorn and stir until evenly coated. Cover and leave to marinate in the refrigerator for 2-3 hours or overnight.

2. To make the sauce, put the coconut in a bowl, add the boiling water and stir until dissolved. Add the remaining ingredients and mix thoroughly. Cover and set aside.

3. Thread the quorn on to 16 bamboo skewers. Brush with a little vegetable oil then cook under a very hot grill, turning occasionally, for about 3-4 minutes or until lightly browned. Serve hot on a bed of noodles with the cold peanut sauce, accompanied by a mixed salad. Garnish with fresh coriander or parsley and lime wedges.

Vegetable, Fruit and Nut Stir-Fry (left)
Quorn Satay (right)

Vegetable Chilli

Serves 8

2 × 15 ML TBS VEGETABLE OIL
2 ONIONS, SKINNED AND CHOPPED
2 GARLIC CLOVES, SKINNED AND CRUSHED
1-2 FRESH GREEN CHILLIES, SEEDED AND CHOPPED
1 BAY LEAF
1 CINNAMON STICK
4 CLOVES
1 × 15 ML TBS MILD PAPRIKA
2 × 5 ML TSP CUMIN POWDER
½ × 5 ML TSP CHILLI POWDER, OR TO TASTE
1 × 5 ML TSP DRIED MARJORAM
2 × 15 ML TBS TOMATO PURÉE
225 G (8 OZ) BUTTON MUSHROOMS, WIPED AND SLICED
1 LARGE GREEN PEPPER, SEEDED AND CHOPPED
900 G (2 LB) MIXED VEGETABLES, PREPARED AS NECESSARY AND CUT INTO CHUNKS
2 × 400 G CANS CHOPPED TOMATOES
2 × 430 G CANS RED KIDNEY BEANS, DRAINED
3 × 15 ML TBS CHOPPED FRESH CORIANDER
SALT AND PEPPER
BOILED RICE, SOURED CREAM AND CHOPPED FRESH CORIANDER, TO SERVE

1. Heat the oil in a large saucepan or flameproof casserole. Add the onions, garlic and chillies and fry for 3-4 minutes, stirring continuously. Add the bay leaf, all the spices, the marjoram and the tomato purée, and fry for a further 2 minutes, stirring.
2. Add all the fresh vegetables and stir to coat in the spice mixture. Fry for 1-2 minutes, then add the tomatoes. Increase the heat and bring to the boil, stirring occasionally. Add enough water just to cover the vegetables, half cover the pan or casserole with a lid and simmer for 35-45 minutes.
3. Add the kidney beans with half the coriander. Season with salt and pepper. Bring back to the boil, then lower the heat and simmer for 15 minutes, stirring occasionally. If the chilli looks very wet, leave the lid off during this time. If it is dry, add a little water and cover completely. Remove the bay leaf.
4. Stir in the remaining coriander, then leave to stand for 5 minutes. Taste and adjust the seasoning. Serve with boiled rice, topped with soured cream and coriander.

Vegetable Chilli

Stuffed Vine Leaves

Serves 6

175 G (6 OZ) LONG-GRAIN BROWN RICE
SALT AND PEPPER
50 G (2 OZ) BUTTER OR MARGARINE
450 G (1 LB) LEEKS, TRIMMED, WASHED AND CUT INTO THIN SLICES
175 G (6 OZ) UNSALTED PEANUTS, ROUGHLY CHOPPED
115 G (4 OZ) NO-SOAK DRIED APRICOTS, SNIPPED INTO SMALL PIECES
2 × 15 ML TBS FRESH CHOPPED THYME OR 1 × 5 ML TSP DRIED
GRATED RIND AND JUICE OF 1 LEMON
1 EGG, BEATEN
225 G PACKET VINE LEAVES IN BRINE
450 ML (16 FL OZ) VEGETABLE STOCK (SEE PAGE 13)
GREEN SALAD, TO ACCOMPANY

1. Cook the rice in boiling salted water until just tender (about 30 minutes). Drain.
2. Heat the butter in a frying pan, add the leeks and nuts and fry for a few minutes until the leeks have softened. Transfer to a bowl; stir in the rice, apricots, thyme and lemon rind. Season well and stir the beaten egg in.
3. Meanwhile, drain the vine leaves and boil for 5 minutes; drain and rinse under the cold tap. Cool.
4. Divide the stuffing between the vine leaves. Fold up to form parcels and place, seam side down, in ovenproof dishes. The parcels should be placed close together in a single layer but not jammed together too tightly. Pour the stock and lemon juice over the parcels. Cover tightly and bake in the oven at 220°C/425°F/Gas Mark 7 for about 30 minutes until piping hot.
5. Serve with a green salad.

COOK'S TIP

If the leaves have any holes, fold them carefully to prevent the filling bursting out.

Stuffed Vine Leaves

Vegetarian Medley

Serves 4

25 G (1 OZ) BUTTER

2 CARROTS, PEELED AND SLICED

1 LARGE ONION, SKINNED AND CHOPPED

1 GREEN PEPPER, SEEDED AND SLICED

2 TOMATOES, SKINNED AND CHOPPED

1 LARGE COOKING APPLE, PEELED, IF WISHED, AND CHOPPED

1 GARLIC CLOVE, SKINNED AND CRUSHED

1×15 ML TBS CHOPPED FRESH SAGE OR 1×5 ML TSP DRIED

115 G (4 OZ) LENTILS, BOILED RAPIDLY FOR 10 MINUTES, THEN DRAINED

1×15 ML TBS RAISINS

2×15 ML TBS UNSALTED PEANUTS

SALT AND PEPPER

300 ML (10 FL OZ) LOW-FAT NATURAL YOGURT

25 G (1 OZ) CREAM CHEESE

FRESH SAGE LEAVES, TO GARNISH

1. Melt the butter in a large frying pan and lightly fry the carrots, onion, green pepper, tomatoes, apple, garlic and sage for 15 minutes, until softened. Add the lentils, raisins and peanuts. Season to taste.
2. Stir the yogurt into the cream cheese and mix well to blend. Stir into the vegetable mixture. Reheat gently for 5 minutes. Serve at once, garnished with sage leaves.

Hot Spinach Soufflé

Serves 3-4

2×15 ML TBS GRATED PARMESAN CHEESE

450 G (1 LB) FRESH SPINACH, COOKED, OR 225 G (8 OZ) CHOPPED FROZEN SPINACH, THAWED

50 G (2 OZ) BUTTER OR MARGARINE

3×15 ML TBS PLAIN FLOUR

200 ML (7 FL OZ) MILK

SALT AND PEPPER

3 EGGS, SEPARATED, AND 1 EXTRA EGG WHITE

115 G (4 OZ) GRUYÈRE CHEESE, GRATED

1. Grease a 1.3 lt (2¼ pt) soufflé dish and dust with the Parmesan cheese. Place the spinach in a sieve and press to remove all moisture.
2. Melt butter in a saucepan, add spinach and cook for a few minutes to evaporate any liquid. Stir the flour in and cook gently for 1 minute, stirring. Remove the pan from the heat and gradually stir in the milk and seasoning. Bring to the boil slowly, and continue to cook, stirring, until thickened. Cool slightly. Beat in the yolks one at a time and 75 g (3 oz) grated Gruyère.
3. Stiffly whisk the egg whites and fold into the mixture. Spoon into the soufflé dish, Sprinkle with the remaining cheese.
4. Stand dish on a baking tray and bake in the oven at 190°C/375°/Gas Mark 5 for 30 minutes or until well risen and just set. Serve immediately.

Vegetarian Medley

Stuffed Tomatoes

Serves 4

115 G (4 OZ) CRACKED WHEAT

150 ML (5 FL OZ) BOILING WATER

4 LARGE BEEF TOMATOES, EACH WEIGHING ABOUT 175 G (6 OZ)

25 G (1 OZ) NUTS, SUCH AS HAZELNUTS OR CASHEWS, TOASTED AND CHOPPED

50 G (2 OZ) STONED BLACK OLIVES, ROUGHLY CHOPPED

2×15 ML TBS PESTO, SAUCE

3×15 ML TBS CHOPPED FRESH BASIL

SALT AND PEPPER

— TO SERVE —

LOW-FAT NATURAL YOGURT

PESTO SAUCE OR HOUMOUS

CHOPPED FRESH BASIL

1. Put the cracked wheat in a bowl and pour the boiling water over it. Leave to soak for about 30 minutes or until the water has been absorbed and the cracked wheat has softened.
2. Cut the tops off the tomatoes and reserve. Scoop out the tomato centres with a spoon and finely chop half the tomato flesh. (Discard the remainder.)
3. Add the chopped tomato to the cracked wheat with the remaining ingredients and season with salt and pepper. Use to fill the tomato shells. To serve, top each tomato with a spoonful of yogurt and a little pesto or a spoonful of houmous. Sprinkle with chopped fresh basil and then carefully replace the tomato tops.

COOK'S TIP

Serve these stuffed tomatoes as part of a summer lunch with a selection of salads.

Spiced Eggs with Cauliflower and Coconut

Serves 6

675 G (1½ LB) OLD POTATOES, SCRUBBED

SALT AND PEPPER

6 HARD-BOILED EGGS

50 G (2 OZ) CREAMED COCONUT

4×15 ML TBS VEGETABLE OIL

225 G (8 OZ) ONIONS, SKINNED AND ROUGHLY CHOPPED

1 SMALL CAULIFLOWER, DIVIDED INTO SMALL FLORETS

1×15 ML TBS GROUND CORIANDER

1×15 ML TBS GROUND CUMIN

½×5 ML TSP GROUND TURMERIC

½×5 ML TSP CHILLI POWDER

1×15 ML TBS PLAIN FLOUR

300 ML (10 FL OZ) VEGETABLE STOCK (SEE PAGE 13)

2×15 ML TBS MANGO CHUTNEY

450 G (1 LB) TOMATOES, SKINNED AND ROUGHLY CHOPPED

CHOPPED FRESH CORIANDER

BROWN RICE, TO ACCOMPANY

1. Cook the potatoes in their skins in boiling, salted water until tender; drain and cool. When quite cold, cut into small chunks. Shell the hard-boiled eggs and chop. Break up the coconut in a measuring jug and make up to 300 ml (10 fl oz) with boiling water.
2. Heat the oil in a large, heavy-based saucepan. Add the onions, cauliflower and spices and stir over a moderate heat for a minute or two.
3. Mix in the flour, stock, coconut liquid, chutney and seasoning. Bring to the boil, cover and simmer for 10 minutes.
4. Stir in the potatoes, tomatoes and eggs, then cover and simmer for 5 minutes. Adjust seasoning; stir fresh coriander in. Serve with freshly boiled brown rice.

Vegetable Toad in the Hole

Serves 2

175 G (6 OZ) PREPARED MIXED VEGETABLES, SUCH AS CARROTS, COURGETTES, GREEN BEANS AND BROCCOLI

4 CHERRY TOMATOES

WHITE VEGETABLE FAT

50 G (2 OZ) PLAIN FLOUR

PINCH OF SALT

1 EGG

175 ML (6 FL OZ) FULL-FAT MILK AND WATER MIXED

1. Cut the vegetables into small or large chunks. Steam or boil the vegetables until just tender. Prick the tomatoes with a fork.
2. Put a knob of fat into each compartment of a four-hole Yorkshire pudding tin. Put the tin in the oven at 220°C/425°F/Gas Mark 7 for about 5 minutes to heat the fat.
3. Meanwhile, sift the flour and salt into a bowl and make a well in the centre. Break the egg into the well, then add half the liquid. Gradually mix the flour into the liquid to make a smooth, thick paste, then gradually work in the remaining liquid. Beat until smooth. If necessary, remove any lumps with a balloon whisk.
4. Divide the vegetables between the compartments in the pudding tin and pour over the batter. Bake on the top shelf in the oven for 30-35 minutes or until well risen and golden brown.

Vegetable Toad in the Hole

Broad Bean Bake

Serves 2-3

675 G (1½ LB) FRESH BROAD BEANS, SHELLED, OR 225 G (8 OZ) FROZEN

SALT AND PEPPER

2 CARROTS, PEELED AND CUT INTO CHUNKS

2 PARSNIPS, PEELED AND CUT INTO CHUNKS

25 G (1 OZ) BUTTER

25 G (1 OZ) PLAIN WHOLEMEAL FLOUR

300 ML (10 FL OZ) MILK

2×15 ML TBS CHOPPED FRESH MIXED HERBS

1×5 ML TSP MILD MUSTARD

2×15 ML TBS PORRIDGE OATS

50 G (2 OZ) DOUBLE GLOUCESTER CHEESE, GRATED

25 G (1 OZ) CHOPPED MIXED NUTS

1. Cook the fresh broad beans, if using, in boiling salted water for 5 minutes. Add the carrots and parsnips to the beans and continue to cook for 10-15 minutes or until the vegetables are tender. If using frozen beans, add for the last 5 minutes of cooking. Drain well.
2. Melt the butter in a small saucepan. Stir the flour in and cook for 2 minutes. Remove from the heat, gradually add the milk, then cook, stirring, until the sauce thickens, boils and is smooth. Simmer the sauce for 1-2 minutes.
3. Stir in the herbs, mustard and the vegetables. Add seasoning to taste. Simmer for 2-3 minutes, until heated through, then divide between 2-3 individual flameproof dishes.
4. Mix the oats, cheese and nuts together and sprinkle on top of the vegetables. Brown for 2-3 minutes under a hot grill.

Root Vegetable Stew

Serves 6

335 G (12 OZ) CELERIAC, TRIMMED AND CUT INTO LARGE CHUNKS

LEMON JUICE

25 G (1 OZ) BUTTER OR MARGARINE

2 ONIONS, SKINNED AND SLICED

2 GARLIC CLOVES, SKINNED AND CRUSHED

450 G (1 LB) CARROTS, PEELED AND CUT INTO 0.6 CM (¼ IN) THICK SLICES

450 G (1 LB) PARSNIPS, PEELED AND CUT INTO 0.6 CM (¼ IN) THICK SLICES

335 G (12 OZ) BUTTON MUSHROOMS, WIPED

450 ML (16 FL OZ) VEGETABLE STOCK (SEE PAGE 13)

SALT AND PEPPER

4×15 ML TBS SINGLE CREAM

2×15 ML TBS CHOPPED FRESH PARSLEY

1. Drop the celeriac chunks immediately into cold water lightly mixed with a little lemon juice to prevent discolouration.
2. Melt the margarine or butter in a large flameproof casserole. Add the onions and garlic and fry for 2-3 minutes or until beginning to soften, stirring constantly. Stir in the carrots, parsnips and mushrooms and fry for a further 4-5 minutes, stirring, then add the stock and seasoning. Bring to the boil, cover and cook in the oven at 160°C/325°F/Gas Mark 3 for about 50 minutes, or until vegetables are tender.
3. Meanwhile, remove the celeriac from the water and cook in boiling salted water for about 35 minutes or until very tender. Drain and purée in a blender or food processor with a little of the casserole juices. Stir the celeriac purée into the casserole, return to the boil, taste and adjust the seasoning, if necessary. Stir in the cream and parsley just before serving.

Boston Baked Beans

Serves 6-8

450 G (1 LB) DRIED HARICOT OR KIDNEY BEANS, SOAKED OVERNIGHT IN COLD WATER, DRAINED, THEN RINSED
2 ONIONS, SKINNED AND CHOPPED
2×15 ML TBS DIJON MUSTARD
2×15 ML TBS SOFT DARK BROWN SUGAR
5×15 ML TBS BLACK TREACLE
450 ML (16 FL OZ) TOMATO JUICE
450 ML (16 FL OZ) LAGER
4×15 ML TBS TOMATO PURÉE
2×15 ML TBS LIGHT SOY SAUCE
2×15 ML TBS CHILLI SAUCE
1 GARLIC CLOVE, SKINNED AND CRUSHED
SALT AND PEPPER

1. Put the beans in a large flameproof casserole and add enough fresh cold water to cover. Bring to the boil and boil rapidly for 10 minutes, then simmer for 45 minutes. Drain and return to the casserole with the remaining ingredients. Mix thoroughly together, season with salt and pepper, cover with a tightly fitting lid and cook in the oven at 150°C/300°F/Gas Mark 2 for 4 hours or until the beans are very tender.
2. Check and stir the beans occasionally during cooking and add a little extra tomato juice or water, if necessary, to prevent them drying out. Taste and adjust the seasoning before serving.

COOK'S TIP

There are many versions of this classic dark, rich New England dish and they all vary enormously, so much that beans and black treacle or molasses seem to be the only constants. The chilli sauce and garlic are not particularly traditional and may be omitted if you prefer your beans less spicy.

Boston Baked Beans

Vegetable Bake

Serves 10

1.8 KG (4 LB) AUBERGINES, ROUGHLY CHOPPED
6×15 ML TBS VEGETABLE OIL
450 G (1 LB) ONIONS, SKINNED AND ROUGHLY CHOPPED
225 G (8 OZ) CELERY, TRIMMED AND ROUGHLY CHOPPED
2 BAY LEAVES
8×15 ML TBS CHOPPED FRESH BASIL
6×15 ML TBS TOMATO PURÉE
300 ML (10 FL OZ) WHITE WINE
300 ML (10 FL OZ) VEGETABLE STOCK (SEE PAGE 13)
225 G (8 OZ) STONED BLACK OLIVES
900 G (2 LB) TOMATOES, SKINNED, SEEDED AND CHOPPED
2×400 G CANS ARTICHOKE HEARTS, QUARTERED
PEPPER
115 G (4 OZ) BUTTER OR MARGARINE
115 G (4 OZ) PLAIN FLOUR
1.2 LT (2 PT) MILK
225 G (8 OZ) FETA CHEESE, GRATED
4 EGGS, SEPARATED
2×15 ML TBS CHOPPED FRESH PARSLEY

1. Place the aubergines in a large saucepan and cover with cold water. Bring to the boil and simmer for 3-4 minutes. Drain well and pat dry. Transfer aubergines to a baking tray and drizzle 2×15 ml tbs oil over them. Brown the aubergines under a hot grill, turning occasionally.
2. Heat the remaining oil in two large saucepans. Sauté the onions, celery and aubergines with the bay leaves for 2-3 minutes. Add 6×15 ml tbs basil, the tomato purée, wine and stock. Bring to the boil. Cover and simmer for 10-15 minutes, or until the aubergines are tender. Off the heat, stir in the olives, tomatoes and artichokes. Discard the bay leaves. Season with pepper. Transfer the vegetable mixture to two 2.8 lt (5 pt) ovenproof dishes.
3. Melt the butter or margarine in a large saucepan. Stir the flour in. Cook, stirring, for 1-2 minutes before adding the milk. Bring to the boil, stirring, then simmer for 2-3 minutes. Off the heat, beat in 175 g (6 oz) feta cheese, the remaining basil and the egg yolks. Season with pepper. Whisk the egg whites until they just hold their shape, then fold them into the sauce.
4. Spoon the feta sauce evenly over the vegetables. Sprinkle with the remaining grated cheese and the parsley. Bake in the oven at 180°C/350°F/Gas Mark 4 for about 45 minutes. Brown under a hot grill before serving, if wished.

COOK'S TIP
Serve this dish with hot garlic bread and a spinach or mixed green salad.

Golden Cheese Pudding

Golden Cheese Pudding

Serves 4

600 ML (20 FL OZ) MILK
3 EGGS
4×15 ML TBS FRESHLY GRATED PARMESAN CHEESE
½×5 ML TSP CHILLI SEASONING, NOT POWDER
FRESHLY GRATED NUTMEG
SALT AND PEPPER
5 LARGE THICK SLICES WHITE CRUSTY BREAD, ABOUT 225 G (8 OZ)
BUTTER, FOR GREASING
225 G (8 OZ) GRUYÈRE OR EMMENTHAL CHEESE, GRATED
TOMATO SALAD, TO ACCOMPANY

1. Whisk together the milk, eggs, 3×15 ml tbs Parmesan, the chilli seasoning and nutmeg. Season.
2. Halve the bread slices if very big, and place half of them in a liberally buttered 2 lt (3½ pt) deep ovenproof dish. Cover with two-thirds of the Gruyère cheese and top with the remaining bread. Pour the egg and milk mixture over the top. Press the bread gently into the milk.
3. Sprinkle the remaining Gruyère cheese and Parmesan over the bread and allow to stand for at least 30 minutes to absorb most of the liquid.
4. Place in a roasting tin with enough boiling water to come halfway up the sides of the dish. Bake in the oven at 220°C/425°F/Gas Mark 7 for about 30 minutes or until puffed, set and well browned, covering loosely with foil, if necessary, to prevent overbrowning. Serve with a tomato salad.

Tarte au Chèvre et Menthe

Serves 6

175 G (6 OZ) PLAIN WHITE FLOUR
SALT AND FRESHLY GROUND BLACK PEPPER
75 G (3 OZ) BUTTER OR MARGARINE
40 G (1½ OZ) HAZELNUTS, VERY FINELY CHOPPED
3-4 × 15 ML TBS WATER
175 G (6 OZ) MILD FRESH CREAMY GOAT'S CHEESE (CHÈVRE)
300 G (10 OZ) FROMAGE FRAIS
2 EGGS
SMALL HANDFUL OF FRESH MINT LEAVES

1. Put the flour and a pinch of salt in a bowl. Rub the butter in until the mixture resembles fine breadcrumbs. Stir in the chopped hazelnuts, then add enough of the water to form a dough.
2. Roll out the pastry on a lightly floured surface and use to line a greased 23 cm (9 in) shallow, loose-bottomed, fluted flan tin. Cover and chill while making the filling.
3. To make the filling, beat the cheese until smooth. Gradually beat in the fromage frais, followed by the eggs. Season with salt and pepper.
4. Line the pastry case with foil or greaseproof paper weighed down with baking beans and bake blind in the oven at 200°C/400°F/Gas Mark 6 for 10–15 minutes, then remove the paper and beans and bake for a further 5 minutes until the pastry base is cooked through.
5. Stir the filling, then pour it into the pastry case. Sprinkle with the mint leaves and grind a little black pepper over the top. Bake in the oven at 200°C/400°F/Gas Mark 6 for about 15 minutes or until firm to the touch. Cook under a hot grill for 2-3 minutes until browned. Serve warm or cold.

COOK'S TIP

This delicately flavoured, creamy tart is delicious served for lunch with a salad, or in thinner slices as a starter, garnished with extra mint leaves.

Tarte au Chèvre et Menthe

Catalan Pie

Serves 6

175 G (6 OZ) STRONG WHITE FLOUR, PLUS EXTRA FOR SPRINKLING

50 G (2 OZ) CORNMEAL (MAIZE MEAL), PLUS EXTRA FOR SPRINKLING

1×15 ML TBS SUGAR

SALT AND PEPPER

1×5 ML TSP FAST-ACTION DRIED YEAST

ABOUT 150 ML (5 FL OZ) WARM WATER

2×15 ML TBS OLIVE OIL, PLUS EXTRA FOR BRUSHING

335 G (12 OZ) ONIONS, SKINNED AND ROUGHLY CHOPPED

2 GARLIC CLOVES, SKINNED AND CRUSHED

1×15 ML TBS MILD CHILLI POWDER

450 G (1 LB) RIPE TOMATOES, ROUGHLY CHOPPED

225 G (8 OZ) COURGETTES, TRIMMED AND ROUGHLY CHOPPED

3 HARD-BOILED EGGS, SHELLED AND CHOPPED

25 G (1 OZ) SULTANAS OR RAISINS

2×15 ML TBS CAPERS

25 G (1 OZ) CASHEW NUTS, CHOPPED

1. Put the flour, cornmeal, sugar, 1×5 ml tsp salt and the yeast in a bowl. Mix together, then make a well in the centre and add the warm water. Stir together to make a dough, adding a little extra liquid if necessary.
2. Turn the dough on to a lightly floured surface and knead for 5-10 minutes or until smooth and elastic. Cover and leave to rise in a warm place for about 35 minutes or until doubled in size.
3. Meanwhile, heat the 2×15 ml tbs olive oil in a heavy-based saucepan with a lid. Add the onions, garlic and chilli powder and cook over a high heat for 5 minutes, stirring all the time. Cover the pan, reduce the heat and cook for 15-20 minutes or until the onion is soft. Add the tomatoes and courgettes and cook for 5 minutes, stirring occasionally. If the mixture is very wet, cook over a high heat for a little longer to evaporate excess moisture. Add the eggs, sultanas or raisins, capers and nuts, season with salt and pepper, and leave to cool.
4 Turn the dough out on to a lightly floured surface and knead for 1-2 minutes. Divide it in half and roll one half into a rectangle measuring about 33×25 cm (13×10 in). Transfer the dough to an oiled baking tray and cover with the filling, spreading it almost to the edges.
5 Roll out the remaining dough to the same size and place on top of the filling. Twist the edges together to seal. Brush the pie with olive oil, cover loosely with a clean tea-towel and leave in a warm place until slightly risen.
6 Mark small indentations all over the pie with the end of a chopstick or your little finger. Sprinkle with cornmeal and bake in the oven at 230°C/450°F/Gas Mark 8 for about 20 minutes or until well risen and golden brown. Serve warm or cold.

COOK'S TIP

Before rolling out the pastry, check the size of your baking tray. If the measurements given in the recipe are too large, make a

Catalan Pie

shorter, squarer pie that will fit neatly on to your baking tray.

VARIATIONS

For a vegan version of this delicious pie, omit the eggs and replace with one of the following: 115 g (4 oz) chopped tofu; 115 g (4 oz) roughly chopped nuts; 115 g (4 oz) cooked and slightly mashed red kidney beans; 115 g (4 oz) cooked black-eyed beans.

Sweet Pepper and Basil Flan

Serves 4

SHORTCRUST PASTRY MADE WITH 175 G (6 OZ) FLOUR (SEE PAGE 212)

2 LARGE RED PEPPERS (ABOUT 335 G/12 OZ TOTAL WEIGHT)

FEW SAFFRON THREADS

150 G (5 OZ) FULL-FAT SOFT CHEESE WITH GARLIC AND HERBS

2 EGGS

2×15 ML TBS CHOPPED FRESH BASIL

1×15 ML TBS CHOPPED FRESH PARSLEY

SALT AND PEPPER

BASIL SPRIG, TO GARNISH

1. Roll out the pastry and use to line a 20 cm (8 in) plain flan ring. Bake blind (see page 212) until set and lightly browned.
2. Meanwhile, place the peppers under a hot grill for 10-15 minutes, turning frequently, until the skins are charred and black. Cool slightly, then peel off the skins. Halve the peppers and remove the seeds. Cut into 5 cm (2 in) pieces.
3. Grind the saffron with a pestle and mortar or in a small heavy bowl with the end of a rolling pin. Whisk together the cheese, eggs, herbs and saffron. Stir in the peppers and season with salt and pepper.
4. Spoon the pepper mixture into the prepared flan case. Bake in the oven at 180°C/350°F/Gas Mark 4 for 25-30 minutes or until just set. Brown under a hot grill for 1-2 minutes, if wished. Serve warm, garnished with a sprig of basil.

Wholemeal Vegetable and Herb Pie

Serves 4

90 G (3½ OZ) BUTTER

3 CARROTS, PEELED AND SLICED

40 G (1½ OZ) PLAIN WHITE FLOUR

300 ML (10 FL OZ) MILK

SALT AND PEPPER

1 SMALL CAULIFLOWER, BROKEN INTO FLORETS

115 G (4 OZ) BROCCOLI, BROKEN INTO FLORETS

50 G (2 OZ) PEARL BARLEY, COOKED

2×15 ML TBS CHOPPED FRESH PARSLEY

115 G (4 OZ) PLAIN WHOLEMEAL FLOUR

3×15 ML TBS WATER

MILK, TO GLAZE

1. Melt 40 g (1½ oz) of the butter in a medium saucepan and lightly fry the carrots for 7 minutes. Stir the white flour in and cook for 1 minute. Gradually add the milk, then cook, stirring continuously, until the sauce thickens, boils and is smooth. Simmer for 1-2 minutes. Season with salt and pepper to taste.
2. Blanch the cauliflower and broccoli in boiling salted water for 5 minutes. Drain.
3. Mix the sauce with the cauliflower, broccoli, pearl barley and parsley. Spoon into a 1.2 lt (2 pt) pie dish.
4. Put the wholemeal flour and ½×5 ml tsp salt in a bowl. Rub in the remaining 50 g (2 oz) butter until the mixture resembles fine breadcrumbs. Add the water to mix and form a dough.
5. Roll out the pastry on a lightly floured work surface to 5 cm (2 in) wider than the top of the pie dish. Cut a 2.5 cm (1 in) wide strip from the outer edge and place on the dampened rim of the dish. Brush the strip with water. Cover with the pastry lid, press the edges lightly to seal. Trim off excess pastry. Knock the edges back to seal and crimp. Decorate with pastry leaves and brush with milk.
6. Bake in the oven at 200°C/400°F/Gas Mark 6 for 30 minutes until golden.

Avocado Pie

Serves 6

225 G (8 OZ) WHOLEMEAL BREADCRUMBS

75 G (3 OZ) CASHEW NUTS, ALMONDS OR HAZELNUTS, CHOPPED

LARGE PINCH OF DRIED THYME

1 GARLIC CLOVE, SKINNED AND CRUSHED

115 G (4 OZ) BUTTER OR MARGARINE, MELTED

SALT AND PEPPER

2 LARGE RIPE AVOCADOS

1×15 ML TBS RASPBERRY VINEGAR OR LIME JUICE

1×15 ML TBS TAHINI (SESAME SEED PASTE)

½ CUCUMBER, FINELY CHOPPED

2 SALAD ONIONS, TRIMMED AND FINELY CHOPPED

2 FIRM TOMATOES, CHOPPED

1×5 ML TSP CASTER SUGAR

TABASCO OR CHILLI SAUCE, TO TASTE

A FEW BLACK OLIVES

CHOPPED FRESH CORIANDER, CHIVES, PARSLEY OR MINT

1. To make the crust, mix together the breadcrumbs, nuts, thyme, garlic and margarine or butter. Season with salt and pepper. Press over the bottom and sides of a 23 cm (9 in) flan dish or loose-bottomed flan tin. Bake in the oven at 200°C/400°F/Gas Mark 6 for 25–30 minutes or until golden and firm to the touch. Leave to cool.
2. To make the filling, halve, stone and peel the avocados and mash the flesh. Mix with all the remaining ingredients, except the olives and herbs. Spoon into the flan case and sprinkle the olives and herbs on top of the pie. Serve within 2 hours.

COOK'S TIP

The nutty, garlicky crust for this pie can be made in advance and frozen or stored in an airtight container for up to 2 days. However, the filling will discolour if left for too long, so make it no more than 2 hours before you intend to serve it.

AUBERGINE TART

Serves 6-8

— PASTRY —

225 G (8 OZ) PLAIN WHITE FLOUR

SALT AND PEPPER

1 EGG, BEATEN

4×15 ML TBS OLIVE OIL

2-3×15 ML TBS TEPID WATER

— FILLING —

2×15 ML TBS DIJON MUSTARD

275 G (10 OZ) AUBERGINES, VERY THINLY SLICED

1 SMALL GREEN PEPPER, HALVED AND SEEDED

OLIVE OIL FOR BRUSHING

3 EGG YOLKS

350 ML (12 FL 0Z) DOUBLE CREAM

1 SMALL GARLIC CLOVE, SKINNED AND CRUSHED

175 G (6 OZ) CHEDDAR CHEESE, GRATED

2 LARGE TOMATOES

A FEW BLACK OLIVES

1×15 ML TBS CHOPPED FRESH HERBS

FRESH BASIL SPRIGS AND TOMATO WEDGES, TO GARNISH

1. First make the pastry. Put the flour and a pinch of salt in a bowl. Make a well in the centre and add the egg, olive oil and tepid water. Mix vigorously with a fork or your fingers until the pastry forms a dough.
2. Knead the dough lightly, then form into a ball, cover with a damp tea-towel and leave to rest for 30 minutes.
3. Roll out the pastry on a lightly floured surface and use to line a greased shallow 28 cm (11 in) round loose-bottomed, fluted flan tin. Spread the mustard over the pastry case, cover and chill while making the filling.
4. Spread the aubergines in a single layer on an oiled baking tray. Lay the green pepper halves, cut side down, on a chopping board and cut into very fine slices. Sprinkle over the aubergine and brush with a little olive oil. Bake in the oven at 200°C/400°F/Gas Mark 6 for 20 minutes or until the vegetables are slightly softened and tinged with brown.
5. Beat together the egg yolks, cream, garlic and cheese, and season with salt and pepper. Slice the tomatoes thickly and, using a sharp knife, remove and discard the seeds.
6. Arrange the tomato slices in a single layer in the pastry case. Top with the aubergine and pepper slices and sprinkle with the olives. Carefully pour the custard mixture over the vegetables so that it just comes to the top of the pastry case. Stand the tart on a baking tray and bake in the oven at 200°C/400°F/Gas Mark 6 for 30 minutes. Sprinkle with the herbs, then continue cooking for 15-20 minutes or until the custard has set. Serve warm or cold, garnished with basil and tomato.

Aubergine Tart

MUSHROOM AND BASIL FLAN

Serves 6

115 G (4 OZ) BUTTER OR MARGARINE

225 G (8 OZ) PLAIN WHITE FLOUR

3-4×15 ML TBS WATER

3×15 ML TBS OLIVE OIL

115 G (4 OZ) ONION, SKINNED AND CHOPPED

1 SMALL GREEN PEPPER, SEEDED AND CHOPPED

1 SMALL RED PEPPER, SEEDED AND CHOPPED

225 G (8 OZ) BUTTON OR CUP MUSHROOMS, WIPED AND THICKLY SLICED

3 EGGS

150 ML (5 FL OZ) SOURED CREAM

50 G (2 OZ) FRESHLY GRATED PARMESAN CHEESE

3×15 ML TBS CHOPPED FRESH BASIL

SALT AND PEPPER

1. Cut or rub the fat into the flour. Bind to a firm dough with the water. Roll out and use to line a 25 cm (10 in) loose-based fluted flan tin. Bake blind (see page 212) until set and lightly browned.
2. Heat the oil in a frying pan, add the onion and peppers and soften.
3. Add the sliced mushrooms and cook gently for 1-2 minutes.
4. Whisk together the eggs, soured cream, half the Parmesan, the basil and seasoning. Stir in the cooled mushrooms and then spoon into the cooked flan case. Sprinkle with the remaining cheese.
5. Bake in the oven at 180°C/350°F/Gas Mark 4 for about 25-35 minutes or until set and tinged with colour. Serve warm.

BEAN AND POTATO PIE

Serves 6

450 G (1 LB) FLOURY POTATOES (SUCH AS KING EDWARD OR MARIS PIPER), PEELED AND ROUGHLY CUT UP

SALT AND PEPPER

2×15 ML TBS VEGETABLE OIL

1 LARGE ONION, SKINNED AND CHOPPED

450 G (1 LB) LEEKS, TRIMMED, WASHED AND SLICED

225 G (8 OZ) MUSHROOMS, WIPED AND SLICED

115 G (4 OZ) FRESH SPINACH, TRIMMED AND WASHED

150 G (5 OZ) FULL-FAT SOFT CHEESE WITH GARLIC AND HERBS

225 G (8 OZ) COOKED BLACK-EYED BEANS OR 1×430 G CAN BLACK-EYED BEANS, DRAINED AND RINSED

FRESHLY GRATED NUTMEG

2×340 G PACKETS CHILLED PUFF PASTRY

WATER, MILK OR BEATEN EGG, TO GLAZE

SESAME SEEDS

1. Cook the potatoes in boiling salted water for 10-15 minutes or until tender. Drain well and leave to cool.
2. Meanwhile, heat the oil in a large saucepan, add the onion and leeks and fry for 5-10 minutes or until soft. Add the mushrooms and continue cooking until the mushrooms are soft. Add the spinach and cook for 1 minute or until the spinach has just wilted. Add the soft cheese, the beans and potatoes and season generously with salt, pepper and nutmeg. Leave to cool.
3. Thinly roll out one packet of pastry on a lightly floured surface to a rectangle measuring about 33×25 cm (13×10 in). Transfer the pastry to a baking tray.
4. Spoon the filling on to the pastry, leaving a 2.5 cm (1 in) border around the edges. Roll out the second piece of pastry and use to cover the first. Brush the edges with water, milk or beaten egg and press together to seal. Lightly mark squares on the pastry with the back of a knife. Brush with milk or beaten egg and sprinkle with sesame seeds. Bake in the oven at 200°C/400°F/Gas Mark 6 for 30–35 minutes or until well risen and golden brown.

Cheese and Leek Tart

Serves 4

175 G (6 OZ) PLAIN WHITE FLOUR

SALT AND PEPPER

115 G (4 OZ) BUTTER

1×5 ML TSP PARMESAN CHEESE

2 EGGS AND 1 EGG YOLK

2×15 ML TBS WATER

1×15 ML TBS VEGETABLE OIL

450 G (1 LB) LEEKS, TRIMMED, WASHED AND CUT INTO THIN RINGS

PINCH OF NUTMEG

75 G (3 OZ) CAMEMBERT, RINDED AND ROUGHLY CHOPPED OR MASHED

150 ML (5 FL OZ) SINGLE CREAM

50 ML (2 FL OZ) MILK

1. Place the flour and salt in a bowl. Rub in 75 g (3 oz) butter, cut into small pieces, until the mixture resembles fine breadcrumbs. Stir the Parmesan cheese in. Bind with the egg yolk and water. Knead lightly, then wrap and chill for about 15 minutes.
2. Meanwhile, heat the remaining butter and oil in a large sauté pan, and add the leeks and nutmeg. Cover and cook gently for about 10 minutes, or until the leeks have softened but not coloured; cool.
3. Roll out the pastry on a lightly floured surface and use to line a 20 cm (8 in) flan ring, placed on a baking tray. Chill for 15 minutes, then bake blind (see page 212) in the oven at 200°C/400°F/Gas Mark 6 for 12 minutes or until set but not browned.
4. Place the Camembert in a bowl with the cream and whisk until almost smooth. Whisk in the eggs and milk and season well. Using a slotted spoon, pile the leeks into the baked flan case then pour the custard mixture over the top. Bake in the oven at 180°C/350°F/Gas Mark 4 for about 35 minutes or until just set. Stand for about 10 minutes before serving.

COOK'S TIP

Butter gives a wonderful flavour to the pastry. Polyunsaturated margarine can be used but cut it in with a fork rather than rubbing in by hand.

Cheese and Leek Tart

Mushroom Strudels

Serves 8

225 G (8 OZ) LONG-GRAIN BROWN RICE

SALT AND PEPPER

450 G (1 LB) MIXED MUSHROOMS, SUCH AS SHIITAKE, FLAT AND BUTTON

65 G (2½ OZ) MARGARINE OR BUTTER

450 G (1 LB) LEEKS, TRIMMED, WASHED AND FINELY CHOPPED

65 G (2½ OZ) WALNUT PIECES, FINELY CHOPPED

2×5 ML TSP CHOPPED FRESH OREGANO

4×5 ML TSP SOY SAUCE

1×5 ML TSP YEAST EXTRACT

8 SHEETS OF FILO PASTRY, EACH MEASURING ABOUT 23×30 CM (9×12 IN)

SESAME SEEDS

1. Cook the rice in boiling salted water for about 20 minutes or until tender. Drain and cool. Finely chop the mushrooms.
2. Melt 25 g (1 oz) of the margarine or butter in a large frying pan. Add the leeks and fry for 1-2 minutes. Stir the mushrooms in and continue cooking for about 8 minutes or until they are quite tender and all excess moisture has been driven off. Mix in the walnuts, oregano, soy sauce, yeast extract and rice. Season with salt and pepper, transfer to a bowl and leave to cool.
3. Melt the remaining margarine or butter. Layer up three sheets of pastry, brushing each sheet with melted margarine or butter. Repeat with another stack of three sheets.
4. Spoon the filling over the two stacks of sheets, leaving a narrow border around the edge of each. Fold in the sides and roll up the strudels. Transfer to a lightly greased baking tray and brush with melted margarine or butter. Crumple the remaining pastry decoratively on top, brush with the remaining margarine or butter and sprinkle with sesame seeds.
5. Bake in the oven at 220°C/425°F/Gas Mark 7 for 25-30 minutes or until the pastry is crisp and golden

Mushroom Strudels

Rice, Grains and Pasta

Rice and pasta are cheap, nutritious and extremely versatile. They can be served as accompaniments to other dishes or used as the main ingredient with meat and fish or in a vegetarian dish. Also included in this chapter are recipes using couscous, which is widely used in Middle Eastern cooking, and egg noodles, which are a staple ingredient in both Japanese and Chinese cooking.

Top left: Vegetable Biryani (page 137)
Bottom left: Penne with Tomatoes and Chilli (page 139)
Right: Pasta with Mushroom Sauce (page 139)

Risotto Castles

Serves 6

— RISOTTO —

115 G (4 OZ) ONION OR SHALLOTS, PEELED AND FINELY CHOPPED

2×15 ML TBS OLIVE OIL

225 G (8 OZ) ARBORIO (RISOTTO) RICE

115 G ML (4 FL OZ) DRY WHITE WINE OR VERMOUTH

750 ML (1¼ PT) CHICKEN STOCK (SEE PAGE 13)

SALT AND PEPPER

50 G (2 OZ) FRESHLY GRATED PARMESAN CHEESE

2 EGGS, BEATEN

BUTTER FOR GREASING

3×15 ML TBS DRY WHITE BREADCRUMBS

115 G (4 OZ) REBLOCHON CHEESE (OR TALEGGIO, PONT L'EVÊQUE, OR CAMEMBERT), RINDED AND CUT INTO 6 CUBES

— TOMATO SAUCE —

2×15 ML TBS OLIVE OIL

450 G (1 LB) FRESH, VERY RIPE TOMATOES, SKINNED AND DICED

2×15 ML TBS WHITE WINE

2×15 ML TBS CHOPPED FRESH BASIL OR DILL OR 1×5 ML TSP DRIED DILL WEED

1. Soften the onion in the oil in a non-stick saucepan. Add the rice and wine, bring to the boil and cook, stirring, until the wine is absorbed. Add the hot stock, 150 ml (5 fl oz) at a time, and cook over a medium heat, stirring often, until all the stock is absorbed. Season well and stir in the Parmesan. Cool; add the eggs.
2. Butter six 150 ml (5 fl oz) ramekin dishes; dust out with breadcrumbs.
3. Line the bottom and sides of the ramekins with risotto. Place a cube of cheese in the centre and top with the remaining risotto, packing down well. Cover with greased foil. Place the ramekins on a baking tray. Bake in the oven at 220°C/425°F/ Gas Mark 7 for 20-25 minutes or until firm to the touch and slightly puffed up.
4. Meanwhile, prepare the sauce. Heat the oil in a saucepan, add the tomatoes and wine and cook over a high heat for 2-3 minutes. Stir in the basil; season.
5. Cool the castles for 5-10 minutes, then turn out and serve with the sauce.

COOK'S TIP

Italian Arborio rice is a fat grained rice that produces a thick, creamy risotto. You can use long-grain or pudding rice, but give them longer to absorb the liquid in step 1 and don't expect such a creamy finish.

Risotto Castles

Mushroom Risotto

Serves 4

ABOUT 1.5 LT (2½ PT) VEGETABLE STOCK (SEE PAGE 13)

115 G (4 OZ) BUTTER OR MARGARINE

1 ONION, SKINNED AND VERY FINELY CHOPPED

1 GARLIC CLOVE, SKINNED AND CRUSHED

225 G (8 OZ) MUSHROOMS, WIPED AND SLICED

335 G (12 OZ) ARBORIO (RISOTTO) RICE

50 G (2 OZ) FRESHLY GRATED PARMESAN CHEESE

SALT AND PEPPER

1. Put the stock in a large saucepan and bring to the boil. Reduce the heat and keep at barely simmering point.
2. Meanwhile, melt half the butter in a large heavy-based saucepan. Add the onion and garlic, and cook for about 5 minutes or until soft. Do not let them burn.
3. Add the mushrooms to the onion and garlic and cook for 3-4 minutes, stirring all the time. Add the rice and cook for 1 minute.
4. Slowly pour on about one-third of the stock. Cook gently, stirring occasionally, until the stock has been absorbed. Continue cooking and adding more stock, using a ladle, as soon as each addition has been absorbed, stirring frequently. You may not need all the stock, but continue cooking for about 20 minutes or until the rice is soft. Then add three-quarters of the Parmesan cheese, with the remaining butter, and season with salt and pepper. Serve sprinkled with the remaining Parmesan.

VARIATIONS

Pea and Saffron Risotto

Omit the mushrooms. Shell 675 g (1½ lb) fresh peas. Soak a large pinch of saffron threads in a little of the warm stock for about 10 minutes. Add to the onions in step 3 with 150 ml (5 fl oz) dry white wine and the peas. Continue as above. Alternatively, use 335 g (12 oz) frozen petits pois and add them about 5 minutes before the end of the cooking time.

Asparagus Risotto

Cook as for Pea and Saffron Risotto, but substitute 225 g (8 oz) asparagus tips for the peas. Steam until just tender and stir into the risotto 5 minutes before the end of the cooking time.

Almond and Courgette Risotto

Cook as Pea and Saffron Risotto, but substitute 450 g (1 lb) courgettes, trimmed and thinly sliced, for the peas. Add them about 5 minutes before the end of the cooking time with 3×15 ml tbs ground almonds. Continue as above but omit the cheese. Serve the risotto sprinkled with toasted flaked almonds and sesame seeds.

Sesame Pilaff with Fennel

Serves 4

4×15 ML TBS SESAME SEEDS

175 G (6 OZ) FENNEL, TRIMMED AND FINELY CHOPPED, RESERVING THE FEATHERY TOPS

50 G (2 OZ) BUTTER OR MARGARINE

1 ONION, SKINNED AND FINELY CHOPPED

1 LARGE GREEN PEPPER, SEEDED AND CHOPPED

PINCH OF GROUND TURMERIC

335 (12 OZ) ARBORIO (RISOTTO) RICE

ABOUT 1.3 LT (2¼ PT) VEGETABLE STOCK (SEE PAGE 13)

SALT AND PEPPER

1. Toast the sesame seeds under a hot grill until golden brown, then leave to cool. Finely chop the fennel tops and set aside.
2. Melt the butter or margarine in a saucepan and add the onion, pepper, fennel and turmeric. Fry for 2-3 minutes or until beginning to soften, stirring constantly. Stir the rice in and continue to cook, stirring, for 1 minute, then add the stock and toasted sesame seeds. Season with salt and pepper.
3. Bring to the boil, cover and simmer very slowly for about 45 minutes or until all the liquid has been absorbed and the rice is tender. Stir in the fennel tops and serve.

COOK'S TIP

If fennel is not available, use only 1.2 lt (2 pt) stock and stir in 2×15 ml tbs chopped fresh parsley or salad onion tops just before serving. It's important to use Arborio rice as it soaks up the liquid, becoming plump and tender rather than mushy.

Lamb and Rosemary Pilaff

Serves 4

3×15 ML TBS VEGETABLE OIL

450 G (1 LB) LEAN BONELESS LAMB, CUT INTO SMALL CUBES

1×15 ML TBS DRIED ROSEMARY

225 G (8 OZ) ONIONS, SKINNED AND SLICED

225 G (8 OZ) LONG-GRAIN BROWN RICE

750 ML (25 FL OZ) BEEF STOCK (SEE PAGE 13)

SALT AND PEPPER

225 G (8 OZ) COURGETTES, TRIMMED AND CUT INTO FAT STICKS

75 G (3 OZ) NO-SOAK DRIED APRICOTS, SLICED

LEMON SLICES, TO GARNISH

1. Heat the oil in a medium-sized flameproof casserole. Add the meat and rosemary and fry together over a high heat until the meat is beginning to brown. Remove from the pan.
2. Add the onion and lightly brown. Rinse and drain the rice then stir into the pan with the stock and seasoning.
3. Replace the meat, cover the pan and simmer for about 25 minutes. Stir the courgettes and the apricots into the casserole.
4. Cover again and simmer for a further 15-20 minutes, or until most of the liquid is absorbed and the meat is quite tender. Adjust seasoning and serve garnished with lemon slices.

COOK'S TIP

Letting the rice absorb the juices as it cooks gives this dish a slightly stodgy finished appearance but a delicious flavour.

Almond and Sesame Pilaff

Serves 6-8

50 G (2 OZ) BUTTER OR MARGARINE

50 G (2 OZ) SALAD ONIONS, TRIMMED AND ROUGHLY CHOPPED

450 G (1 LB) LONG-GRAIN BROWN RICE

800 ML (1 PT 7 FL OZ) CHICKEN STOCK (SEE PAGE 13)

2 BAY LEAVES

SALT AND PEPPER

50 G (2 OZ) TOASTED FLAKED ALMONDS

2×15 ML TBS TOASTED SESAME SEEDS

1. Melt half the butter in a shallow, flameproof casserole. Sauté the salad onions for 2-3 minutes. Stir the rice in and continue to cook for 1 minute before adding the stock, bay leaves and seasoning.
2. Bring to the boil, cover tightly and cook in the oven at 180°C/350°F/Gas Mark 4 for about 35-40 minutes or until the rice is tender and all the liquid absorbed.
3. Stir in the remaining butter, almonds and sesame seeds, remove bay leaves and adjust seasoning before serving.

Perfect Pilaff

Serves 4

335 G (12 OZ) LAMB'S LIVER, CUT INTO FINE STRIPS

2×15 ML TBS VEGETABLE OIL

175 G (6 OZ) ONION, SKINNED AND SLICED

1 GREEN PEPPER, SEEDED AND THINLY SLICED

2×15 ML TBS SUNFLOWER SEEDS

225 G (8 OZ) LONG-GRAIN WHITE RICE

ABOUT 450 ML (15 FL OZ) VEGETABLE STOCK (SEE PAGE 13)

2×15 ML TBS LEMON JUICE

1 GARLIC CLOVE, SKINNED AND CRUSHED

SALT AND PEPPER

CHOPPED FRESH PARSLEY

SLICED TOMATO AND ONION SALAD, TO ACCOMPANY

1. Brown the liver quickly in the hot oil in a large, flameproof casserole or heavy-based sauté pan. Lift out of the pan using a slotted spoon; drain on absorbent kitchen paper.
2. Add the onion and pepper to the pan together with the sunflower seeds and stir-fry for 1-2 minutes.
3. Mix the rice in followed by the stock, lemon juice, garlic and seasoning. Bring to the boil; cover tightly and simmer for 10 minutes.
4. Stir the liver in, re-cover and simmer for about 5 minutes longer, or until the rice is tender and most of the liquid is absorbed. Adjust seasoning and stir in plenty of chopped parsley to serve. Accompany with a sliced tomato and onion salad.

Perfect Pilaff

Fragrant Saffron Pilaff

Serves 6

335 G (12 OZ) BASMATI RICE

4×15 ML TBS VEGETABLE OIL

225 G (8 OZ) BUTTON MUSHROOMS, WIPED AND SLICED

3 CLOVES

6 GREEN CARDAMOM PODS

1 STICK CINNAMON

½×5 ML TSP SAFFRON THREADS

2×5 ML TSP CASTER SUGAR

SALT AND PEPPER

1. Wash the rice in several changes of cold water. Place in a bowl, add 1 lt (1¾ pt) cold water and soak for 30 minutes. Drain and set aside.
2. Heat the oil in a large pan. Add the mushrooms, cloves, cardamom pods, cinnamon and rice. Stir over the heat for 1-2 minutes.
3. Add 600 ml (20 fl oz) cold water, the saffron, sugar and seasoning. Bring to the boil, stirring. Reduce the heat, cover tightly and cook very gently for about 15 minutes or until all the liquid is absorbed and the rice is tender.
4. Adjust seasoning and fluff the rice with a fork before serving.

Basmati Pilaff

Serves 8

450 G (1 LB) EASY-COOK BASMATI RICE, WASHED

8 CARDAMOM PODS, SPLIT

8 BLACK PEPPERCORNS

6 WHOLE CLOVES

2.5 CM (1 IN) STICK CINNAMON

1×15 ML TBS CUMIN SEEDS

3×15 ML TBS VEGETABLE OIL

1 LARGE ONION, SKINNED AND FINELY CHOPPED

2×5 ML TSP TURMERIC

3 BAY LEAVES, TORN IN PIECES

SALT AND PEPPER

75 G (3 OZ) SHELLED PISTACHIO NUTS, ROUGHLY CHOPPED

50 G (2 OZ) RAISINS (OPTIONAL)

1. Put the rice in a bowl, cover with cold water and leave to soak for 30 minutes. Drain off the water, transfer the rice to a sieve and rinse under cold running water until the water runs clear.
2. Put the cardamom pods, peppercorns, cloves, cinnamon stick and cumin seeds in a large, heavy flameproof casserole and dry fry over moderate heat for 2-3 minutes, stirring all the time until they pop and release their flavour. Add the oil and stir until hot, then add the onion and turmeric and cook gently, stirring frequently, for 10 minutes until the onion is softened.
3. Add the rice and stir until coated in the spiced onion mixture, then slowly pour in 1.2 lt (2 pt) boiling water. (Take care as the water may sizzle and splash.) Add the bay leaves and salt and pepper to taste, bring to the boil and stir well. Lower the heat, cover and cook very gently for 15 minutes, without lifting the lid. Remove from the heat and leave to stand for 15 minutes.
4. Uncover the rice, add half the pistachio nuts and raisins, if using, and gently fork through, to fluff up the grains. Taste and adjust seasoning. Spoon the pilaff on to a warmed serving platter, moulding it up in the centre, then sprinkle the remaining pistachios over the top. Serve hot.

COOK'S TIP

For a luxurious touch, you can fork a good-sized knob of butter into the pilaff at the same time as the pistachios.

Prawns and Rice with Dill

Serves 4

175 G (6 OZ) LONG-GRAIN BROWN RICE

SALT AND PEPPER

450 G (1 LB) RAW PRAWNS, IN THEIR SHELLS

2×15 ML TBS SUNFLOWER OIL

1 LARGE BULB FENNEL, TRIMMED AND THINLY SLICED

2 LARGE COURGETTES, TRIMMED AND DICED

150 ML (5 FL OZ) FISH OR VEGETABLE STOCK (SEE PAGE 13)

25 G (1 OZ) BUTTER OR MARGARINE

2×15 ML TBS CHOPPED FRESH DILL

1 GARLIC CLOVE, SKINNED AND CRUSHED

1. Cook the rice in boiling salted water for about 30 minutes or until tender. Rinse with boiling water and drain well.
2. Meanwhile, peel the prawns, cut down their backs and remove the black vein. Wash well and dry on absorbent kitchen paper. Halve, or divide into three if large.
3. Heat 1 × 15 ml tbs of the oil in a frying pan. Add the prawns and stir-fry until they have turned pink. Remove from the pan.
4. Heat the remaining oil in the pan. Add the fennel and stir-fry for 2-3 minutes until slightly softened. Mix the courgettes in and stir-fry briefly. Stir in the rice and seasoning and heat through thoroughly, stirring.
5. Return the prawns to the pan with the stock and bring to the boil. Cover the pan and cook gently for about 3-4 minutes, or until the prawns are cooked and just firm.
6. Adjust seasoning. Just before serving, stir in the butter, dill and garlic.

Thai Fried Rice

Serves 8

450 G (1 LB) BASMATI RICE

SALT

75 ML (3 FL OZ) VEGETABLE OIL

1×15 ML TBS NAM PLA FISH SAUCE

2 HOT CHILLIES, CHOPPED

4 SALAD ONIONS, CHOPPED

3 EGGS, BEATEN (OPTIONAL)

2×15 ML TBS SOY SAUCE

2×5 ML TSP BROWN SUGAR

FRESH CORIANDER SPRIG, TO GARNISH

1. Cook the rice, following the packet instructions, until almost tender. Drain, then rinse with boiling water. Spread out on a tray and leave to cool.
2. Heat the oil in a wok, then add the fish sauce, chillies and onions and stir-fry for 1-2 minutes to flavour the oil.
3. Add the eggs, if using, and stir-fry until the egg scrambles, stirring all the time so that the egg sets in small pieces.
4. Stir the rice with a fork to separate the grains, then tip into the hot oil. Stir-fry with the eggs for 5-8 minutes until really hot (the time will depend on whether the rice was cold or warm before stir-frying). Mix the soy sauce with the sugar, then stir into the rice. Serve immediately, garnished with a sprig of coriander.

Thai Fried Rice

Special Fried Rice

Serves 8

450 G (1 LB) LONG-GRAIN WHITE RICE

SALT AND PEPPER

3-4×15 ML TBS VEGETABLE OIL

3 CARROTS, PEELED AND COARSELY GRATED

2 GARLIC CLOVES, SKINNED AND CRUSHED

115 G (4 OZ) FROZEN PEELED PRAWNS, THAWED

175 G (6 OZ) FROZEN PEAS, THAWED

175 G (6 OZ) FRESH BEANSPROUTS, SOAKED IN COLD WATER FOR 10 MINUTES AND DRAINED BEFORE USING

3×15 ML TBS LIGHT SOY SAUCE

1 BUNCH OF SALAD ONIONS, THINLY SLICED DIAGONALLY

1-2×5 ML TSP SESAME OIL

1. Cook the rice, following the packet instructions, until almost tender. Drain, then rinse with boiling water. Spread out on a large tray and leave to cool.
2. Just before serving, heat the oil in a wok or large frying pan (you may need to do this in two batches). Add the carrots and garlic and stir-fry for 2 minutes. Add the prawns, peas and beansprouts and stir-fry for 1 minute. Stir in the rice and stir-fry for 3 minutes. Stir in the soy sauce and seasoning, to taste, and the salad onions: remove from heat and place in a serving dish. Sprinkle with the sesame oil and serve at once.

Nasi Goreng

Serves 4

50 ML (2 FL OZ) VEGETABLE OIL

115 G (4 OZ) ONION, SKINNED AND CHOPPED

1 RED CHILLI, SEEDED AND CHOPPED

1 GARLIC CLOVE, SKINNED AND CRUSHED

450 G (1 LB) MIXTURE OF PRAWNS, CHOPPED COOKED CHICKEN OR HAM, TOASTED CASHEW NUTS AND WIPED, SLICED MUSHROOMS

175 G (6 OZ) RICE, BOILED

2×15 ML TBS SOY SAUCE

2×5 ML TSP SOFT LIGHT BROWN SUGAR

SALT AND PEPPER

SLICED CUCUMBER AND CHOPPED CORIANDER, TO GARNISH

1. Heat the oil in a large frying pan or wok. Add the onion, chilli and garlic and stir-fry for 2 minutes.
2. Add the mix of prawns, chicken or ham, toasted cashews and mushrooms, and stir well.
3. Add the rice, soy sauce, sugar and seasoning. Stir-fry for another 4-5 minutes or until heated through, adding more oil if necessary.
4. Serve immediately, garnished with sliced cucumber and chopped coriander.

COOK'S TIP

This fried rice dish makes an ideal supper on its own, or is delicious served as an accompaniment.

VEGETABLE BIRYANI

Serves 4

335 G (12 OZ) BASMATI RICE
SALT AND PEPPER
50 G (2 OZ) BUTTER
1 LARGE ONION, SKINNED AND CHOPPED
2.5 CM (1 IN) PIECE OF FRESH ROOT GINGER, PEELED AND GRATED
1-2 GARLIC CLOVES, SKINNED AND CRUSHED
1×5 ML TSP GROUND CORIANDER
2×5 ML TSP GROUND CUMIN
1×5 ML TSP GROUND TURMERIC
½×5 ML TSP CHILLI POWDER
3 CARROTS, TRIMMED, PEELED AND THINLY SLICED
225 G (8 OZ) FRENCH BEANS, TRIMMED AND HALVED
225 G (8 OZ) SMALL CAULIFLOWER FLORETS
1×5 ML TSP GARAM MASALA
JUICE OF 1 LEMON
HARD-BOILED EGG SLICES, LEMON WEDGES AND CORIANDER SPRIGS, TO GARNISH

1. Put the rice in a sieve and rinse under running cold water until the water runs clear.
2. Put the rice in a saucepan with 600 ml (20 fl oz) water and 1×5 ml tsp salt. Bring to the boil, then reduce the heat and simmer for 10 minutes or until only just tender.
3. Meanwhile, melt the butter in a large heavy-based saucepan, add the onion, ginger and garlic and fry gently for 5 minutes or until soft but not coloured. Add the coriander, cumin, turmeric and chilli powder and fry for 2 minutes more, stirring constantly to prevent the spices catching and burning.
4. Remove the rice from the heat and drain. Add 900 ml (1½ pt) water to the onion and spice mixture and season with salt and pepper. Stir well and bring to the boil. Add the carrots and beans and simmer for 15 minutes, then add the cauliflower and simmer for a further 10 minutes. Lastly, add the rice. Fold gently to mix and simmer until reheated.
5. Stir the garam masala and lemon juice into the biryani and simmer for a few minutes more to reheat and allow the flavours to develop. Taste and adjust the seasoning, if necessary, then place in a warmed serving dish. Garnish with egg slices, lemon wedges and coriander. Serve immediately.

VEGETABLE COUSCOUS

Serves 6

115 G (4 OZ) CHICK-PEAS, SOAKED OVERNIGHT IN COLD WATER
335 G (12 OZ) COUSCOUS (NOT PRE-COOKED)
115 G (4 OZ) BUTTER OR MARGARINE
2 MEDIUM LEEKS, WASHED, TRIMMED AND THICKLY SLICED
1 CARROT, TRIMMED, PEELED AND THICKLY SLICED
1 PARSNIP, TRIMMED, PEELED AND ROUGHLY CHOPPED
225 G (8 OZ) SWEDE, PEELED AND ROUGHLY CHOPPED
1×5 ML TSP GROUND CUMIN
1×5 ML TSP GROUND CORIANDER
½×5 ML TSP PAPRIKA
1.2 LT (2 PT) VEGETABLE STOCK (SEE PAGE 13)
2×15 ML TBS TOMATO PURÉE
CHILLI SAUCE, TO TASTE
SALT AND PEPPER
1 RED PEPPER, SEEDED AND DICED
1 GREEN PEPPER, SEEDED AND DICED
450 G (1 LB) TOMATOES, SKINNED AND QUARTERED
225 G (8 OZ) COURGETTES, TRIMMED AND SLICED
1 SMALL CAULIFLOWER, DIVIDED INTO FLORETS
CHOPPED FRESH PARSLEY, TO GARNISH

1. Drain the chick-peas and rinse well in cold water. Put in a large saucepan, cover with fresh water, bring to the boil and boil rapidly for 10 minutes. Continue to cook, for 1 hour in all. Drain well.
2. Place the couscous in a bowl and pour 200 ml (7 fl oz) warm water over. Work the water into the couscous with your fingertips, using a 'rubbing-in' motion to ensure all the grains are separate. Leave to stand for 15 minutes, then repeat the process twice more, using a total of 600 ml (20 fl oz) water.
3. Melt half the butter or margarine in a large saucepan with a capacity of at least 4.2 lt (7 pt), over which a perforated steamer will fit snugly. Add the leeks, carrot, parsnip and swede and sprinkle the spices over the top. Fry gently until lightly browned, then add the chick-peas with the stock, tomato purée and chilli sauce. Season with salt and pepper and bring to the boil.
4. Line a steamer with a double thickness of muslin and spoon the couscous in, seasoning well with salt and pepper. Place over the vegetables and cover the steamer tightly. Bring the vegetables to a fast boil, then lower the heat and simmer gently for about 30 minutes.
5. Take the pan and steamer off the heat and spoon the couscous into a large bowl. Cut the remaining margarine or butter into small pieces and add to the couscous. Stir well until the butter has melted and every grain is separate. Season again, if necessary.
6. Add the remaining prepared vegetables to the pan and stir well. Add a little extra chilli sauce, if liked. Return to the heat and bring slowly to the boil. Spoon the couscous back into the lined steamer and place over the pan. Cover the steamer tightly, lower the heat and simmer for another 15 minutes.
7. Turn the couscous into a dish and fork through. Serve the vegetable mixture separately, sprinkled with parsley.

COOK'S TIP

Couscous is traditionally served with a fiery hot sauce called Harissa sauce which is made from red peppers and chillies flavoured with garlic and spices.

Mushroom Fricassée

Mushroom Fricassée

Serves 2

150 ML (5 FL OZ) WATER
115 G (4 OZ) COUSCOUS
GRATED RIND AND JUICE OF 1 LEMON
SALT AND PEPPER
75 G (3 OZ) BUTTER OR MARGARINE
225-275 G (8-10 OZ) FLAT OR CUP MUSHROOMS, WIPED AND SLICED
2×5 ML TSP PLAIN FLOUR
150 ML (5 FL OZ) MILK
2×5 ML TSP DIJON MUSTARD
50 G (2 OZ) CASHEW NUTS
PARSLEY AND LEMON WEDGES, TO GARNISH

1. Bring the water to the boil and pour over the couscous. Add lemon rind and salt and pepper, then leave to soak for 5 minutes.
2. Heat 50 g (2 oz) of the butter in a frying pan and quickly fry the mushrooms until just beginning to soften.
3. Stir in the flour and milk and bring to the boil. Cook for 1-2 minutes, adding a little more milk if it is too thick. Remove from the heat and stir in the mustard and 1 × 5 ml tsp lemon juice. Adjust the seasoning.
4. Meanwhile, heat the remaining butter in a separate frying pan. Add the cashew nuts and couscous and cook over a high heat, stirring occasionally, until piping hot. Season and serve with the mushrooms, garnished with parsley and lemon wedges.

COOK'S TIP

Couscous is produced by moistening grains of semolina and forming them into tiny pellets. It's a staple food in North African countries, where it is served with a meat or vegetable stew. The couscous grains are steamed above the stew in a *couscousière* or steamer.

Flat mushrooms give a delicious flavour to this fricassée, but can make the sauce very dark – a half-and-half mixture of cup and flat mushrooms is best.

HOT NOODLES WITH SESAME DRESSING

Serves 6

335 G (12 OZ) CHINESE EGG NOODLES

SALT AND PEPPER

1 SMALL GREEN CHILLI, SEEDED AND FINELY CHOPPED

3×15 ML TBS TOASTED SESAME SEEDS

3×15 ML TBS VEGETABLE OIL

2×15 ML TBS SESAME OIL

1 GARLIC CLOVE, SKINNED AND CRUSHED

4×15 ML TBS SOY SAUCE

4×15 ML TBS CHOPPED, FRESH CORIANDER OR PARSLEY

1. Cook the noodles in boiling salted water, according to the packet instructions.
2. Meanwhile, mix together all the remaining ingredients except the coriander.
3. Drain the noodles well and toss in the sesame dressing and the coriander. Adjust the seasoning and serve immediately.

PENNE WITH TOMATO AND CHILLI

Serves 4

2×15 ML TBS OLIVE OIL

2 CELERY STICKS, TRIMMED AND FINELY CHOPPED

1 SMALL CARROT, TRIMMED, PEELED AND FINELY CHOPPED

1 ONION, SKINNED AND FINELY CHOPPED

1-2 GARLIC CLOVES, SKINNED AND CRUSHED

2×15 ML TBS TOMATO PURÉE

1×5 ML TSP DRIED HERBS

1-2 FRESH RED CHILLIES, SEEDED AND CHOPPED

2×400 G CANS CHOPPED TOMATOES

150 ML (5 FL OZ) DRY RED WINE OR VEGETABLE STOCK (SEE PAGE 13)

A HANDFUL OF FRESH PARSLEY (INCLUDING SOME STALKS), CHOPPED

SALT AND PEPPER

450 G (1 LB) DRIED PENNE

FRESH BASIL SPRIGS AND SHAVINGS OF PARMESAN CHEESE, TO GARNISH

1. Heat the oil in a large heavy-based saucepan. Add the celery, carrot, onion and garlic and cook over a high heat for 2-3 minutes, stirring all the time. Lower the heat and continue cooking for about 5 minutes or until the vegetables are beginning to soften without browning.
2. Add the tomato purée, dried herbs and chillies, increase the heat and fry for 1-2 minutes. Add the tomatoes, red wine or stock and half the parsley. Season with salt and pepper and bring to the boil, then lower the heat, cover and simmer for 45 minutes.
3. Cook the pasta in boiling salted water until just tender.
4. While the pasta is cooking, remove the lid from the sauce, increase the heat and cook vigorously until it is reduced and thickened. Add the remaining parsley, taste and adjust the seasoning, if necessary.
5. Drain the pasta and tip it into the sauce. Toss together to mix and serve immediately, garnished with basil and shavings of Parmesan cheese.

COOK'S TIP

This simple sauce is equally delicious if made in advance, cooled and then reheated when required. It is also good served with baked potatoes, nut roasts, burgers or a different type of pasta. Should you need to make it in a hurry, from store cupboard ingredients, some or all of the vegetables may be omitted.

PASTA WITH MUSHROOM SAUCE

Serves 2

1×15 ML TBS OLIVE OIL

1 GARLIC CLOVE, SKINNED AND FINELY CHOPPED

4×15 ML TBS CHOPPED FRESH PARSLEY

225 G (8 OZ) FRESH MUSHROOMS, SUCH AS SHIITAKE, OYSTER, CHESTNUT, FLAT OR CLOSED CUP, ROUGHLY CHOPPED OR BROKEN

SALT AND FRESHLY GROUND BLACK PEPPER

200 G CARTON LOW-FAT FROMAGE FRAIS

250 G PACKET FRESH PASTA

SPRIGS OF FRESH PARSLEY, TO GARNISH

GRATED PARMESAN CHEESE (OPTIONAL)

TOMATO SALAD, TO ACCOMPANY

1. Heat the oil in a large non-stick frying pan. Add the garlic and parsley and cook for 1 minute, stirring all the time. Add the mushrooms and pepper and cook for 2-3 minutes, stirring frequently. As soon as the mushrooms have released their juice, turn the heat up to high and cook for a further 3 minutes, stirring frequently. Remove from the heat and stir in the fromage frais.
2. Meanwhile, in a large saucepan, cook the pasta in boiling salted water. Drain well.
3. Serve pasta immediately, topped with the sauce, reheated, if necessary. Garnish with parsley and sprinkle with Parmesan cheese, if liked. Serve with a tomato salad.

NOODLES WITH FRIED EGGS

Serves 2

115-175 G (4-6 OZ) FINE EGG NOODLES

SALT

2×15 ML TBS SESAME OIL

1 ONION, SKINNED AND SLICED

1 LARGE CARROT, TRIMMED, PEELED AND VERY THINLY SLICED

1 SMALL GARLIC CLOVE, SKINNED AND CRUSHED

ABOUT 3 LARGE CHINESE LEAVES OR A HANDFUL OF SPINACH, WASHED AND ROUGHLY CHOPPED

3×15 ML TBS LIGHT SOY SAUCE

1×5 ML TSP SUGAR

1×15 ML TBS WHITE WINE VINEGAR

VEGETABLE OIL FOR FRYING

2 EGGS

1. Cook the noodles according to the packet instructions.
2. Meanwhile, heat the sesame oil in a large frying pan. Add the onion, carrot and garlic and fry over a very high heat until tinged with brown and softened, stirring all the time. Add the Chinese leaves or spinach and the soy sauce, sugar and vinegar, reduce the heat and simmer very gently while cooking the eggs.
3. Heat a little vegetable oil in a frying pan and fry the eggs. Meanwhile, drain the noodles and stir into the vegetable mixture, tossing everything together to mix.
4. Divide the noodles between two plates and top each portion with an egg. Serve immediately.

Salads and Vegetable Accompaniments

The variety of vegetables available in supermarkets has never been greater than it is today. New varieties are constantly being introduced to provide a diverse range of colours, shapes and sizes – including an increasing number of very appealing baby vegetables – all perfect for using in the delicious selection of salads and vegetable accompaniments in this chapter.

Top left: Crisp Vegetable Salad (page 145)
Bottom left: Cracked Wheat Salad with Peppers (page 143)
Right: Sliced Tomato and Asparagus Salad (page 143)

LEMON PEPPER SALAD

Serves 8

335 G (12 OZ) MANGETOUT, TRIMMED, OR FINE ASPARAGUS TIPS

SALT AND PEPPER

2 BUNCHES OF SALAD ONIONS, TRIMMED AND FINELY SLICED

4 GREEN PEPPERS, SEEDED AND CUT INTO THIN STRIPS

GRATED RIND AND JUICE OF 1 LEMON

PINCH OF CASTER SUGAR

115 ML (4 FL OZ) OLIVE OIL

1. Cook the mangetout or asparagus in boiling, salted water for 2-3 minutes or until just tender. Drain and refresh under cold water. Toss with the salad onions and peppers in a bowl.
2. Whisk together the rind and strained lemon juice, the sugar, olive oil and seasoning. Stir into the salad before serving.

COOK'S TIP

It's worth taking the time to shred the onions and peppers finely; use a very sharp knife to make it easier.

SLICED TOMATO AND ASPARAGUS SALAD

Serves 10

335 G (12 OZ) ASPARAGUS TIPS

SALT AND PEPPER

6×15 ML TBS OLIVE OIL

5×5 ML TSP RASPBERRY OR RED WINE VINEGAR

1×5 ML TSP CLEAR HONEY

ABOUT 1.1 KG (2½ LB) RIPE BEEF TOMATOES, THINLY SLICED

1 SHALLOT, SKINNED AND FINELY CHOPPED

A FEW SUN-DRIED TOMATOES, SHREDDED

1. Blanch the asparagus tips in boiling salted water until just tender. Drain and refresh the vegetables under the cold tap.
2. Whisk together the oil, vinegar, honey and seasoning.
3. Just before serving, arrange the sliced tomatoes on a large serving platter and scatter the shallots and sun-dried tomatoes over the top. Pile the asparagus tips in the centre. Spoon the dressing over the salad.

COOK'S TIP

Choose deep red, ripe beef tomatoes as they have the best flavour. If asparagus is unavailable, try stick beans, trimmed and halved.

Lemon Pepper Salad (top)
Courgette and Almond Salad (bottom)

CRACKED WHEAT SALAD WITH PEPPERS

Serves 6

225 G (8 OZ) CRACKED WHEAT

300 ML (10 FL OZ) BOILING WATER

½ CUCUMBER, ROUGHLY CHOPPED

SALT AND PEPPER

½ GREEN PEPPER, SEEDED AND DICED

½ RED PEPPER, SEEDED AND DICED

1 BUNCH OF SALAD ONIONS, TRIMMED AND CHOPPED

115 G (4 OZ) FETA CHEESE, DICED

2×15 ML TBS CHOPPED FRESH MINT

2×15 ML TBS CHOPPED FRESH PARSLEY

4×15 ML TBS OLIVE OIL

3×15 ML TBS LEMON JUICE

1 GARLIC CLOVE, SKINNED AND CRUSHED

LEMON WEDGES AND FRESH MINT SPRIGS, TO GARNISH

1. Soak the cracked wheat in the boiling water for about 30 minutes or until the water has been absorbed, stirring the wheat occasionally.
2. Meanwhile, sprinkle the cucumber with salt and leave for 15 minutes. Rinse, drain and dry. Blanch the peppers in boiling water for 1 minute, then drain.
3. If necessary, drain the cracked wheat. Mix with all the other ingredients. Season with salt and pepper, cover and refrigerate until required. Serve garnished with lemon wedges and mint sprigs.

VARIATION

Serve on a bed of sliced tomatoes, topped with toasted hazelnuts.

COURGETTE AND ALMOND SALAD

Serves 8

450 G (1 LB) COURGETTES, TRIMMED AND THINLY SLICED

SALT AND PEPPER

½ HEAD OF ENDIVE

2 ORANGES

4×15 ML TBS SUNFLOWER OR OLIVE OIL

2×15 ML TBS LEMON JUICE

1×15 ML TBS CHOPPED FRESH PARSLEY (OPTIONAL)

2×15 ML TBS FLAKED ALMONDS

2 TART, GREEN EATING APPLES, SUCH AS GRANNY SMITH'S

1. Blanch the courgettes in boiling, salted water for 1 minute. Drain and refresh under cold water. Leave to cool completely, then pat dry with absorbent kitchen paper and refrigerate, covered. Wash the endive, dry it and refrigerate in a polythene bag.
2. With a serrated knife and holding the fruit over a bowl to catch the juice, cut all the peel and pith away from the oranges. Cut down between the membranes to release the segments into the bowl.
3. Whisk together the oil, lemon juice, parsley, if using, and seasoning. Toss into the orange segments with the almonds.
4. Just before serving, halve, core and thinly slice the apples. Add to the dressing mixture with the courgettes and endive. Stir well. Adjust seasoning, if necessary, and serve immediately.

COOK'S TIP

If you have any nut oils in the store cupboard, such as hazelnut or walnut, substitute one or two spoonfuls in the dressing. The salad can be prepared to the end of step 3 the day before, then covered and kept in the refrigerator until required. Add the slices of apple just before serving the salad to prevent discolouring.

Roasted New Potato Salad

Serves 6

675 G (1½ LB) SMALL NEW POTATOES, SCRUBBED
50 ML (2 FL OZ) OLIVE OIL
3 OR 4 SPRIGS OF FRESH ROSEMARY
115 G (4 OZ) RINDLESS, SMOKED STREAKY BACON, CHOPPED
50 G (2 OZ) MUSHROOMS, PREFERABLY BROWN CAP, WIPED, TRIMMED AND SLICED
2×15 ML TBS DRY RED WINE
1×15 ML TBS RED WINE VINEGAR
2×15 ML TBS TOASTED PINE KERNELS
SALT AND PEPPER
FRESH ROSEMARY, TO GARNISH

1. Boil the potatoes for 1-2 minutes; drain well. Place in a roasting tin with the oil and rosemary. Cook in the oven at 200°C/400°F/Gas Mark 6 for 35-40 minutes or until tender, turning once during cooking.
2. Meanwhile, sauté the bacon and mushrooms in a non-stick pan. Cook, stirring, for 2-3 minutes until the mushrooms have softened. Off the heat add the wine, vinegar and pine kernels. Season to taste.
3. Place the hot cooked potatoes and roasting oil in a large heat-proof bowl, removing the rosemary sprigs. Reheat the bacon dressing if necessary and pour over the potatoes. Stir together well. Serve the salad warm or cold, garnished with one or two sprigs of fresh rosemary.

COOK'S TIP

This is a good salad to serve with barbecued or grilled meats, and the bacon dressing is delicious served with roast beef. It can be made the day before and reheated in a hot oven for 10-12 minutes.

Roasted New Potato Salad

Simple Potato Salad

Serves 8

1.4 KG (3 LB) SMALL NEW POTATOES, SCRUBBED
SALT AND PEPPER
300 ML (10 FL OZ) MAYONNAISE
150 ML (5 FL OZ) SOURED CREAM
CHOPPED FRESH HERBS

1. Cut any large potatoes in half. Cook them gently in lightly salted boiling water until just tender. Drain and cool.
2. Mix the mayonnaise and cream together and season to taste with salt and pepper. Toss the potatoes in the dressing. Sprinkle with fresh herbs to serve.

Cucumber Ribbon and Asparagus Salad

Serves 8

675 G (1½ LB) FRESH ASPARAGUS SPEARS
SALT AND PEPPER
2 LARGE CUCUMBERS
150 ML (5 FL OZ) VEGETABLE OIL
4×15 ML TBS LEMON JUICE
1×15 ML TBS CASTER SUGAR
½ BUNCH OF CHIVES
ALFALFA SPROUTS, TO GARNISH

1. With a sharp knife or vegetable peeleer, scrape each asparagus stalk from tip to base, then trim off any woody parts at the stem base. Tie the stalks in bundles of about 10 and stand upright in a saucepan of boiling, salted water. Cover the tips with a tent of foil. Simmer for 8–12 minutes, or until just tender. Drain and cool.
2. Peel the cucumbers. With a swivel peeler, 'shave' off ribbons of cucumber into a bowl until all the cucumber is used, discarding the central core. Add the asparagus. Cover and refrigerate.
3. Whisk together the oil, lemon juice and sugar. Season. Snip the chives into 2.5 cm (1 in) lengths and stir into the dressing. Spoon over the cucumber and asparagus mixture. Garnish with alfalfa.

CRISP VEGETABLE SALAD

Serves 8

900 G (2 LB) FRENCH BEANS, TOPPED, TAILED AND CUT IN HALF

SALT AND PEPPER

2 SMALL HEADS FENNEL, THINLY SLICED, WITH FEATHERY TOPS RESERVED

300 ML (10 FL OZ) OLIVE OIL

115 ML (4 FL OZ) WHITE WINE VINEGAR

1×15 ML TBS DIJON MUSTARD

2 AVOCADOS

1 LARGE CUCUMBER, PEELED, HALVED AND THICKLY SLICED

ABOUT 20 BLACK OLIVES

1. Cook the French beans in boiling salted water until just tender. Drain; refresh under cold water. Blanch the fennel in boiling water for 1 minute. Drain and refresh.
2. Whisk together the oil, vinegar, mustard and most of the fennel tops, chopped. Season. Peel, halve and stone the avocados. Thickly slice into the dressing.
3. Toss together all the prepared vegetables, olives, avocado and dressing. Serve garnished with remaining fennel tops.

CUCUMBER AND YOGURT SALAD

Serves 8

2 LARGE CUCUMBERS

SALT AND PEPPER

1 HEAD OF FENNEL, TRIMMED AND SHREDDED

1 BUNCH OF SALAD ONIONS, TRIMMED AND FINELY CHOPPED

450 ML (16 FL OZ) NATURAL YOGURT

1. Thinly peel the cucumbers, cut them in half lengthways and scoop out the seeds. Cut the cucumber halves crossways into slices about 0.6 cm (¼ in) thick. Put the slices into a large mixing bowl and sprinkle lightly with salt. Cover and leave to stand for at least 1 hour.
2. Rinse the cucumber and drain well in a colander, or pat dry.
3. Put the cucumber, fennel and onions in a large salad bowl. Add the yogurt and seasoning. Mix together well.

Spinach and Watercress Salad with Bacon

SPINACH AND WATERCRESS SALAD WITH BACON

Serves 8

225 G (8 OZ) SMOKED STREAKY BACON

5×15 ML TBS OLIVE OIL

1×15 ML TBS HAZELNUT OIL

4×5 ML TSP WHITE WINE VINEGAR

1×15 ML TBS WHOLEGRAIN MUSTARD

SALT AND PEPPER

225 G (8 OZ) YOUNG SPINACH LEAVES, RINSED AND DRIED, SHREDDING ANY LARGE LEAVES

2 BUNCHES OF WATERCRESS, RINSED AND DRIED, DISCARDING ANY COARSE STALKS

1. Grill the streaky bacon until really crisp. Drain on absorbent kitchen paper to absorb any excess oil. Snip into small pieces, discarding the rind.
2. Whisk together both types of oil with the white wine vinegar, wholegrain mustard and seasoning.
3. Just before serving, toss all the ingredients together and serve in a large salad bowl.

TOMATO, FENNEL AND AVOCADO SALAD

Serves 6

12×15 ML TBS LOW-CALORIE MAYONNAISE

1×5 ML TSP LEMON JUICE

1×5 ML TSP TABASCO SAUCE

1×5 ML TSP GROUND PAPRIKA

SALT AND PEPPER

2×15 ML TBS WHOLEGRAIN MUSTARD

1 BUNCH SALAD ONIONS, TRIMMED AND CUT INTO 1 CM (½ IN) LENGTHS

675 G (1½ LB) CHERRY TOMATOES, HALVED

335 G (12 OZ) FENNEL OR ONION, THINLY SLICED, RESERVING ANY FEATHERY TOPS FOR GARNISH

2 AVOCADOS, RIPE BUT FIRM, PEELED, HALVED, STONED AND THICKLY SLICED

1. Whisk together the first six ingredients.
2. Stir the salad onions into the dressing then pour it over the tomatoes and fennel or onion; stir to prevent discoloration.
3. Then add the avocados and stir carefully to coat with the dressing. Transfer to a large shallow platter. Garnish with fennel tops and serve immediately.

Grilled Vegetable Salad

Serves 4-6

1 RED PEPPER, HALVED AND SEEDED

1 GREEN PEPPER, HALVED AND SEEDED

ABOUT 6 WHOLE GARLIC CLOVES

335 G (12 OZ) BABY COURGETTES, TRIMMED AND SLICED LENGTHWAYS

1 BUNCH OF ASPARAGUS, TRIMMED

OLIVE OIL FOR BRUSHING

A FEW CHERRY TOMATOES

CHOPPED FRESH HERBS, SUCH AS BASIL, MARJORAM, PARSLEY AND CHIVES (OPTIONAL)

— DRESSING —

2×5 ML TSP BALSAMIC OR GARLIC VINEGAR

1×5 ML TSP CLEAR HONEY

1×5 ML TSP DIJON MUSTARD

5×15 ML TBS OLIVE OIL

SALT AND PEPPER

1. Cut each half of pepper into four. Remove the loose, papery outer skins from the garlic cloves, but leave the inner skins attached.

2. Pour enough water to come to a depth of about 5 cm (2 in) into a saucepan, and bring to the boil. When the water is boiling fast, add the peppers and the garlic. Bring back to the boil and boil for 1 minute. Remove the peppers with a slotted spoon (leaving the garlic in the water), refresh under cold running water and leave to drain. Repeat this process with the courgettes, using the same water. Remove the garlic from the pan and drain.

3. Steam the asparagus until just tender (see Cook's Tip). Drain, arrange on a serving plate and leave to cool. Brush the blanched peppers, courgettes and garlic with a little olive oil and cook under a hot grill until the vegetables are flecked with brown. Turn the vegetables over, brush with more oil and cook the other side. Leave to cool, then arrange on the serving plate with the asparagus. Halve some of the tomatoes, if wished, and scatter over the vegetables.

4. To make the dressing, put the vinegar, honey and mustard in a small bowl, and whisk together with a fork until well blended. Gradually whisk in the olive oil to make a very thick dressing. Season.

5. Just before serving, drizzle the dressing over the vegetables and sprinkle the herbs, if using, over the top.

COOK'S TIP

To steam asparagus, stand it, tied in a bundle, tips upwards, in about 5 cm (2 in) of simmering salted water in a saucepan. Cover the tips with a tent of foil and cook for 8–12 minutes (depending on thickness). The stems cook in the simmering water, while the delicate tips are gently steamed.

Grilled Vegetable Salad

Coconut, Rice and Lentil Salad

Serves 8

4×15 ML TBS VEGETABLE OIL

225 G (8 OZ) ONION, SKINNED AND FINELY CHOPPED

2 BAY LEAVES

1 CINNAMON STICK

4 WHOLE GREEN CARDAMOM PODS, SPLIT OPEN

175 G (6 OZ) RED LENTILS, RINSED, DRAINED AND BOILED RAPIDLY FOR 10 MINUTES

50 G (2 OZ) CREAMED COCONUT, CHOPPED

175 G (6 OZ) LONG-GRAIN WHITE RICE

ABOUT 1.8 LT (3 PT) COLD WATER

SALT AND PEPPER

3×15 ML TBS CHOPPED FRESH PARSLEY AND 25 G (1 OZ) TOASTED FLAKED ALMONDS OR CASHEW NUTS, TO SERVE

1. Heat the oil in a large saucepan and sauté the onion with the bay leaves, cinnamon and cardamoms until golden.
2. Stir in the red lentils, coconut and rice. Add the cold water and ½×5 ml tsp salt. Bring to the boil. Boil gently for about 10 minutes or until the rice and lentils are just cooked.
3. Drain well and rinse under cold running water. Leave to drain. Stir and season.
4. To serve, add the parsley and nuts.

Christmas Salad

Serves 8

2 RED ONIONS

1 POMEGRANATE

1 LARGE BUNCH OF ROQUETTE OR 3 BUNCHES OF WATERCRESS, OR A MIXTURE OF BOTH

50 ML (2 FL OZ) OLIVE OIL

2×5 ML TSP RED WINE VINEGAR

2×5 ML TSP DIJON MUSTARD

SALT AND PEPPER

1. Skin and thinly slice the onions into rings. Halve and open the pomegranate and separate out the seeds, discarding all the pith and membrane. Trim, rinse, drain and dry the salad leaves.
2. Whisk together the oil, vinegar, mustard and seasoning. Toss with the salad leaves, onion and pomegranate. Serve immediately.

COOK'S TIP

Roquette has a strong peppery flavour. Watercress makes an excellent substitute, but you could try any mixture of salad leaves. The important thing is to choose very green leaves to provide a good contrast with the red-skinned onions and pomegranate seeds.

Stir-Fried Courgettes with Sesame Seeds

Serves 6

2×15 ML TBS VEGETABLE OIL

4 GARLIC CLOVES, SKINNED AND CRUSHED

900 G (2 LB) COURGETTES, TRIMMED AND THINLY SLICED

1 SALAD ONION, TRIMMED AND THICKLY SLICED

½×5 ML TSP SALT

1×15 ML TBS SESAME OIL

BLACK PEPPER

2×15 ML TBS TOASTED SESAME SEEDS

1. Heat the vegetable oil in a wok or large frying pan. Add the garlic; fry for 2 minutes.
2. Add the courgettes; stir-fry for 7-8 minutes. Stir in the onion, salt and sesame oil. Season with black pepper. Cook for 1 minute, then stir in the sesame seeds.

Stir-Fried Chinese Leaves

Serves 6

2×15 ML TBS SUNFLOWER OIL

1 HEAD CHINESE LEAVES, COARSELY CHOPPED, RINSED AND DRIED

450 G (1 LB) FIRM TOMATOES, SKINNED AND QUARTERED AND SEEDED

SALT AND PEPPER

1. Heat the oil in a wok or large frying pan and stir-fry the Chinese leaves for 3-4 minutes until they are transparent but still crisp.
2. Stir in the tomatoes and season. Stir again, then transfer to a warmed serving dish.

Steamed Runner Beans and Courgettes

Serves 8

900 G (2 LB) SMALL RUNNER BEANS, TOPPED AND TAILED AND CUT IN HALF DIAGONALLY

450 G (1 LB) COURGETTES, TRIMMED AND SLICED DIAGONALLY

SALT AND PEPPER

VINAIGRETTE (OPTIONAL)

1. Place the beans and courgettes in a colander or steamer basket over a pan of gently simmering water. Cover tightly with foil or a lid. Steam for 6 minutes or until tender. (Cook in two batches if necessary.)
2. Season and keep warm, covered, or, if serving as a salad, allow to cool slightly and toss in vinaigrette to serve.

COOK'S TIP

If you don't want to cook the vegetables at the last minute, serve them as a salad (ie, cook ahead, and toss them in vinaigrette).

Steamed Cucumber

Serves 4-6

1 LARGE CUCUMBER, ABOUT 335 G (12 OZ)

SALT AND PEPPER

CHOPPED FRESH PARSLEY, TO GARNISH

1. Peel off the cucumber skin lengthways at 0.6 cm (¼ in) intervals with a paring knife, if wished. Cut the cucumber into 5 cm (2 in) slices and divide each one lengthways into eight pieces.
2. Place cucumber in a steamer or metal colander over a pan of gently boiling water. Cover with a tight fitting lid or foil. Steam for 7-10 minutes, or until just tender. Season and serve sprinkled with parsley.

COOK'S TIP

The pieces of cucumber quickly flop if overcooked, so keep a careful eye on them while they're steaming.

CABBAGE WITH PINE KERNELS

Serves 8

25 ML (1 FL OZ) OLIVE OIL

900 G (2 LB) RED CABBAGE, FINELY SHREDDED

2.5 CM (1 IN) PIECE OF FRESH ROOT GINGER, PEELED AND GRATED (OPTIONAL)

150 ML (5 FL OZ) VEGETABLE STOCK (SEE PAGE 13)

SALT AND PEPPER

40 G (1½ OZ) BUTTER

2×15 ML TBS BALSAMIC VINEGAR OR RED WINE VINEGAR MIXED WITH 2×5 ML TSP MUSCOVADO SUGAR

50 G (2 OZ) TOASTED PINE KERNELS

1. Heat the oil in a large saucepan and sauté the cabbage with the ginger over a high heat for 3-4 minutes or until reduced in bulk, stirring occasionally.
2. Add the stock and seasoning, bring to the boil, then cover and cook over a low heat for about 20 minutes. Stir occasionally.
3. When the cabbage is just tender, uncover and bubble down any excess liquid. Off the heat, stir in the butter, vinegar and pine kernels. Adjust seasoning, cover and keep warm.

COOK'S TIP

Balsamic vinegar is a wonderful sweet-and sour vinegar, which gives a delicious flavour to this dish.

BAKED TOMATO AND FENNEL

Serves 8-10

900 G (2 LB) FENNEL BULBS, TRIMMED AND CUT INTO HALVES OR QUARTERS, DEPENDING ON SIZE

5×15 ML TBS WHITE WINE

3×15 ML TBS CHOPPED FRESH THYME OR 1×5 ML TSP DRIED

5×15 ML TBS OLIVE OIL

900 G (2 LB) RIPE BEEF TOMATOES, HALVED OR QUARTERED

1. Remove the core from each section of fennel by make a 'V' in the base of the bulb,

Cabbage with Pine Kernels

but make sure that the layers are held together.

2. Place the fennel in a roasting tin. Pour the white wine over and sprinkle with thyme. Brush with olive oil.

3. Bake in the oven at 200°C/400°F/Gas Mark 6 for 45 minutes. Add the tomatoes, skin side up, and continue to cook for a further 30 minutes or until tender, basting twice during the cooking time. Cover and keep warm.

Aubergine in a Hot Sweet and Sour Sauce

Serves 4

3×15 ML TBS OLIVE OIL

200 G (7 OZ) ONIONS, SKINNED AND SLICED

2.5 CM (1 IN) PIECE OF FRESH ROOT GINGER,PEELED AND FRESHLY CHOPPED

2 RED CHILLIES, SEEDED AND FINELY CHOPPED

1½×5 ML TSP CUMIN SEEDS

1½×5 ML TSP CORIANDER SEEDS

3 CLOVES

5 CM (2 IN) CINNAMON STICK

300 ML (10 FL OZ) WATER

1×15 ML TBS GROUND PAPRIKA

3×15 ML TBS FRESH LIME JUICE

3-4×15 ML TBS DARK MUSCOVADO SUGAR

1-2×5 ML TSP SALT

450 G (1 LB) AUBERGINES, CUT INTO 2.5 CM (1 IN) CUBES

WHOLE RED CHILLIES, TO GARNISH (OPTIONAL)

1. Heat the oil in a large wok, add the onions, ginger and chillies and stir-fry until softened, about 4 minutes. Add the next four spices, and cook for 2-3 minutes.

2. Add the water to the wok and reduce the heat. Stir in the paprika, lime juice, sugar and salt with the aubergine. Bring to the boil. Simmer, covered, for about 20 minutes until the aubergine is tender.

3. Uncover and bring to the boil. Reduce the liquid until it coats the aubergine pieces, about 3-4 minutes. Garnish with whole red chillies if wished.

Aubergine and Courgette Fingers

Serves 8

4 SMALL AUBERGINES, CUT LENGTHWAYS INTO 2.5 CM (1 IN) SLICES AND EACH SLICE CUT ACROSS INTO 1 CM (½ IN) WIDE FINGERS

SALT AND PEPPER

3×15 ML TBS OLIVE OIL

450 G (1 LB) COURGETTES, TRIMMED AND CUT INTO FINGERS, AS FOR THE AUBERGINES

2×15 ML TBS CHOPPED FRESH OREGANO OR MARJORAM, TO GARNISH

1×15 ML TBS TOASTED SESAME SEEDS, TO GARNISH

1. Put the aubergines in a colander and sprinkle generously with salt. Leave for at least 30 minutes. Rinse the aubergines and dry thoroughly.

2. Heat the oil in a large, heavy-based frying pan and sauté the aubergines for 3 minutes. Add the courgettes and continue cooking for 3-4 minutes or until just tender but not soggy. Season with salt and pepper.

3. Serve garnished with oregano or marjoram and sprinkle with the sesame seeds.

COOK'S TIP

Choose small aubergines, in preference to the larger variety, as they are less bitter.

Chestnut and Sprout Sauté

Serves 8

900 G (2 LB) CHESTNUTS

600 ML (20 FL OZ) CHICKEN STOCK (SEE PAGE 13)

900 G (2 LB) BRUSSELS SPROUTS, TRIMMED

SALT AND PEPPER

115 G (4 OZ) BUTTER

225 G (8 OZ) CELERY, TRIMMED AND CUT INTO 2.5 CM (1 IN) LENGTHS

450 G (1 LB) ONIONS, SKINNED AND QUARTERED, SEPARATING THE LAYERS

GRATED RIND OF 1 LEMON

CHOPPED FRESH PARSLEY, TO GARNISH

1. Nick the brown outer skins of the chestnuts with a sharp knife. Cook in boiling water for about 10 minutes. Drain, cool and peel off the shells and inner skins. Cover with the stock and simmer for 20 minutes or until tender. Drain the chestnuts well.

2. Meanwhile, cook the sprouts in boiling, salted water for 3-4 minutes only; drain well.

3. Melt the butter in a large sauté or frying pan. Sauté the celery and onions with the lemon rind until beginning to soften.

4. Add the cooked chestnuts, Brussels sprouts and seasoning. Sauté over a high heat for a further 2-3 minutes or until piping hot, stirring frequently; cover and keep warm. Sprinkle with chopped parsley to garnish.

Artichoke and Chive Bake

Serves 4

900 G (2 LB) JERUSALEM ARTICHOKES, SCRUBBED AND LEFT WHOLE

SALT AND PEPPER

1×5 ML TSP LEMON JUICE

2 EGGS, SEPARATED

1×15 ML TBS CHOPPED FRESH CHIVES OR ½×5 ML TSP DRIED

50 G (2 OZ) CHEDDAR CHEESE, GRATED

1. Cover the artichokes with salted water. Add the lemon juice. Bring to the boil, then cover and simmer for about 12 minutes or until the artichokes are quite tender.

2. Drain and run under a cold tap. Peel off the skins, then mash the flesh until almost smooth, leaving a few small pieces of artichoke to add texture to the bake. Return the purée to a saucepan and stir over a moderate heat to drive off excess moisture; leave to cool slightly.

3. Stir the egg yolks into the purée with the chives and seasoning. Fold in the whisked egg whites, then place the mixture in a greased 1.2 lt (2 pt) shallow ovenproof dish. Sprinkle the grated cheese over the top.

4. Bake in the oven at 190°C/375°F/Gas Mark 5 for 25-30 minutes or until lightly set and golden. Serve straightaway.

Sautéed Artichokes with Orange

Serves 4

900 G (2 LB) JERUSALEM ARTICHOKES, SCRUBBED AND LEFT WHOLE OR CUT INTO LARGE CHUNKS

SALT AND PEPPER

1×5 ML TSP LEMON JUICE

2×15 ML TBS OIL

25 G (1 OZ) BUTTER OR MARGARINE

FINELY GRATED RIND AND SEGMENTED FLESH OF 1 ORANGE

CHOPPED FRESH PARSLEY (OPTIONAL)

1. Cover the artichokes with salted water. Add the lemon juice. Bring to the boil, cover and simmer until the artichokes are barely tender – about 8-10 minutes.
2. Drain the artichokes and run under the cold tap. Peel off the skins.
3. Heat the oil and butter in a sauté pan; add the artichokes with the orange rind. Fry over a moderate heat, turning frequently until golden brown.
4. Stir in the orange segments and parsley if wished; adjust seasoning. Keep warm, uncovered, in a low oven.

Sautéed Leeks with Cream

Serves 6

2×15 ML TBS OLIVE OIL

25 G (1 OZ) BUTTER

900 G (2 LB) TRIMMED LEEKS, CUT INTO FINE STRIPS, WASHED AND DRAINED

SALT AND PEPPER

75 ML (3 FL OZ) SINGLE CREAM

LEMON JUICE

1. Using two large frying pans, heat the oil then add the butter. As it begins to froth, add half the leeks to each pan with plenty of seasoning. Fry over a high heat for several minutes, until tinged with colour and just beginning to wilt.
2. Mix in the cream and heat through, adding lemon juice and seasoning to taste.

Leek and Potato Bake

Serves 4-6

225 G (8 OZ) TRIMMED LEEKS, SPLIT AND RINSED, THEN CUT INTO 1 CM (½ IN) SLICES

SALT AND PEPPER

900 G (2 LB) OLD POTATOES, PEELED AND THINLY SLICED (IN A FOOD PROCESSOR IF YOU HAVE ONE)

1 GARLIC CLOVE, SKINNED AND CRUSHED

ABOUT 300 ML (10 FL OZ) VEGETABLE STOCK

BUTTER OR MARGARINE

1. Cook the leeks in boiling salted water for 2 minutes; drain.
2. Grease a 1.2 lt (2 pt) shallow ovenproof dish. Layer up the potatoes, leeks, garlic and seasoning, ending with a layer of potato. Pour the stock over just to cover the vegetables and dot the surface of the top layer with butter.
3. Stand the dish on a baking tray. Bake in the oven at 180°C/350°F/Gas Mark 4 for 1¼-1½ hours or until the potatoes are tender and the top is golden.

Sliced Beetroot and Onion Bake

Serves 4

450 G (1 LB) BEETROOT, PEELED AND THINLY SLICED

225 G (8 OZ) ONION, SKINNED AND THINLY SLICED

1×15 ML TBS REDCURRANT JELLY

1×15 ML TBS RED WINE VINEGAR

115 ML (4 FL OZ) VEGETABLE STOCK (SEE PAGE 13)

25 G (1 OZ) BUTTER OR MARGARINE

SALT AND PEPPER

SPRIG OF FRESH PARSLEY, TO GARNISH

1. Place the beetroot and onion in a shallow ovenproof dish. Warm together the jelly, vinegar, stock, butter and seasoning and pour over the beetroot. Mix well.
2. Cover the dish tightly and bake in the oven at 200°C/400°F/Gas Mark 6 for about 1¼ hours or until the beetroot is tender. Garnish with sprig of parsley to serve.

Potato and Garlic Purée

Serves 4

675 G (1½ LB) OLD POTATOES, PEELED AND CUT INTO CHUNKS

2 GARLIC CLOVES, SKINNED AND CHOPPED

SALT AND PEPPER

150 ML (5 FL OZ) MILK, WARMED

15 G (½ OZ) BUTTER OR MARGARINE

SNIPPED FRESH CHIVES

1. Place the potatoes and garlic in a pan and cover with water, adding a little salt. Bring to the boil, cover and simmer for 20 minutes or until the potatoes are tender.
2. Drain the potatoes and garlic, then return them to the pan with the lid on to dry them a little. Mash thoroughly and add the warmed milk and butter. Season. Just before serving, beat in the chives.

Potatoes with Roast Garlic

Serves 8

1.8 KG (4 LB) POTATOES, PEELED AND CUT INTO LARGE, EVEN-SIZED PIECES

SALT AND PEPPER

LARD, DRIPPING OR OLIVE OIL

2 WHOLE BULBS OF GARLIC, SEPARATED INTO CLOVES, REMOVING THE LOOSE, PAPERY SKINS AND LEAVING THE INNER SKINS ATTACHED

CHOPPED FRESH PARSLEY, TO GARNISH

1. Cover the potatoes with cold salted water and bring to the boil. Boil for 2 minutes then drain thoroughly.
2. Heat the fat in a roasting tin in the oven. Add the potatoes and baste with the fat until well coated. Scatter the garlic over the potatoes. Cook in the oven at 180°C/350°F/Gas Mark 4 for 1½ hours, turning occasionally.
3. Turn up the heat to 220°C/425°F/Gas Mark 7 and continue roasting for 15 minutes until crisp and golden. Place on a serving dish. Season and sprinkle with parsley.

Potatoes with Roast Garlic (top)
Sliced Beetroot and Onion Bake (bottom)

Lemon Sesame Potatoes

Serves 8

1.8 KG (4 LB) SMALL NEW POTATOES, SCRUBBED BUT NOT PEELED

SALT

4×15 ML TBS SOY SAUCE

4×15 ML TBS VEGETABLE OIL

4×15 ML TBS LEMON JUICE

25 G (1 OZ) SESAME SEEDS

1. Halve any large potatoes. Cook in boiling salted water for 5 minutes only, then drain.
2. Put the potatoes in one or two shallow roasting tins. Drizzle the soy sauce, oil and lemon juice over the top. Sprinkle with the sesame seeds.
3. Bake in the oven at 200°C/400°F/Gas Mark 6 for about 45 minutes.

Mashed Potato with Olive Oil and Parmesan

Serves 6

1.8 KG (4 LB) OLD POTATOES, PEELED AND ROUGHLY CHOPPED

SALT

4×15 ML TBS OLIVE OIL OR MELTED BUTTER

150 ML (5 FL OZ) SINGLE CREAM

1×15 ML TBS COARSELY MILLED BLACK PEPPER

25 G (1 OZ) COARSELY GRATED PARMESAN CHEESE

OLIVE OIL AND BLACK PEPPER, TO SERVE

1. Cook the potatoes in boiling salted water for 15-20 minutes until tender. Drain well. Push the potatoes through a sieve or potato ricer (like a large garlic press) to make a purée, or use a potato masher for a coarser texture.
2. Place the oil, potatoes, cream and black pepper in a saucepan and stir over a moderate heat until piping hot. Beat in all but 1×15 ml tbs Parmesan cheese.
3. Pile the potatoes into a warm serving dish. Drizzle with a little oil. Serve with black pepper and the remaining grated Parmesan cheese.

Bay-Roasted Potatoes

Serves 8

1.4 KG (3 LB) SMALL, EVEN-SIZED POTATOES, SCRUBBED IF NECESSARY BUT NOT PEELED

SALT AND PEPPER

ABOUT 10-12 FRESH OR DRIED BAY LEAVES

ABOUT 75 ML (3 FL OZ) OLIVE OIL

2 GARLIC CLOVES, SKINNED

1. Cook the potatoes in boiling salted water for 2 minutes. Drain and cool for 1-2 minutes. Slit 10-12 of the potatoes and insert a bay leaf.
2. Meanwhile, place the olive oil and garlic together in one large or two medium roasting tins. Heat them in the oven at 190°C/375°F/Gas Mark 5 for 3-4 minutes. Toss in the hot potatoes, then shake them well in the tins until they are coated in olive oil. Season with the salt and pepper
3. Roast the potatoes for about 35-40 minutes or until they are golden and tender. Serve hot, with or without bay leaves, with some extra salt sprinkled over, if wished.

COOK'S TIP

The bay leaves inserted in the potatoes add a really delicious flavour. If you're short of time, simply add a few bay leaves to the roasting tin with the oil and garlic.

Sweet Potatoes Dauphinoise

Serves 4-6

BUTTER OR MARGARINE, FOR GREASING

1 GARLIC CLOVE, SKINNED AND CRUSHED

900 G (2 LB) SWEET POTATOES, PEELED AND THINLY SLICED

SALT AND PEPPER

FRESHLY GRATED NUTMEG

350 ML (12 FL OZ) SINGLE CREAM

75 ML (3 FL OZ) MILK

1. Lightly grease a shallow 1.2 lt (2 pt) ovenproof dish. Sprinkle with the crushed garlic. Blanch the sweet potatoes in boiling water for 1 minute; drain well.
2. Arrange a layer of potato slices in the bottom of the dish. Season with salt, pepper and nutmeg. Whisk together the cream and milk. Add 2×15 ml tbs of the mixture to the potato layer and spread to cover.
3. Continue layering the potatoes with the cream and seasoning, finishing with the cream. Bake, uncovered, in the oven at 150°C/300°F/Gas Mark 2 for about 2 hours, or until the potatoes are tender and the top is crisp and golden.

Gratin Dauphinoise

Serves 6

900 G (2 LB) WAXY POTATOES, SUCH AS MARIS BARD OR WILJA, PEELED AND CUT INTO VERY THIN SLICES

1.2 LT (2 PT) MILK

BUTTER OR MARGARINE FOR GREASING

1 SMALL GARLIC CLOVE, SKINNED AND HALVED

600 ML (20 FL OZ) DOUBLE CREAM

SALT AND PEPPER

FRESHLY GRATED NUTMEG

115 G (4 OZ) GRUYÈRE CHEESE, GRATED

1. Put the potatoes in a large saucepan and add the milk. Bring to the boil and simmer very gently for 10-12 minutes or until just soft. Drain well and reserve the milk.
2. Grease a large gratin dish and rub the bottom and sides of the dish with garlic. Put the cream in a pan and bring to the boil.
3. Arrange the potatoes in the prepared dish in an even layer. Cover the potatoes with the cream, adding a little of the reserved milk. Season generously and sprinkle with the nutmeg and grated cheese.
4. Bake, uncovered in the oven at 180°C/350°F/Gas Mark 4 for 1-1½ hours or until the potatoes are very tender and the top is brown.

COOK'S TIP

For this unorthodox version of a classic dish, it is vital that the potatoes are sliced wafer-thin, so that they cook until melt-in-the-mouth tender.

Bay-Roasted Potatoes (top)
Sweet Potatoes Dauphinoise (bottom)

Game Chips

Serves 4

450 G (1 LB) POTATOES, PEELED AND CUT INTO VERY THIN SLICES

VEGETABLE OIL FOR DEEP-FRYING

1. Put the potato slices into a bowl of cold water and leave for 30 minutes to remove excess starch. Drain and dry in a tea-towel.
2. In a deep frying pan or deep-fat fryer, heat the oil to 190°C/375°F. Put enough of the potato slices into the frying basket to quarter-fill it, lower it into the oil and cook until the chips are golden. Drain on absorbent kitchen paper and keep warm while cooking the remaining slices.

Crispy Potato Galette

Serves 8

900 G (2 LB) OLD POTATOES, PEELED AND CUT INTO VERY THIN SLICES

50 G (2 OZ) BUTTER

1×15 ML TBS OLIVE OIL

SALT AND PEPPER

1. Dry the potato slices thoroughly on a clean tea towel. Melt the butter with the oil in a 20 cm (8 in) non-stick frying pan or skillet with a lid (see Cook's Tip). Heat until foaming, then remove the pan from the heat and add the potato slices, overlapping them in a circular pattern. Season well with salt and pepper, then press the potatoes down firmly with a metal spatula.
2. Cover the potatoes with a sheet of buttered greaseproof paper, then with the pan lid. Cook over a moderate heat for 10-15 minutes until the potatoes are golden brown on the underside.
3. Transfer the covered pan to the oven. Bake in the oven at 200°C/400°F/Gas Mark 6 for 30 minutes or until the potatoes feel tender when pierced with a skewer. Remove from the oven and leave to rest, covered, for 10 minutes.
4. Uncover the potatoes and place a warmed flat serving plate on top. Invert the potato galette on to the plate. Serve hot, cut into eight equal wedges.

COOK'S TIP

In French cookery, a galette is a kind of flat round cake made from flaky pastry. This version is made of very thinly sliced potatoes arranged in an attractive circular pattern. You will need a frying pan or skillet with an ovenproof handle and lid to make this galette – the French cast iron type is ideal. if your pan handle and lid knob are not ovenproof, cover them with several thicknesses of foil for protection, or bake the galette in a sandwich tin.

Curried Potato and Cauliflower

Serves 4-6

VEGETABLE OIL

675 G (1½ LB) OLD POTATOES, PEELED AND CUT INTO BITE-SIZED PIECES

225 G (8 OZ) ONIONS, SKINNED AND ROUGHLY CHOPPED

225 G (8 OZ) CAULIFLOWER FLORETS – 1 SMALL CAULIFLOWER, DIVIDED INTO PIECES

1×15 ML TBS MILD CURRY POWDER

50 G (2 OZ) CREAMED COCONUT, CHOPPED

400 ML (15 FL OZ) WARM WATER

400 G CAN CHOPPED TOMATOES

1×15 ML TBS LEMON JUICE

SALT AND PEPPER

3×15 ML TBS CHOPPED FRESH CORIANDER

FRESH CORIANDER SPRIG, TO GARNISH

1. Heat a little oil in a medium-sized flameproof casserole. Add the potatoes, onions, cauliflower and curry powder and fry gently for 2-3 minutes, stirring frequently.
2. Meanwhile, blend the coconut until smooth with the warm water. Stir into the casserole with the tomatoes, lemon juice and seasoning. Bring to the boil.
3. Cover the casserole and simmer for 20-25 minutes or until the vegetables are quite tender, stirring occasionally to prevent sticking.
4. Stir in the chopped coriander and adjust the seasoning. Serve garnished with a coriander sprig.

COOK'S TIP

Serve this strong, well-flavoured dish with grilled bacon or chicken.

Sautéed Potatoes with Celery

Serves 4

675 G (1½ LB) MEDIUM-SIZED OLD POTATOES, SCRUBBED BUT NOT PEELED

SALT AND PEPPER

3×15 ML TBS VEGETABLE OIL

50 G (2 OZ) BUTTER OR MARGARINE

4 LARGE CELERY STICKS, TRIMMED AND SLICED

50 G (2 OZ) WALNUT PIECES

CHOPPED FRESH PARSLEY

1. Cook the potatoes in boiling salted water until almost tender – about 20 minutes. Drain and, while still warm, peel off the skins and cut the flesh into large chunks.
2. Heat the oil and butter in a large frying pan. Add the celery and potatoes and cook over a high heat, turning, until golden.
3. Add the nuts and fry for 1-2 minutes longer. Stir in the parsley and season.

Carrots with Honey

Serves 8

50 G (2 OZ) BUTTER

900 G (2 LB) CARROTS, PEELED AND CUT INTO THICK DIAGONAL SLICES

450 G (1 LB) BUTTON ONIONS OR SHALLOTS, SKINNED

GRATED RIND AND JUICE OF 1 LEMON

1 CM (½ IN) PIECE OF FRESH ROOT GINGER, PEELED AND FINELY CHOPPED

1×15 ML TBS CLEAR HONEY

200 ML (7 FL OZ) WATER

2×15 ML TBS CHOPPED FRESH PARSLEY

1. Melt the butter in a large saucepan and sauté the carrots and onions, stirring, for 2-3 minutes. Add the lemon rind, strained lemon juice, ginger, honey and water.
2. Bring to the boil, cover tightly and cook gently for 15 minutes or until just tender. Uncover and bubble down the juices until the carrots are lightly glazed, shaking the pan occasionally to prevent the carrots sticking. Stir in the parsley before serving.

Curried Potato and Cauliflower

Glazed Carrots with Turnips

Serves 8

900 G (2 LB) CARROTS, PEELED AND CUT INTO THICK STICKS

900 G (2 LB) TURNIPS, PEELED AND CUT INTO THICK STICKS

50 G (2 OZ) BUTTER OR MARGARINE

2×15 ML TBS LEMON JUICE

4×15 ML TBS GRANULATED SUGAR

SALT AND BLACK PEPPER

1. Place the vegetables in a medium saucepan and just cover with cold water. Add the butter, lemon juice, sugar and seasoning to taste.
2. Bring to the boil and boil rapidly over a high heat for about 15 minutes or until all the liquid has evaporated and the vegetables are tender and lightly glazed. Shake the pan occasionally to prevent them sticking.
3. Cover and keep warm until required. Season with black pepper just before serving, adding extra butter, if wished.

Glazed Carrots with Dill

Serves 4

450 G (1 LB) CARROTS, PEELED AND CUT INTO THIN STICKS

THICKLY GRATED RIND OF 1 ORANGE

25 G (1 OZ) BUTTER OR MARGARINE

1×15 ML TBS SUGAR

1 CM (½ IN) PIECE OF FRESH ROOT GINGER, PEELED AND FINELY CHOPPED OR 1 GARLIC CLOVE, SKINNED AND CRUSHED

SALT AND PEPPER

A FEW FRESH DILL SPRIGS, ROUGHLY CHOPPED

1. Place the carrots in a small saucepan with the orange rind, butter, sugar, ginger or garlic and seasoning. Just cover with cold water.
2. Bring to the boil, then cook over a moderate to high heat for about 12 minutes or until the carrots are tender and all the liquid has evaporated. Shake the pan to prevent the carrots sticking. Stir in the dill and serve at once.

Glazed Carrots with Dill

Celeriac Purée

Serves 8

1.4 KG (3 LB) CELERIAC, PEELED AND CHOPPED

SALT AND WHITE PEPPER

600 ML (20 FL OZ) MILK

50 G (2 OZ) UNSALTED BUTTER

3×15 ML TBS DOUBLE CREAM

1. Cook the celeriac in simmering salted milk until tender. Drain, reserving the milk, then purée in a blender or food processor.
2. Heat the butter in a non-stick saucepan and stir in the celeriac purée, then heat, stirring constantly to drive off excess moisture. Beat in the cream and enough reserved milk to give a creamy consistency. Season.

Creamed Celeriac and Apple

Serves 4

900 G (2 LB) CELERIAC, PEELED AND THINLY SLICED

SALT AND PEPPER

1×5 ML TSP LEMON JUICE

1 LARGE COOKING APPLE, ABOUT 335 G (12 OZ), PEELED, QUARTERED AND SLICED

2×5 ML TSP CREAMED HORSERADISH

2×15 ML TBS SINGLE CREAM

CHOPPED FRESH PARSLEY

1. Cover the celeriac immediately with cold salted water to which the lemon juice has been added. Bring to the boil, cover and simmer until tender – about 25-30 minutes.
2. Add the apple to the pan and simmer for a further 3-4 minutes or until the apple is tender. Drain well.
3. Mash the celeriac and apple together then return to the pan with the horseradish and seasoning. Reheat, stirring, until the excess moisture has been driven off.
4. Stir in the cream with plenty of chopped parsley, reheat gently and adjust seasoning.

COOK'S TIP

Serve this delicate purée with mild fish or meat dishes rather than spicy ones.

Celeriac 'Straw'

Serves 8

450 G (1 LB) CELERIAC, WASHED AND PEELED

LEMON JUICE

VEGETABLE OIL FOR DEEP-FRYING

SALT

1. Halve the celeriac bulbs and place them, cut sides down, on a board. Slice very thinly and cut these slices into thin strips by stacking and slicing them with a very sharp knife. Drop into a bowl of cold water with a little lemon juice added.
2. Heat the vegetable oil in a deep-fat fryer to 180°C/350°F. Drain and dry the celeriac. Fry in small batches for 1-2 minutes, or until crisp and golden. Drain on absorbent kitchen paper, sprinkle with salt and keep warm while frying the remainder. Serve hot.

Swede and Orange Purée

Serves 4

1.1 KG (2½ LB) SWEDES, PEELED AND THINLY SLICED

SALT AND PEPPER

25 G (1 OZ) BUTTER OR MARGARINE

FINELY GRATED RIND AND JUICE OF 1 ORANGE

3×15 ML TBS SOURED CREAM

1. Cover the swedes with cold salted water and boil until quite tender – about 20 minutes. Drain for several minutes.
2. Mash the swede, then add the butter, seasoning and grated orange rind. Stir over a moderate heat for several minutes until thoroughly hot and all excess moisture has been driven off from the vegetables.
3. Stir in 2 × 15 ml tbs orange juice and the soured cream. Reheat gently, stirring all the time. Adjust the seasoning to serve.

COOK'S TIP

This is perfect with any roast or strongly-flavoured casserole dish. The swedes must be well drained after boiling as they retain a lot of water. It's difficult to mash them until completely smooth, but any remaining pieces of swede usually break down as the mixture is stirred over the heat.

Roast Swedes

Serves 4

VEGETABLE OIL

1.1 KG (2½ LB) SWEDES, PEELED AND DIVIDED INTO LARGE, WEDGE-SHAPED PIECES

SALT AND FRESHLY GROUND PEPPER

CHOPPED FRESH PARSLEY (OPTIONAL)

1. Heat a thin film of oil in a large roasting tin. Add the swedes. Season to taste, and turn the swede over in the oil to coat completely.
2. Bake in the oven at 200°C/400°F/Gas Mark 6 for 1-1¼ hours or until tender and golden. Turn once or twice while cooking. Sprinkle with plenty of milled pepper and chopped parsley, if wished.

COOK'S TIP

Cooked swedes have a similar texture to roast parsnips – soft on the inside with a golden outer side.

Turnips Stir-Fried with Leeks

Serves 2-3

2×15 ML TBS OLIVE OIL

25 G (1 OZ) BUTTER

75 G (3 OZ) STREAKY BACON, RINDED AND CUT INTO SMALL PIECES

450 G (1 LB) TURNIPS, PEELED AND THINLY SLICED

225 G (8 OZ) TRIMMED LEEKS, SPLIT, RINSED AND CUT INTO 1 CM (½ IN) SLICES

1×5 ML TSP SUGAR

SALT AND PEPPER

1×15 ML TBS LEMON JUICE

THICKLY GRATED LEMON RIND AND FRESH CORIANDER SPRIG, TO GARNISH

1. Heat the oil and butter in a large frying pan. Add the bacon and heat gently until the fat runs.
2. Increase the heat. Add the turnips, leeks, sugar and seasoning. Fry over a high heat, stirring until golden and tender.
3. Stir in the lemon juice and adjust the seasoning. Serve garnished with lemon rind and coriander.

Turnips with Mushroom Sauce

Serves 4

675 G (1½ LB) TURNIPS, PEELED AND CUT INTO BITE-SIZE WEDGES

SALT AND PEPPER

40 G (1½ OZ) BUTTER OR MARGARINE

115 G (4 OZ) BUTTON MUSHROOMS, WIPED, TRIMMED AND QUARTERED IF LARGE

2×15 ML TBS PLAIN WHITE FLOUR

300 ML (10 FL OZ) MILK

3×15 ML TBS SOURED CREAM

3×15 ML TBS CHOPPED FRESH PARSLEY

1×15 ML TBS LEMON JUICE

1 HARD-BOILED EGG, SHELLED AND CHOPPED

1. Cook the turnips in boiling salted water until just tender, about 10 minutes. Drain.
2. Meanwhile, melt the butter. Add the mushrooms and cook for a minute or two until beginning to soften.
3. Mix in the flour, milk, soured cream and seasoning. Bring to the boil, stirring all the time, until the sauce has thickened.
4. Stir in the parsley, lemon juice, chopped egg and turnips. Heat gently and adjust seasoning to serve.

Spiced Parsnips

Serves 6

900 G (2 LB) PARSNIPS, PEELED AND CUT INTO STICKS

1 SMALL GREEN CHILLI, HALVED, SEEDED AND FINELY CHOPPED

SALT AND PEPPER

1×5 ML TSP SUGAR

1×5 ML TSP GROUND CORIANDER

25 G (1 OZ) BUTTER

CHOPPED FRESH CORIANDER, TO GARNISH

1. Place all the ingredients, except the fresh coriander, into a sauté pan and just cover with cold water.
2. Bring to the boil, then boil uncovered until all the liquid has evaporated and the parsnips are quite tender – about 8-12 minutes. Shake the pan occasionally to prevent the parsnips from sticking.
3. Adjust seasoning, adding plenty of chopped coriander and serve.

Golden Parsnip Galette

Serves 4-6

900 G (2 LB) PARSNIPS, PEELED AND THINLY SLICED

1 GARLIC CLOVE, SKINNED AND CRUSHED

SALT AND PEPPER

50 G (2 OZ) MELTED BUTTER OR MARGARINE

1. Grease and base-line a 20 cm (8 in) sandwich tin with greaseproof paper. Layer up the parsnips with the garlic and seasoning, pressing down the parsnips as you go. Pour the melted butter over.
2. Cover with foil and bake in the oven at 220°C/425°F/Gas Mark 7 for 1-1¼ hours or until the parsnips are quite tender. Invert the galette on to a flameproof plate and brown under a hot grill.

Parsnip and Ginger Bake

Serves 4

900 G (2 LB) PARSNIPS, PEELED AND THINLY SLICED

SALT AND PEPPER

15 G (½ OZ) PIECE OF FRESH ROOT GINGER, PEELED AND FINELY CHOPPED

4×15 ML TBS SINGLE CREAM

2 EGGS, BEATEN

25 G (1 OZ) BUTTER OR MARGARINE

GRATED RIND AND JUICE OF ½ LEMON

FLAKED ALMONDS

1. Cover the parsnips with cold salted water and bring to the boil; cover and simmer for about 15 minutes or until tender. Drain the parsnips, then mash them.
2. Stir the ginger into the parsnip purée with the cream, eggs, butter, lemon rind and juice. Beat well and adjust seasoning.
3. Place in a lightly greased 1.2 lt (2 pt) shallow ovenproof dish. Sprinkle the surface lightly with almonds.
4. Bake in the oven at 200°C/400°F/Gas Mark 6 for 20-25 minutes or until golden and lightly set.

Turnips Stir-Fried with Leeks

Desserts

From classic baked puddings to refreshing light fruit desserts, this chapter provides a collection of the most popular desserts. Recipes include such family favourites as pies made with a choice of fruits and nuts, charlottes and ice cream, plus exotic meringue desserts served with cream or summer fruit, soufflés and mouthwatering chocolate creations for when you want to entertain or for other special occasions.

Left: Lemon Curd Creams (page 168) Right: Fudge Nut Tart (page 182)

GULAB JAMUN

Serves 8

175 G (6 OZ) SELF-RAISING FLOUR

¼×5 ML TSP SALT

175 G (6 OZ) GROUND ALMONDS

75 G (3 OZ) UNSALTED BUTTER, CUT INTO SMALL PIECES

ABOUT 150 ML (5 FL OZ) NATURAL YOGURT

FLOUR, FOR DUSTING

225 G (8 OZ) GRANULATED SUGAR

600 ML (20 FL OZ) COLD WATER

V EGETABLE OIL FOR DEEP-FRYING

ROSE PETALS, TO DECORATE

1. Sift the flour and salt into a bowl, then stir in the ground almonds. Cut in the butter, then rub in with the fingertips until the mixture resembles fine breadcrumbs. Stir in enough yogurt to make a firm dough.

2. Roll the dough into 32 small balls, dust lightly with flour and place in a single layer on a tray. Chill in the refrigerator for at least 30 minutes.

3. Meanwhile, put the sugar in a heavy metal saucepan, pour in the cold water and heat gently until the sugar has dissolved. Increase the heat and bring to the boil. Lower the heat to moderate and simmer for 7-10 minutes until the mixture is syrupy. Remove from the heat, pour into a large, shallow serving bowl.

4. Heat the oil in a deep-fat fryer or deep saucepan to 190°C/375°F or until a cube of stale bread turns golden in 30 seconds. With a slotted spoon, lower the balls one at a time into the hot oil and deep-fry in batches for 2-3 minutes until light golden all over. Remove with a slotted spoon and drain on absorbent kitchen paper while deep-frying the remainder.

5. When all the balls have been deep-fried, gently lower them into the warm sugar syrup. Leave until lukewarm, shaking the bowl occasionally and spooning over the syrup so that all the balls become impregnated with syrup. Serve lukewarm or chill in the refrigerator overnight and serve chilled. Sprinkle with rose petals just before serving.

COOK'S TIP

These Indian sweetmeats should be steeped in the warm sugar syrup while they are still hot after deep-frying.

Gulab Jamun

Citrus Fruits Poached in Wine

Serves 4

150 ML (5 FL OZ) MEDIUM WHITE WINE
150 ML (5 FL OZ) WATER
50 G (2 OZ) CASTER SUGAR
PARED RIND AND JUICE OF 2 LEMONS
1 LIME, VERY THINLY SLICED
1 LARGE ORANGE, VERY THINLY SLICED
2 GRAPEFRUITS, 1 PINK, BOTH PEELED
1 TANGERINE, PEELED
1 MINEOLA OR OTHER EASY-PEELER, PEELED
50 G (2 OZ) KUMQUATS, THICKLY SLICED
MOUSSE OR SYLLABUB, TO ACCOMPANY

1. Place the wine in a large shallow pan with the water. Add the sugar and heat gently until dissolved. Add the lemon rind and about 5-6×15 ml tbs juice. Bring to the boil and boil for 1 minute.
2. Prepare the fruits. Leave the skin on the lime and orange for added shape and colour. Segment the peeled grapefruits, tangerine and mineola with a serrated knife over a bowl to catch the juices. Place the kumquat, lime and orange slices into the pan. Cover and simmer very gently until tender – about 20-25 minutes.
3. Add the other fruit segments and juices and warm through gently for 1-2 minutes. (The fruits will disintegrate if cooked too harshly.) Serve hot with a mousse or syllabub.

Orchard Fruit in Strawberry Syrup

Serves 8

75 G (3 OZ) SUGAR
600 ML (20 FL OZ) WATER
450 G (1 LB) VERY RIPE STRAWBERRIES, THINLY SLICED
PARED RIND OF 1 LEMON
4 PEACHES, HALVED AND STONED
4 NECTARINES, HALVED AND STONED
PINK ROSE PETALS, TO DECORATE

1. Place the sugar in a heavy-based saucepan and heat gently, without stirring, until completely dissolved. Increase heat and bubble gently until golden. Pour on the water (it will splutter furiously). Stir over a low heat until the caramel has completely dissolved.
2. Add the strawberries and lemon rind. Simmer gently, stirring, for 4-5 minutes. Leave until cool then strain into a large glass serving bowl. (Don't be tempted to press the strawberries through a strainer as this makes the syrup cloudy; instead save the cooked berries and use them to accompany ice cream, or stir into fresh fruit salads.)
3. Place the peach and nectarine halves in the strawberry syrup. Submerge with a wooden spoon to coat all cut surfaces in the syrup. Cover and chill in the refrigerator for at least 1 hour. Sprinkle over the rose petals to decorate just before serving.

COOK'S TIP
Take great care when adding the water to the hot sugar as it does splutter.

Red Fruit Sundae

Red Fruit Sundae

Serves 4

225 G (8 OZ) MIXED RED FRUIT
1×15 ML TBS CLEAR HONEY
1 ORANGE
300 G (11 OZ) FROMAGE FRAIS FROZEN DESSERT
RED FRUIT AND MINT SPRIGS, TO DECORATE

1. Pick over the fruit. Bring to the boil in a saucepan with the honey, grated orange rind and juice. Simmer for 3-4 minutes.
2. Blend in a blender or food processor until smooth, then push through a nylon sieve. Cover and chill.
3. Serve with fromage frais frozen dessert, decorated with fruit and mint sprigs.

Quick Apple Charlotte

Serves 8

675 G (1½ LB) EATING APPLES, PEELED, QUARTERED, CORED AND THICKLY SLICED

675 G (1½ LB) COOKING APPLES, PEELED, QUARTERED, CORED AND THICKLY SLICED

75 G (3 OZ) BUTTER OR MARGARINE

½×5 ML TSP GROUND CINNAMON

GRATED RIND AND JUICE OF 1 LEMON

3×15 ML TBS APRICOT JAM

4×15 ML TBS CASTER SUGAR

400 G (14 OZ) MIXED-GRAIN LOAF (UNSLICED) OR A SMALL BROWN LOAF

CUSTARD, TO SERVE

1. Place the eating and cooking apples in a large saucepan with 25 g (1 oz) butter or margarine and the cinnamon. Add the lemon rind and strained juice with the jam and half the sugar. Cover the pan tightly and cook gently until the apples are beginning to soften – about 15 minutes. Uncover and stir over a high heat for a minute or two to drive off excess moisture. (The apples should not be completely broken down.)

2. Meanwhile, make 50 g (2 oz) breadcrumbs from the loaf and stir into the apple mixture. Place in a 1.8 lt (3 pt) shallow ovenproof dish.

3. Cut about nine slices of bread 0.3-0.6 cm (⅛-¼ in) thick and remove the crusts. Spread one side of each slice with the remaining butter or margarine and sprinkle the remaining sugar over this side. Halve each slice diagonally then arrange sugar-side up over the apple until it is more or less completely covered. Don't overlap the slices of bread too closely or they will not crisp up properly.

4. Place the dish on a baking tray and bake in the oven at 220°C/425°F/Gas Mark 7 for about 20 minutes – the bread should be brown and crisp. Cool for about 10 minutes. Serve with custard.

Fresh Pineapple and Apricots

Serves 8

225 G (8 OZ) NO-SOAK DRIED APRICOTS, SNIPPED INTO STRIPS

JUICE OF 3 ORANGES

3×15 ML TBS COINTREAU

1 LARGE PINEAPPLE, SLICED INTO 8 PIECES ABOUT 1 CM (½ IN) THICK

40 G (1½ OZ) FLAKED ALMONDS, TOASTED

1. Place the apricot strips in a bowl. Strain the orange juice over the apricots. Add the Cointreau and stir gently to mix. Cover tightly and refrigerate for several hours or overnight.

2. Meanwhile, stamp out the cores from the pineapple slices and trim away the skin. Cover the slices and refrigerate until required.

3. To serve, arrange the pineapple on a flat-edged platter and top with apricots and juices. Scatter the almonds over the top.

Fresh Pineapple and Apricots

Grapefruit and Mint Ice Cream

Serves 4-6

600 ML (20 FL OZ) MILK

25 G (1 OZ) FRESH MINT LEAVES, RINSED, DRAINED AND ROUGHLY CHOPPED

25 G (1 OZ) CUSTARD POWDER

75 G (3 OZ) CASTER SUGAR

FINELY GRATED RIND AND JUICE OF 2 PINK GRAPEFRUIT

150 ML (5 FL OZ) DOUBLE CREAM, LIGHTLY WHIPPED

FRESH MINT SPRIGS AND GRAPEFRUIT SEGMENTS AND GRATED RIND, TO DECORATE

1. Bring 450 ml (16 fl oz) milk to the boil with the chopped mint; take off the heat, cover and leave to infuse for 10 minutes.

2. Whisk together the custard powder, sugar and remaining milk until smooth. Strain on the mint-infused milk, then return to the pan. Bring to the boil, stirring constantly, and cook for 1-2 minutes. Pour into a bowl and allow to cool, whisking occasionally to prevent a skin forming.

3. Stir the grapefruit rind and about 300 ml (10 fl oz) of juice into the cold custard with the cream.

4. Pour the mixture into a shallow freezer container and freeze until mushy – about 3 hours. Whisk to break down the ice, then freeze again until mushy and repeat the whisking process. Freeze until firm.

5. To serve, leave to soften in the refrigerator for about 45 minutes. Scoop into serving dishes and decorate with mint leaves, grapefruit segments and grated rind.

COOK'S TIP

The ice cream will be smoothest if you can freeze the mixture in a churn that breaks down the ice crystals as it mixes.

Grapefruit and Mint Ice Cream

Hot Vanilla Soufflé

Serves 4

1 VANILLA POD, SPLIT TO REVEAL SEEDS, OR 1×5 ML TSP VANILLA FLAVOURING

300 ML (10 FL OZ) MILK

50 G (2 OZ) BUTTER, PLUS EXTRA FOR GREASING

40 G (1½ OZ) PLAIN WHITE FLOUR

50 G (2 OZ) CASTER SUGAR

5 EGGS, SEPARATED

ICING SUGAR, TO DUST

SINGLE CREAM, TO SERVE

1. Place the vanilla pod in a saucepan with the milk and bring to the boil. Take off the heat; cover and leave to infuse for about 20 minutes before straining.
2. Tie a collar of greaseproof paper around a 1.5 lt (2½ pt) soufflé dish so that it stands about 8 cm (3 in) above the dish. Brush the inside of the dish and the paper with melted butter.
3. Melt 50 g (2 oz) butter in a large, heavy-based saucepan. Add the flour and cook for 1 minute before blending in the strained milk. Bring to the boil, stirring all the time; cook for about 1 minute. Take the pan off the heat and allow the mixture to cool lightly, then beat in the sugar, egg yolks and vanilla flavouring, if used.
4. Whisk the egg whites until stiff but not dry. Beat one spoonful into the sauce mixture, then lightly fold in the remaining egg whites. Pour the mixture gently into the prepared dish. Level with a palette knife and make a few cuts through the outer edges of the mixture – this helps it to rise evenly.
5. Stand the dish on a baking tray and cook in the oven at 190°C/375°F/Gas Mark 5 for 35-40 minutes or until well risen, just set and well browned on top. (It can take as long as 50 minutes in a gas oven.) Snip the string and carefully ease off the paper. Dust lightly with icing sugar and serve straightaway, accompanied by single cream.

Chocolate Cinnamon Soufflé

Serves 4-6

50 G (2 OZ) BUTTER, PLUS EXTRA FOR GREASING

75 G (3 OZ) PLAIN CHOCOLATE, BROKEN INTO PIECES

315 ML (10½ FL OZ) MILK

40 G (1½ OZ) PLAIN WHITE FLOUR

½×5 ML TSP GROUND CINNAMON

5 EGGS, SEPARATED

25 G (1 OZ) CASTER SUGAR

WHIPPED CREAM AND NATURAL YOGURT, MIXED, TO SERVE

1. Tie a collar of greaseproof paper around a 1.5 lt (2½ pt) soufflé dish so that it stands 8 cm (3 in) above the dish. Brush the inside of the dish and paper with melted butter.
2. Place the chocolate in a small bowl with 1×15 ml tbs milk. Stand the bowl in a saucepan of simmering water and heat gently until the chocolate is evenly melted, stirring occasionally. Take off the heat.
3. Melt 50 g (2 oz) butter in a heavy-based saucepan. Add the flour and cook for 1 minute before gradually blending in 300 ml (10 fl oz) milk and the cinnamon. Bring to the boil, stirring all the time. Cook for about 1 minute. Take off the heat, allow to cool slightly, then gradually beat in the egg yolks, caster sugar and melted chocolate.
4. Whisk the egg whites until stiff but not dry. Beat one spoonful into the sauce mixture to lighten it, then carefully fold in the remaining egg whites. Gently pour the soufflé mixture into the prepared dish. Level the top with a palette knife and make a few cuts through the outer edges of the mixture – this helps it to rise evenly.
5. Stand the dish on a baking tray and cook in the oven at 190°C/375°F/Gas Mark 5 for 35-40 minutes or until well risen, just set and well browned on top. (It can take as long as 50 minutes in a gas oven.) Snip the string and carefully ease off the paper. Serve straightaway, accompanied by whipped cream and yogurt.

COOK'S TIP

This soufflé is especially delicious served with a few sliced strawberries.

Individual Apple Soufflés

Serves 6

ICING SUGAR, FOR DUSTING

335 G (12 OZ) COOKING APPLES

50 G (2 OZ) BUTTER OR MARGARINE

25 G (1 OZ) CASTER SUGAR

2×15 ML TBS PLAIN FLOUR

150 ML (5 FL OZ) MILK

3 EGGS, SEPARATED

2×15 ML TBS APPLE BRANDY

APPLE SLICES, TO DECORATE (OPTIONAL)

SINGLE CREAM, TO SERVE

1. Lightly grease six 150 ml (5 fl oz) ramekin dishes. Dust them with icing sugar.
2. Peel, quarter, core and roughly chop the apples. Place in a small saucepan with 25 g (1 oz) of the butter and the sugar. Cover tightly and cook gently until the apples are very soft. Uncover and cook over a moderate heat, stirring frequently until all excess moisture evaporates. Mash or beat until smooth; cool slightly.
3. Melt the remaining butter in a pan, add the flour and cook for 2 minutes. Remove from the heat and stir in the milk. Cook, stirring, for 2-3 minutes.
4. Remove from the heat, cool slightly, then stir in the apple purée and egg yolks. Gently mix in the apple brandy. Whisk the egg whites until stiff but not dry. Stir one large spoonful into the apple mixture, then gently fold in the remaining egg whites. Divide between the prepared ramekin dishes so that each is three-quarters full.
5. Bake in the oven at 180°C/350°F/Gas Mark 4 for about 30 minutes or until just set and golden brown. Dust quickly with icing sugar and decorate with apple slices, if using. Serve straight away with single cream.

COOK'S TIP

The apple sauce mixture can be prepared ahead, ready to add the whisked egg whites at the last minute.

Individual Apple Soufflés

Grand Marnier Soufflé

Serves 4

50 G (2 OZ) BUTTER, PLUS EXTRA FOR GREASING

40 G (1½ OZ) PLAIN WHITE FLOUR

300 ML (10 FL OZ) MILK

4×15 ML TBS FINELY CHOPPED ORANGE MARMALADE

25 G (1 OZ) SUGAR

5 EGGS, SEPARATED

5×15 ML TBS GRAND MARNIER

ICING SUGAR, TO DUST

SINGLE CREAM, TO SERVE (OPTIONAL)

1. Tie a collar of greaseproof paper around a 1.5 lt (2½ pt) soufflé dish so that it stands about 8 cm (3 in) above the dish. Brush the inside of the dish and the paper with melted butter.

2. Melt 50 g (2 oz) butter in a large, heavy-based saucepan. Add the flour and cook for 1 minute before blending in the milk. Bring to the boil, stirring all the time. Cook for about 1 minute.

3. Remove from the heat and cool slightly before beating in the marmalade, sugar and egg yolks. Carefully stir in the Grand Marnier.

4. Whisk the egg whites until stiff but not dry. Beat one spoonful into the sauce mixture to lighten it, then lightly fold in the remaining egg whites. Gently pour the soufflé mixture into the prepared dish. Level the top with a palette knife and make a few cuts through the outer edges of the mixture – this helps it to rise evenly.

5. Stand the dish on a baking tray and cook in the oven at 190°C/375°F/Gas Mark 5 for 35-40 minutes or until well risen, just set and the top is well browned. (It can take as long as 50 minutes in a gas oven.) Snip the string and carefully ease off the paper. Dust lightly with icing sugar. Serve straightaway, accompanied by single cream, if wished.

Crêpes Suzette

Makes 8

115 G (4 OZ) PLAIN FLOUR

PINCH OF SALT

1 EGG

300 ML (10 FL OZ) MILK

VEGETABLE OIL FOR FRYING

CREAM, TO SERVE

— SAUCE —

50 G (2 OZ) BUTTER OR MARGARINE

25 G (1 OZ) CASTER SUGAR

GRATED RIND AND JUICE OF 1 LARGE ORANGE

2×15 ML TBS GRAND MARNIER OR OTHER ORANGE FLAVOURED LIQUEUR

3×15 ML TBS BRANDY OR RUM

1. Sift the flour and salt into a bowl and make a well in the centre. Break in the egg and beat well with a wooden spoon, then gradually beat in the milk, drawing in the flour from the sides of the bowl to make a smooth batter.

2. Heat a little oil in an 18 cm (7 in) heavy-based frying pan, running it around the base and sides of the pan, until hot. Pour off any surplus.

3. Pour in just enough batter to thinly coat the base of the pan. Cook for 1-2 minutes until golden brown. Turn or toss and cook the second side until golden.

4. Transfer the pancake to a plate and keep hot. Repeat with the remaining batter to make a total of eight pancakes. Pile the cooked pancakes on top of each other with greaseproof paper in between.

5. To make the sauce, melt the butter in a large frying pan. Remove from the heat and add the sugar, orange rind and juice and the liqueur. Heat gently to dissolve the sugar.

6. Fold each pancake in half and then in half again to form a fan shape. Place the pancakes in the frying pan in overlapping lines. Pour the orange sauce over the pancakes in the pan.

7. Warm the brandy, pour it over the pancakes and set alight. Shake gently, then serve at once with cream.

COOK'S TIP

Pancake batter may also be made in a blender or food processor. Put the egg and liquid in first, then add the flour and process for a few seconds only.

Lemon Curd Creams

Serves 6

6×15 ML TBS LEMON CURD

500 G CARTON FRESH CUSTARD SAUCE

300 ML (10 FL OZ) DOUBLE CREAM

— TO FINISH —

150 ML (5 FL OZ) DOUBLE CREAM, WHIPPED

FLAKED ALMONDS

1. Spoon the lemon curd into the base of six 150 ml (5 fl oz) ramekin dishes.

2. Mix together the custard sauce and cream, then gently pour the mixture into the ramekins, being careful not to disturb the lemon curd.

3. Stand the ramekins on a baking tray and cover with foil.

4. Bake at 180°C/350°F/Gas Mark 4 for about 40-45 minutes or until the custards are just set. If you know that your oven is hot check earlier.

5. Take the ramekins off the baking tray and cool. When cold, cover and chill. Decorate with whipped cream and flaked almonds.

Berried Treasure Chest

Serves 4

3 EGG WHITES

175 G (6 OZ) ICING SUGAR

45 G (1½ OZ) CASTER SUGAR

3×15 ML TBS COLD WATER

50 G (2 OZ) BLANCHED ALMONDS

OIL

150 ML (5 FL OZ) DOUBLE CREAM

335 G (12 OZ) MIXED SUMMER FRUIT, PICKED OVER AND RINSED WELL

1. Line two baking trays with non-stick baking parchment and draw two rectangles 18×10 cm (7×4 in) on one sheet and one on the other.

2. Place the egg whites and icing sugar in a large bowl. Stand the bowl over a pan of barely simmering water and continue whisking with an electric whisk until very

Berried Treasure Chest

stiff and shiny. This will take about 10 minutes. Do not allow the bowl to become too hot or the mixture will cook. Remove from the heat and continue whisking until the mixture is quite cold. Spoon into a piping bag fitted with a 1 cm (½ in) plain nozzle.

3. Pipe a solid base into one rectangle, then pipe around the edge of another to form an empty rectangle for the sides of the chest, and lastly, pipe a lattice filled with dots in the final one to make the lid. Bake in the oven at 100°C/200°F/Gas Mark Low (your oven's lowest setting) for 2-2½ hours or until quite dry. Cool, then peel off the paper.

4. Place the caster sugar in a small saucepan and add the cold water and heat slowly, without boiling, until the sugar dissolves. Bring to the boil and boil rapidly until the sugar turns golden. Stir in the almonds and pour on to an oiled tray. Cool, then process in a food processor to make a fine praline.

5. Whip the cream until it forms soft peaks. Stir in the praline.

6. Place the meringue base on a serving dish and use a little cream to fix the meringue rectangle to the base to form the chest. Fill with the cream and top with half the fruit. Set the lid on top at an angle to resemble an open chest. Arrange the remaining fruit around the treasure chest and serve within 1 hour of making.

COOK'S TIP

This is a meringue 'basket' containing all the treasures of the summer. The base, sides and top of the chest must be assembled at the last minute.

Chocolate Coconut Cream Roulade

Serves 8

165 G (5½ OZ) PLAIN CHOCOLATE, BROKEN INTO PIECES

5 EGGS, SEPARATED

175 G (6 OZ) CASTER SUGAR

1×15 ML TBS WATER

15 G (½ OZ) COCOA POWDER, SIFTED

CASTER SUGAR, FOR DUSTING

300 ML (10 FL OZ) DOUBLE CREAM

50 G (2 OZ) CREAMED COCONUT, GRATED OR FINELY CHOPPED

25 G (1 OZ) FLAKED OR SHREDDED COCONUT, TOASTED

1. Grease a 33×23 cm (13×9 in) swiss roll tin and line with greased greaseproof paper. Melt 115 g (4 oz) chocolate in a heatproof bowl set over a saucepan of hot water. Leave the chocolate to cool.
2. Whisk the egg yolks with the sugar until pale and fluffy. Add the water, melted chocolate and cocoa and whisk well to combine. Stiffly whisk the egg whites and lightly fold them into the mixture. Place in the prepared tin and level the surface.
3. Bake in the oven at 180°C/350°F/Gas Mark 4 for 20 minutes until well risen and firm to the touch. Remove from the oven, but do not turn out of the tin. Cover with a sheet of greaseproof paper and a damp teatowel and leave the roulade overnight at room temperature.
4. Have ready a large sheet of greaseproof paper dusted with caster sugar. Turn the cake out on to the paper and remove the lining paper.
5. Stiffly whip the cream and fold in the creamed coconut. Spread half of the cream over the chocolate cake and roll up like a swiss roll. (Don't worry when it cracks during rolling, as this won't show once the roll is complete).
6. Cover the roll with the remaining coconut cream and arrange the toasted coconut down the centre. Melt the remaining chocolate and drizzle over the roll. Leave to set before serving.

Chocolate Coconut Cream Roulade

Rhubarb and Orange Suedoise

Serves 10

900 G (2 LB) FRESH RHUBARB, WIPED, TRIMMED AND CUT INTO SHORT LENGTHS

GRATED RIND AND JUICE OF 2 LARGE ORANGES

½×5 ML TSP GROUND CINNAMON

115 G (4 OZ) SOFT LIGHT BROWN SUGAR

RED FOOD COLOURING (OPTIONAL)

2×15 ML TBS POWDERED GELATINE

2 EGG WHITES

115 G (4 OZ) CASTER SUGAR

150 ML (5 FL OZ) DOUBLE CREAM

150 ML (5 FL OZ) SINGLE CREAM

1. Place the rhubarb in a large saucepan and add the grated rind of one orange. Grate the rind of the second orange straight into a small bowl, cover the bowl tightly and refrigerate.
2. Add the juice from both oranges to the pan. Pour in 300 ml (10 fl oz) water and sprinkle in the cinnamon and soft light brown sugar. Cover the pan tightly then simmer until the fruit is soft and mushy; cool slightly.
3. In a blender or food processor purée the pan ingredients until quite smooth – there should be about 1.5 lt (2½ pt). Pour the purée into a large bowl; add a little food colouring if wished.
4. Spoon 6×15 ml tbs water into a small bowl then sprinkle the gelatine over the water. Leave to stand for about 5 minutes, or until sponge-like in texture. Stand the basin in a pan of simmering water until the gelatine mixture is liquid and quite clear. Stir into the rhubarb. Ladle the mixture into 10 individual dessert dishes, preferably glass. Cover and refrigerate to set, preferably overnight.
5. Meanwhile, make the small meringues. Whisk the egg whites until stiff but not dry. Whisk in 2×15 ml tbs caster sugar until the mixture returns to its former stiffness. Fold in remaining caster sugar. Spoon or pipe the mixture into small meringue shapes on baking trays lined with non-stick baking parchment. (There should be about 50 meringues.) Dry out in the oven at 100°C/200°F/Gas Mark Low (your oven's lowest setting) for about 1½ hours. Cool on

a wire rack then store the meringues in an air-tight container.

6. To serve the suedoise, lightly whip the creams together until they hold their shape then fold in the reserved orange rind, keeping a little for decoration. Spoon over the rhubarb in the serving dishes and top with meringues. Decorate with orange rind.

Ricotta and Almond Cheesecake

Serves 8

FLOU[illegible] [illegible]USTING

335 G [illegible] [illegible]ESE

[illegible] [illegible]DS

75 G [illegible] [illegible]R

FINELY GRATED RIND AN[illegible] [illegible]E OF 2 LEMONS

75 G (3 OZ) SUL[illegible]ANAS

40 G (1½ OZ) CUT MIXED PEEL, FINELY CHOPPED

4 RIPE NECTARINES OR PEACHES, HALVED AND STONED

450 ML (16 FL OZ) DRY RED WINE

ICING SUGAR, FOR DUSTING

1. Grease and base-line an 18 cm (7 in) shallow round cake tin. Dust with flour.

2. In a food processor blend the cheese, almonds, sugar and egg yolks until smooth. Add the lemon rind and 2×15 ml tbs lemon juice; blend again until mixed.

3. Place the cheese mixture in a bowl and stir in the sultanas and peel. Spoon into the prepared tin, levelling the surface.

4. Bake in the oven at 180°C/350°F/Gas Mark 4 for about 50-55 minutes or until firm.

5. Meanwhile, slice the unpeeled nectarines or peaches and place them in a saucepan. Cover with the red wine and slowly heat until barely boiling. Turn off the heat and leave in the wine to cool completely. Cover and chill.

6. Cool the cheesecake in the tin for about 30 minutes. Turn out and serve slightly warm or chilled, dusted with icing sugar. Serve with the chilled nectarines or peaches.

Rhubarb and Orange Suedoise

Creamy Meringues

Serves 8

3 EGG WHITES

175 G (6 OZ) CASTER SUGAR

— FILLING —

225 G (8 OZ) CLOTTED CREAM, OR 300 ML (10 FL OZ) DOUBLE OR WHIPPING CREAM, WHIPPED

CRYSTALLISED ROSE PETALS, TO DECORATE

1. Mark eight 6 cm (2½ in) circles on a sheet of non-stick baking parchment. Place on a baking tray, pencil side down.

2. Whisk the egg whites until stiff but not dry. Add half of the sugar, and whisk until thick and glossy. Fold in the remaining sugar.

3. Transfer the meringue to a piping bag fitted with a 1 cm (½ in) plain or star-shaped nozzle. Starting at the centre of each circle, pipe the meringue in a spiral out to the edge of the marked circles. Pipe another ring on top of the edge of each round to form small nest shapes.

4. Bake in the oven at 140°C/275°F/Gas Mark 1 for about 1-1½ hours or until firm and dried out. Leave to cool on the baking tray. To serve, fill with the cream and decorate with cystallised rose petals.

COOK'S TIP

Unfilled meringue nests keep well in an air-tight container for several weeks. Once filled, meringues should be eaten right away.

Ginger Meringues with Rhubarb Sauce

Serves 6

4 EGG WHITES

225 G (8 OZ) CASTER SUGAR

4 × 15 ML TBS ADVOCAAT LIQUEUR

2 × 15 ML TBS FINELY CHOPPED PRESERVED STEM GINGER

2 × 5 ML TSP PRESERVED STEM GINGER SYRUP

300 ML (10 FL OZ) DOUBLE CREAM

450 G (1 LB) RHUBARB, CUT INTO 4 CM (1½ IN) LENGTHS

50 G (2 OZ) GRANULATED SUGAR

1 × 5 ML TSP ARROWROOT

ICING SUGAR, TO DUST

1. Line two baking trays with non-stick baking parchment. Whisk the egg whites until stiff but not dry. Add 2 × 15 ml tbs caster sugar and whisk again until very stiff and shiny. Fold in the remaining caster sugar.
2. Spoon or pipe the meringue mixture into 48 walnut-sized rounds, well spaced on the baking trays.
3. Bake in the oven at 130°C/250°F/Gas Mark ½ for 2 hours or until completely dried out. Cool on a wire rack and store in an air-tight container until required.
4. Mix together the Advocaat, chopped preserved stem ginger and syrup. Whip the cream until it just begins to hold its shape and fold into the ginger mixture into the cream. Whip again for 1 minute. Cover the mixture and refrigerate.
5. Place the rhubarb in a medium-sized saucepan with the granulated sugar and 300 ml (10 fl oz) water. Cook, covered, over a very gentle heat until tender, about 20 minutes. Cool slightly before puréeing. Sieve the purée back into the rinsed out pan. Blend the arrowroot with 1 × 15 ml tbs water. Stir into the rhubarb purée and bring to the boil, stirring all the time. Boil for 1-2 minutes until thickened. Cool.
6. To serve the meringues, sandwich the rounds together with a little of the ginger cream. Refrigerate for about 30 minutes to soften slightly. Dust with icing sugar and serve with the rhubarb sauce.

Steamed Orange and Coconut Sponge

Serves 6

175 G (6 OZ) SOFTENED BUTTER

75 G (3 OZ) DARK SOFT BROWN SUGAR

75 G (3 OZ) CASTER SUGAR

4 LARGE ORANGES

3 EGGS, BEATEN

50 G (2 OZ) DESICCATED COCONUT

225 G (8 OZ) SELF-RAISING WHITE FLOUR, SIFTED

TOASTED SHREDDED COCONUT, TO DECORATE (OPTIONAL)

— CUSTARD —

2 × 15 ML TBS CUSTARD POWDER

2 × 15 ML TBS CASTER SUGAR

450 ML (16 FL OZ) MILK

JUICE OF 3 LARGE ORANGES

1. Grease and base-line a 1.5 lt (2½ pt) pudding basin. Put a large pan of water on to boil over which a steamer will fit.
2. Beat together the butter, brown sugar, caster sugar and the finely grated rind of one orange until light and fluffy. Gradually beat in the eggs, keeping the mixture stiff. Gently fold in the coconut, flour and 3 × 15 ml tbs orange juice. Spoon into the prepared basin, then cover with pleated and greased greaseproof paper and foil. Tie down securely. Place the bowl in the steamer; cover and steam for about 2 hours.
3. Meanwhile, prepare the custard. Mix the powder to a smooth paste with the caster sugar and a little milk. Heat the remaining milk, then stir into the custard mixture. Return to the pan and bring to the boil, stirring all the time; cook for 1-2 minutes. Pour out into a bowl and cool slightly, then whisk in the orange juice. Leave to cool further, whisking occasionally.
4. Using a serrated knife, cut all peel and pith away from the remaining 3 oranges. Slice the flesh, discarding the pips.
5. Turn out the pudding to serve with the orange custard and slices of fresh orange. Decorate with the shredded coconut, if you wish.

Christmas Puddings

Makes 2 × 900 g (2 lb) puddings

225 G (8 OZ) SHREDDED SUET

225 G (8 OZ) FRESH WHITE BREADCRUMBS

50 G (2 OZ) PLAIN FLOUR

450 G (1 LB) SULTANAS

225 G (8 OZ) RAISINS

50 G (2 OZ) CHOPPED MIXED PEEL

GRATED RIND OF 2 LEMONS

50 G (2 OZ) GLACÉ CHERRIES, HALVED

¼ × 5 ML TSP SALT

225 G (8 OZ) SOFT DARK BROWN MUSCOVADO SUGAR

1 × 5 ML TSP GROUND MIXED SPICE

5 EGGS, WELL BEATEN

50 ML (2 FL OZ) BRANDY

50 ML (2 FL OZ) RUM

HOLLY LEAVES, TO DECORATE

ORANGE WHISKY BUTTER, TO SERVE (SEE RIGHT)

1. In a large bowl, mix together all the ingredients except the eggs, brandy and rum. Then add the eggs and liquor and beat vigorously.
2. Divide the mixture between two 40 cm (16 in) squares of foil, each inside a double thickness of butter muslin, and gather up around the mixture. Shape the puddings into firm rounds. Secure with string.
3. To keep the round shape, the puddings should be boiled suspended by a string so that they don't touch the bottom of the pan. Choose a large pan that will hold the puddings easily, leaving a good 2.5 cm (1 in) space around, below and above when suspended. Tie the puddings to a long-handled wooden spoon or cooling rack laid across the top of the pan. Pour in enough boiling water to cover the puddings. Cover the pan with a lid of foil. Simmer for 5 hours. Top up the water to keep the puddings submerged.
4. Drain off the water and leave the puddings suspended until cold. Rewrap in clean, dry muslin then overwrap with foil. Store in the refrigerator for up to 6 weeks.
5. To serve, remove the foil. Suspend and boil the pudding as before. Boil for 4 hours. Lift out, unwrap, decorate with holly leaves and serve with orange whisky butter.

COOK'S TIP

The puddings are boiled rather than steamed, which makes them rich and moist. However, they must be stored in the refrigerator or frozen or they will go mouldy. If you don't want to make round puddings, pack the mixture into two 1.2 lt (2 pt) pudding basins. Cover with greased greaseproof paper and foil. Secure with string. Boil for 5 hours, cool, then cover with fresh greaseproof paper and foil. Store and boil to reheat, as in recipe.

Orange Whisky Butter

Serves 8

115 G (4 OZ) UNSALTED BUTTER, SOFTENED

115 G (4 OZ) SOFT LIGHT BROWN MUSCOVADO SUGAR

GRATED RIND OF 1 SMALL ORANGE

½×5 ML TSP MIXED SPICE

PINCH OF GROUND GREEN CARDAMOM

3×15 ML TBS WHISKY

1×5 ML TSP LEMON JUICE

1. Cream the butter and sugar until pale and soft. Add the orange rind and spices.
2. Gradually beat in the whisky and lemon juice. Spoon into small, wide-necked pots. Cover and store in the refrigerator for up to one week.

Baked Orange and Almond Pudding

Serves 6

115 G (4 OZ) BUTTER

115 G (4 OZ) CASTER SUGAR

FINELY GRATED RIND AND JUICE OF 1 ORANGE

2 EGGS, BEATEN

1×5 ML TSP VANILLA FLAVOURING

115 G (4 OZ) BLANCHED ALMONDS, CUT INTO SLIVERS AND LIGHTLY TOASTED

75 G (3 OZ) WHITE SELF-RAISING FLOUR, SIFTED

1×5 ML TSP BAKING POWDER

JUICE OF 1 LEMON

50 G (2 OZ) ICING SUGAR, SIEVED

1. Soften the butter in a medium-sized bowl. Add the caster sugar and orange rind. Beat until pale and fluffy.
2. Gradually beat in the eggs with the vanilla flavouring.
3. Fold 75 g (3 oz) almonds into the mixture with the sifted flour and the baking powder. Add about 1-2×15 ml tbs orange juice to obtain a soft dropping consistency. Place the mixture in a 1.2 lt (2 pt) greased and floured kugelhopf or ring mould and level the surface. Bake in the oven at 190°C/375°F/Gas Mark 5 for 40-50 minutes or until well risen, golden and firm to the touch. Turn out on to a wire rack.
4. Place 2×15 ml tbs lemon juice in a bowl. Add the icing sugar and whisk well. Spoon the mixture over the warm cake to glaze it. Sprinkle the top with the remaining toasted almonds. Serve warm or cold.

Christmas Puddings

Warm Lemon Syrup Cake

Serves 12

225 G (8 OZ) BUTTER OR MARGARINE, SOFTENED
FINELY GRATED RIND AND JUICE OF 2 LEMONS
225 G (8 OZ) CASTER SUGAR
4 EGGS, BEATEN
225 G (8 OZ) SELF-RAISING WHITE FLOUR
POACHED FRUIT, TO ACCOMPANY

— SYRUP —

175 G (6 OZ) CASTER SUGAR
STRAINED JUICE OF 3 LEMONS
75 ML (3 FL OZ) WATER

1. Grease and base-line a 21 cm (8½ in) base measurement moule à manqué tin. (This is a deep cake tin with sloping sides; if unavailable, use a deep round cake tin of a similar size.)
2. Cream together the butter and lemon rind. Gradually beat in the caster sugar, followed by the eggs, keeping the mixture stiff. Lastly, fold in the flour and 2 × 15 ml tbs lemon juice.
3. Spoon into the prepared tin and bake at 180°C/350°F/Gas Mark 4 for about 1 hour, or until well browned.
4. Meanwhile, prepare the syrup. Place the sugar, lemon juice and water in a saucepan. Warm gently until the sugar dissolves; bring to the boil and bubble for 1 minute. Cool.
5. As soon as the cake is cooked, turn out on to an edged dish and immediately spoon over the syrup. Leave for about 30 minutes for the syrup to soak in. Serve warm with poached fruit.

COOK'S TIP

This lemon cake is simply delicious warm, but if you can resist the temptation, it will keep well for several days in an air-tight tin.

Warm Lemon Syrup Cake

Apricot and Pistachio Rolls

Serves 6

400 G (14 OZ) NO-SOAK DRIED APRICOTS
1 BAY LEAF
GRATED RIND AND JUICE OF 1 ORANGE
3 × 15 ML TBS GRAND MARNIER
50 G (2 OZ) BUTTER
PINCH OF GRATED NUTMEG
6 SHEETS FILO PASTRY, ABOUT 23 × 30 CM (9 × 12 IN)
25 G (1 OZ) PISTACHIO NUTS, SKINNED AND ROUGHLY CHOPPED
ICING SUGAR
300 ML (10 FL OZ) SINGLE CREAM
FRESH MINT SPRIGS AND GRATED ORANGE RIND, TO DECORATE (OPTIONAL)

1. Cover the apricots with cold water and leave to soak overnight. Drain, reserving the soaking liquid. Place the apricots in a medium-sized saucepan with the bay leaf and 150 ml (5 fl oz) soaking liquid. Bring to the boil and simmer for 2-3 minutes until most of the liquid has evaporated. Discard the bay leaf. Stir in the orange rind, 2 × 15 ml tbs juice and 1 × 15 ml tbs Grand Marnier. Purée in a blender or food processor and allow to cool.
2. Melt the butter with the nutmeg. Brush the filo pastry sheets lightly with half the melted butter. Divide the apricot mixture between the pastry sheets, placing it in a line along one of the shorter edges but leaving about 2.5 cm (1 in) of uncovered pastry at each side of the mixture.
3. Fold the sides of the pastry over slightly, then carefully roll up to form thin rolls. Place on a lightly oiled baking tray and brush with the remaining melted butter. Sprinkle with pistachio nuts, dust lightly with icing sugar. Bake in the oven at 200°C/400°F/Gas Mark 6 for 20-25 minutes, or until golden and crisp.
4. Meanwhile, stir together the cream, remaining Grand Marnier and 1 × 5 ml tsp icing sugar. Chill well and serve with the hot apricot and pistachio rolls. Decorate, if you wish, with mint sprigs and grated orange rind.

Apricot and Pistachio Rolls

Peach and Walnut Tortes

Serves 4

50 G (2 OZ) WALNUT PIECES

115 G (4 OZ) CASTER SUGAR

50 G (2 OZ) PLAIN WHITE FLOUR, SIFTED

2 EGGS

675 G (1½ LB) SMALL RIPE PEACHES

1×15 ML TBS WATER

ABOUT 115 ML (4 FL OZ) DOUBLE CREAM

1-2×15 ML TBS LEMON JUICE

ICING SUGAR, FOR DUSTING

BRANDY

1. Toast the walnuts until just beginning to brown; cool. Grind to a powder through a nut mouli or using a food processor. Grease and base-line a sandwich tin (21 cm (8½ in) top measurement, 20 cm (8 in) base measurement). Dust the tin with a little caster sugar and flour, shaking out any excess.
2. With an electric whisk, beat the eggs with 75 g (3 oz) caster sugar until the mixture is thick and mousse-like. When the beaters are lifted out, the mixture should leave a thick trail. Fold in the flour with 40 g (1½ oz) of the ground nuts. Spoon into the prepared tin and bake in the oven at 190°C/375°F/ Gas Mark 5 for 20-25 minutes or until firm to the touch. Turn out of the tin and cool.
3. Meanwhile, roughly chop two-thirds of the peaches, discarding the stones. Place in a small pan with the remaining caster sugar and the water. Cover tightly and simmer until tender. Purée, then push through a nylon sieve; cool.
4. Whip the cream until it holds its shape, then whisk in 5-6×15 ml tbs fruit purée, keeping the mixture firm enough to spread. Quarter the remaining peaches and reserve about eight thin slices for decoration. Skin and roughly chop the remaining peaches. Toss them all lightly in lemon juice.
5. Using a 10 cm (4 in) oval cutter, stamp out four shapes from the cold cake. (Freeze any cake trimmings for use in trifles.) Split each oval into two then sandwich together again with the cream mixture and chopped peaches. Dust with icing sugar and decorate with the peach slices and remaining ground walnuts. Stir a little brandy into the remaining fruit purée and divide between four small serving plates. Place a peach torte in the centre of each plate. Cover and refrigerate until required. Remove from the refrigerator at least half an hour before serving.

Crisp Palmiers

Crisp Palmiers

Serves 6

115 G (4 OZ) CHILLED PUFF PASTRY

CASTER SUGAR

150 ML (5 FL OZ) DOUBLE CREAM, WHIPPED

— **FRUIT SAUCE** —

675 G (1½ LB) SMALL STRAWBERRIES OR RASPBERRIES, HULLED

335 G (12 OZ) CASTER SUGAR

4×15 ML TBS LEMON JUICE

1. Roll the pastry out to a rectangle measuring about 51×13 cm (20×5 in) and 0.3 cm (⅛ in) thick. Sprinkle generously with sugar.
2. Fold the short ends over to the centre until they meet and press down firmly. Sprinkle with sugar as before and fold the short ends to the centre again. Press down and sprinkle with sugar. Fold one side of the roll on top of the other and press together.
3. Using a sharp knife, cut into 12 slices, each just under 1 cm (½ in) thick. Place cut side down on non-stick baking trays. Press down firmly, allowing room to spread.
4. Bake in the oven at 220°C/425°F/Gas Mark 7 for about 6 minutes or until golden. Turn over and bake for a further 3-4 minutes. Cool.
5. About 2 hours before serving, sandwich together with the whipped cream.
6. To make the fruit sauce, lightly crush the hulled fruit with a fork, then stir in the sugar and lemon juice. Cover and leave for about 1½ hours, stirring occasionally, until the sugar has dissolved. Serve with the cream-filled palmiers.

Spiced Pear Strudel

Serves 8

75 G (3 OZ) FRESH WHITE BREADCRUMBS

150 G (5 OZ) UNSALTED BUTTER

50 G (2 OZ) SOFT LIGHT BROWN SUGAR

50 G (2 OZ) SULTANAS

½×5 ML TSP MIXED SPICE

½×5 ML TSP GROUND CINNAMON

450 G (1 LB) PEARS, PEELED, CORED AND SLICED

4 LARGE SHEETS OF FILO PASTRY

50 G (2 OZ) BLANCHED ALMONDS, TOASTED AND CHOPPED

1×15 ML TBS REDCURRANT JELLY (OPTIONAL)

ICING SUGAR, FOR DUSTING

1. Fry the breadcrumbs in 50 g (2 oz) of the butter, stirring frequently until crisp and golden. Mix together the brown sugar, sultanas, mixed spice, cinnamon and pear slices.
2. Melt the remaining butter. Brush one sheet of filo pastry with a little of the melted butter. Cover with a second sheet of pastry and brush with a little more melted butter.
3. Cover the pastry with half the fried breadcrumbs, leaving a 5 cm (2 in) border on all sides. Arrange half the pear mixture over the crumbs and sprinkle with half the chopped almonds. Dot with half the redcurrant jelly, if using.
4. Fold the edges over the filling and brush with a little melted butter. Roll up, like a swiss roll, starting from a long side. Place the strudel on a lightly greased baking tray (with raised edges) and brush with melted butter. Make a second strudel in the same way using the remaining ingredients.
5. Bake in the oven at 190°C/375°F/Gas Mark 5 for 35 minutes until crisp and golden, covering with foil during cooking if necessary, to prevent overbrowning. Brush halfway through cooking, with butter from the baking tray.
6. Allow the strudels to cool slightly, then sprinkle liberally with sifted icing sugar. Serve warm or cold, cut into chunky slices.

COOK'S TIP

For convenience, make the strudel in advance, ready to reheat just before serving.

French Apple Flan

Serves 6

2 QUANTITIES RICH SHORTCRUST PASTRY (SEE PAGE 212)

900 G (2 LB) COOKING APPLES

50 G (2 OZ) BUTTER OR MARGARINE

2×15 ML TBS WATER

9×15 ML TBS APRICOT JAM

50 G (2 OZ) SUGAR

FINELY GRATED RIND OF ½ LEMON

2×15 ML TBS CALVADOS OR BRANDY

225 G (8 OZ) DESSERT APPLES

ABOUT 2×15 ML TBS LEMON JUICE

1×5 ML TSP CASTER SUGAR

1. Roll out the pastry on a floured surface and use to line a 20 cm (8 in) loose-based fluted flan tin placed on a baking tray. Chill in the refrigerator for 30 minutes.
2. Bake blind at 200°C/400°F/Gas Mark 6 for 10-15 minutes, then remove paper and beans and bake for a further 5 minutes.
3. Meanwhile, cut the cooking apples into quarters, core, then chop the flesh. Melt the butter in a saucepan and add the apples with the water. Cover and cook gently for about 15 minutes until soft and mushy.
4. Rub the apples through a sieve into a large clean pan. Add half the apricot jam with the sugar, lemon rind and Calvados or brandy. Cook over a high heat for about 15 minutes, stirring, until all excess liquid has evaporated and the mixture is thickened.
5. Spoon the thick apple purée into the flan case and smooth the surface. Peel, quarter, core and slice the dessert apples very thinly. Arrange in an overlapping circle over the apple purée. Brush lightly with lemon juice; sprinkle with the caster sugar.
6. Return the flan to the oven and bake at 200°C/400°F/Gas Mark 6 for a further 25-30 minutes, or until the pastry and apples are lightly coloured. Transfer to a serving plate. Cool for 10 minutes.
7. Gently warm the remaining jam with 1×15 ml tbs lemon juice, then sieve. Brush over the top and sides of the flan.

Deep-Dish Apple Flan

Serves 6-8

1½ QUANTITIES QUICK SWEET PASTRY (SEE PAGE 213)

1.4 KG (3 LB) COOKING APPLES, PEELED, QUARTERED AND THICKLY SLICED

3 CLOVES

50 G (2 OZ) BUTTER

1×5 ML TSP MIXED SPICE

1 CINNAMON STICK

75 G (3 OZ) CASTER SUGAR

1 EGG, BEATEN

1-2×15 ML TBS FLAKED ALMONDS

1-2×15 ML TBS DEMERARA SUGAR

ICING SUGAR, FOR DUSTING

1. Follow the recipe for Quick Sweet Pastry to the end of step 3, but using a 5 cm (2 in) deep, 21 cm (8½ in) loose-based, fluted flan tin. Refrigerate the pastry trimmings, wrapped in clingfilm.
2. Meanwhile, put the apples into a medium saucepan. Add the cloves, butter, mixed spice, cinnamon and caster sugar. Cook, stirring, over a high heat until the apples are soft. Off the heat, remove the cloves and cinnamon stick then allow the apples to cool slightly.
3. Spoon the apple mixture into the prepared flan case. Make pastry leaves from the trimmings. Arrange neatly over the apple filling and brush the pastry lightly with beaten egg. Sprinkle with flaked almonds and demerara sugar.
4. Bake in the oven at 180°C/350°F/Gas Mark 4 for about 35 minutes or until golden and crisp. Leave to cool for 10 minutes before removing from the tin. Serve warm dusted with icing sugar.

Glazed Nut Flan (left)
Deep-Dish Apple Flan (centre)
Apricot and Cardamon Flan (right)

Apricot and Cardamom Flan

Serves 6

115 G (4 OZ) NO-SOAK DRIED APRICOTS
6 GREEN CARDAMOMS, SPLIT
2 BAY LEAVES
1½ QUANTITIES QUICK SWEET PASTRY (SEE PAGE 213)
150 ML (5 FL OZ) SINGLE CREAM
1 WHOLE EGG AND 1 EGG YOLK
25 G (1 OZ) CASTER SUGAR
4×15 ML TBS APRICOT JAM
1×15 ML TBS WATER

1. Place the apricots, cardamoms and bay leaves in a bowl. Cover with cold water and leave to soak overnight in the refrigerator.
2. Follow the recipe for Quick Sweet Pastry to the end of step 1, chilling for at least 30 minutes. Roll out on a lightly floured surface and use to line a 34×11 cm (13½×4½ in) loose-based fluted tranche tin. Chill for 10-15 minutes. Place on a flat baking tray and bake blind for about 20 minutes.
3. Drain the apricots, discard the bay leaves and cardamoms. Cut the apricots in half; pat dry with kitchen paper.
4. Whisk cream, eggs and sugar together. Arrange the apricots, cut-side down, in the pastry case. Pour the cream mixture over the top. Bake in the oven at 180°C/350°F/Gas Mark 4 for 35 minutes or until just set. Brown under the grill. Cool before removing the flan case.
5. In a saucepan, melt the apricot jam with the water over a gentle heat. Bring to the boil. Brush evenly over the warm flan. Serve warm or cold.

Glazed Nut Flan

Serves 6-8

1 QUANTITY QUICK SWEET PASTRY (SEE PAGE 213)
50 G (2 OZ) HAZELNUTS
25 G (1 OZ) PISTACHIO NUTS, SHELLED
1 EGG
25 G (1 OZ) CASTER SUGAR
25 G (1 OZ) BUTTER, MELTED
GRATED RIND AND JUICE OF 1 LEMON
PINCH OF GRATED NUTMEG
4×15 ML TBS GOLDEN SYRUP
1×15 ML TBS PLAIN FLOUR
75 G (3 OZ) WALNUT PIECES
75 G (3 OZ) BRAZIL NUTS
50 G (2 OZ) PECAN NUTS

1. Follow the recipe for Quick Sweet Pastry to the end of step 3, only very lightly browning the pastry.
2. Meanwhile, brown the hazelnuts under a hot grill. Place in a clean tea-towel and rub well to remove the skins. Dip the pistachio nuts in boiling water for 1 minute. Drain and remove the skins; dry on kitchen paper.
3. With an electric whisk beat the egg and sugar together until very thick and pale – about 5 minutes. Quickly stir in the melted butter, lemon rind, nutmeg and half the golden syrup. Fold in the flour and finally all the nuts.
4. Spoon the nut mixture into the prepared flan case. Bake in the oven at 180°C/350°F/Gas Mark 4 for about 35 minutes or until golden and firm to the touch; cool for 10-15 minutes.
5. Heat together the remaining golden syrup and 2×15 ml tbs lemon juice. Boil for 2-3 minutes until syrupy. Brush over the warm flan. Leave in the tin for 10-15 minutes before removing to a wire rack to cool. Serve warm or cold.

Warm Lemon and Apple Flan

Serves 8

115 G (4 OZ) BUTTER OR MARGARINE, CUT INTO SMALL PIECES
225 G (8 OZ) PLAIN WHITE FLOUR
125 G (4½ OZ) CASTER SUGAR
3-4×15 ML TBS WATER
3 EGGS
150 ML (5 FL OZ) SINGLE CREAM
FINELY GRATED RIND AND JUICE OF 2 LEMONS
450 G (1 LB) CRISP EATING APPLES, PEELED, CORED AND COARSELY GRATED
ICING SUGAR, FOR DUSTING
SINGLE CREAM, TO SERVE

1. Rub or fork the fat into the flour until the mixture resembles fine breadcrumbs. Stir in 40 g (1½ oz) caster sugar then bind to a firm dough with the water. Knead lightly, roll out and use to line a 25 cm (10 in) fluted flan tin. Chill for 30 minutes.
2. Prick pastry base then line with greaseproof paper and baking beans. Bake at 200°C/400°F/Gas Mark 6 for about 15 minutes or until set. Remove the paper and beans and return to the oven until golden and well dried out.
3. Place the eggs, cream and remaining caster sugar in a bowl and whisk well. Add the lemon rind and 5-6×15 ml tbs strained lemon juice, whisking again until smooth. Add the apple to the lemon mixture; stir to mix.
4. Spoon the mixture into the flan case. Bake at 180°C/350°F/Gas Mark 4 for about 45-50 minutes, or until set and golden. Dust with icing sugar and serve warm with single cream.

Spiced Lemon Syrup Tart

Serves 6

75 G (3 OZ) BUTTER, CUT INTO SMALL PIECES
175 G (6 OZ) PLAIN WHOLEMEAL FLOUR
1×5 ML TSP GROUND MIXED SPICE
5×15 ML TBS WATER
225 G (8 OZ) GOLDEN SYRUP
150 G (5 OZ) FRESH WHITE BREADCRUMBS
FINELY GRATED RIND AND JUICE OF 1 LEMON

1. Rub the butter into the flour mixed with half the spice. Bind to a soft dough with the water. Roll out thinly and use to line a 20 cm (8 in) loose-based flan tin; chill for 15 minutes. Reserve the pastry trimmings.
2. Bake the flan case blind in the oven at 200°C/400°F/Gas Mark 6 for about 12 minutes or until thoroughly dried out.
3. Mix the syrup with the breadcrumbs, remaining spice, finely grated lemon rind and 1 × 15 ml tbs juice. Spoon into the flan case and decorate with a lattice made from strips of pastry trimmings.
4. Bake at 200°C/400°F/Gas Mark 6 for about 25 minutes or until the pastry is crisp and golden. Cool for about 1 hour before serving.

Papaya Pie

Serves 6

275 G (10 OZ) PLAIN WHITE FLOUR
1×5 ML TSP GROUND CINNAMON
150 G (5 OZ) SOFTENED BUTTER, CUT INTO SMALL PIECES
CASTER SUGAR
1 EGG, SEPARATED, AND 1 EGG YOLK
GRATED RIND AND JUICE OF 1 LARGE ORANGE
2 MEDIUM-SIZED RIPE PAPAYAS, PEELED, HALVED, SEEDED AND THINLY SLICED
300 ML (10 FL OZ) DOUBLE OR WHIPPING CREAM, LIGHTLY WHIPPED

1. Sift the flour and cinnamon on to a clean, dry work surface. Make a well and in it place the butter, 65 g (2½ oz) sugar, the egg yolks and orange rind with 3 × 15 ml tbs orange juice (reserve the remaining juice). With the fingers of one hand only, 'pinch' the well ingredients together until evenly blended. Gradually draw in the flour, using a palette knife, and knead gently until just smooth. Wrap and chill for about 20 minutes.
2. Roll out two-thirds of the dough to line a 24 cm (9½ in) loose-based fluted flan tin. Arrange the papayas in the flan case. Top with remaining pastry, sealing well.
3. Bake in the oven at 180°C/350°F/Gas Mark 4 for about 25 minutes, or until just set but not browned. Brush with beaten egg white and dust with caster sugar. Bake for 20-25 minutes more, until well browned. Serve warm. Stir about 3 × 15 ml tbs orange juice into the cream and serve with the pie.

Papaya Pie

Orchard Lattice Pie

Serves 6

150 G (5 OZ) BUTTER, CUT INTO SMALL PIECES
275 G (10 OZ) PLAIN WHITE FLOUR
90 G (3½ OZ) SOFT LIGHT BROWN SUGAR
1 EGG, SEPARATED
ABOUT 3×15 ML TBS WATER
GRATED RIND AND JUICE OF 1 LEMON
½×5 ML TSP GROUND CINNAMON
1×15 ML TBS SEMOLINA
675 G (1½ LB) COOKING APPLES, PEELED, CORED AND CHOPPED INTO LARGE PIECES
225 G (8 OZ) BLACKBERRIES
CASTER SUGAR
CUSTARD, TO SERVE

1. Rub the butter into the flour until the mixture resembles breadcrumbs. Stir in 40 g (1½ oz) brown sugar then bind to a soft dough with the egg yolk mixed with the water. Knead, then roll out on a floured surface to an oblong about 25 × 10 cm (10 × 4 in). Fold into three, then give it a half turn. Repeat the rolling and folding twice more; wrap and chill.
2. In a bowl, put the lemon rind, 2 × 15 ml tbs juice, 50 g (2 oz) brown sugar, the cinnamon and semolina. Stir well. Stir the apple into the bowl with the blackberries.
3. Roll out two-thirds of the pastry and use to line a 900 ml (1½ pt) pie plate 21 cm (8 ½ in) top measurement. Pile the apple mixture into the dish, then decorate with a lattice made from the remaining pastry.
4. Stand the dish on a baking tray. Bake in the oven at 200°C/400°F/Gas Mark 6 for 15 minutes. Brush the pastry with beaten egg white; sprinkle with caster sugar.
5. Bake at 200°C/400°F/Gas Mark 6 for a further 25 minutes, covering lightly with foil when well browned. Serve with custard.

Orchard Lattice Pie

PRUNE AND PEAR TART

Serves 8

— PASTRY —

115 G (4 OZ) ICING SUGAR

SALT

5 EGG YOLKS

1×5 ML TSP VANILLA FLAVOURING

175 G (6 OZ) BUTTER, SOFTENED

335 G (12 OZ) PLAIN WHITE FLOUR

— FILLING —

450 G (1 LB) LARGE NO-SOAK PRUNES

RUM

CASTER SUGAR

450 G (1 LB) PEARS, PEELED, CORED AND CUT INTO LARGE CHUNKS

1 EGG, BEATEN WITH SALT, TO GLAZE

1. To make the pastry, place the icing sugar, salt, egg yolks, vanilla flavouring and butter in a food processor and blend until smooth. Add the flour and blend intermittently until the dough begins to come together. Turn out to a floured work surface and knead lightly until smooth. The dough will be quite soft. Wrap and chill for at least 1 hour.

2. Place the prunes in a large saucepan and cover with water. Simmer for about 15 minutes, or until soft. Drain and cool.

3. Cut the pastry in two; roll out half and use it to line a 23 cm (9 in) flan tin or dish. Wrap the other half and chill the flan case for 15-20 minutes. Bake the base blind in the oven at 200°C/400°F/Gas Mark 6 until it has set but is not too coloured.

4. Sieve half the prunes, and stir in rum and sugar to taste. Spread this purée over the tart base and arrange the whole prunes and pears on top.

5. Roll out the remaining pastry and cover the tart with it; seal the edges well. Brush with beaten egg then, using a sharp knife, make a large cross in the centre of the pie. Carefully lift and fold the edges back loosely to reveal the filling. Brush these flaps lightly with egg glaze and sprinkle with caster sugar. Chill for about 30 minutes.

6. Bake at 190°C/375°F/Gas Mark 5 for about 45 minutes, or until the tart is well browned. Serve warm or cold.

SOUFFLÉED PEAR TRANCHE

Serves 8

175 G (6 OZ) PLAIN FLOUR, PLUS 1×15 ML TBS

75 G (3 OZ) GROUND ALMONDS

150 G (5 OZ) CASTER SUGAR

115 G (4 OZ) BUTTER, SOFTENED, PLUS A KNOB OF BUTTER

4 EGGS

675 G (1½ LB) RIPE PEARS, PEELED, HALVED, CORED AND FINELY CHOPPED

225 G (8 OZ) GRANNY SMITH APPLES, PEELED, HALVED, CORED AND FINELY CHOPPED

GRATED RIND OF 1 LEMON

1×15 ML TBS POWDERED GELATINE

75 ML (3 FL OZ) MILK

FEW DROPS OF VANILLA FLAVOURING

ICING SUGAR, FOR DUSTING

SINGLE CREAM, GRATED NUTMEG AND SLICES OF FRESH PEAR, TO SERVE

1. Sift the 175 g (6 oz) flour on to a work surface. Add the ground almonds. Make a well in the centre and add 75 g (3 oz) caster sugar, 115 g (4 oz) butter, 1 egg and 1 egg yolk. Work the sugar, butter and eggs together with the fingertips of one hand until combined. With a palette knife, work in the flour and almonds and knead lightly, forming a smooth paste. Wrap in clingfilm and chill for 20 minutes before using.

2. Put the pears and apples into a medium-sized saucepan. Add 4×15 ml tbs water, lemon rind and 25 g (1 oz) caster sugar. Cover and cook over a gentle heat until soft and pulpy, stirring occasionally. Uncover and stir over a high heat until any excess liquid has evaporated. Cool and purée.

3. In a small bowl, sprinkle the gelatine over 3× 15 ml tbs water and leave to soak for 5 minutes. Place over a saucepan of gently simmering water until dissolved. Stir into the fruit purée.

4. Thinly roll out the pastry and use to line a 35×11 cm (14×4½ in) oblong flan frame; chill for 15 minutes. Bake blind at 190°C/375°F/Gas Mark 5 for 20 minutes.

5. Mix the remaining 1× 15 ml tbs flour with 3× 15 ml tbs of the milk to form a smooth paste. Heat the remaining milk with 25 g (1 oz) caster sugar and the vanilla flavouring. Add the flour mixture and boil, stirring, until thickened. Off the heat, beat in the knob of butter and 2 egg yolks. Cool slightly. Whisk the remaining 3 egg whites until stiff but not dry. Fold into the sauce.

6. Spoon the purée evenly into the flan case. Top with the soufflé mixture and bake at 200°C/400°F/Gas Mark 6 for 15-20 minutes. Cool and dust with icing sugar before serving with single cream, grated nutmeg and slices of fresh pear.

FUDGE NUT TART

Serves 8

225 G (8 OZ) BUTTER, HALF OF IT CUT INTO SMALL PIECES

175 G (6 OZ) PLAIN WHITE FLOUR

25 G (1 OZ) CASTER SUGAR

2-3×15 ML TBS WATER

115 G (4 OZ) SKINNED HAZELNUTS

115 G (4 OZ) PECAN NUTS

75 G (3 OZ) SOFT LIGHT BROWN SUGAR

150 ML (5 FL OZ) DOUBLE CREAM

FINELY GRATED RIND AND JUICE OF 1 LEMON

1 EGG, BEATEN

WHOLE PECAN NUTS, TO DECORATE

2×15 ML TBS WARM APRICOT JAM, TO GLAZE

1. Rub the butter pieces into the flour until the mixture resembles fine breadcrumbs. Stir in the caster sugar and bind to a dough with the water. Roll out and use to line a 23 cm (9 in) fluted flan tin or a 34×11 cm (13½×4½ in) loose-based fluted tranche tin. Bake blind in the oven at 200°C/400°F/Gas Mark 6 until golden and well dried out.

2. Meanwhile, toast the nuts until lightly browned; cool, then roughly chop. Warm the remaining butter with the brown sugar and the cream until evenly mixed.

3. Cool slightly, then stir in the chopped nuts, lemon rind, 2× 15 ml tbs lemon juice and the beaten egg. Mix well.

4. Pour into the flan case. Arrange the whole nuts over the flan. Bake at 180°C/350°F/Gas Mark 4 for 25-30 minutes, or until lightly set.

5. Brush the flan evenly with the warm apricot jam.

Souffléed Pear Tranche

Peach and Banana Millefeuille

Serves 6

213 G PACKET CHILLED PUFF PASTRY

40 G (1½ OZ) BUTTER, MELTED

450 G (1 LB) RIPE PEACHES OR NECTARINES, QUARTERED, STONED AND ROUGHLY SLICED

335 G (12 OZ) FIRM BANANAS, PEELED AND ROUGHLY SLICED

3×15 ML TBS DEMERARA SUGAR

4×15 ML TBS APRICOT JAM, WARMED

1. Roll out the pastry to a 28 cm (11 in) round. Place on a non-stick baking tray and prick well. Bake in the oven at 230°C/450°F/Gas Mark 8 for 8-10 minutes or until well browned and cooked through.
2. Brush melted butter over the pastry and scatter the fruit over the top. Sprinkle with sugar and drizzle with remaining butter. Grill for 8 minutes or until the fruit is tinged with colour. Cool slightly.
3. Brush warm apricot jam over the fruit to glaze; leave to cool completely.
4. Refrigerate for a maximum of 2 hours before serving.

COOK'S TIP

Don't worry if the bananas discolour sightly – even when sliced at the last minute, they tend to turn brown.

Walnut Pear Slice

Serves 6

115 G (4 OZ) PLAIN WHITE FLOUR

½×5 ML TSP GROUND CINNAMON, PLUS EXTRA FOR SPRINKLING

25 G (1 OZ) GROUND WALNUTS

GRATED RIND AND JUICE OF ½ LEMON

1 EGG

50 G (2 OZ) CASTER SUGAR, PLUS EXTRA FOR SPRINKLING

50 G (2 OZ) SOFTENED BUTTER OR POLYUNSATURATED MARGARINE

3×15 ML TBS FRESH BROWN BREADCRUMBS

3 RIPE PEARS, PEELED, QUARTERED AND CORED, EACH QUARTER CUT INTO 4 OR 5 SLICES

CREAM AND YOGURT MIXED, TO SERVE

1. Sift the flour with ½×5 ml tsp ground cinnamon on to a clean dry work surface. Sprinkle the walnuts and lemon rind over the flour. Make a well in the centre and into this place the egg, 50 g (2 oz) caster sugar and the fat. With the fingertips of one hand only, pinch the ingredients from the well together until evenly blended. Draw in the flour gradually, with the help of a palette knife; knead until smooth. Wrap and chill for about 30 minutes.
2. Roll out the pastry to an oblong about 30×10 cm (12×4 in), trimming the edges. Lift the pastry on to a baking sheet; sprinkle the breadcrumbs over the top. Toss the pieces of pear gently in a little lemon juice. Drain and arrange in overlapping lines across the dough. Sprinkle over a little sugar and cinnamon.
3. Bake in the oven at 190°C/375°F/Gas Mark 5 for about 30 minutes or until the pastry is well browned and crisp around the edges. Allow to cool slightly. Cut into slices; serve topped with cream and yogurt.

Peach and Banana Millefeuille (left)
Walnut Pear Slice (right)

The smell of freshly baked bread, a home-made cake or a batch of warm scones for tea is quite irresistible. In this chapter there are cakes and bakes for every occasion from small cakes, brownies, scones and biscuits to rich fruit cakes for Christmas and other festive occasions, creamy gâteaux for dinner parties or simply for tea or coffee time, plus a choice of delicious breads and savoury biscuits.

Top left: Viennese Chocolate Cake (page 204)
Bottom left: Olive and Walnut Bread (page 206)
Coconut Cherry Fingers (page 198)

Golden Biscuits

Makes 32

150 G (5 OZ) CASTER SUGAR
150 G (5 OZ) SOFT TUB MARGARINE
FEW DROPS OF VANILLA FLAVOURING
GRATED RIND OF 1 LEMON
1 EGG, BEATEN
225 G (8 OZ) PLAIN FLOUR

1. Lightly grease two baking trays
2. Cream together the sugar and margarine until pale and fluffy. Beat in the vanilla flavouring, lemon rind and egg.
3. Stir in the flour and mix to a firm paste. Knead lightly, wrap and chill in the refrigerator for 30 minutes.
4. Roll the dough to a sausage shape about 5 cm (2 in) in diameter and 20 cm (8 in) long. Wrap in greaseproof paper. Refrigerate for at least 30 minutes.
5. When required, cut off 0.6 cm (¼ in) slices, place on the baking trays and bake in the oven at 190°C/375°F/Gas Mark 5 for 12-15 minutes. Leave the biscuits to cool on a wire rack.

VARIATION

Honey Jumbles

Follow the basic recipe above as far as the end of step 4. Slice off 0.6 cm (¼ in) rounds. Roll into pencil-thin strips 10 cm (4 in) long. Twist into 'S' shapes and place on lightly greased baking trays. Chill for 30 minutes. Bake as above. While still warm, glaze well with clear honey, sprinkle with demerara sugar and grill for 1-2 minutes until caramelised, then cool.

Golden Biscuits (top); Honey Jumbles (bottom)

Pinwheel Biscuits

Makes 18

115 G (4 OZ) BUTTER OR BLOCK MARGARINE
50 G (2 OZ) CASTER SUGAR
50 G (2 OZ) CORNFLOUR
115 G (4 OZ) PLAIN FLOUR
FINELY GRATED RIND OF ½ LEMON
1×15 ML TBS LEMON JUICE
1×15 ML TBS COFFEE ESSENCE
MILK FOR BRUSHING

1. Grease two baking trays.
2. Cream half of the butter or margarine and half of the sugar together in a bowl until pale and fluffy. Gradually work in half the flours with the lemon rind and juice. Knead well, then wrap in foil and chill in the refrigerator for 30 minutes.
3. Meanwhile, cream the remaining butter and sugar together as before. Add the remaining flours and the coffee flavouring. Knead, wrap and chill as before.
4. Roll out both pieces of dough to oblongs 25×18 cm (10×7 in). Brush a little milk over one layer and top with second piece of dough. Roll up from the narrow edge, wrap in foil and chill for 30 minutes.
5. Cut the roll into 18 slices and place on baking trays. Bake in the oven at 180°C/350°F/Gas Mark 4 for about 20 minutes. Cool on a wire rack.

Chocolate Nut Snaps

Makes 24

1 EGG, SEPARATED
115 G (4 OZ) CASTER SUGAR
150 G (5 OZ) PLAIN CHOCOLATE
115 G (4 OZ) HAZELNUTS, SKINNED AND FINELY CHOPPED
40 G (1½ OZ) PLAIN FLOUR
200 G (7 OZ) ICING SUGAR, SIFTED

1. Grease two baking trays.
2. Whisk the egg white until stiff but not dry. Fold in the caster sugar.
3. Grate 75 g (3 oz) chocolate into the mixture and stir in with the nuts, flour and egg yolk. Knead lightly on a well floured surface. Wrap and chill in the refrigerator for 30 minutes.
4. Roll out the dough to about 0.6 cm (¼ in) thick. Using a 5 cm (2 in) star cutter, stamp out 24 shapes. Knead lightly and re-roll dough as necessary. Place on the baking trays. Chill again for 30 minutes.
5. Bake in the oven at 190°C/375°F/Gas Mark 5 for about 20 minutes. Immediately ease off the baking trays and cool on a wire rack.
6. Blend the icing sugar to a smooth paste with about 2×15 ml tbs water. Spoon 3×15 ml tbs into a small greaseproof paper piping bag. Melt remaining chocolate with 4×5 ml tsp water and stir into remaining icing.
7. Coat the surface of each biscuit with chocolate icing. Pipe on the white icing and pull a skewer back and forth through the icing to create a feathered effect. Leave to set.

Chocolate Hazelnut Brownies

Makes about 16

115 G (4 OZ) PLAIN CHOCOLATE, BROKEN INTO PIECES
115 G (4 OZ) BUTTER OR MARGARINE, CUT INTO SMALL PIECES
75 G (3 OZ) SELF-RAISING FLOUR
225 G (8 OZ) SOFT LIGHT BROWN SUGAR
75 G (3 OZ) HAZELNUTS, TOASTED, SKINS RUBBED OFF, THEN ROUGHLY CHOPPED
3 EGGS
½×5 ML TSP VANILLA FLAVOURING

1. Place the chocolate and butter or margarine together in a small bowl and stand the bowl over a pan of simmering water. Stir the chocolate occasionally until melted and blended with the butter.
2. In a large bowl, mix together the flour, sugar and nuts, then whisk in the eggs, melted chocolate and vanilla flavouring. Beat until evenly mixed.
3. Place in a greased and base-lined 28×18 cm (11×7 in) cake tin. Bake in the oven at 180°C/350°F/Gas Mark 4 for 35-40 minutes, or until just firm to the touch.
4. Cool in the tin for about 15 minutes, then invert the brownie slab on to a wire rack. Cool, then cut into fingers to serve.

VARIATION

Coconut Brownies

Omit the chopped hazelnuts and stir 75 g (3 oz) desiccated coconut into the mixture.

Chocolate Date Bars

Makes 12

175 G (6 OZ) STONED DATES, CHOPPED
2×5 ML TSP PLAIN FLOUR
115 G (4 OZ) PLAIN CHOCOLATE
150 ML (5 FL OZ) WATER
115 G (4 OZ) SELF-RAISING FLOUR
150 G (5 OZ) ROLLED OATS
115 G (4 OZ) SOFT LIGHT BROWN SUGAR
175 G (6 OZ) BUTTER OR MARGARINE

1. Grease a shallow 18 cm (7 in) square tin and line the base with greaseproof paper.
2. Put the dates, plain flour, chocolate and water in a small saucepan and cook gently for 5 minutes until the chocolate has melted and the mixture thickened slightly. Leave to cool.
3. Meanwhile, mix together the self-raising flour, oats and sugar and rub in the butter. Spread half of the mixture over the base of the prepared tin, pressing down well. Cover with the cooled date and chocolate mixture, then the remainder of the oat mixture. Press down with a round-bladed knife.
4. Bake in the oven at 190°C/375°F/Gas Mark 5 for about 25 minutes until golden brown. Cool in the tin for 15 minutes then mark into 12 fingers. Cool completely in the tin.

Grantham Gingerbreads

Makes 30

115 G (4 OZ) BUTTER OR BLOCK MARGARINE
335 G (12 OZ) CASTER SUGAR
1 EGG, BEATEN
250 G (9 OZ) SELF-RAISING FLOUR
1×5 ML TSP GROUND GINGER

1. Cream the butter or margarine and sugar in a bowl until pale and fluffy. Gradually beat in the egg.
2. Sift the flour and ginger into the mixture. Work in with a fork to a firm dough.
3. Roll the dough into small balls about the size of a walnut and put them on two or three greased baking trays, spaced apart.
4. Bake in the oven at 150°C/300°F/Gas Mark 2 for 40-45 minutes until crisp, well risen, hollow and very lightly browned. Cool on a wire rack.

Cherry and Walnut Biscuits

Makes 24

225 G (8 OZ) PLAIN FLOUR
PINCH OF SALT
75 G (3 OZ) BUTTER OR BLOCK MARGARINE
115 G (4 OZ) CASTER SUGAR
GRATED RIND OF ½ LEMON
1 EGG, SEPARATED
3-4×15 ML TBS MILK
115 G (4 OZ) WALNUT PIECES, FINELY CHOPPED
12 GLACÉ CHERRIES, HALVED

1. Sift the flour with the salt, rub in the butter or margarine until the mixture resembles fine breadcrumbs, then stir in the sugar, lemon rind, egg yolk and milk to give a fairly firm dough.
2. Form the dough into small balls, dip these in the lightly whisked egg white and roll them in the chopped walnuts.
3. Place the biscuits on two greased baking trays and top each with a cherry half.
4. Bake in the oven at 180°C/350°F/Gas Mark 4 for about 20-25 minutes until firm and lightly browned. Cool on a wire rack.

Almond Crisps

Makes 24

115 G (4 OZ) BUTTER OR BLOCK MARGARINE
75 G (3 OZ) CASTER SUGAR
1 EGG YOLK
FEW DROPS OF ALMOND FLAVOURING
150 G (5 OZ) SELF-RAISING FLOUR
75 G (3 OZ) CHOPPED ALMONDS

1. Cream the butter or margarine and sugar until pale and fluffy. Beat in the egg yolk and almond flavouring, then the flour to give a smooth dough.
2. Form into a neat log shape and cut into 24 even slices. Shape each into a barrel, then roll in chopped almonds.
3. Place well apart on two or three greased baking trays and bake in the oven at 190°C/375°F/Gas Mark 4 for about 15-20 minutes. Cool on a wire rack.

Shrewsbury Biscuits

Makes 20-24

115 G (4 OZ) BUTTER OR BLOCK MARGARINE
150 G (5 OZ) CASTER SUGAR
2 EGG YOLKS
225 G (8 OZ) PLAIN FLOUR
GRATED RIND OF 1 LEMON OR ORANGE

1. Cream the butter or margarine and sugar until pale and fluffy. Add the egg yolks and beat well.
2. Stir in the flour and grated lemon rind and mix to a fairly firm dough.
3. Turn out on to a lightly floured surface and knead lightly.
4. Roll out to about 0.6 cm (¼ in) thick. Cut into rounds with a 6 cm (2½ in) fluted cutter and place on greased baking trays.
5. Bake in the oven at 180°C/350°F/Gas Mark 4 for about 15 minutes until firm and a very light brown colour.

VARIATIONS

Spice Biscuits

Omit the lemon rind and add 1×5 ml tsp ground mixed spice and 1×5 ml tsp ground cinnamon, sifted with the flour.

Fruit Biscuits

Add 50 g (2 oz) chopped dried fruit to the mixture with the flour.

Fruit Squares

Makes 18-20

Divide the dough in half. Roll out both portions into oblongs and sprinkle 115 g (4 oz) chopped dried fruit over one piece. Cover with the other piece and roll out the mixture 0.6 cm (¼ in) thick. Cut into squares.

Chocolate Cream Sandwiches

Makes 10-12

Replace 3×15 ml tbs flour with cocoa powder. Sandwich the cool, cooked biscuits together with Butter Cream (see page 213).

Raspberry Rings

Makes 10-12

Follow the recipe to the end of step 4. Remove the centres of half the biscuits, using a 2.5 cm (1 in) plain cutter, then bake. When cool, spread the solid rounds with jam and dip the rings into white Glacé Icing (see page 213). Place the iced rings on top of the rounds so the jam shows through.

Madeleines

Makes 18

150 G (5 OZ) SELF-RAISING FLOUR
50 G (2 OZ) SEMOLINA
50 G (2 OZ) CORNFLOUR
225 G (8 OZ) BUTTER OR BLOCK MARGARINE
75 G (3 OZ) ICING SUGAR, PLUS EXTRA TO DREDGE

1. Into a bowl, sift the flour, semolina and cornflour. Cream the butter or margarine and icing sugar together until pale and fluffy. Stir in the flour mixture, using a fork to form a soft paste.
2. Grease 18 madeleine moulds and press a little mixture into each. Smooth off the top. Bake in the oven at 180°C/350°F/Gas Mark 4 for 15-20 minutes. Cool a little in the tins before gently easing out. When cold, dredge with icing sugar.

Almond Crisps (top)
Cherry and Walnut Biscuits (middle)
Shrewsbury Biscuits (bottom)

Apple Shorties

Makes 16 squares

75 G (3 OZ) SOFTENED BUTTER OR MARGARINE
40 G (1½ OZ) CASTER SUGAR
75 G (3 OZ) PLAIN WHITE FLOUR
40 G (1½ OZ) FINE SEMOLINA
1 COOKING APPLE, ABOUT 175 G (6 OZ)
115 G (4 OZ) SULTANAS
½×5 ML TSP MIXED SPICE
2×15 ML TBS SOFT LIGHT BROWN SUGAR
1×5 ML TSP LEMON JUICE

1. Grease a square, shallow baking tin measuring 18 cm (7 in) along the top. Beat together butter or margarine, caster sugar, flour and semolina until the mixture is blended. Press into the prepared tin and level the surface. Bake in the oven at 190°C/375°F/Gas Mark 5 for 15 minutes.
2. Meanwhile, peel and grate the apple and mix with the remaining ingredients.
3. Spoon over the shortbread and return to the oven for a further 15 minutes. Cool slightly before cutting into 16 squares. Cool completely, then remove from tin.

VARIATION

Caramel and Walnut Topping

Omit the apple topping. Melt together 75 g (3 oz) butter, 75 g (3 oz) sugar, 50 ml (2 fl oz) single cream and 1×15 ml tbs flour. Bring to the boil and simmer, stirring constantly, until thickened. Stir in 75 g (3 oz) chopped walnuts and spoon evenly over the shortbread. Return to the oven for 15 minutes. Cool.

Easter Biscuits

Makes 16-18

115 G (4 OZ) BUTTER OR BLOCK MARGARINE
75 G (3 OZ) CASTER SUGAR
1 EGG, SEPARATED
200 G (7 OZ) PLAIN FLOUR
PINCH OF SALT
½×5 ML TSP GROUND MIXED SPICE
½×5 ML TSP GROUND CINNAMON
50 G (2 OZ) CURRANTS
1×15 ML TBS CHOPPED MIXED PEEL
1-2×15 ML TBS MILK OR BRANDY
A LITTLE CASTER SUGAR

1. Grease two baking trays.
2. Cream together the butter or margarine and sugar until pale and fluffy and beat in the egg yolk.
3. Sift the flour with salt and spices and fold into the creamed mixture, with the currants and peel. Add enough milk or brandy to give a fairly soft dough.
4. Knead lightly on a floured surface and roll out to about 0.6 cm (¼ in) thick.
5. Cut into rounds using a 5 cm (2 in) fluted cutter. Place on the baking trays and then bake the biscuits in the oven at 200°C/400°F/Gas Mark 6 for 10 minutes
6. Remove from the oven, brush with beaten egg white and sprinkle lightly with caster sugar.
7. Return to the oven for 10 minutes until golden brown. Cool on a wire rack.

Shortbread Rounds

Makes about 20

115 G (4 OZ) BUTTER OR BLOCK MARGARINE
50 G (2 OZ) CASTER SUGAR
115 G (4 OZ) PLAIN FLOUR
50 G (2 OZ) GROUND RICE
CASTER SUGAR, TO DREDGE

1. Grease two baking trays.
2. Cream the butter or margarine until soft. Add the caster sugar and beat until pale and fluffy.
3. Stir in the flour and ground rice, until the mixture binds together. Knead well to form a smooth dough.
4. On a lightly floured surface, roll out the dough thinly. Using a 8 cm (3 in) fluted cutter, stamp out about 20 rounds, re-rolling the dough as necessary.
5. Place the rounds on the baking trays and prick over the surface with a fork. Bake in the oven at 180°C/350°F/Gas Mark 4 for about 15 minutes, or until pale golden and just firm to the touch.
6. Transfer to a wire rack to cool. Dredge with caster sugar to serve.

COOK'S TIP

Shortbread can also be made in a floured shortbread mould which is turned out on to the baking tray before baking.

Almond Biscuits

Makes about 18

115 G (4 OZ) BUTTER
115 G (4 OZ) CASTER SUGAR
150 ML (5 OZ) PLAIN FLOUR
½×5 ML TSP ALMOND FLAVOURING
50 G (2 OZ) BLANCHED ALMONDS, CHOPPED

1. Cream the butter and sugar together until pale and fluffy. Fold in the flour, almond flavouring and blanched almonds, and mix to make a stiff dough.
2. Place in small heaps on a floured baking tray. Bake in the oven at 180°C/350°F/Gas Mark 4 for 12-15 minutes until golden brown. Cool on a wire rack.

Langues de Chat

Makes 48

75 G (3 OZ) MARGARINE
75 G (3 OZ) CASTER SUGAR
1 EGG
50 G (2 OZ) PLAIN WHITE FLOUR
25 G (1 OZ) GROUND ALMONDS

1. Place all the ingredients in a mixing bowl and whisk together until blended.
2. Spoon the mixture into a piping bag fitted with a 0.6-1 cm (¼-½ in) plain nozzle. Pipe thin 5 cm (2 in) lengths on to baking trays lined with non-stick baking parchment; there should be about 48 biscuits. Allow plenty of room to spread – you'll need three or four baking trays or simply bake them in rotation, putting one batch in the oven as the last one is cooked. Bake in the oven at 200°C/400°F/Gas Mark 6 for 6-7 minutes or until tinged with colour.
3. Using a palette knife, immediately ease the biscuits off the parchment and cool on wire racks. Store them in an air-tight container until required.

COOK'S TIP

Allow the biscuits plenty of room to spread while baking or the mixture will run together forming one enormous biscuit!

Apple Shorties (top)
Langues de Chat and Easter Biscuits (bottom)

Date and Oat Slices

Makes 14 slices

225 G (8 OZ) STONED DATES, ROUGHLY CHOPPED
GRATED RIND AND JUICE OF 1 ORANGE
175 G (6 OZ) PORRIDGE OATS
175 G (6 OZ) PLAIN WHOLEMEAL FLOUR
75 G (3 OZ) SOFT LIGHT BROWN SUGAR
1×15 ML TBS BAKING POWDER
½×15 ML TBS GRATED NUTMEG
175 G (6 OZ) BUTTER OR MARGARINE, CUT INTO PIECES

1. Place the dates in a small saucepan with the rind and juice of the orange and enough water to just cover. Bring to the boil and simmer gently for about 10 minutes until soft. Allow to cool. Drain well. Grease a 28×18 cm (11×7 in) shallow tin.
2. Place the oats, flour, sugar, baking powder and nutmeg in a medium bowl. Add the butter or margarine and rub in until the mixture resembles breadcrumbs.
3. Press half the oat mixture into the tin, and spoon the drained dates on top. Spread the remaining oat mixture over the top.
4. Bake in the oven at 180°C/350°F/Gas Mark 4 for 30-35 minutes, or until beginning to colour.
5. Leave to cool in the tin for a good 5 minutes to firm up, then cut into 14 bars and ease out of the tin. Complete the cooling on a wire rack.

Nut and Raisin Chocolate Bars

Makes about 12

2×15 ML TBS GOLDEN SYRUP
75 G (3 OZ) BUTTER OR MARGARINE
50 G (2 OZ) PLAIN CHOCOLATE
175 G (6 OZ) DIGESTIVE BISCUITS, FINELY CRUSHED
50 G (2 OZ) MIXED NUTS, SUCH AS WALNUTS, BRAZIL NUTS, ROUGHLY CHOPPED
75 G (3 OZ) RAISINS

1. Grease and base-line a 15-18 cm (6-7 in) shallow square tin.
2. Melt the syrup, butter or margarine and chocolate gently. Stir in the biscuits, nuts and raisins, ensuring that they are evenly mixed in.
3. Spoon into the prepared tin, pressing down with the back of a spoon to level. Place in the refrigerator to set for approximately 2 hours.
4. Turn out of the tin and cut into fingers. These can then be stored in an air-tight container for a week or more.

Toasted Oat and Raisin Biscuits

Makes about 48

75 G (3 OZ) ROLLED OATS
115 G (4 OZ) BUTTER
50 G (2 OZ) CASTER SUGAR
50 G (2 OZ) SOFT DARK BROWN SUGAR
1 EGG, BEATEN
175 G (6 OZ) PLAIN FLOUR
½×5 ML TSP SALT
½×5 ML TSP BICARBONATE OF SODA
½×5 ML TSP VANILLA FLAVOURING
75 G (3 OZ) SEEDLESS RAISINS
50 G (2 OZ) SHELLED UNSALTED PEANUTS, ROUGHLY CHOPPED

1. Grease three baking trays. Toast the oats for a few minutes under the grill, until golden brown.
2. Cream the butter and sugars together until light and fluffy. Beat in the egg. Sift in the flour, salt and bicarbonate of soda and fold into the creamed mixture with the remaining ingredients.
3. Drop heaped teaspoonfuls of the mixture, about 5 cm (2 in) apart, on to the baking trays, flattening them lightly with the back of the spoon.
4. Bake in the oven at 180°C/350°F/Gas Mark 4 for 12-15 minutes until lightly browned. Transfer from the baking trays on to a wire rack and leave to cool. Store in an air-tight container.

VARIATION

These toasted oat biscuits can be varied according to your taste. Replace the raisins with sultanas, stoned chopped dates or chocolate chips, if you prefer.

Dutch Spiced Biscuits

Makes 18

115 G (4 OZ) PLAIN WHITE FLOUR
½×5 ML TSP GROUND CLOVES
½×5 ML TSP GROUND CINNAMON
½×5 ML TSP GROUND GINGER
PINCH OF GRATED NUTMEG
PINCH OF BAKING POWDER
PINCH OF SALT
50 G (2 OZ) SOFT DARK BROWN SUGAR
1×15 ML TBS MILK
65 G (2½ OZ) BUTTER OR MARGARINE
2×15 ML TBS VERY FINELY CHOPPED CANDIED PEEL
FLAKED BLANCHED ALMONDS, TO DECORATE

1. Sift the flour, spices, baking powder and salt into a bowl. Put the sugar and milk in a small saucepan and heat gently, stirring, until the sugar has dissolved.
2. Stir the sugar mixture into the bowl. Add the butter or margarine in pieces, then the candied peel. Work to a smooth dough.
3. Turn the dough on to a floured surface and knead lightly until no longer sticky. Roll out the dough to a thickness of 0.6 cm (¼ in).
4. Cut the dough into 18 shapes using a 6 cm (2½ in) biscuit cutter (see Cook's Tip) and place on greased baking trays. Press a few almonds pieces into each biscuit, then bake in the oven at 180°C/350°F/Gas Mark 4 for 15 minutes.
5. Leave to settle on the trays for a few minutes, then transfer to a wire rack and leave to cool completely. Store in an air-tight tin for up to 2 weeks.

COOK'S TIP

These biscuits are known as *speculaas*. Traditional *speculaas* dough is pressed into special carved wooden moulds and then turned out on to baking trays. At Christmas time in Holland, baker's shops are full of intricately 'carved' *speculaas*, some as heavy as 450 g (1 lb), and special moulds (mostly in the shape of men and women) are available for home baking. If you are making them at home without a special mould, you can use gingerbread men cutters, in which case you will be able to make about six men.

Hazelnut Florentines

Makes 24

50 G (2 OZ) BUTTER OR MARGARINE
50 G (2 OZ) CASTER SUGAR
3 GLACÉ CHERRIES, ROUGHLY CHOPPED
2×15 ML TBS CUT MIXED PEEL, ROUGHLY CHOPPED
1×15 ML TBS SULTANAS, ROUGHLY CHOPPED
50 G (2 OZ) HAZELNUTS, TOASTED UNDER A GRILL, SKINS RUBBED OFF AND ROUGHLY CHOPPED
2×5 ML TSP MILK
115 G (4 OZ) PLAIN CHOCOLATE, ROUGHLY BROKEN

1. Place the butter or margarine in a small saucepan and melt over a low heat. Stir in the sugar and bring to the boil, stirring. Take the pan off the heat immediately and stir in the fruit and nuts with the milk. Allow to cool slightly, stirring occasionally until evenly blended and no longer oily in appearance.
2. Line three baking trays with non-stick baking parchment. Divide the mixture between them, spooning it into small neat rounds about 2 cm (¾ in) in diameter. Leave plenty of room for the mixture to spread.
3. Bake in the oven at 180°C/350°F/Gas Mark 4 for about 12 minutes or until evenly golden brown. Leave to cool and firm on the trays for 1-2 minutes. Carefully lift off with a fish slice and place on a rack to cool. (Wipe the paper clean and reserve.)
4. Put the chocolate into a small bowl and set it over a pan of gently simmering water until completely melted. Remove from the heat and stir until cool and of spreading consistency. Dip the edges of the Florentines into the chocolate. Return to the paper-lined baking trays and refrigerate to set. Store in the refrigerator for up to 1 week in air-tight containers, interleaved with greaseproof paper.

Hazelnut Florentines (right)
Dutch Spiced Biscuits (left)

Cigarettes Russes

Makes 8

25 G (1 OZ) BUTTER OR BLOCK MARGARINE
1 EGG WHITE
50 G (2 OZ) CASTER SUGAR
25 G (1 OZ) PLAIN FLOUR

1. Grease the handles of several wooden spoons and line two baking trays with non-stick baking parchment.
2. Melt the butter or margarine and leave to cool. Whisk the egg white until stiff and fold in the sugar.
3. Gently stir in the butter with the flour.
4. Spread small spoonfuls of mixture into oblongs about 8×6 cm (3×2½ in) on the baking trays, not more than two per baking tray. Bake one tray at a time in the oven at 190°C/375°F/Gas Mark 5 for 6-7 minutes.
5. Allow to stand for 1-2 seconds, then remove with a fish slice and place upside down on a flat surface.
6. Wind the biscuits tightly round a greased wooden spoon handle. Cool slightly, then ease the biscuits off the spoon handles and place them on a wire rack to finish cooling.

Chocolate Peanut Cookies

Makes about 34

115 G (4 OZ) SOFTENED BUTTER OR MARGARINE
150 G (5 OZ) CASTER SUGAR
1 EGG
150 G (5 OZ) PLAIN WHITE FLOUR
2×5 ML TSP COCOA POWDER
½×5 ML TSP BAKING POWDER
½×5 ML TSP SALT
175 G (6 OZ) CHOCOLATE DROPS
75 G (3 OZ) SALTED PEANUTS, ROUGHLY CHOPPED

1. Grease two or three baking trays.
2. Beat together all the ingredients. Place large spoonfuls of the mixture on to the baking trays, leaving room for the cookies to spread. Flatten out the cookies slightly, using the back of a damp teaspoon.
3. Bake in the oven at 190°C/375°F/Gas Mark 5 for about 15 minutes or until the cookies are golden and just firm to the touch. Allow to cool on a wire rack.

VARIATIONS

Coconut and Raisin Cookies
Omit the cocoa, chocolate drops and salted peanuts. Reduce the sugar to 75 g (3 oz) and stir in 50 g (2 oz) desiccated coconut and 115 g (4 oz) roughly chopped raisins.

Oat and Ginger Cookies
Omit the cocoa, chocolate drops and salted peanuts. Add 1×5 ml tsp vanilla flavouring, 1×5 ml tsp ground ginger and 50 g (2 oz) rolled oats.

Chocolate Chip Cookies (top)
Coconut Macaroons (middle)
Cigarettes Russes (bottom)

Chocolate Chip Cookies

Makes 20

75 G (3 OZ) BUTTER OR BLOCK MARGARINE
75 (3 OZ) CASTER SUGAR
75 G (3 OZ) SOFT LIGHT BROWN SUGAR
FEW DROPS OF VANILLA FLAVOURING
1 EGG
175 G (6 OZ) SELF-RAISING FLOUR
PINCH OF SALT
50 G (2 OZ) WALNUT PIECES, CHOPPED
50-115 G (2-4 OZ) CHOCOLATE CHIPS

1. Cream together the butter or margarine, sugars and vanilla flavouring until pale and fluffy, then gradually beat in the egg.
2. Sift the flour and salt together and fold into the creamed mixture with the nuts and chocolate chips.
3. Drop spoonfuls of mixture on to two greased baking trays and bake in the oven at 180°C/350°F/Gas Mark 4 for 12-15 minutes until firm.
4. Cool on the baking trays for 1 minute, then transfer to a wire rack to finish cooling.

Peanut Butter Cookies

Makes 25-30

50 G (2 OZ) CRUNCHY PEANUT BUTTER
GRATED RIND OF ½ ORANGE
50 G (2 OZ) CASTER SUGAR
3×15 ML TBS SOFT LIGHT BROWN SUGAR
50 G (2 OZ) BUTTER OR BLOCK MARGARINE
1 EGG
2×15 ML TBS SEEDLESS RAISINS, CHOPPED
115 G (4 OZ) SELF-RAISING FLOUR, SIFTED

1. Cream together the peanut butter, orange rind, sugars and butter or margarine until pale and fluffy.
2. Beat in the egg, add the raisins and stir in the flour to give a fairly firm dough.
3. Roll the dough into balls about the size of a walnut. Place well apart on an ungreased baking tray. Mark each with a fork.
4. Bake in the oven at 180°C/350°F/Gas Mark 4 for 25 minutes until risen and golden brown. Cool on a wire rack.

Coconut Macaroons

Makes 18

2 EGG WHITES
115 G (4 OZ) ICING SUGAR, SIFTED
115 G (4 OZ) GROUND ALMONDS
FEW DROPS OF ALMOND FLAVOURING
115 G (4 OZ) DESICCATED COCONUT
2×15 ML TBS SHREDDED COCONUT

1. Line two baking trays with non-stick baking parchment. Whisk the egg whites until stiff but not dry. Lightly fold in the icing sugar.
2. Gently stir in the almonds, almond flavouring and desiccated coconut until the mixture forms a sticky dough.
3. Spoon walnut-sized pieces of mixture on to the baking trays. Press a few strands of shredded coconut on to the top of each one.
4. Bake in the oven at 150°C/300°F/Gas Mark 2 for about 25 minutes. The outer crust should be golden and the inside soft. Cool on a wire rack.

Apple Rock Cakes

Makes about 12

175 G (6 OZ) PLAIN WHOLEMEAL FLOUR
175 G (6 OZ) PLAIN WHITE FLOUR
2×5 ML TSP BAKING POWDER
½×5 ML TSP GRATED NUTMEG
¼×5 ML TSP MIXED SPICE
115 G (4 OZ) SOFT LIGHT BROWN SUGAR
175 (6 OZ) BUTTER OR MARGARINE
115 G (4 OZ) DRIED STONED DATES, ROUGHLY CHOPPED
1 COOKING APPLE, ABOUT 175 G (6 OZ), PEELED AND COARSELY GRATED
1 EGG, BEATEN
2-4×15 ML TBS MILK

1. In a bowl, mix together the flours, baking powder, nutmeg, spice and sugar. Rub in the butter or margarine until blended.
2. Stir in the dates, apple, egg and enough milk until the mixture forms a soft dough.
3. Place large spoonfuls on to two greased baking trays. Bake in the oven at 190°C/375°F/Gas Mark 5 for about 20 minutes. Cool, then transfer to a wire rack.

Sultana Rock Cakes

Makes 12-14

225 G (8 OZ) PLAIN WHITE FLOUR
2×5 ML TSP BAKING POWDER
½×5 ML TSP GROUND MIXED SPICE
115 G (4 OZ) BUTTER OR POLYUNSATURATED MARGARINE, CUT INTO SMALL PIECES
50 G (2 OZ) DEMERARA SUGAR
115 G (4 OZ) SULTANAS
1 EGG
1-2×15 ML TBS MILK

1. Mix together the flour, baking powder and spice; rub or fork in the fat until blended. Mix in the sugar and sultanas.
2. Whisk the egg and milk together, then mix with the flour ingredients to form a firm dough. Spoon into about 12-14 'blobs' of dough on greased baking trays, forking up the surface.
3. Bake in the oven at 200°C/400°F/Gas Mark 6 for about 15 minutes, or until well browned. Serve warm.

VARIATIONS

Date and Lemon Rock Cakes

Omit the spice, sultanas and milk. Add 115 g (4 oz) chopped dates and the grated rind of 1 lemon to the rubbed-in ingredients. Mix it to a firm dough with the egg and 2×15 ml tbs lemon juice.

Ginger Rock Cakes

Omit the spice and sultanas. Stir ½×5 ml tsp ground ginger and 50 g (2 oz) chopped stem ginger into the rubbed-in ingredients. Mix it to a firm dough with the egg and 1×15 ml tbs stem ginger syrup and milk.

Coconut Cherry Fingers

Makes about 16

115 G (4 OZ) PLAIN WHITE FLOUR
115 G (4 OZ) PLAIN WHOLEMEAL FLOUR
2×5 ML TSP BAKING POWDER
115 G (4 OZ) BUTTER OR POLYUNSATURATED MARGARINE, CUT INTO SMALL PIECES
50 G (2 OZ) SOFT LIGHT BROWN SUGAR
75 G (3 OZ) DESICCATED COCONUT
175 G (6 OZ) GLACÉ CHERRIES, CHOPPED
200 ML (7 FL OZ) MILK
1 EGG, BEATEN
2×15 ML TBS LEMON JUICE
SHREDDED COCONUT, TO FINISH

1. Mix the flours and baking powder together, then rub or fork in the fat until blended. Stir in the sugar and coconut.
2. Stir in the cherries with the milk, egg and lemon juice. Mix to a wet dough.
3. Place in a greased and base-lined 28×18 cm (11×7 in) cake tin. Sprinkle a little shredded coconut over the surface.
4. Bake in the oven at 180°C/350°F/Gas Mark 4 for 40-45 minutes, or until golden brown and firm. Cover lightly with foil if necessary to prevent browning.
5. Turn out on to a wire rack, cool, then cut into fingers to serve.

VARIATION

Almond Cherry Fingers

Replace desiccated coconut with 75 g (3 oz) ground almonds and sprinkle flaked almonds over the top in place of coconut.

Spicy Eccles Cakes

Makes about 15

50 G (2 OZ) SOFTENED BUTTER OR POLYUNSATURATED MARGARINE
50 G (2 OZ) SOFT LIGHT BROWN SUGAR
50 G (2 OZ) CUT MIXED PEEL
115 G (4 OZ) CURRANTS
1×5 ML TSP GROUND MIXED SPICE
GRATED RIND OF 1 LEMON
340 G PACKET CHILLED PUFF PASTRY
1 EGG WHITE, BEATEN
CASTER SUGAR, TO SPRINKLE

1. Mix together the butter or margarine, brown sugar, peel, currants, spice and lemon rind.
2. Roll out the pastry thinly and stamp out about fifteen 13 cm (5 in) circles, folding and rerolling as necessary.
3. Moisten the edges of the pastry rounds and spoon the fruit mixture into the centre. Fold over the pastry edges to enclose the filling completely.
4. Turn the cakes over, seam-side down, then roll out gently so that the fruit just breaks the surface. Make three shallow cuts across the top. Place on greased baking trays; brush with egg white and sprinkle with the sugar.
5. Bake in the oven at 220°C/425°F/Gas Mark 7 for 10-12 minutes, or until crisp and golden brown. Cool on a wire rack for about 30 minutes.

VARIATION

Apricot Eccles

Replace the mixed peel and currants with 175 g (6 oz) no-soak apricots, snipped into small pieces. Substitute cinnamon for the mixed spice.

COOK'S TIP

These flaky pastry cakes are best served while still slightly warm.

Chocolate, Coffee and Raspberry Éclairs

Makes 24

— CHOUX PASTRY —

65 G (2½ OZ) PLAIN FLOUR
PINCH OF SALT
150 ML (5 FL OZ) WATER
50 G (2 OZ) BUTTER, CUT INTO PIECES
2 EGGS, BEATEN

— FILLINGS —

300 ML (10 FL OZ) DOUBLE CREAM
2 PIECES STEM GINGER, CHOPPED
1×15 ML TBS SEEDLESS RASPBERRY JAM
2×5 ML TSP ICING SUGAR
¼×5 ML TSP GROUND CINNAMON

— CHOCOLATE GINGER ICING —

25 G (1 OZ) PLAIN CHOCOLATE, BROKEN INTO PIECES
7 G (¼ OZ) BUTTER
1×15 ML TBS WARM WATER
75 G (3 OZ) ICING SUGAR
1×5 ML TSP STEM GINGER SYRUP

— RASPBERRY ICING —

75 G (3 OZ) ICING SUGAR
1×15 ML TBS SEEDLESS RASPBERRY JAM
2-3×5 ML TSP WATER

— COFFEE ICING —

1×5 ML TSP COFFEE GRANULES
1×15 ML TBS HOT WATER
75 G (3 OZ) ICING SUGAR

Chocolate, Coffee and Raspberry Eclairs

1. To make the choux pastry, sift the flour and salt on to a piece of greaseproof paper. Put the water and butter in a saucepan and heat gently until the butter melts. (Do not allow the water to boil before the butter has melted.) Quickly bring to the boil, remove from the heat and immediately add the flour all at once. Stir quickly, using a wooden spoon, until the dough is smooth.

2. Return the pan to a medium heat and beat the dough with a wooden spoon until it forms a ball and leaves the sides of the pan clean. Remove from the heat and cool slightly. Gradually add the beaten eggs, a spoonful at a time, beating well after each addition. Continue beating to form a shiny dough which holds its shape, but is not stiff.

3. Transfer the choux pastry to a piping bag fitted with a large star nozzle. Pipe twenty-four 5 cm (2 in) lengths, about 5 cm (2 in) apart on lightly greased baking trays, cutting off at the ends with a wet knife.

4. Bake in the oven at 200°C/400°F/Gas Mark 6 for 12-15 minutes until well risen and lightly golden. Reduce oven temperature to 180°C/350°F/Gas Mark 4 and continue cooking for a further 10-15 minutes until crisp and golden brown. Slit along the side of each éclair to allow the steam to escape and return to the oven for 5 minutes. Leave to cool on a wire rack.

5. Whip the cream until thick, then divide into three portions. To one portion, add the chopped ginger; stir the raspberry jam into another portion and the icing sugar and cinnamon into the remaining portion. Pipe or spoon each mixture into eight éclairs.

6. To make the chocolate and ginger icing, melt the chocolate and butter in a small heatproof bowl set over a pan of hot water. Stir in the warm water and icing sugar and mix well. Add the ginger syrup and stir to combine. (Stir icing occasionally to keep it smooth.) Dip the tops of the ginger cream-filled éclairs in the icing and leave to set.

7. To make the raspberry icing, mix the icing sugar with the raspberry jam and water to form a smooth icing. Dip the raspberry-cream-filled éclairs in the icing; leave to set.

8. To make the coffee icing, dissolve the coffee in the hot water and mix with the icing sugar to form a smooth icing. Dip the cinnamon-cream-filled éclairs into the coffee icing and leave to set before serving.

HONEY AND SPICE CAKE

Makes about 24 slices

225 G (8 OZ) CLEAR HONEY
225 G (8 OZ) SOFT LIGHT BROWN SUGAR
225 G (8 OZ) BUTTER OR MARGARINE
115 G (4 OZ) PLAIN WHITE FLOUR
115 G (4 OZ) PLAIN WHOLEMEAL FLOUR
1×5 ML TSP GROUND CINNAMON
1×5 ML TSP GROUND GINGER
2×5 ML TSP GROUND MIXED SPICE
1×5 ML TSP BICARBONATE OF SODA
GRATED RIND AND JUICE OF 2 ORANGES
225 G (8 OZ) MEDIUM OATMEAL
ABOUT 115 ML (4 FL OZ) MILK
2 EGGS

1. Gently heat the honey, sugar and butter or margarine together in a small saucepan. Allow to cool slightly. Grease and base-line a 23 cm (9 in) square cake tin.
2. Sift the flours, spices and bicarbonate of soda into a medium-sized bowl. Add the rind of the oranges and the oatmeal; stir to mix. Measure the orange juice and make up to 175 ml (6 fl oz) with milk. Add the eggs and whisk together.
3. Pour the cooled honey and egg mixtures into the flour mixture. Mix well to form a smooth batter. Pour into the tin. Bake in the oven at 180°C/350°F/Gas Mark 4 for about 1 hour, or until well risen, golden and springy to the touch.
4. Cool for about 10 minutes before turning out and cooling on a wire rack. Store in an air-tight container for up to 5 days.

COOK'S TIP

This cake is very crumbly but delicious. The mixture makes a big cake – you can always store half and freeze the rest.

ORANGE AND POPPY SEED CAKE

Makes about 12 slices

225 G (8 OZ) MARGARINE OR BUTTER
175 G (6 OZ) GOLDEN CASTER SUGAR
3 EGGS
335 G (12 OZ) SELF-RAISING WHOLEMEAL FLOUR
1×5 ML TSP BAKING POWDER
PINCH OF SALT
FINELY GRATED RIND AND JUICE OF 2 ORANGES
50 G (2 OZ) POPPY SEEDS

1. Grease and line a 1.5 lt (2½ pt) loaf tin. Put all the ingredients except the poppy seeds in a blender or food processor and process until smooth and well mixed. Fold in the poppy seeds.
2. Spoon the mixture into the prepared tin.

Orange and Poppy Seed Cake

Bake in the oven at 180°C/350°F/Gas Mark 4 for 50 minutes-1 hour or until well risen and firm to the touch. Turn out and cool on a wire rack.

COOK'S TIP

The finished loaf could be decorated with a little glacé icing made by blending sifted icing sugar with enough orange juice to give a smooth coating consistency. Decorate the iced top with blanched orange rind strips.

Hazelnut and Carrot Cake

Makes about 8 wedges

3 EGGS, SEPARATED

150 G (5 OZ) CASTER SUGAR

225 G (8 OZ) CARROTS, PEELED AND COARSELY GRATED

FINELY GRATED RIND OF 1 LEMON

150 G (5 OZ) HAZELNUTS WITH SKINS, FINELY CHOPPED

50 G (2 OZ) PLAIN WHOLEMEAL FLOUR

½×5 ML TSP BAKING POWDER

1×5 ML TSP GROUND MIXED SPICE

1. Grease and base-line a 20 cm (8 in) round deep cake tin.
2. Place the egg yolks and sugar in a medium bowl and whisk until thick and pale. Stir in the prepared carrots, lemon rind and nuts. Fold in the flour, baking powder and mixed spice.
3. Whisk the egg whites until stiff but not dry and fold lightly into the cake mixture. Spoon into the prepared tin.
4. Bake in the oven at 180°C/350°F/Gas Mark 4 for 45-50 minutes or until golden and springy to the touch. Allow to cool in the tin for a few minutes before turning out on to a wire rack to cool completely. Store in an air-tight container for up to a week.

COOK'S TIP

This is a light but very moist mixture, where the skins are left on the hazelnuts to add colour to the finished cake. Spread each wedge with a little soft cheese mixed with honey, if wished.

Nutty Christmas Cake

Nutty Christmas Cake

Serves 16-20

50 G (2 OZ) NO-SOAK DRIED APRICOTS, ROUGHLY CHOPPED

115 G (4 OZ) GLACÉ CHERRIES, QUARTERED

225 G (8 OZ) EACH CURRANTS, SULTANAS AND SEEDLESS RAISINS

50 G (2 OZ) MIXED CHOPPED PEEL

75 ML (3 FL OZ) RUM

LARD FOR GREASING

225 G (8 OZ) BUTTER OR MARGARINE

225 G (8 OZ) SOFT DARK BROWN MUSCOVADO SUGAR

FINELY GRATED RIND OF 1 LEMON

4×SIZE 1 EGGS, BEATEN

225 G (8 OZ) PLAIN WHITE FLOUR

PINCH OF SALT

½×5 ML TSP GROUND MACE

½×5 ML TSP GROUND CINNAMON

50 G (2 OZ) BLANCHED ALMONDS, ROUGHLY CHOPPED

2×15 ML TBS MILK

175 G (6 OZ) MIXED NUTS, TO DECORATE, SUCH AS WALNUTS, HAZELNUTS, BRAZIL NUTS, BLANCHED ALMONDS

— TO FINISH —

4×15 ML TBS APRICOT JAM

FINELY GRATED RIND AND JUICE OF 1 ORANGE

1. Place all the dried fruit and the peel in a bowl. Pour the rum over it; cover and leave to soak overnight.
2. Brush a 20 cm (8 in) round cake tin with melted lard then line the base and sides with a double layer of greaseproof paper. Tie a double thickness of brown paper around the outside of the tin.
3. Beat the butter or margarine until soft. Gradually beat in the sugar with the lemon rind until light in colour. Add the eggs, a little at a time, beating well each time.
4. Sieve together the flour, salt and spices. Using a large metal spoon, fold the flour into the creamed ingredients along with the soaked fruit, chopped almonds and milk.
5. Spoon the mixture into the prepared tin and level the surface. Gently push the mixed nuts on to the top of the cake.
6. Bake in the oven at 150°C/300°F/Gas Mark 2 for about 3½ hours or until a skewer inserted into the centre comes out clean. Cover lightly with foil during baking, if necessary, to prevent overbrowning. Leave to cool in the tin. Turn out and wrap tightly in greaseproof paper and foil to store for at least 2 weeks before eating.
7. To complete, warm the apricot jam with the orange rind and 1×15 ml tbs juice. Sieve, then brush over the nuts to glaze.

30-Minute Fruit Cake

Makes 18 squares

115 G (4 OZ) SOFTENED BUTTER
115 G (4 OZ) SOFT LIGHT BROWN SUGAR
GRATED RIND OF 1 LEMON
2 EGGS
FEW DROPS OF VANILLA FLAVOURING
150 G (5 OZ) SELF-RAISING WHITE FLOUR
1×5 ML TSP BAKING POWDER
1-2×15 MLT BS LEMON JUICE (OPTIONAL)
50 G (2 OZ) GLACÉ CHERRIES, CHOPPED
175 G (6 OZ) MIXED DRIED FRUIT
25 G (1 OZ) DESICCATED COCONUT
25 G (1 OZ) DEMERARA SUGAR
50 G (2 OZ) FLAKED ALMONDS

1. Grease a shallow, oblong baking tin measuring 28×18 cm (11×7 in) along the top, then line the base with greaseproof paper.
2. Beat together the first seven ingredients. Add a little lemon juice, if necessary, to form a soft dropping consistency. Stir in the cherries, dried fruit and coconut.
3. Spoon into the tin and sprinkle the demerara sugar and almonds over the top. Bake in the oven at 190°C/375°F/Gas Mark 5 for 30 minutes or until golden.
4. Cool in the tin for a few minutes before turning out on to a wire rack to cool.

Black Forest Gâteau

Serves 8-10

115 G (4 OZ) BUTTER
6 EGGS
225 G (8 OZ) CASTER SUGAR
75 G (3 OZ) PLAIN FLOUR
50 G (2 OZ) COCOA POWDER
½×5 ML TSP VANILLA FLAVOURING
2×425 G CANS STONED BLACK CHERRIES, DRAINED AND SYRUP RESERVED
4×15 ML TBS KIRSCH
600 ML (20 FL OZ) WHIPPING CREAM
115 G (4 OZ) CHOCOLATE CARAQUE (SEE RIGHT), TO DECORATE
1×5 ML TSP ARROWROOT

Black Forest Gâteau

1. Grease and base-line a 23 cm (9 in) round cake tin. Put the butter into a bowl, place the bowl over a pan of warm water and beat it until really soft but not melted.
2. Put the eggs and sugar into a large bowl, place over a pan of hot water and whisk until pale and creamy and thick enough to leave a trail on the surface when the whisk is lifted.
3. Sift the flour and cocoa together, then lightly fold into the egg mixture with a metal spoon. Fold in the vanilla flavouring and softened butter.
4. Turn the mixture into the tin and tilt the tin to spread the mixture evenly. Bake in the oven at 180°C/350°F/Gas Mark 4 for about 40 minutes, until well risen, firm to the touch and beginning to shrink away from the sides of the tin.
5. Turn out the cake on to a wire rack, covered with greaseproof paper and leave to cool for 30 minutes.
6. Cut the cake into three horizontally. Place a layer on a flat plate. Mix together 5×15 ml tbs cherry syrup and the Kirsch. Spoon 3×15 ml tbs over the cake.
7. Whip the cream until it just holds its shape, then spread a little thinly over the soaked sponge. Reserve a quarter of the cherries for decoration and scatter half the remainder over the cream.
8. Repeat the layers of sponge, syrup, cream and cherries. Top with the third cake round and spoon the remaining Kirsch-flavoured syrup over the top of the cake.
9. Spread a thin layer of cream around the sides of the cake, reserving a third to decorate. Coat the sides with chocolate caraque.
10. Spoon the remaining cream into a piping bag fitted with a large star nozzle and pipe whirls of cream around the top edge of the cake.
11. Fill the centre with the reserved cherries. Blend the arrowroot with 3×15 ml tbs cherry syrup, place in a small saucepan, bring to the boil and boil, stirring, for a few minutes until the mixture is thickened and clear. Brush the glaze over the cherries.

CHOCOLATE CARAQUE

Melt chocolate in a double boiler or a bowl placed over a pan of hot water, then pour it on to a cold surface (ideally a marble slab) and spread into a rectangular shape, using a palette knife. Leave to cool until just firm, but not hard or brittle. Hold a sharp long-bladed knife at a slight angle and draw it across the chocolate to make long, thin scrolls. Use chocolate caraque to decorate cakes, mousses and soufflés.

For a less dramatic, though simpler version of chocolate caraque, shave a bar of chilled chocolate with a vegetable peeler or canelle knife to make chocolate curls.

COFFEE GÂTEAU

Serves 6-8

75 G (3 OZ) CASTER SUGAR

3 EGGS

100 G (3½ OZ) PLAIN FLOUR

— FILLING —

225 G (8 OZ) BUTTER, SOFTENED

4×15 ML TBS GOLDEN SYRUP

1×15 ML TBS INSTANT COFFEE GRANULES DISSOLVED IN 1×15 ML TBS BOILING WATER

— PRALINE —

50 G (2 OZ) UNBLANCHED ALMONDS

50 G (2 OZ) CASTER SUGAR

1. Grease a 33×23 cm (13×9 in) swiss roll tin and line the base and sides with greaseproof paper.
2. To make the sponge, whisk the sugar and eggs in a bowl placed over a pan of hot water, using an electric whisk, until pale and creamy and thick enough to leave a trail on the surface when the whisk is lifted. Remove the bowl from the heat and whisk the mixture until cool.
3. Sift the flour over the mixture and fold in lightly using a metal spoon. Pour the mixture into the prepared tin and gently level the surface.
4. Bake in the oven at 190°C/375°F/Gas Mark 5 for 10-12 minutes until risen and golden brown. Have ready a large sheet of greaseproof paper, sprinkled with a little caster sugar. Turn the sponge out on to the paper, remove the lining paper and leave to cool.
5. To make the filling, put the butter in a bowl and mix in the golden syrup and dissolved coffee granules.
6. To make the praline, gently heat the almonds and sugar in a non-stick frying pan until the sugar melts and turns a rich dark golden brown. Carefully pour on to a well-buttered baking tray. Quickly coat and separate eight almonds and leave to one side to set individually; leave the rest of the praline to cool and set.
7. Roughly crush the praline in a blender, or between two sheets of greaseproof paper with a rolling pin.
8. Cut the sponge crossways into three equal strips. Sandwich them together with half of the filling. Spread the remainder over the top and sides of the gâteau, reserving a little for piping on the top. Cover the sides with crushed praline. Put the reserved filling into a piping bag fitted with a small star nozzle and pipe on top of the gâteau. Decorate the centre of the iced top with the caramel coated almonds.

Coffee Gâteau

VIENNESE CHOCOLATE CAKE

Serves 12

300 G (11 OZ) PLAIN CHOCOLATE, BROKEN UP
150 G (5 OZ) UNSALTED BUTTER, SOFTENED
115 G (4 OZ) CASTER SUGAR
½×5 ML TSP VANILLA FLAVOURING
5 EGGS, SEPARATED
75 G (3 OZ) GROUND ALMONDS
40 G (1½ OZ) CORNFLOUR
6×15 ML TBS APRICOT JAM
1×15 ML TBS WATER
200 ML (7 FL OZ) DOUBLE CREAM
4 TRUFFLE-LIKE CHOCOLATES, HALVED, OR
25 G (1 OZ) MILK CHOCOLATE, TO DECORATE

1. Cut out a disc of non-stick baking parchment to fit the base of a 21 cm (8½ in) spring-form or loose-based cake tin. Lightly grease the base and sides of the tin; line the base with the paper and grease this too. Allow to set, then dust with flour.
2. Put half the plain chocolate into a small bowl and place it over a pan of gently simmering water until the chocolate has melted. Don't overheat the chocolate or allow any moisture to come into contact with it, or it will become granular. Take the bowl off the heat and cool slightly.
3. Meanwhile beat the butter until really soft, preferably using an electric whisk. Gradually beat in the caster sugar until the mixture is light and fluffy. Add the cooled chocolate and vanilla flavouring and whisk well until thoroughly combined.
4. Beat the egg yolks one by one into the chocolate mixture. Gently stir in the ground almonds and cornflour. Whisk the egg whites until stiff but not dry. Add about one-third to the cake mixture and stir in vigorously to lighten it. Gently fold in the remaining egg whites, ensuring that they're evenly combined. Spoon the mixture into the prepared tin and level the surface.
5. Bake in the oven at 180°C/350°F/Gas Mark 4 for 55 minutes-1 hour or until risen and firm to the touch. The cake may be slightly cracked on top. Leave to cool in the tin for 5 minutes, then loosen the edges with a blunt-edged knife. Invert on a wire rack; slide a baking tray underneath. Peel off the lining paper and leave to cool.
6. Heat the jam with the water, stirring occasionally until evenly blended, then sieve. Allow to cool and thicken slightly, then brush quite generously over the top and sides of the cake to give an even layer. Put to one side to allow to set.
7. Put the remaining plain chocolate into a medium bowl and add the cream. Stand the bowl over a saucepan of simmering water and heat gently, stirring occasionally until evenly blended. Do not overheat. Cool for 2 minutes to allow the icing to thicken a little. Pour all the icing into the centre of the cake then, using a large palette knife, quickly ease it out to run down the sides. Do not overwork it. Leave at room temperature until the icing has set.
8. Decorate with the chocolates. Alternatively, melt the milk chocolate over simmering water (as above). Spoon into a small paper icing bag and pipe *Sacher* across the cake. Store in an air-tight container for up to a week.

REAL OATCAKES

Makes 16

450 G (1 LB) MEDIUM OATMEAL
LARGE PINCH OF SALT
¼×5 ML TSP BICARBONATE OF SODA
50 G (2 OZ) BEEF DRIPPING OR LARD, MELTED
3-5×15 ML TBS HOT WATER

1. In a large bowl, mix together the oatmeal, salt and bicarbonate of soda. Make a well in the centre and pour the melted dripping into it. Stir in enough hot water to form a stiff, but not too dry, dough.
2. Bring the dough together with hands dipped in extra oatmeal. Knead on a surface dusted with oatmeal until smooth.
3. Divide the dough into four and roll out each quarter to a rough 20 cm (8 in) circle, about 0.6 cm (¼ in) thick, using a plate as a guide to neaten the circle. Cut each circle into four quarters and place on greased baking trays.
4. Bake in the oven at 160°C/325°F/Gas Mark 3 for 25-30 minutes until firm but not coloured. Cool on a wire rack. Store in an airtight container. To crisp before serving, spread on a baking tray and heat in the oven at 200°C/400°F/Gas Mark 6 for 2-3 minutes.

CINNAMON SUGAR BUNS

Makes 8

280 G PACKET WHITE BREAD MIX OR
180 G PACKET PIZZA BASE MIX
200 ML (7 FL OZ) TEPID WATER
50 G (2 OZ) BUTTER, MELTED
115 G (4 OZ) SOFT LIGHT BROWN SUGAR
1½×5 ML TSP GROUND CINNAMON
75 G (3 OZ) FLAKED ALMONDS
2×15 ML TBS GOLDEN SYRUP, WARMED

1. Put the bread mix into a bowl, add the water and mix to form a dough. Knead thoroughly on a lightly floured surface for 5 minutes until smooth and elastic (or use an electric mixer fitted with a dough hook).
2. Roll out the dough on a lightly floured surface to form a rectangle measuring 35×23 cm (14×9 in). Brush all over with some of the melted butter, reserving a little for later. Mix half the sugar with half the cinnamon and two-thirds of the almonds. Sprinkle over the dough.
3. Starting from a long side, roll up like a swiss roll. Damp the edge with water and press down firmly to seal the roll. Cut the roll into eight equal slices. Put the slices cut-sides down and press fairly firmly with the palm of your hand to form neat pinwheels.
4. Generously butter a 23 cm (9 in) round sandwich tin and coat with a little of the remaining sugar and cinnamon. Arrange slices of roll, cut-sides down, in the prepared cake tin. Brush all over with the remaining melted butter and sprinkle with the remaining cinnamon, sugar and flaked almonds.
5. Cover with lightly oiled polythene bag and leave to prove in a warm place until doubled in size (the buns should fill the tin). Bake in the oven at 190°C/375°F/Gas Mark 5 for 25 minutes. Cover with foil to prevent overbrowning and cook for a further 5 minutes. Drizzle, or lightly brush, with the warmed golden syrup while still hot. Serve warm.

Cinnamon Sugar Buns

Cheese and Herb Scones

Makes about 12

225 G (8 OZ) SELF-RAISING FLOUR
PINCH OF SALT
1×5 ML TSP MUSTARD POWDER
1×5 ML TSP BAKING POWDER
40 G (1½ OZ) BLOCK MARGARINE OR BUTTER
2×5 ML TBS CHOPPED FRESH MIXED HERBS
115 G (4 OZ) STRONG CHEDDAR CHEESE, FINELY GRATED
ABOUT 150 ML (5 FL OZ) MILK

1. Grease a baking tray. Sift the flour, salt, mustard powder and baking powder together into a bowl. Rub in the margarine or butter until the mixture resembles fine breadcrumbs. Stir in the herbs, half the cheese and enough milk to give a soft, light dough.
2. On a lightly floured surface, roll out to about 2 cm (¾ in) thick and cut into rounds with a 5 cm (2 in) plain cutter. Put on the baking tray, brush the tops with milk and sprinkle with the remaining cheese.
3. Bake in the oven at 200°C/400°F/Gas Mark 7 for 10 minutes. Cool on a wire rack.

VARIATIONS

Olive and Herb Scones
Omit the cheese and mustard. Finely chop 25 g (1 oz) stoned black or green olives, or a mixture, and stir them into the rubbed-in ingredients with the chopped mixed fresh herbs. Push half an olive into the top of each scone and sprinkle with a few herbs before baking.

Tomato and Garlic Scones
Omit the cheese, herbs and mustard. Finely chop 25 g (1 oz) sun-dried tomatoes and stir them into the rubbed-in ingredients. Add half a small garlic clove, skinned and crushed, to the milk. Sprinkle the scones with a few herbs or a little grated Parmesan cheese before baking.

Nut Scones
Omit the herbs and mustard. The cheese may be omitted or left in as preferred. Add 50 g (2 oz) chopped mixed nuts to the rubbed-in ingredients. Sprinkle the scones with sesame or poppy seeds before baking.

Plain Scones
To make plain scones, for serving with jam and cream, follow the basic recipe but omit the herbs, cheese and mustard (you should still add a pinch of salt to sweet scones).

Sweet Fruit Scones
Add 50 g (2 oz) dried mixed fruit to the plain scone mixture above.

COOK'S TIP

Scones are quick to throw together at a moment's notice if you run short of bread. Serve them as an accompaniment to salads and soups, or for lunch, split and filled with salad, cheese or houmous. They really are best served fresh and warm from the oven.

Olive and Walnut Bread

Makes 2 loaves, 12 slices each

115 G (4 OZ) STONED BLACK OLIVES, ROUGHLY CHOPPED
75 G (3 OZ) WALNUTS, FINELY CHOPPED
600 G (1 LB 5 OZ) STRONG WHITE FLOUR
2×5 ML TSP SALT
7 G SACHET FAST-ACTION DRIED YEAST
5×15 ML TBS CHOPPED FRESH PARSLEY
375 ML (13 FL OZ) TEPID WATER
3×15 ML TBS OLIVE OIL

1. Mix the olives and walnuts together with the flour, salt, yeast and parsley. Make a well in the centre and add the water mixed with the oil. Stir together to form a soft dough, adding a little more water if necessary.
2. Turn the dough on to a well-floured surface and knead well until it is smooth and elastic – about 10 minutes.
3. Divide the dough in half and shape each piece into a roll 18-20 cm (7-8 in) long. Place rolls of dough on separate oiled baking trays and cover loosely with lightly oiled clingfilm. Leave in a warm place for 30-40 minutes or until doubled in size. Lightly slash the top of each loaf with a sharp knife.
4. Bake in the oven at 220°C/425°F/Gas Mark 7 for 12 minutes. Lower the temperature to 180°C/350°F/Gas Mark 4 for a further 25 minutes or until well browned and sounding hollow when tapped. Leave to cool for a few minutes on wire racks. Serve warm, thickly sliced.

Rustic Walnut Bread

Makes 2 loaves

600 G (1 LB 5 OZ) STRONG WHITE FLOUR
1×5 ML TSP SALT
25 G (1 OZ) BUTTER OR MARGARINE
7 G SACHET FAST-ACTION DRIED YEAST
115 G (4 OZ) SHELLED WALNUTS, ROUGHLY CHOPPED
ABOUT 350 ML (12 FL OZ) TEPID WATER

1. Sift the flour and salt into a warmed large mixing bowl. Rub in the margarine or butter with your fingertips, then stir in the yeast and chopped walnuts.
2. Pour in enough tepid water to make a smooth dough, mixing with a wooden spoon, then form the mixture into a ball of dough with your hands.
3. Turn the dough out on to a floured surface and knead for 10 minutes until smooth and elastic, adding a little more flour if the dough becomes too sticky.
4. Divide the dough in half and shape each piece into a roll. Place on oiled baking sheets, cover with a clean tea-towel and leave to rise in a warm place for about 1 hour, or until doubled in size.
5. Uncover the loaves and slash the tops with a sharp knife. Bake in the oven at 220°C/425°F/Gas Mark 7 for 10 minutes, then reduce the oven temperature to 190°C/375°F/Gas Mark 5 and bake for a further 25 minutes, or until the loaves are crusty on top and feel hollow when tapped on the bottom, swapping over oven shelves halfway through to ensure even cooking. If the loaves become too brown during baking, cover them with a sheet of greaseproof paper or foil.
6. Leave the loaves to cool on a wire rack before serving.

Herbed Granary Bread

Makes 1 loaf

450 G (1 LB) GRANARY FLOUR
1×5 ML TSP SALT
2×15 ML TBS CHOPPED FRESH PARSLEY
2×15 ML TBS CHOPPED MIXED FRESH HERBS, SUCH AS MINT, THYME, MARJORAM, ROSEMARY AND CHIVES
7 G SACHET FAST-ACTION DRIED YEAST
1 GARLIC CLOVE, SKINNED AND CRUSHED (OPTIONAL)
2×5 ML TSP CLEAR HONEY
300 ML (10 FL OZ) WARM WATER
FINE OATMEAL FOR SPRINKLING

1. Put the flour, salt, herbs and yeast in a bowl and mix together. Make a well in the centre. Stir the garlic, if using, and the honey into the warm water, then pour it into the centre of the dry ingredients. Beat together until the dough leaves the sides of the bowl clean. Turn the dough on to a lightly floured surface and knead well for about 10 minutes.
2. Shape the dough into a sausage shape about 40 cm (16 in) long and place on a greased baking tray. Cut several slashes on the top of the loaf. Cover and leave in a warm place for 30 minutes, or until doubled in size.
3. Brush with a little milk and sprinkle with oatmeal. Bake in the oven at 230°C/450°F/Gas Mark 8 for 10 minutes, then reduce the oven temperature to 200°C/400°F/Gas Mark 6 and bake for a further 15-20 minutes, or until the loaf sounds hollow when tapped on the base. Leave to cool on a wire rack.

COOK'S TIP

This is one recipe in which dried herbs are no substitute for fresh.

Soda Bread

Makes 1 large loaf

450 G (1 LB) PLAIN WHOLEMEAL FLOUR
115 G (4 OZ) PLAIN WHITE FLOUR
50 G (2 OZ) ROLLED OATS
1×5 ML TSP BICARBONATE OF SODA
1×5 ML TSP SALT
ABOUT 450 ML (16 FL OZ) SKIMMED MILK

1. Put the flours, oats, bicarbonate of soda and salt in a large bowl and mix together. Add enough skimmed milk to mix to a soft dough.
2. Knead very lightly, then shape into a large round and place it on a greased baking tray. Cut a deep cross in the top. Bake in the oven at 230°C/450°F/Gas Mark 8 for 15 minutes, then reduce the oven temperature to 200°C/400°F/Gas Mark 6 and bake for a further 20-25 minutes or until the loaf sounds hollow when tapped on the bottom. Eat while still warm.

COOK'S TIP

Round loaves of soda bread were traditionally baked on a hot griddle over an open fire, and had a lovely crisp crust. The bread is moist, close-textured and delicious.

Herbed Granary Bread

Tomato Herb Focaccia

Makes 1 loaf

50 G (2 OZ) SUN-DRIED TOMATOES IN OLIVE OIL, DRAINED AND CHOPPED

200 ML (7 FL OZ) BOILING WATER

450 G (1 LB) STRONG WHITE FLOUR

½×5 ML TSP SALT

50 G (2 OZ) VEGETABLE MARGARINE OR BUTTER

7 G SACHET FAST-ACTION DRIED YEAST

1×15 ML TBS CHOPPED FRESH THYME OR ROSEMARY

3×15 ML TBS OLIVE OIL

1 EGG

COARSE SALT (OPTIONAL)

CHOPPED FRESH THYME OR ROSEMARY, TO SERVE

1. Put the tomatoes in a bowl and pour the boiling water over them. Leave to soak for 15 minutes.
2. Put the flour and salt in a bowl and rub in the margarine or butter. Stir in the yeast. Drain the tomatoes, reserving the liquid, and stir into the flour with the herbs.
3. Beat together the reserved liquid, the olive oil and egg. Make a well in the centre of the flour mixture, pour the egg mixture into it and mix to a dough. Turn the dough on to a floured surface and knead for 5 minutes or until smooth.
4. Put the dough on a greased baking tray and press into a square measuring at least 25 cm (10 in) across. Cover with a clean tea-towel and leave in a warm place for about 30 minutes or until doubled in size. Brush with salt water. Slash the top with a sharp knife, or make indentations with a wooden spoon, and sprinkle with salt, if using.
5. Bake in the oven at 220°C/425°F/Gas Mark 7 for 15-20 minutes or until golden brown. Sprinkle with chopped fresh thyme or rosemary before serving.

COOK'S TIP

Sun-dried tomatoes lend a delicious flavour and a distinctive colour to this Italian bread.

Olive Sourdough Bread

Makes 1 loaf, to serve 8

— SOURDOUGH STARTER —

1½×5 ML TSP ACTIVE DRIED YEAST

450 ML (16 FL OZ) TEPID WATER

A PINCH OF SUGAR

225 G (8 OZ) STRONG WHITE FLOUR

— BREAD —

400 G (14 OZ) STRONG WHITE FLOUR

175 G (6 OZ) STRONG WHOLEMEAL FLOUR

1×5 ML TSP SALT

3×15 ML TBS CHOPPED FRESH MIXED HERBS

3×15 ML TBS VIRGIN OLIVE OIL

225 ML (8 FL OZ) TEPID WATER

225 G (8 OZ) MIXED STONED BLACK AND GREEN OLIVES, ROUGHLY CHOPPED

1. To make the sourdough starter, in a large bowl, sprinkle the yeast on to 150 ml (5 fl oz) of the water with the pinch of sugar and leave in a warm place until frothy.
2. Mix in the remaining water and enough of the flour to form a thick, pourable mixture. Don't worry if it's not perfectly smooth, as the yeast will break down lumps. Tightly cover the bowl with a damp cloth. Leave at warm room temperature for 3 days to ferment and develop the sourdough flavour. (Ring out the cloth in cold water when it dries out.)
3. To make the bread, put the flours, salt and herbs in a bowl and mix together. Add 200 ml (7 fl oz) of the starter and the olive oil and tepid water, or enough water to make a soft dough.
4. On a lightly floured surface, knead the dough for about 10 minutes until smooth and elastic. Put the dough in a large oiled bowl, cover with a clean tea-towel and leave in a warm place for about 1 hour, or until doubled in size.
5. Knock back the dough on a lightly floured surface, then carefully knead in the olives. Shape into a long sausage then curl it round to form a coil. Wrap one end of the dough over the other and pinch with your fingers to mould them together.
6. Transfer the coil to a greased baking tray and cover loosely with a clean tea-towel. Leave in a warm place for about 20 minutes or until doubled in size.
7. Remove the tea-towel and with a sharp pair of scissors, snip around the top of the loaf to make a zig-zag pattern. Brush with water and bake in the oven at 230°C/450°F/Gas Mark 8 for 15 minutes. Reduce the temperature to 190°C/375°F/Gas Mark 5 and bake for a further 20-25 minutes or until the loaf sounds hollow when tapped. Cool on a wire rack.

Olive Sourdough Bread

CORNBREAD

Makes 2 loaves

335 G (12 OZ) CORNMEAL
450 G (1 LB) STRONG WHITE FLOUR
115 G (4 OZ) SOFT LIGHT BROWN SUGAR
2×5 ML TSP SALT
7 G SACHET FAST-ACTION DRIED YEAST
50 G (2 OZ) MARGARINE OR BUTTER
ABOUT 375 ML (13 FL OZ) TEPID MILK
CORN OR MAIZE MEAL FOR SPRINKLING

1. Put the cornmeal, flour, sugar and salt and yeast in a bowl. Rub in the margarine or butter. Make a well in the centre, then add and mix in enough milk to make a soft dough. Knead on a floured surface for 10 minutes or until smooth and elastic.
2. Put the dough in an oiled bowl, cover with a clean tea-towel and leave to rise in a warm place for about 1 hour or until doubled in size. Turn the dough on to a floured surface and knead for 5 minutes.
3. Divide the dough into two and put each piece into a 450 g (1 lb) loaf tin or shape into 15 cm (6 in) rounds and place on greased baking trays. Cover and leave in a warm place until doubled in size.
4. Brush with water, then sprinkle generously with corn or maize meal. Bake in the oven at 230°C/450°F/Gas Mark 8 for 15 minutes, then reduce the temperature to 190°C/375°F/Gas Mark 5 for 15 minutes or until well risen and loaves sound hollow if tapped on the bottom. Cool on a wire rack.

Tomato Herb Focaccia

PARATHAS

Makes 12

335 G (12 OZ) PLAIN WHOLEMEAL FLOUR
1×15 ML TBS CUMIN SEEDS
1×5 ML TSP SALT
¼×5 ML TSP CHILLI POWDER
ABOUT 300 ML (10 FL OZ) COLD WATER
VEGETABLE GHEE, BUTTER OR VEGETABLE MARGARINE, MELTED FOR BRUSHING

1. Put the flour, cumin seeds, salt and chilli powder in a bowl and mix well together. Add the cold water and bind to a soft pliable dough – it may be slightly sticky.
2. Turn the dough on to a lightly floured surface and knead with floured hands for 6-8 minutes or until smooth and elastic. Cover the dough with a clean damp cloth and leave to rest for about 15 minutes.
3. Divide the dough into 12 pieces. Take a piece of dough and shape it into a smooth ball. Roll it out on a lightly floured surface into a round about 15 cm (6 in) across.
4. Brush a little ghee, butter or margarine over the paratha, then roll it into a long sausage shape. Hold the rolled paratha upright and place one end in the centre of your hand. Wind the rest of the roll carefully around the centre point to form a small fat disc.
5. Press the disc lightly together and roll out on a floured surface to a round about 15 cm (6 in) in diameter. Cover with a clean damp cloth and roll out the remaining dough to make 12 parathas altogether.
6. Heat a heavy frying pan or griddle. Place one paratha in the pan and cook over a low heat until small bubbles appear on the surface. Turn the paratha over and brush the top with melted ghee, butter or margarine. Cook for about 30 seconds or until golden brown.
7. Turn the paratha again and brush with more fat. Press down the edges of the paratha with a spatula to ensure even cooking, and cook the other side until it is golden brown. Brush with more fat and serve at once or wrap in foil and keep warm while cooking the remainder.

Naan-Style Bread

Makes 6

450 G (1 LB) PLAIN FLOUR
1×5 ML TSP BAKING POWDER
1×5 ML TSP SALT
7 G SACHET FAST-ACTION DRIED YEAST
2×5 ML TSP CASTER SUGAR
1 EGG, BEATEN
2×15 ML TBS VEGETABLE OIL
4×15 ML TBS NATURAL YOGURT
200 ML (7 FL OZ) TEPID MILK
VEGETABLE GHEE OR MELTED BUTTER, FOR BRUSHING

1. Sift the flour, baking powder and salt into a large bowl. Stir in the yeast. Make a well in the centre and stir in the sugar, egg, oil, yogurt and milk.
2. Mix to a soft dough, adding more milk if necessary. Turn the dough on to a lightly floured surface and knead for 10 minutes or until smooth and elastic.
3. Put the dough in a bowl, cover with a clean cloth and leave to rise in a warm place for about 1 hour or until doubled in size.
4. Knead the dough on a lightly floured surface for 2-3 minutes, then divide into six equal pieces. Roll out each piece and shape into a teardrop about 25 cm (10 in) long.
5. Place one naan on a baking tray and put under a preheated hot grill. Cook for 1½-2 minutes on each side or until golden brown and puffy. Brush the cooked naan with melted ghee or butter. Cook the remaining naan in the same way. Serve warm.

VARIATION

Peshawari Naan

(Naan with Sultanas and Almonds) Follow the recipe above to the beginning of step 4. To make the filling, mix together 115 g (4 oz) sultanas, 115 g (4 oz) ground almonds, 4×15 ml tbs vegetable ghee or butter and 3×15 ml tbs chopped fresh coriander. Knead the dough on a lightly floured surface and divide into six equal pieces. Roll each piece into a round about 15 cm (6 in) in diameter. Spoon the filling into the centre of each naan and fold over the dough to enclose the filling completely. Press the edges well together to seal. Cook for 1½ minutes on one side, turn over, brush with plenty of melted ghee or butter and sprinkle with a few flaked almonds. Cook for 1½ -2 minutes or until golden brown and puffy. Serve warm, sprinkled with chopped fresh coriander.

COOK'S TIP

This flat, teardrop-shaped bread is traditionally baked on the side of a tandoor oven. This version is not entirely authentic, but it does produce a soft, puffy naan-style bread that's perfect for mopping up curries and Indian foods.

Pitta Bread

Makes 16

675 G (1½ LB) STRONG WHITE FLOUR
1×5 ML TSP SALT
7 G SACHET FAST-ACTION DRIED YEAST
1×15 ML TBS SUGAR
450 ML (16 FL OZ) TEPID WATER
1×15 ML TBS OLIVE OIL

1. Put the flour, salt, yeast and sugar in a bowl, make a well in the centre and pour in the water with the olive oil. Mix to a smooth dough, then turn out on to a floured surface and knead for 10 minutes until smooth and elastic.
2. Divide the dough into 16 pieces and roll each into an oval shape about 20 cm (8 in) long. Place on floured baking trays, cover with a clean tea-towel and leave in a warm place for about 30 minutes, or until slightly risen and puffy.
3. Bake in batches in the oven at 240°C/475°F/Gas Mark 9 for 5-8 minutes only. The pittas should be just lightly browned on top. Remove from the oven and wrap in a clean tea-towel.
4. Repeat with the remaining pittas. When the pittas are warm enough to handle, but not completely cold, transfer them to a plastic bag and leave until cold. This will ensure that they have a soft crust.
5. To serve, warm in the oven, or toast lightly. Split and fill with salads, cheese, cold meats or your favourite sandwich filling. Or cut into strips and serve with dips.

COOK'S TIP

Homemade pitta bread is not quite the same as the perfectly pocketed manufactured kind. However, if you follow this recipe exactly most of your pittas, if not all, should have a pocket, and they will all retain a soft, pliable crust.

Sesame and Cumin Breadsticks

Makes about 32

7 G SACHET FAST-ACTION DRIED YEAST
450 G (1 LB) STRONG WHITE FLOUR
1½×5 ML TSP SALT
1×5 ML TSP GROUND CUMIN
50 G (2 OZ) MARGARINE OR BUTTER
2×15 ML TBS SESAME OIL
2×15 ML TBS VEGETABLE OIL
200 ML (7 FL OZ) TEPID WATER
1 EGG, BEATEN
3×15 ML TBS SESAME SEEDS
2×15 ML TBS CUMIN SEEDS

1. Put the yeast, flour, salt and ground cumin in a large bowl. Put the margarine or butter and oils in a small saucepan and heat gently until the butter has melted. Make a well in the centre of the dry ingredients and pour in the fat and tepid water. Mix to make a dough, adding a little extra water if necessary. Turn the dough out on to a floured surface and knead for 10 minutes or until smooth and elastic.
2. Divide the dough into 32 pieces. Roll each into a sausage shape about 20 cm (8 in) long and place on greased baking trays.
3. Brush the dough sticks with beaten egg and sprinkle the sesame and cumin seeds over the top. Bake in the oven at 200°C/400°F/Gas Mark 6 for 15-20 minutes or until golden brown. Turn off the oven and leave the bread sticks to cool in the oven. When cold they should be crisp. Store in an air-tight container.

COOK'S TIP

These crisp, slightly spicy bread sticks are perfect for serving with dips.

Sesame and Cumin Breadsticks (top)
Pitta Bread (bottom)

Shortcrust Pastry

Makes 335 g (12 oz) pastry

225 G (8 OZ) PLAIN FLOUR

PINCH OF SALT

50 G (2 OZ) BUTTER OR BLOCK MARGARINE, CHILLED AND DICED

50 G (2 OZ) LARD, CHILLED AND DICED

3-4×15 ML TBS CHILLED WATER

1. Place the flour and salt in a bowl and add the butter or margarine and lard to the flour.
2. Using both hands, rub the fat lightly into the flour until the mixture resembles fine breadcrumbs.
3. Add the water, sprinkling it evenly over the surface. (Uneven addition may cause blistering when the pastry is cooked.)
4. Stir in with a round-bladed knife until mixture begins to stick together in lumps.
5. With one hand, collect the dough mixture together to form a ball.
6. Knead lightly for a few seconds to give a firm, smooth dough. Do not overhandle.
7. To roll out, sprinkle a very little flour on a working surface and the rolling pin (not on the pastry) and roll out the dough evenly in one direction only, turning it occasionally. The usual thickness is 0.3 cm (⅛ in). Do not pull or stretch the pastry.
8. The pastry can be baked straightaway, but it is better if allowed to 'rest' for about 30 minutes in the tin or dish, covered with foil or greaseproof paper, in the refrigerator.
9. Bake in the oven at 200-220°C/400-425°F/Gas Mark 6-7, except where otherwise specified, until lightly browned.

COOK'S TIPS

This plain short pastry is probably the most widely used of all pastries. For shortcrust pastry, the proportion of flour to fat is 2:1, or twice the quantity. Therefore, for a recipe using quantities of shortcrust pastry other than 335 g (12 oz) simply use half the quantity of fat to the flour weight specified.

This quantity, made with 225 g (8 oz) flour, is approximately equivalent to one 340 g packet ready-made shortcrust pastry.

This is the classic shortcrust pastry recipe, but many people now prefer to use all butter or margarine, omitting the lard.

VARIATIONS

Wholemeal Pastry

Follow the recipe and method for Shortcrust Pastry but use plain wholemeal flour instead of white. You may need a little extra water due to the greater absorbency of wholemeal flour. For a lighter result, use a mixture of half wholemeal and half white flour.

Nut Pastry

Follow the recipe and method for Shortcrust Pastry but stir in 25 g (1 oz) very finely chopped shelled walnuts, peanuts, cashew nuts, hazelnuts or almonds before adding the water. When using salted nuts, do not add salt to the flour.

Cheese Pastry

Follow the recipe and method for Shortcrust Pastry, but stir in 115 g (4 oz) finely grated Cheddar or other hard cheese and a pinch of mustard powder before adding the water.

Herb Pastry

Follow the recipe and method for Shortcrust Pastry, but stir in 1-2×15 ml tbs finely chopped fresh herbs, such as parsley, sage or thyme, or 1-2×5 ml tsp dried herbs to the flour before adding the water.

Rich Shortcrust Pastry

Makes 200 g (7 oz)

75 G (3 OZ) BUTTER OR BLOCK MARGARINE, CUT INTO SMALL PIECES

115 G (4 OZ) PLAIN WHITE FLOUR

PINCH OF SALT

1 EGG, BEATEN

1. Rub the butter or margarine into the flour and salt until the mixture resembles breadcrumbs. Add the egg, stirring with a round-bladed knife, until the mixture begins to come together. Turn out on to a floured surface and knead lightly together. Wrap the dough in foil or clingfilm and chill for 10-15 minutes.
2. Roll out the pastry on a floured surface and use it to line a 20 cm (8 in) shallow loose-based flan tin. Chill for 10-15 minutes before baking.
3. Prick the pastry base, then line with greaseproof paper and baking beans. Place the flan tin on a flat baking tray and bake blind in the oven at 200°C/400°F/Gas Mark 6 for about 15-20 minutes, or until just cooked through.

BAKING BLIND

This is the term used to describe the cooking of pastry cases without any filling. The pastry may be partially pre-baked to be cooked for a further period when filled, or completely cooked if the filling doesn't need further cooking. All shortcrust and puff pastries may be baked blind as follows.

The pastry shell is lined with foil or greaseproof paper and then, for larger cases, filled with baking beans before cooking. Baking beans may be any dried pulse or ceramic 'beans'.

1. Make the pastry and line the flan case. Chill in the refrigerator for 30 minutes if possible, to 'rest' the pastry.
2. Cut out a piece of foil or greaseproof paper rather larger than the tin. Remove the case from the refrigerator and prick the base thoroughly all over with a fork.
3. Press the paper or foil against the pastry, then add a 1 cm (½ in) layer of beans.
4. For partially pre-baked cases, bake in the oven at 200°C/400°F/Gas Mark 6 for 10-15 minutes until set. Lift out the paper or foil and beans, and bake for a further 5 minutes, until the base is just firm and lightly coloured.

Pastry cases which need complete baking should be returned to the oven for a further 15 minutes, or until firm and pale golden brown.

For small pastry cases, it is usually sufficient to prick the pastry well with a fork before baking. Pastry cases which have been baked keep several days in an airtight tin, or they may be frozen.

QUICK SWEET PASTRY

Makes 225 g (8 oz)

2 EGG YOLKS
50 G (2 OZ) SOFTENED BUTTER
FEW DROPS OF VANILLA FLAVOURING
50 G (2 OZ) CASTER SUGAR
115 G (4 OZ) PLAIN WHITE FLOUR

1. In a medium bowl, cream together the egg yolks, butter, vanilla flavouring and sugar until smooth. Add the flour and stir quickly together with a large metal spoon. Turn out on to a floured surface and knead lightly together. Wrap in foil or clingfilm and chill for 20-25 minutes.
2. Roll out the pastry on a lightly floured surface and use it to line a 20 cm (8 in) loose-based flan tin. Chill for 15 minutes.
3. Prick the pastry base then line with greaseproof paper and baking beans. Place the flan tin on a baking tray and bake blind in the oven at 200°C/400°F/Gas Mark 6 for about 15-20 minutes until just cooked.

BUTTER CREAM

Makes 250 g (9 oz)

75 G (3 OZ) BUTTER, SOFTENED
175 G (6 OZ) ICING SUGAR
FEW DROPS OF VANILLA FLAVOURING
1-2 × 15 ML TBS MILK OR WARM WATER

Put the butter in a bowl and cream it until soft. Sift the icing sugar and gradually beat it into the mixture, then add the vanilla flavouring and milk or water.

VARIATIONS

Orange or Lemon
Replace the vanilla flavouring with a little finely grated orange or lemon rind. Add a little juice from the fruit instead of the milk, beating well to avoid curdling the mixture.

Coffee
Replace the vanilla flavouring with 2 × 5 ml tsp instant coffee granules dissolved in some of the hot liquid; cool the coffee before adding it to the mixture.

Chocolate
Dissolve 1 × 15 ml tbs cocoa powder in a little hot water and cool before adding to the mixture.

Mocha
Dissolve 1 × 5 ml tsp cocoa powder and 2 × 5 ml tsp instant coffee granules in a little hot water taken from the measured amount. Cool before adding to the mixture.

Almond
Add 2 × 15 ml tbs finely chopped toasted almonds and mix thoroughly.

TO USE BUTTER CREAM

It can be used as a filling or icing. Spread it over the top of the cake only, or over the top and sides. Decorate by making swirls with a palette knife and mark with the prongs of a fork. Butter cream can be piped in a pattern on top of the cake as well.

GLACÉ ICING

Makes about 115 g (4 oz)

115 G (4 OZ) ICING SUGAR
FEW DROPS OF VANILLA OR ALMOND FLAVOURING (OPTIONAL)
1 × 15 ML TBS HOT WATER
COLOURING (OPTIONAL)

1. Sift the icing sugar into a bowl. Add a few drops of vanilla or almond flavouring if wished.
2. Gradually add the hot water. The icing should be thick enough to coat the back of a spoon. If necessary, add more water or sugar to adjust consistency. Add colouring, if liked, and use at once.

VARIATIONS

Orange or Lemon
Replace the water with 1 × 15 ml tbs strained orange or lemon juice.

Mocha
Dissolve 1 × 5 ml tsp cocoa powder and 2 × 5 ml tsp instant coffee granules in the 1 × 15 ml tbs hot water.

Liqueur
Replace 2-3 × 5 ml tsp of the water with the same amount of any liqueur.

Chocolate
Dissolve 2 × 5 ml tsp cocoa powder in the 1 × 15 ml tbs hot water.

TO USE GLACÉ ICING

1. If coating both top and sides of cake, stand the cake on a wire rack with a tray underneath to catch the drips. As soon as the icing reaches a coating consistency and looks smooth and glossy, pour it from the bowl on to the centre of the cake.
2. Allow the icing to run down the sides, guiding it with a palette knife. Keep a little icing to fill the gaps. Scrape up any icing which falls under the rack and use this, making sure there are no cake crumbs or it will ruin the appearance.
3. If the sides are decorated and only the top is to have glacé icing, pour the icing on to the centre of the cake and spread it with a palette knife, stopping just inside the edges to prevent it dripping down the sides.
4. If the top is to be iced and the sides left plain, protect them with a band of greaseproof paper tied around the cake and projecting a little above it. Pour on the icing and let it find its own level. Peel off the paper when the icing is hard.
5. Arrange any ready-made decorations, such as nuts, cherries or sweets, in position as soon as the icing has thickened and formed a skin.

TO FEATHER ICE

1. Make a quantity of glacé icing to a coating consistency. Make up a second batch of icing using half the quantity of sugar and enough warm water to mix it to a thick piping consistency.
2. Tint the second batch with food colouring and spoon into a greaseproof paper piping bag.
3. Coat the top of the cake with the large quantity of icing. Working quickly, before it has time to form a skin, snip the end off the piping bag and pipe parallel lines of coloured icing about 1-2 cm (½-¾ in) apart, over the surface.
4. Quickly draw the point of a skewer or a sharp knife across the piped lines, first in one direction then in the other, spacing them evenly apart.

Entertaining

Entertaining family and friends should always be a pleasure rather than a chore. If you do plan your entertaining in the right way, you will be able to enjoy their company and your guests will feel at ease.

The first thing to do is to decide what type of party you want to have – a five-course dinner for eight with all the trimmings, a casual help-yourself supper for a few friends or a Sunday lunch get-together with children welcome. There are numerous possibilities to choose from, depending on how many people you want to invite and how much you want to spend. Whichever type you choose, careful advance planning will make all the difference.

The Menu

Having decided on the type of occasion and the number of guests, you can plan the menu. It's most important to keep the menu simple and within your capabilities. Whether catering for a large or small gathering, your plan of action should be the same: Choose the dishes you want to serve and list them. Read through the recipes, plan when to cook each one and start to make shopping lists.

Don't forget to add any garnishes and 'extras' like bread and butter, coffee, sugar and milk. It's a good idea to separate the list into non-perishables, which can be bought in advance, and perishables that must be bought nearer the time.

Choosing the Dishes

The choice of dishes depends on a variety of factors. Are any of your guests vegetarian? Do any of them dislike particular foods?

Try to achieve a balance of flavours, textures and colours in the food you serve. The 'wet and dry' rule is a good one to follow when planning actual dishes; that is a 'wet' course, such as a soup or casserole, should preceded a 'dry' one, such as grilled steak or an apple tart. Aim, too, for balance in 'weight' of the courses. A thick soup with dumplings, followed by steak pie and a steamed dessert may be traditional country fare, but is far too filling for all but the heartiest of appetites. Select accompaniments to complement the main dish, taking colour, texture and flavour into consideration.

Pay attention to variety and the balance of flavours throughout the courses. If serving fish as a main course, then fish is inappropriate to start. A chilled soup or a salad would be better instead. Similarly, one course based on a vegetable or fruit (such as avocado or melon), and one based on meat or fish makes a well-balanced combination. Fruit puddings go well with most menus, but avoid creamy desserts if either of the preceding courses have been served with a cream sauce. If fruit was served in either of the first courses, it is best to choose an alternative, such as a chocolate-based recipe for dessert.

Avoid putting together a meal that consists of several rich courses. If your main dish is heavy and filling, serve it with lightly cooked fresh vegetables or a salad and keep your starter and dessert simple, light and refreshing.

The time of year will suggest the food you choose to serve and seasonal food will always be the cheapest and freshest. In summer, when soft fruits are plentiful, make the most of them. Foods that are only available fresh for a short season, such as home-grown asparagus and new potatoes, are a treat your guests will certainly enjoy.

Last but not least, plan the menu so that you leave plenty of time to be with your guests. A dish that needs careful timing, such as steak or soufflé, will not allow for the fact that guests may not be punctual or that people linger over their food longer than you had originally anticipated.

Setting the Scene

Whether the scene of your party is your own home or a hired hall, room or marquee, it is important to create a party atmosphere that will make your guests feel welcome and relaxed as soon as they walk through the front door.

Lighting

The lighting in a room can make all the difference to the atmosphere. Harsh overhead lighting is far too bright for a party mood: it's better to use side lights and table lamps that create shadow as well as light. At dinner, candles on the table, with one or two side lights in the background, may be all that is required, but remember your guests will want to be able to see what they are eating!

Flowers

It's always lovely to have flowers on the table for a formal dinner party, but practical considerations must come first. Make sure that there's room for all the table settings, serving dishes, sauces, accompaniments and glasses for each guest. Your guests should be able to see each other easily, so tall arrangements are unsuitable.

For a buffet, the flower arrangement on the table should be higher than the level of the food, and quite flamboyant.

Seating at Dinner Parties

There are no hard and fast seating rules. Your top priority is to make sure people get a chance to enjoy the company of others, and at a small dinner party it won't matter who sits where because the conversation can range across the table without any difficulty. Couples, married or otherwise, are generally separated, on the grounds that they have plenty of opportunity to talk to each other the rest of the time. You can alternate men and women around the table if you wish, and if the party consists of even numbers of sexes. Otherwise spread out members of whichever is the minority fairly evenly.

Laying the Table

When laying each place setting, arrange the knives and forks (and spoons) so that they are used from the outside inwards. Knife blades should always face inwards. The dessert spoon and fork can be placed on either side of the setting, or less formally, above it so that the handle of the dessert spoon points towards the knife blades. Arrange glasses for water and wine above the knives.

Napkins

Plain white linen napkins always look good, but napkins can be made of other fabric in a colour or pattern to complement the table setting. For less formal occasions paper napkins can be used, but make them good quality, thick ones of a generous size. Bear in mind that coloured paper napkins can stain clothes if food or drink is spilled on them.

Choosing the Wine

To gain the maximum enjoyment from both the food and the wine, as well as the occasion, and to avoid wasting money or suffering a disappointment, you need to make sure you serve an appropriate wine with the food. Follow these guidelines:

- match the quality and style of the wine to the quality and style of the food i.e. serve a light wine with light food, a full-bodied one with full-flavoured dishes.

- serve white wines before red, dry before sweet, light bodied before more full-bodied, young before old, less expensive before expensive ones.

- wines of a region are the best accompaniments for the foods from the region

- if a wine has been used in the making of a dish, it will be the most suitable one to serve with it

- select wines that are appropriate for the occasion, i.e. lesser quality wines for informal affairs reserving the finer wines for special occasions where the guests will appreciate the qualities of the wine.

First courses

Consommés, meat and game soups – fino Sherry, sercial Madeira.

Light fish soups – good quality light dry white wines.

Vegetable purées – more full-bodied white such as Graves, Pinot Grigio or mature white Rioja.

Mixed hors d'oeuvres and antipasto – fairly assertive white such as those made from the sauvignon grape or semillon if the wine is dry, or perhaps a fruity light red such as Bardolino, Valpolicella, Bandol or a young Zinfandel.

Cold meats, smoked meats and sausages such as salami – strong rosé such as Tavel or a medium weight white such as Chilean or New Zealand Sauvignon Blanc.

Meat pâté – medium-fuller bodied red, from light young Vin de Pays to Minervois and Côtes du Rhône Villages, depending on spiciness.

Fish and Shellfish
Served plainly cooked and simply presented – a full-bodied white wine, such as Soave, Loire Chenin Blanc or Pouilly Fuissé.

Lighter fish with a creamy, not too rich, sauce – Mosel.

Oily fish – with sardines Vinho Verde, *with trout* Alsace Sylvaner or Riesling, *with salmon* dry white Graves or Burgundy, Californian or Australian Chardonnay.

Mussels are good partnered by dry white wine such as a Muscadet de Sèvre et Maine or Gros Plant, *scallops* with Saviennières or Alsace Riesling or other good dry Riesling.

Shellfish need a completely dry but medium-bodied wine such as good Burgundy and other Chardonnays or good white Rhône.

Smoked salmon – Sancerre or a Fumé Blanc or a fairly full-flavoured sparkling wine.

Poultry
Chicken plainly cooked or cold – a fairly light, dry white in any price basket. With cream or full-flavoured sauce or stuffing a more full-bodied white with some acidity such as an Alsace Pinot Blanc or Pinot Gris.

Turkey simply cooked and served – fairly full-bodied white such as white Burgundy or other Chardonnay, white Rioja, white Rhône.

Cooked in a richer or more flavoured way, try a light red such as a light Cabernet Sauvignon, Italian or Bulgarian Merlot, Chianti Classico.

Duck – medium-bodied Bordeaux, like Fronsac, Saint-Émilion or a good Bourgogne Rouge..

Meat
Lamb – with plain roast lamb Bordeaux or other Cabernet Sauvignon, *with chops* Bulgarian, Lebanese or Chilean Cabernet Sauvignon, *with barbecued lamb and Mediterranean-style lamb dishes* the many warm ripe southern French wines, like Corbières, Roussillon, Côtes du Ventoux and Côtes du Lubéron.

Beef – with a plain roast or fairly simply cooked steaks red Burgundy, *with richly flavoured beef dishes* red Rhône, Dao, Barolo, Australian Syrah/Shiraz.

Pork and veal – plainly roasted a light elegant Burgundy such as Beaune or a soft claret such as Saint-Émilion, *with grilled or fried pork chops* a dry white with some acidity such as Alsace Pinot Gris, *with creamy sauced or casseroled dishes* Maçon Blanc or a full-bodied oaky Portuguese wine such as white Bairrada..

Desserts
Gâteau-type, non-citrus and not too creamy desserts – a sweet white wine such as Sauternes, German Auslese or a southern French Muscat.

Rich-cream desserts and pastries – Port, Madeira or sweet Sherry.

Difficult Foods
Acidity in foods makes wine taste sharp, so avoid using too much dressing on a salad and use lemon juice instead of vinegar to make the dressing; avoid too much lemon with fish, citrus fruits, gherkins, chutneys and tomatoes. Eggs and egg-based dishes can cause problems and chocolate spells death to almost any wine as it completely coats the mouth. Really strong cheeses can overpower all but the most robust wines. Red wines do not go with desserts, with the exception of some pears, peaches and strawberries.

Serving Temperatures

Generally, coolness enhances the crisp acidity of white wines, whether sweet or dry, whilst a certain degree of warmth is usually needed to bring out the aroma and flavour of red ones. About an hour in the refrigerator is enough for any white wine. Fruity light red wines such as Beaujolais, red Loire and Valpolicella can also be served cool, after perhaps 20-30 minutes in the refrigerator. Serve most red wines at about 15-16°C/60°F and guard against any heating process being used – wines should only come to temperature by standing in the room, not near a cooker, radiator or fire, or even in the microwave!.

Glossary

A brief guide to the cooking methods, terms and ingredients which occur throughout the book.

Arrowroot Can be used as an alternative to cornflour as a thickening agent in liquids, such as sauces. It gives a clear gloss to a sauce, unlike cornflour which produces a cloudy sauce.

Aspic Jelly Savoury jelly used for setting and garnishing savoury dishes.

Au gratin Describes a dish which has been coated with sauce, sprinkled with breadcrumbs or cheese and finished by browning under the grill or in the oven. Low-sided *gratin* dishes are used.

Baking Cooking in the oven by dry heat.

Baking blind The method used for cooking flans and tarts without their fillings (see page 212).

Baking Powder A raising agent consisting of an acid, usually cream of tartar and an alkali (bicarbonate of soda) which react to produce carbon dioxide. This expands during baking and makes cakes and breads rise.

Barding Covering dry meat or the breast of poultry or game birds with pieces of bacon or fat to prevent the flesh drying out during roasting.

Basting Spooning the juices and melted fat over meat, poultry or game during roasting to keep it moist. The term is also used to describe spooning over a marinade. Use a large spoon.

Beating A method of incorporating air into an ingredient or mixture by agitating it vigorously with a spoon, fork, whisk or electric mixer. Also used to soften ingredients.

Beurre manié Equal parts of flour and butter kneaded together to form a paste. Used for thickening soups, stews and casseroles. It is whisked into the hot liquid a little at a time at the end of cooking.

Bicarbonate of soda Sometimes used in baking to act as a raising agent.

Blender An electric machine usually consisting of a goblet with rotating blades in the base. Used for puréeing wet mixtures and grinding dry ingredients. Ideal for making fresh breadcrumbs.

Boiling Cooking in liquid at 100°C/212°F. The main foods that are boiled are vegetables, rice and pasta. Syrups and glazes that need reducing and thickening are also boiled, as are some sauces.

Boning Removing the bones from meat or poultry, cutting the flesh as little as possible, so that it can be rolled or stuffed.

Bouquet garni Small bunch of herbs – usually a mixture of parsley stems, thyme and a bay leaf – tied in muslin and used to flavour stocks, soups and stews.

Braising A slow cooking method used for cuts of meat, poultry and game which are too tough to roast. It is also good for some vegetables. A pan or casserole with a tightly fitting lid should be used so that little liquid is lost through evaporation. The meat is first browned, then cooked on a bed of chopped vegetables (called a *mirepoix*), with just enough liquid to cover the vegetables. It may be cooked on the hob or in the oven.

Brochette Fish, meat or vegetables, cooked on a skewer or spit.

Brûlée A French term, literally meaning 'burnt' applied to a dish with a crisp coating of caramelised sugar.

Calorie Scientific term used to describe the quantity of heat required to raise the temperature of 1 g of water by 1°C. The body's energy requirements and the energy value of foods are measured as kilocalories (one kilocalorie is equivalent to 100 Calories) or kilo-joules (a kilojoule is a metric calorie 1 kcal = 4.183 kj). In practice the term calorie is used to describe what is in actual fact a kilocalorie, while the term kilojoule (kj) is rarely used in this country.

Caramel Substance obtained by heating sugar syrup very slowly until a rich brown colour.

Casserole Strictly speaking, a dish with a tightly fitting lid used for cooking meat and vegetables. Now applied to the food cooked in this way.

Celsius Also known as Centigrade. A scale for measuring temperature in which the freezing point of water is 0° and the boiling point 100°. Now used for the oven settings on electric cookers, replacing the Fahrenheit scale which is gradually becoming obsolete in Europe.

Charlotte A hot or cold moulded dessert. For a hot charlotte the mould is lined with bread and for a cold charlotte it is lined with sponge fingers.

Chilling Cooling food without freezing.

Chining Applied to joints of meat, this means severing the rib bones from the backbone by sawing through the ribs close to the spine. Joints such as loin or neck of lamb, veal or pork are best chined as this makes them easier to carve into chops or cutlets after cooking.

Chopping Cutting food into small neat pieces without damaging the tissues.

Chorizo Spanish sausage made of smoked pork and pimiento. Sold ready cooked.

Clarifying Process of removing sediment or impurities from a food. Butter and dripping may be clarified so that they can be used for frying at higher temperatures.

To clarify butter, heat until melted and all bubbling stops. Remove from the heat and stand until the salt and sediment have sunk to the bottom, then gently pour off the fat, straining it through muslin. Chill and use as required. Clarified butter is also known as ghee.

To clarify dripping, melt the fat, then strain it to remove any particles. Pour over two to three times its volume of boiling water and allow to cool. Lift it off and wipe the underside with absorbent kitchen paper to remove any sediment. Clarifying also means to clear a liquid or jelly, such a consommé, usually by adding egg white. The coagulation of the egg white throughout the liquid gathers up all the impurities and forms a scum on the surface which can be discarded.

Consistency Term used to describe the texture of a mixture, e.g. firm, dropping or soft.

Consommé Concentrated stock which has been clarified.

Couscous Processed semolina in tiny pellets. Staple food in North African countries.

Crackling The crisp skin on roasting pork.

Cream of tartar (tartaric acid) A raising agent which is an ingredient of baking powder and self-raising flour.

Creaming Beating together fat and sugar until the mixture resembles whipped cream in texture and colour (pale and fluffy). Used in cakes and puddings which contain a high proportion of fat and require the incorporation of a lot of air.

Crêpe French term of a pancake.

Crimping Decorating the edges of a pie, tart or shortbread by pinching it at regular intervals to give a fluted effect. The term may also refer to trimming cucumber, radishes, etc with a canelle knife of fork to produce a deckled cut finish.

Croûte A circle or rectangle of fried or toasted bread on which game and some main dishes and savouries are served. The term may also refer to a pastry crust, usually crescent shaped, served with savoury dishes.

Croûtons Small pieces of fried or toasted bread which are served with salads and soup.

Curd The parts of milk which coagulate when natural fermentation takes place, or when a curdling agent, such as rennet or an acid is added. The term also refers to a creamy preserve made from fruit (usually lemon or orange) and sugar, eggs and butter.

Curdle To separate fresh milk or a sauce either by adding acid (such as lemon juice) or by heating excessively. Also used to refer to creamed mixtures which have separated when the egg has been beaten in too quickly.

Cure To preserve fish, meat or poultry by salting, drying or smoking.

Deep-fat Hot oil or fat in which food is totally immersed for deep-frying.

Deglaze To heat stock, wine or other liquid with the cooking juices left in the pan after roasting or sautéeing meat, stirring to dissolve the sediment.

Dégorge To draw out moisture from food, e.g. salting aubergines to remove bitter juices.

Dice To cut food into small cubes.

Dough A thick mixture of uncooked flour and liquid, usually combined with other ingredients. The term is used to refer to mixtures such as pastry, scones and biscuits as well as those made with yeast.

Dredging Sprinkling food lightly with flour, sugar or other powdered coating. Fish and meat are often dredge with flour before frying, while cakes, biscuits and pancakes may be sprinkled with caster or icing sugar after cooking.

Dressing Plucking, drawing and trussing poultry and game. The term is also used to describe garnishing a dish, and coating a salad.

Dripping Fat obtained from roasting meat or pieces of fat which are rendered down deliberately.

Dropping consistency Term used to describe the correct texture of a cake or pudding mixture just before cooking. Test for it by taking a spoonful of the mixture and holding the spoon on its side above the bowl. The mixture should fall off of its own accord within 5 seconds.

Drying Preserving food by dehydration. This is usually done commercially for foods such as rice, pasta and pulses, but it is possible to dry herbs and fruit at home.

Emulsion A mixture of two liquids which do not automatically dissolve into each other, e.g. oil and water. They can be made to emulsify by vigorous beating or shaking together as when combining oil and vinegar in a French dressing.

En croûte Term describing food which is wrapped in pastry before cooking.

En papillote A French term applied to food which is baked and/or served in baking parchment or greaseproof paper for a brief period and served in the parcel.

Enzyme Substances present in all foods which have not been subjected to processing. They work within foods continuously and are responsible for changes in food condition. Most enzymes are killed by cooking.

Escalope A thin slice of meat, such as veal, turkey or pork, cut from the top of the leg and often egged and crumbled, then fried or grilled.

Fahrenheit System of measuring temperature which is being replaced with Celsius. Its freezing point is 32° and boiling point 212°.

Fillet A term used for the undercut of a loin of beef, veal, pork or game; boned breasts of birds; and boned sides of fish.

Fine herbes Classic French mixture of chopped herbs, i.e. parsley, tarragon, chives and chervil.

Flambé Flavouring a dish with alcohol, usually brandy or rum, which is then ignited so that the actual alcohol content is burned off.

Folding in (cutting and folding) Method of combining a whisked or creamed mixture with other ingredients so that it retains its lightness. Used mainly for meringues, soufflés and certain cake mixtures. Folding is best done with a metal spoon.

Frying Method of cooking food in hot fat or oil. There are various methods: shallow-frying in a little fat in a shallow pan; deep-frying where the food is totally immersed in oil; dry-frying in which fatty foods, such as bacon and sausages, are cooked in a non-stick pan without extra fat; see also Stir-frying.

Garnish A decoration, usually edible, such a parsley, watercress, or lemon which is added to a savoury dish to enhance its appearance.

Gelatine An animal-derived gelling agent sold in powdered form in sachets, and as leaf gelatine.

Glaze Food used to give a glossy coating to sweet and savoury dishes to improve their appearance and sometimes flavour. Ingredients for glazes accounts for the different textures of cakes and breads.

Gluten A protein constituent of wheat and other cereals. The amount present in flours varies and accounts for the different textures of cakes and breads.

Grating Shredding cheese, carrots and other hard foods with a grater or food processor attachment.

Griddle A flat, heavy, metal plate used on top of the cooker for cooking scones, crumpets etc.

Grinding Reducing foods to small particles in a food mill, pestle and mortar, electric grinder or food processor. Foods ground include coffee beans, nuts and spices.

Grissini Long, slim, brittle Italian bread sticks.

Gut To clean out the inside of a fish, removing all the entrails.

Hulling Removing the calyx from soft fruits, e.g. strawberries.

Infusing Method of imparting flavour to a liquid. Flavourings, such as aromatic vegetables, herbs, spices, vanilla pod or coffee beans, are added to milk or water, sometimes brought to the boil, then left to soak.

Julienne Vegetables or fruit rind cut into very fine strips to use as a garnish or ingredient.

Kebab General name for a dish comprising cubes of meat, fish, shellfish, fruit and vegetables which are cooked on skewers under a grill on a barbecue.

Knead To work dough by pummelling with the heel of the hand.

Knock back To knead a yeast dough for a second time after rising, to ensure an even texture.

Langues de chats Literally means cats' tongues. Small thin flat crisp biscuits served with ice creams and mousses.

Larding Inserting small strips of fat bacon into the flesh of game birds, poultry and dry meat before cooking. It is done with a special larding needle.

Leaven The raising agent in dough, usually yeast or baking powder.

Liaison Term used to describe any combination of ingredients which is used for thickening or binding. The ingredients of a liason are usually flour, cornflour, arrowroot, rice or potato flour, or alternatively an egg yolk.

Lukewarm In cookery, this term is used to describe the temperature of a substance, usually a liquid, when it is about blood temperature, i.e. approximately 37°C/98.4°F.

Macerate To soften and flavour raw or dried foods by soaking in a liquid.

Marinate To soak meat, poultry or game in a mixture of oil, wine, vinegar and flavourings to tenderise it and add flavour. The mixture, which is known as a *marinade*, may also be used to baste the food during cooking.

Medallions French term for small rounds of meat, usually beef or veal.

Meringue Egg white whisked until stiff, mixed with caster sugar and dried slowly in a low oven until crisp.

Mincing Chopping or cutting food into very small pieces. It may be done with a knife, a manual mincing machine or in a food processor.

Mocca A term which has come to mean a blend of chocolate and coffee.

Monosodium glutamate (MSG) A powder with little flavour of its own, but which enhances the flavour of ingredients it is added to. A principal ingredient in processed foods and Chinese cookery.

Noisettes Neatly trimmed and tied boneless pieces of lamb, not less than 1 cm (½ in) thick, cut from the loin or best end of neck.

Par-boiling A term used to describe boiling food for part of its cooking time before finishing it by another method.

Paring Thinly peeling and trimming vegetables as fruit.

Pasteurising Sterilising milk by heating to 60-92°C/140-180°F to destroy bacteria.

Pâte The French word for pastry, familiar in *pâte sucrée*, a sweet flan pastry.

Pâté A savoury mixture made from minced meat, flaked fish and/or vegetables cooked to form a solid mass. Smoked fish pâtés are rarely cooked.

Paupiettes Slices of meat or fish rolled around a stuffing, usually braised or fried.

Piping Forcing cream, icing, mashed potato, cake mixtures and meringue through a nozzle fitted into the end of a nylon or greaseproof paper piping bag to create fancy patterns.

Pith White lining under the rind of citrus fruit.

Poaching Cooking food gently in liquid at simmering point, so that the surface of the liquid is just trembling.

Pot roasting A method of cooking meat slowly in a covered pan with fat and a little liquid.

Potage The French term for a thick soup.

Praline Almonds caramelised in sugar, then crushed and used to flavour sweet dishes.

Prosciutto Italian raw smoked ham.

Proving The term used for leaving bread dough to rise after shaping.

Pulses The generic name given to all dried peas, beans and lentils. These are valued for their high protein and fibre content.

Purée Fruit, vegetable, meat or fish which has been pounded, sieved or liquidised to a smooth pulp. Purées often form the basis for various kinds of soups, as well as sweet and savoury sauces.

Ramekin Small earthenware, ovenproof container of single portion size.

Reducing Fast-boiling a liquid in an uncovered pan to evaporate water and produce a more concentrated flavour.

Refresh To pour cold water over blanched and drained vegetables to set the colour and stop the cooking process.

Rennet A substance extracted from a calf's stomach which will curdle or coagulate milk. The process is used for junket and cheese-making. Vegetarian rennet is also available.

Roasting Cooking meat by dry heat in an oven or over an open flame.

Roulade Meat, cake or soufflé mixture served in a roll.

Roux A mixture of equal amounts of fat and flour cooked together to form the basis of many sauces.

Rubbing in Method of incorporating fat into flour when a short texture is required. It is used for pastry, cakes, scones and biscuits.

Sautéeing Cooking food in a small quantity of fat in a sauté pan (a frying pan with straight sides and a wide base), which browns the food quickly.

Scalding Pouring boiling water over food to clean it, loosen hairs or remove the skin. Food should not be left in boiling water or it will begin to cook. It is also the term used for heating milk to just below boiling point, to retard souring or infuse it with another flavour.

Scoring To cut narrow parallel lines in the surface of food to improve its appearance or help it cook more quickly.

Searing Browning meat quickly in a little hot fat before grilling or roasting.

Seasoned flour Flour mixed with a little salt and pepper, for dusting meat and fish before frying.

Seasoning Adding salt, pepper, herbs and spices to a dish for added flavour.

Sifting Shaking dry ingredients through a sieve to remove lumps.

Simmering Keeping a liquid just below boiling point.

Skimming Removing froth, scum or fat from the surface of stock, gravy, stews and jam. Use either a skimmer, a spoon or absorbent kitchen paper.

Skinning Removing the skin from meat, fish, poultry, fruit or vegetables.

Steaming Cooking food in the steam of rapidly boiling water.

Steaming Long, slow cooking method where food is placed in liquid which is kept at simmering point. Good for tenderising coarse meat.

Stir-frying Quick method of frying in shallow fat. The food must be cut into small, even-size pieces and moved around constantly until cooked.

Stock The liquid produced when meat, bones, poultry, fish or vegetables are simmered in water with herbs and flavourings for several hours to extract their flavour.

Syrup A concentrated solution of sugar in water, used in making water ices, drinks and fruit juices.

Tenderising Beating raw meat with a spiked mallet or rolling pin to break down the fibres and make it more tender for grilling or frying.

Tepid The term used to describe temperature at approximately blood heat.

Terrine China or earthenware dish used for pâtés. Also used to refer to the food cooked in it.

Tofu Also known as bean curd and widely used in vegetarian and oriental cooking. It is made from a pressed purée of soya beans.

Trussing Tying or skewering into shape before cooking. Applied mainly to poultry and game.

Vanilla sugar Sugar in which a vanilla pod has been stored to release its flavour.

Whipping (whisking) Beating air rapidly into a mixture either with a manual or electric whisk.

Zest The coloured outer layer of citrus fruit which contains essential oil.

INDEX

(page numbers in *italic* refer to the illustrations)

almonds: almond and courgette risotto, 133
almond and sesame pilaff, 135
almond biscuits, 192
almond cherry fingers, 198
almond crisps, 190
baked orange and almond pudding, 173
butter cream, 213
courgette and almond salad, *142*, 143
gulab jamun, 162, *162*
Ricotta and almond cheesecake, 171
anchovies, rib of beef with walnuts and, 82, *82*
Andalusian summer soup, 15
apples: apple rock cakes, 198
apple shorties, 192
braised duckling with apple, 74
chicken and apple casserole, 62, *63*
creamed celeriac and apple, 157
deep-dish apple flan, 178, *178*
French apple flan, 178
individual apple soufflés, 166, *167*
orchard lattice pie, 180, *181*
quick apple charlotte, 164
sausage and apple plait, 110-11
smoked trout and apple mousse, 38, *39*
apricots: apricot and cardamom flan, *178*, 179
apricot and pistachio rolls, 174, *175*
apricot Eccles cakes, 198
chicken and spiced apricot casserole, 62
fresh pineapple and, 164, *164*
artichokes, Jerusalem *see* Jerusalem artichokes
asparagus: asparagus in a citrus dressing, 35
asparagus risotto, 133
cucumber ribbon and asparagus salad, 144
sliced tomato and asparagus salad, 143
aubergines: aubergine and courgette fingers, 149
aubergine and red pepper roulade, *34*, 35
aubergine blinis, 29
aubergine in a hot sweet and sour sauce, 149
aubergine tart, *126*, 127
lamb with peppers and, 102
spicy lamb and aubergines, 92, *92*
three-cheese aubergine tart, 28, *28*
avocados: avocado pie, 125
avocado with fennel and prawns, 40
baked avocado and mushrooms, 32
tomato, fennel and avocado salad, 145

bacon: bacon and pistachio terrine, 37
cheesy chicken and bacon rolls, 68, *68*
duckling and bacon with cranberry, 75
spinach and watercress salad with bacon, 145, *145*
veal and bacon kebabs, 111
veal with bacon and juniper, 111
baking blind, 212
bananas: peach and banana millefeuille, 184, *184*
Basmati pilaff, 135
beans: mixed bean and vegetable soup, 18, *18*
see also individual types of bean
beef: beef and pimiento casserole, 88
beef casserole with kumquats, 88, *89*
beef stock, 13
crispy beef and coconut sauté, 90, *90*
festive fillet of beef, 84
hot carpaccio with salsa verde, 87, *87*
Italian braised beef, 84
peppered beef, 82, *83*
quick beef and onion casserole, 88
rib of beef with anchovies and walnuts, 82, *82*
rich beef and wine casserole, *86*, 87
roast spiced beef, 84, *84*
spiced meat skewers, 88
spicy beef, 84, *84*
stir-fried beef with mixed vegetables, 90, *91*
stir-fried fillet steak with mango, 90
beetroot and onion bake, 150, *151*
berried treasure chest, 168-9
biryani, vegetable 137
biscuits: almond biscuits, 192
almond crisps, 190
apple shorties, 192
caramel and walnut shorties, 192
cherry and walnut biscuits, 190
chocolate chip cookies, 197
chocolate cream sandwiches, 190
chocolate nut snaps, 189
chocolate peanut cookies, 197
cigarettes russes, 197
coconut and raisin cookies, 197
coconut macaroons, 197
date and oat slices, 194
Dutch spiced biscuits, 194
Easter biscuits, 192
golden biscuits, 188, *188*
Grantham gingerbreads, 190
hazelnut florentines, 195
honey jumbles, 188, *188*
langues de chat, 192
madeleines, 190
nut and raisin chocolate bars, 194
oat and ginger cookies, 197
peanut butter cookies, 197
pinwheel biscuits, 189
raspberry rings, 190
shortbread rounds, 192
Shrewsbury biscuits, 190
toasted oat and raisin biscuits, 194
black bean dressing, salmon noisettes with, 47, *47*
black-eye beans: bean and potato pie, 127
Black Forest gâteau, 202, *202*
blackberries: orchard lattice pie, 180, *181*
blinis, aubergine, 29
Boston baked beans, 121, *121*
bread: cornbread, 209
golden cheese pudding, 122, *122*
herb croûtons, 16
herbed granary bread, 206
naan-style bread, 210
olive and walnut bread, 206
olive sourdough bread, 208, *208*
parathas, 209
Peshawari naan, 210
pitta bread, 210, *211*
rustic walnut bread, 206
sesame and cumin breadsticks, 210, *211*
soda bread, 206
tomato bruschetta, 26
tomato herb focaccia, 208
broad bean bake, 120
Brussels sprouts: chestnut and sprout sauté, 149
buns, cinnamon sugar, 204, *205*
butter, orange whisky, 173
butter cream, 213

cabbage with pine kernels, 148, *148*
cakes: almond cherry fingers, 198
apple rock cakes, 198
apricot Eccles cakes, 198
chocolate, coffee and raspberry éclairs, 199
chocolate hazelnut brownies, 189
coconut cherry fingers, 198
coffee gâteau, 203, *203*
date and lemon rock cakes, 198
ginger rock cakes, 198
hazelnut and carrot cake, 201
honey and spice cake, 200
nutty Christmas cake, 201, *201*
orange and poppy seed cake, 200-1, *200*
spicy Eccles cakes, 198
sultana rock cakes, 198
30-minute fruit cake, 202
Viennese chocolate cake, 204
warm lemon syrup cake, 174, *174*
caramel and walnut shorties, 192
carpaccio with salsa verde, 87, *87*
carrots: carrot and coriander syrup, 14-15, *14*
carrots with honey, 154
creamy carrot and celeriac soup, 16, *16*
glazed carrots with dill, *156*, 157
glazed carrots with turnips, 157
hazelnut and carrot cake, 201
cashew nuts: mushroom and cashew nut pâté, 37
Catalan pie, 124-5, *124*
cauliflower: cauliflower and almond cream soup, 17, *17*
cauliflower, soufflés, 32, *33*
curried potato and, 154, *155*
spiced eggs with coconut and, 119
celeriac: celeriac purée, 157
celeriac 'straw', 157
creamed celeriac and apple, 157
creamy carrot and celeriac soup, 16, *16*
celery: celery and Stilton soup, 21
sautéed potatoes with celery, 154
charlotte, quick apple, 164
cheese: blue brie toasts, 28
celery and Stilton soup, 21
cheese and herb scones, 205
cheese and leek tart, 128, *128*
cheese and sesame aigrettes, 29
cheese pastry, 212
cheesy chicken and bacon rolls, 68, *68*
goat's cheese and roasted pepper salad, 24
golden cheese pudding, 122, *122*
golden Parmesan chicken, 64, *65*
Roquefort and watercress soup, *20*, 21
salmon pie with Parmesan crust, 50, *50*
tarte au chèvre et menthe, 123, *123*
warm houmous with feta cheese, 26
cheese, soft: fresh herb cheese, 35
Ricotta and almond cheesecake, 171
sesame cheese pastries, 26, *27*
three-cheese aubergine tart, 28, *28*
cheesecake, Ricotta and almond, 171
cherries: almond cherry fingers, 198
Black Forest gâteau, 202, *202*
cherry and walnut biscuits, 190
coconut cherry fingers, 198
chestnuts: chestnut and roasted garlic soup, 18, *19*
chestnut and sprout sauté, 149
pheasant with chestnuts, 77

roast turkey with chestnut stuffing, 72-3, *73*
venison and chestnut casserole, 78
chick-peas: sausage and bean casserole, 109
warm houmous with feta cheese, 26
chicken: cheesy chicken and bacon rolls, 68, *68*
chicken and apple casserole, 62, *63*
chicken and spiced apricot casserole, 62
chicken soup with dumplings, *12*, 21
chicken stock, 13
chicken-stuffed eggs, 68
chicken with vermouth and olives, 71
golden Parmesan chicken, 64, *65*
marinated chicken with prunes, 64, *64*
mild chicken curry, 66
roasted pecan chicken, 69, *69*
spicy coconut chicken, 66, *67*
yogurt-braised chicken, 62
see also poussins
chillies: chillied pork dim sum, 32, *32*
vegetable chilli, 117, *117*
Chinese leaves, stir-fried, 147
Chinese spiced pork, 108, *108*
chips, game, 154
chocolate: Black Forest gâteau, 202, *202*
butter cream, 213
chocolate caraque, 202
chocolate chip cookies, 197
chocolate cinnamon soufflé, 166
chocolate coconut cream roulade, 170, *170*
chocolate cream sandwiches, 190
chocolate date bar, 189
chocolate hazelnut brownies, 189
chocolate nut snaps, 189
chocolate peanut cookies, 197
éclairs, 199
glacé icing, 213
hazelnut florentines, 195
nut and raisin chocolate bars, 194
Viennese chocolate cake, 204
Christmas cake, nutty, 201, *201*
Christmas puddings, 172-3, *173*
Christmas salad, 147
cigarettes russes, 197
cinnamon sugar buns, 204, *205*
citrus fruits poached in wine, 163
coconut: coconut and raisin cookies, 197
coconut brownies, 189
coconut cherry fingers, 198
coconut macaroons, 197
coconut, rice and lentil salad, 147
crispy beef and coconut sauté, 90, *90*
spiced eggs with cauliflower and, 119
spicy coconut chicken, 66, *67*
steamed orange and coconut sponge, 172
cod: wine-simmered fish, 48
coffee: butter cream, 213
coffee gâteau, 203, *203*
éclairs, 199
consommé, 14
cornbread, 209
courgettes: almond and courgette risotto, 133
aubergine and courgette fingers, 149
courgette and almond salad, *142*, 143
fried courgettes with rosemary aïoli, 29
steamed runner beans and, 147
stir-fried courgettes with sesame seeds, 147
couscous: mushroom fricassée, 138, *138*
vegetable, 137
cracked wheat salad with peppers, 143
crêpes Suzette, 168
croûtons, herb, 16
cucumber: cucumber and yogurt salad, 145
cucumber ribbon and asparagus salad, 144
steamed cucumber, 147
curries: curried parsnip soup, 17
curried potato and cauliflower, 154, *155*
mild chicken curry, 66
Thai prawn curry, 59

dates: chocolate date bars, 189
date and lemon rock cakes, 198
date and oat slices, 194
desserts, 160-84
Dijon-glazed pork medallions, *106-7*, 107
dried fruit: Christmas puddings, 172-3, *173*
fruit biscuits, 190
fruit squares, 190
nutty Christmas cake, 201, *201*
sweet fruit scones, 205
30-minute fruit cake, 202
duck: braised duckling with apple, 74
crispy duck breast with mangetout, 75, *75*
duckling and bacon with cranberry, 75
duckling with orange sauce, 74
roast duckling with honey and grapefruit, 74
Dutch spiced biscuits, 194

Easter biscuits, 192
Eccles cakes, spicy, 198
éclairs: chocolate, coffee and raspberry, 199, *199*
eggs: chicken-stuffed eggs, 68
noodles with fried eggs, 139
spiced eggs with cauliflower and coconut, 119
see also omelettes
feather icing, 213
fennel: avocado with prawns and, 40
baked tomato and fennel, 148-9
fennel and onion soup, 21
sesame pilaff with fennel, 133
tomato, fennel and avocado salad, 145
fish, 42-59
casserole of white fish and vegetables, 51
fish stock, 13
glazed seafood platter, 58, *58*
sliced fish pot, 48
see also individual types of fish
fishcakes, outrageous salmon, 46
flageolet beans, lamb noisettes with, *98*, 99
flans, savoury *see* tarts, savoury
flans, sweet: apricot and cardamom flan, *178*, 179
deep-dish apple flan, 178, *178*
French apple flan, 178
fudge nut tranche, 182
glazed nut flan, *178*, 179
prune and pear tart, 182
souffléed pear tranche, 182, *183*
spiced lemon syrup tart, 180
walnut pear slice, 184, *184*
warm lemon and apple flan, 179
florentines, hazelnut, 195
focaccia, tomato herb, 208
French apple flan, 178
French onion soup, 21
fritters, mushroom, 24
fruit: berried treasure chest, 168-9, *169*
citrus fruits poached in wine, 163
orchard fruit in strawberry syrup, 163
red fruit sundae, 163, *163*
see also dried fruit *and individual types of fruit*
fruit cake, 30-minute, 202
fudge nut tranche, 182

game, 76-9
game chips, 154
gammon with crunchy nut glaze, 109, *109*
gâteaux: Black Forest, 202, *202*
coffee, 203, *203*
gazpacho, 15
ginger: ginger meringues with rhubarb sauce, 172
ginger rock cakes, 198
Grantham gingerbreads, 190
oat and ginger cookies, 197
parsnip and ginger bake, 158
glacé icing, 213
goat's cheese and roasted pepper salad, 24
golden biscuits, 188, *188*
golden-topped fish pie, 52, *53*
granary bread, herbed, 206
Grand Marnier soufflé, 168
Grantham gingerbreads, 190
grapefruit: grapefruit and mint ice cream, 164, *165*
roast duckling with honey and, 74
gratin Dauphinoise, 152
guinea fowl with grapes and Madeira, 77
gulab jamun, 162, *162*

haddock: crispy layered fish pie, 54, *55*
golden-topped fish pie, 52, *53*
potted seafood pâté, 37
seafood roulade, 56
haricot beans: Boston baked beans, 121, *121*
hazelnuts: chocolate hazelnut brownies, 189
chocolate nut snaps, 189
hazelnut and carrot cake, 201
hazelnut florentines, 195
herbs: fresh herb cheese, 35
herb croûtons, 16
herb pastry, 212
honey: carrots with honey, 154
honey and spice cake, 200
honey jumbles, 188, *188*
honeyed lamb noisettes, 102
honeyed pigeon with kumquats, 77
roast duckling with honey and grapefruit, 74
houmous with feta cheese, 26

ice cream, grapefruit and mint, 164, *165*
icings: butter cream, 213
glacé, 213
Italian braised beef, 84

jellied consommé, 14
Jerusalem artichokes: artichoke and chive bake, 149
sautéed artichokes with orange, 150

kebabs: quorn satay, 114, *115*
spiced meat skewers, 88
veal and bacon kebabs, 111
kumquats: beef casserole with, 88, *89*
honeyed pigeon with, 77

lamb: chops with tomato and basil, 97
cinnamon lamb, 100, *101*
fruity lamb, *96-7*, 97
garlic and rosemary rack of, 94
honeyed lamb noisettes, 102
lamb and lentil hotpot, 99
lamb and rosemary pilaff, 133
lamb escalopes with oatmeal, 99
lamb noisettes with flageolet beans, *98*, 99
lamb with coriander marinade, 103
lamb with olive juices, 100
lamb with peppers and aubergines, 102
lamb with spinach, 103
loins of lamb with oatmeal, 94, *95*

minted lamb meatballs, 103
pan-fried lamb, 94
roast fillet with garlic, 92-3, *93*
spiced lamb with potatoes, 100
spicy lamb and aubergines, 92, *92*
langues de chat, 192
leeks: cheese and leek tart, 128, *128*
leek and potato bake, 150
sautéed leeks with cream, 150
stuffed vine leaves, 117
turnips stir-fried with, 158, *159*
lemon: butter cream, 213
date and lemon rock cakes, 198
glacé icing, 213
lemon curd creams, 168
lemon sesame potatoes, 152
lemon-spiced pork, 107
spiced lemon syrup tart, 180
warm lemon and apple flan, 179
warm lemon syrup cake, 174, *174*
lentils: coconut, rice and lentil salad, 147
lamb and lentil hotpot, 99
lettuce and mangetout soup, 15
liqueur glacé icing, 213
liver: perfect pilaff, *134*, 135

macaroons, coconut, 197
mackerel: barbecued fish in satay sauce, 59
lemon and mustard mackerel, 59
madeleines, 190
mangetout: crispy duck breast with, 75, *75*
lettuce and mangetout soup, 15
mango, stir-fried fillet steak with, 90
meat, 80-111
see also individual types of meat
meatballs, minted lamb, 103
Mediterranean seafood cocktail, 40, *40*
Melba toast, 15
melon, saffron prawns with, 40
meringues: berried treasure chest, 168-9, *169*
creamy meringues, 171
ginger meringues with rhubarb sauce, 172
rhubarb and orange suedoise, 170-1, *171*
mineolas: veal escalopes with mineola and herb butter, 111
mocha butter cream, 213
mocha glacé icing, 213
mousse, smoked trout and apple, 38, *39*
mushrooms: baked avocado and, 32
hot salmon and mushroom crisp, 45
mushroom and cashew nut pâté, 37
mushroom fricassée, 138, *138*
mushroom fritters, 24
mushroom risotto, 133
mushroom stock, 13
mushroom strudels, 128, *129*
pasta with mushroom sauce, 139
turnips with mushroom sauce, 158
warm salad of mushrooms, 31, *31*
wild mushroom and basil flan, 127

naan-style bread, 210
nasi goreng, 136-7
noodles: hot noodles with sesame dressing, 139
noodles with fried eggs, 139
nuts: fudge nut tranche, 182
glazed nut flan, *178*, 179
nut and raisin chocolate bars, 194
nut pastry, 212
nut scones, 205
nutty Christmas cake, 201, *201*
see also individual types of nut

oats: date and oat slices, 194
lamb escalopes with oatmeal, 99
loins of lamb with oatmeal, 94, *95*
oat and ginger cookies, 197
pot-roasted poussins with oatmeal stuffing, 66
real oatcakes, 204
toasted oat and raisin biscuits, 194
olives: olive and herb scones, 205
olive and walnut bread, 206
olives sourdough bread, 208, *208*
omelette, prawn and tarragon, 56
onions: brown onion stock, 13
fennel and onion soup, 21
French onion soup, 21
herb sausages with caramelised onions, 110, *110*
lemon and ginger poussins with, *70*, 71
quick beef and onion casserole, 88
sliced beetroot and onion bake, 150, *151*
oranges: baked orange and almond pudding, 173
butter cream, 213
crêpes Suzette, 168
duckling with orange sauce, 74
glacé icing, 213
orange and poppy seed cakes, 200-1, *200*
orange whisky butter, 173
rhubarb and orange suedoise, 170-1, *171*
steamed orange and coconut sponge, 172
venison collops with, 79, *79*
orchard lattice pie, 180, *181*

palmiers, crisp, *176*, 177
pancakes: aubergine blinis, 29
crêpes Suzette, 168
papaya pie, 180, *180*
parathas, 209
parsnips: curried parsnip soup, 17
golden parsnip galette, 158
parsnip and ginger bake, 158
spiced parsnips, 158
pasta with mushroom sauce, 139
see also individual types of pasta
pastries: crisp palmiers, *176*, 177
mushroom strudels, 128, *129*
peach and banana millefeuille, 184, *184*
salmon and prawn rice in filo pastry, 51
sesame cheese pastries, 26, *27*
spiced pear strudel, 177
see also pies
pastry: baking blind, 212
quick sweet, 213
rich shortcrust, 212
shortcrust, 212
pâtés: mushroom and cashew nut, 37
potted seafood, 37
peaches: peach and banana millefeuille, 184, *184*
peach and walnut tortes, 177
peanuts: chocolate peanut cookies, 197
peanut butter cookies, 197
pears: prune and pear tart, 182
souffléed pear tranche, 182, *183*
spiced pear strudel, 177
walnut pear slice, 184, *184*
peas; pea and saffron risotto, 133
Shropshire pea soup, 18
pecan chicken, roasted, 69, *69*
penne with tomato and chilli, 139
peppers: aubergine and red pepper roulade, *34*, 35
cracked wheat salad with, 143
goat's cheese and roasted pepper salad, 24
lamb with aubergines and, 102
lemon pepper salad, *142*, 143
sweet pepper and basil flan, 125
Peshawari naan, 210
pheasant: pheasant with chestnuts, 77
roast pheasant, *76*, *77*
pies: avocado pie, 125
bean and potato pie, 127
Catalan pie, 124-5, *124*
crispy layered fish pie, 54, *55*
orchard lattice pie, 180, *181*
papaya pie, 180, *180*
salmon pie with Parmesan crust, 50, *50*
sausage and apple plait, 110-11
wholemeal vegetable and herb pie, 125
pigeon with kumquats, honeyed, 77
pilaff: almond and sesame, 135
Basmati, 135
fragrant saffron, 135
lamb and rosemary, 133
perfect, *134*, 135
sesame with fennel, 133
pimiento: beef and pimiento casserole, 88
pine kernels, cabbage with, 148, *148*
pineapple and apricots, 164, *164*
pinwheel biscuits, 189
pistachio nuts: apricot and pistachio rolls, 174, *175*
bacon and pistachio terrine, 37
pitta bread, 210, *211*
pizzettas, 24, *25*
plaice: poached plaice and spinach flan, 52
rolled plaice with smoked salmon, 52
poppy seeds: orange and poppy seed cake, 200-1, *200*
pork: chilled pork dim sum, 32, *32*
Chinese spiced pork, 108, *108*
Dijon-glazed pork medallions, *106-7*, 107
fruit-crusted loin of, 105, *105*
lemon-spiced pork, 107
pork tenderloin with watercress sauce, *104*, 105
quick pork cassoulet, 109
potatoes: bay-roasted, 152, *153*
bean and potato pie, 127
crispy potato galette, 154
curried cauliflower and, 154, *155*
game chipes, 154
golden-topped fish pie, 52, *53*
gratin Dauphinoise, 152
leek and potato bake, 150
lemon sesame potatoes, 152
mashed potato with olive oil and Parmesan, 152
potato and garlic purée, 150
potatoes with roast garlic, 150, *151*
roasted new potato salad, 144, *144*
sautéed potatoes with celery, 154
simple potato salad, 144
spiced eggs with cauliflower and coconut, 119
spiced lamb with potatoes, 100
poultry, 60-75
poussins: lemon and ginger poussins with onions, *70*, 71
peppered poussins with lime and sage crumbs, 71
pot-roasted poussins with oatmeal stuffing, 66
prawns: avocado with fennel and, 40
fillets of trout with dill and, 54
nasi goreng, 136-7
potted seafood pâté, 37
prawn and tarragon omelette, 56
prawn puris, 30, *30*
prawns and rice with dill, 136
saffron prawns with melon, 40
salmon and prawn rice in filo pastry, 51
seafood roulade, 56
spicy spinach roulade, 56, *57*
Thai prawn curry, 59
prunes: marinated chicken with, 64, *64*
prune and pear tart, 182

quorn satay, 114, *115*

raisins: coconut and raisin cookies, 197
nut and raisin chocolate bars, 194
toasted oat and raisin biscuits, 194
raspberry jam: éclairs, 199
raspberry rings, 190
red kidney beans: quick pork cassoulet, 109
sausage and bean casserole, 109
red mullet: barbecued mullet cooked in vine leaves, 58-9
rhubarb: ginger meringues with rhubarb sauce, 172
rhubarb and orange suedoise, 170-1, *171*
rice: coconut, rice and lentil salad, 147
nasi goreng, 136-7
prawns and rice with dill, 136
salmon and prawn rice in filo pastry, 51
special fried rice, 136
Thai fried rice, 136, *136*
vegetable biryani, 137
see also pilaff; risotto
Ricotta and almond cheesecake, 171
risotto: almond and courgette, 133
asparagus, 133
mushroom, 133
pea and saffron, 133
risotto castles, 132, *132*
rock cakes: apple, 198
date and lemon, 198
ginger, 198
sultana, 198
root vegetable stew, 120-1
Roquefort and watercress soup, *20*, 21
roulades: aubergine and red pepper, *34*, 35
chocolate coconut cream, 170, *170*
seafood, 56
smoked salmon, 36, *36*
spicy spinach, 56, *57*
turkey and watercress, 72
runner beans and courgettes, steamed, 147
rustic walnut bread, 206

saffron: fragrant saffron pilaff, 135
saffron prawns with melon, 40
salads: Christmas, 147
coconut, rice and lentil, 147
courgette and almond, *142*, 143
cracked wheat with peppers, 143
crisp vegetable, 145
cucumber and yogurt, 145
cucumber ribbon and asparagus, 144
goat's cheese and roasted pepper, 24
grilled vegetable, 146, *146*
lemon pepper, *142*, 143
roasted new potato, 144, *144*
simple potato, 144
sliced tomato and asparagus, 143
spinach and watercress salad with bacon, 145, *145*
tomato, fennel and avocado, 145
warm salad of mushrooms, 31, *31*
salmon: celebration salmon, 46, *46*
dill-glazed salmon, *44*, 45
hot salmon and mushroom crisp, 45
outrageous salmon fishcakes, 46
salmon and prawn rice in filo pastry, 51
salmon noisettes with black bean dressing, 47, *47*
salmon pie with Parmesan crust, 50, *50*
salmon with tarragon, 51
salmon with tomato vinaigrette, 48, *49*
see also smoked salmon
sausages: garlic sausages, 110
herb sausages with caramelised onions, 110, *110*
sausage and apple plait, 110-11
sausage and bean casserole, 109
scones: cheese and herb, 205
nut, 205
olive and herb, 205
plain, 205
sweet fruit, 205
tomato and garlic, 205
seafood cocktail, Mediterranean, 40, *40*
seafood platter, glazed, 58, *58*
seafood roulade, 56
sesame seeds: almond and sesame pilaff, 135
cheese and sesame aigrettes, 29
hot noodles with sesame dressing, 139
lemon sesame potatoes, 152
sesame and cumin breadsticks, 210, *211*
sesame cheese pastries, 26, *27*
sesame pilaff with fennel, 133
stir-fried courgettes with sesame seeds, 147
shellfish: glazed seafood platter, 58, *58*
see also individual types of shellfish
shortbread: apple shorties, 192
caramel and walnut shorties, 192
shortbread rounds, 192
shortcrust pastry, 212
Shrewbury biscuits, 190
Shropshire pea soup, 18
smoked salmon: outrageous salmon fishcakes, 46
rolled plaice with, 52
smoked salmon roulades, 36, *36*
soda bread, 206
smoked trout and apple mousse, 38, *39*
soufflés: cauliflower, 32, *33*
chocolate cinnamon, 166
Grand Marnier, 168
hot spinach, 119
hot vanilla, 166
individual apple, 166, *167*
souffléed pear tranche, 182, *183*
soups, 14-21
sourdough bread, olive, 208, *208*
spice biscuits, 190
spinach: crispy layered fish pie, 54, *55*
hot spinach soufflé, 119
lamb with spinach, 103
poached plaice and spinach flan, 52
spicy spinach roulade, 56, *57*
spinach and watercress salad with bacon, 145, *145*
stocks, 12-13
strawberry syrup, orchard fruit in, 163
strudels: mushroom, 128, *129*
spiced pear, 177
sugar buns, cinnamon, 204, *205*
sultana rock cakes, 198
swedes: roast swedes, 158
swede and orange purée, 157
sweet potatoes Dauphinoise, 152, *153*

tarts, savoury: aubergine tart, *126*, 127
cheese and leek tart, 128, *128*
poached plaice and spinach flan, 52
sweet pepper and basil flan, 125
tarte au chèvre et menthe, 123, *123*
three-cheese aubergine tart, 28, *28*
wild mushroom and basil flan, 127
tarts, sweet *see* flans, sweet
terrines: bacon and pistachio, 37
mixed vegetable, 38, *38*
Thai fried rice, 136, *136*
Thai prawn curry, 59
30-minute fruit cake, 202
toad in the hole, vegetable, 120, *120*
toast: blue brie toasts, 28
Melba, 15
tomatoes: Andalusian summer soup, 15
baked tomato and fennel, 148-9
chilled tomato and basil soup, 15
lamb chops with basil and, 97
penne with tomato and chilli, 139
risotto castles, 132, *132*
salmon with tomato vinaigrette, 48, *49*
sliced tomato and asparagus salad, 143
stuffed tomatoes, 119
tomato and garlic scones, 205
tomato bruschetta, 26
tomato, fennel and avocado salad, 145
tomato herb focaccia, 208
trout: fillets of trout with prawns and dill, 54
see also smoked trout
turkey: roast turkey with chestnut stuffing, 72-3, *73*
turkey and watercress roulades, 72
turnips: glazed carrots with, 157
turnips stir-fried with leeks, 158, *159*
turnips with mushroom sauce, 158

vanilla soufflé, hot, 166
veal: veal and bacon kebabs, 111
veal escalopes with mineola and herb butter, 111
veal with bacon and juniper, 111
vegetables; mixed bean and vegetable soup, 18, *18*
mixed vegetable terrine, 38, *38*
root vegetable stew, 120-1
vegetable bake, 122
vegetable biryani, 137
vegetable chilli, 117, *117*
vegetable couscous, 137
vegetable, fruit and nut stir-fry, 114, *114*
vegetable stock, 13
vegetable toad in the hole, 120, *120*
vegetarian medley, *118*, 119
wholemeal vegetable and herb pie, 125
see salads *and individual types of vegetable*
vegetarian dishes, 112-28
vegetarian medley, *118*, 119
venison: venison and chestnut casserole, 78
venison collops with oranges, 79, *79*
venison escalopes with red wine, 78, *78*
Viennese chocolate cake, 204
vine leaves: barbecued mullet cooked in, 58-9
stuffed vine leaves, 117

walnuts: caramel and walnut shorties, 192
cherry and walnut biscuits, 190
olive and walnut bread, 206
peach and walnut tortes, 177
rib of beef with anchovies and, 82, *82*
rustic walnut bread, 206
walnut pear slice, 184, *184*
watercress: pork tenderloin with watercress sauce, *104*, 105
Roquefort and watercress soup, *20*, 21
spinach and watercress salad with bacon, 145, *145*
turkey and watercress roulades, 72
whisky butter, orange, 173
whitebait, devilled, 40
wholemeal pastry, 212

yogurt: cucumber and yogurt salad, 145
gulab jamun, 162, *162*
yogurt-braised chicken, 62